Translating Nature

THE EARLY MODERN AMERICAS

Peter C. Mancall, Series Editor

Volumes in the series explore neglected aspects of early
modern history in the Western Hemisphere. Interdisciplinary
in character, and with a special emphasis on the Atlantic World
from 1450 to 1850, the series is published in partnership with the
USC-Huntington Early Modern Studies Institute.

Translating Nature

Cross-Cultural Histories of Early Modern Science

EDITED BY

Jaime Marroquín Arredondo
and Ralph Bauer

PENN

UNIVERSITY OF PENNSYLVANIA PRESS

PHILADELPHIA

Copyright © 2019 University of Pennsylvania Press

Published by
University of Pennsylvania Press
Philadelphia, Pennsylvania 19104-4112
www.upenn.edu/pennpress

Printed in the United States of America
on acid-free paper

10 9 8 7 6 5 4 3 2 1

A catalogue record for this book is available from the Library of Congress

ISBN 978-0-8122-5093-0

Contents

Introduction: An Age of Translation

Ralph Bauer and Jaime Marroquín Arredondo

The history of modern science has often been told as the history of discovery—"discovery" in the sense of the finding of new facts and things by empirical means that overturns traditional or received conceptions of nature and the universe. The so-called discovery of America by Europeans in the fifteenth century has hereby become the *paradigm* of modern scientific discovery per se. The classic formulation of this was perhaps the declaration by English statesman and natural philosopher Francis Bacon in the early seventeenth century that Christopher Columbus's discovery of America had announced the coming of a new world of science beyond the book-bound circle of knowledge of the Scholastics. In this new world of science, knowledge would be gained not through the study of books (what Bacon called "received philosophy"), syllogistic reason, or dialectic disputation but instead by the discovery of the secrets of nature through direct observation and empirical experimentation.[1] Since the second part of the twentieth century, however, the modern logic of discovery has been subjected to intense critical scrutiny. On the one hand, the new social history of science has privileged cultural context and social networks over the logic of scientific discovery as an engine of change;[2] on the other hand, postcolonial criticism has insisted that the idea of a New World that lies at the heart of the modern paradigm of discovery is a Eurocentric fiction. It is a fiction predicated on an ontological separation of European subjects doing the discovering from American objects to be discovered, a separation in the process of which non-Western (particularly Amerindian) subjects and knowledge traditions were utterly erased.[3] Scholars today recognize that America was never a tabula rasa—a "New World"—but instead was a world with multiple histories as well as philosophical, historical, and scientific traditions that interacted with those of the European invaders in multiple and complex ways.[4] But while these multicultural entanglements have begun to be reckoned with in contemporary ethnohistorical and anthropological scholarship, the new social history of science has yet to take adequate account of the fact that the knowledge that Europeans gained during the early modern period was often the result not of a discovery of new things but instead of a translation across cultures, that the so-called age of discovery was also an age of translation.[5] As William Eamon aptly notes in the afterword to the present volume, translation often precedes discovery, and in turn discovery is perhaps best characterized as an attribution. By focusing on translation, the history of science can better reckon with its truly global nature and also with the historical reality that scientific discoveries have always had quite different meanings and effects for peoples and ecosystems, often depending on their geopolitical proximity or remoteness from the hegemonic centers of economic, military, and scientific power.

This collection proposes to rethink the history of early modern science as a history not of discovery but of translation. Adopting a transcultural hermeneutics, the chapters assembled here pose the question of what role translation played not only in the history of early modern knowledge but also in the emergence of the modern (empiricist) idea of scientific discovery per se.[6] As Daniela Bleichmar notes in her contribution, in the early modern period, translation still had a dual meaning: the movement of an idea (or a thing) through space and its movement from one language into another. Thus, to explore the role that translation plays in the history of early modern science is to ask how human knowledge about nature is transformed as it travels from one language and cultural context into another. It is, in other words, to attend to what Scott Montgomery has called the "mobility of knowledge."[7] By emphasizing the role that translation played in the history of early modern science, this volume means to highlight the contributions made by the knowledge of "others"—those whose knowledge has often been erased in a historiography of science predicated on a logic of discovery—mainly Native Americans and Catholic Iberians.

This volume thus contributes to current scholarship in the history of science that has challenged the notion of a scientific revolution that allegedly occurred in seventeenth-century Great Britain as the result of a radical break with tradition. But while historians have recently emphasized the considerable continuities of seventeenth-century natural philosophy with its medieval and Renaissance pasts,[8] the history of modern science remains by and large a European story, particularly a Northern European and Protestant one.

This history begins with the dissemination of Aristotelian naturalism during the twelfth and thirteenth centuries, continues with the rise of Ockhamian nominalism at the University of Paris during the fourteenth century, comes of age with Italian humanism in the fifteenth century, and culminates with the sixteenth-century Protestant Reformation, allegedly the "major catalyst" for the development of modern scientific mentalities.[9] To the extent that early modern European expansionism has been recognized as another key catalyst of modern scientific mentalities, the Iberian conquest of America has often been treated as a historical parenthesis—a temporary and aberrant relapse into medievalism and "Inquisition" in a modern age of discovery. As Víctor Navarro Brotóns and William Eamon have pointed out, this notion of Spanish science as being "medieval" or "backward" is the result of the powerful grip that the post-Enlightenment Black Legend has had on the philosophy of modernity generally and the history of science particularly.[10] All too often, it is thereby forgotten that the translation and dissemination of Aristotelian and Arabic naturalism had Iberia as one of its main centers, that the Protestant Reformation was not the only (or even the earliest) reformation, and that the Catholic world, like its Protestant counterpart, was heir to the nominalist, Scotist, neo-Thomist, and humanist currents that gave rise to modern science.

There is now a growing body of scholarship countering the historiographic legacy of the Black Legend by asserting the evident modernity of sixteenth-century Spanish imperial knowledge production.[11] Historians of early modern science have shown that if the decisive factor in the emergence of modern science was the collaboration among natural philosophers, secular and religious humanists, artisans, and government secretaries, this collaboration was inaugurated by the Iberian imperial and commercial networks of expansionism in the fifteenth, sixteenth, and seventeenth centuries. But in their laudable attempt to put to rest once and for all the legacy of the Black Legend in the history of science, historians of early modern Iberian science have generally confined the scope of their investigations to Spanish and Portuguese scientific practices. As a result, more remains to be said about the role that the Iberian models of knowledge production played in the history of modern Western science and epistemologies beyond the Spanish and Portuguese Empires, influencing institutions more typically associated with the scientific revolution such as the British Royal Society of London and the Italian Accademia dei Lincei.[12] As Sara Miglietti notes in her contribution, while scholars have highlighted how these institutions developed comparable strategies for collecting and managing information from the colonial world, the extent to which these institutions communicated with and learned from each other beyond national, imperial, and linguistic borders has not yet been fully considered. Her case in point is the history of climate theory during the seventeenth century, which, she shows, cannot be understood in isolation of any single one of these centers of knowledge production and must be seen in the context of their engagement with methodologies and ideas derived from Spanish travel accounts and natural histories written in the Americas.

One of our claims in this volume is thus that the epistemic developments that led to Francis Bacon's programmatic elaboration of a "new science" were already a crucial part of the Iberian and, in general, Catholic scientific traditions emerging from their encounters with Native American ones. Nobody was more keenly aware of this than Bacon himself. He openly admired the sustained and extensive networks of Spanish imperial knowledge production, writing in his *The Interpretation of Nature* that an implementation of his proposals for collaborative, corporate, and state-sponsored production of knowledge "leadeth us to an administration of knowledge in some such order and policy as the king of Spain in regard of his great dominions useth in state; who though he hath particular councils of State or last resort, that receiveth the advertisements and certificates from all the rest."[13] One of the most important Spanish centers of this "administration of knowledge" admired by Bacon was the Casa de Contratación (House of Trade), the clearinghouse in Seville instituted for the gathering and management of all information about the New World. In *The Principal Navigations, Voyages, Traffiques & Discoveries of the English Nation* (1598), Richard Hakluyt described the creation of the Spanish House of Trade in Seville:

[T]he late Emperour Charles the fifth, considering the rawness of his Seamen, and the manifolde shipwracks which they systeyened in passing and repassing betweene Spaine and the West Indies, with an high reach and great foresight, established not onely a Pilote Major, for the examination of such as sought to take charge of ships in that voyage, but also founded a notable Lecture of the Art of Navigation, which is read to this day in the Contractation house at Sivil. The readers of which Lecture have not only carefully taught and instructed the Spanish Mariners by word of mouth, but also have published sundry exact and worthy treatises concerning Marine causes, for the direction and incouragement of posteritie. The learned works of three of which readers, namely of Alonso de Chavez, of Hieronymo de Chavez, and of Roderigo Zamorano came long ago very happily to my hands, together with the straight and severe examining of all such Masters as desire to take charge of the West Indies.[14]

Although not all of Hakluyt's information is accurate—for example, the House of Trade was already established by Ferdinand II, not by Emperor Charles V—this passage shows that Englishmen such as Hakluyt and Bacon interested in promoting overseas English expansionism were keenly aware of the formidable infrastructure that undergirded Spanish imperial knowledge production and regarded it as a model for their own institutions. In fact, the House of Trade was only one in a variety of Spanish state-sponsored institutions of imperial knowledge production. Others included the Council of the Indies (Consejo de Indias) and the royal court of Philip II itself, especially the treasure house of art and learning he had built outside Madrid at his monastic refuge of the Escorial, which included alchemical laboratories, botanical gardens, and research libraries and archives.[15]

The vast majority of the naturalistic and ethnographic knowledge produced about the Americas ended up in these state archives and provided the informational basis for the official histories written by the appointed royal chroniclers of the Indies. Also, some natural historians collected information at their home base in the Americas and authored massive histories for publication back in Spain. Among the earliest and most important of these was Gonzalo Fernández de Oviedo y Valdés (1478–1557), the first appointed royal chronicler of the Indies and the last one who actually resided in the colonies. Translated into multiple European vernaculars, his works were the point of departure for virtually all subsequent Northern European scientific writings about America. Thus, in his contribution Ralph Bauer explores the translation and transmission of Oviedo's works by the English alchemist Richard Eden, whose synthesis of the languages of classical natural history with that of medieval Christian pilgrimage that he found in the works of the "Pliny of the New World" (as Oviedo was known) provided a model for Francis Bacon's Christian utopia in *New Atlantis*—arguably the first modern work of science fiction. A similar, slightly later, case of early transnational transmission of knowledge is discussed by Marcy Norton in her contribution to this volume involving the enormously influential naturalist research of Francisco Hernández, Philip II's *protomédico*, who arrived in New Spain in 1570 to conduct the systematic study of American flora and fauna as well as materia medica. Partially published in a Latin edition after sitting in the archives for several decades, Hernández's works became one of the key sources for some of the most famous English naturalists of the seventeenth century, including Francis Willughby and John Ray.

Besides the dissemination through print, there were other routes in which knowledge was transmitted beyond the channels of Spanish knowledge production. Thus, Daniela Bleichmar discusses the odyssey of the *Codex Mendoza*, a Mexican pictographic manuscript that had been prepared in New Spain circa 1541. The manuscript was shipped to the court of Charles V but was intercepted on its way by French privateers; it was later purchased by Hakluyt and included in Samuel Purchas's massive travel collection *Hakluytus posthumus: Or Purchas his pilgrimes* (1625). Significantly, it was through the Protestant clergyman's publication that in the seventeenth century the *Codex Mendoza* reached not only the Mexican Creole savant Carlos de Sigüenza y Góngora but also the famous German Jesuit polymath Athanasius Kircher (1602–1680), the "last man who knew everything" and used the codex for comparative material in his *Oedipus Aegyptiacus* (1652–1654), one of the most important works in seventeenth-century Egyptology inspired by Renaissance Hermeticism.[16]

Indeed, as several chapters in this collection emphasize, it was the Jesuits who had created the first truly global transnational scientific corporate network that spanned the planet from their center in Rome to viceregal Peru in one direction and Japan in the other. Thus, Luis Millones Figueroa illustrates the workings of this global Jesuit network of knowledge dissemination by focusing on the seventeenth-century Jesuit Bernabé Cobo (1580–1657), working in South America. Similarly, Sarah Rivett explores the comparatist philosophical speculations of Joseph-François Lafitau, the eighteenth-century French Jesuit working in Canada, in the context of a well-established network of Jesuit linguistic scholarship about non-European languages throughout the globe. And Ruth Hill focuses on the remarkably cosmopolitan cartographic knowledge produced about the Philippines by the eighteenth-century Jesuit historian, geographer, jurist, catechist, and cartographer Pedro Murillo Velarde (1696–1753). If the rise of modern science must primarily be understood as the history of social networks (as Bruno Latour has argued), these chapters show that the Jesuits were among the earliest and most sophisticated pioneers to implement such a "science in action" on a global scale.[17]

Yet, the cross-cultural mobility of naturalist knowledge within these networks connecting men of science across the globe could also give rise to anxiety, suspicion, rivalry, and even suppression and resistance that could be motivated by geopolitical, patriotic, or epistemological concerns.[18] The practice of secrecy imposed on the production of natural knowledge by the Spanish imperial state beginning with the suppression and redaction of the letters of Columbus from his first transatlantic voyage is a case in point.[19] Another form of resistance to the translation and appropriation of natural knowledge is discussed by John Slater in his chapter. There, he investigates a distinct but understudied tradition of early modern natural history written in the Spanish vernacular and deliberately kept out of print by their authors. They did so to distinguish their works from the increasingly theoretical and taxonomical approach that characterized works of cosmopolitan Northern European armchair naturalists writing in Latin. Similar criticisms of speculative natural philosophy not based in original firsthand ethnographic knowledge were voiced from those with direct experience of the colonial contact zones of the Spanish Empire. Thus, as Millones Figueroa notes, Cobo argued that only knowledge of American nature that is acquired on the ground through an indispensable familiarity with indigenous languages would regenerate a "new philosophy" that had been perverted by the arrogance of European men of science who appropriated the knowledge of those working in the colonial trenches.

Despite the sophistication and expansiveness of these early modern networks of knowledge production—and despite the porousness of national and imperial borders with regard to the dissemination of knowledge about the Americas—we have only begun to appreciate the important role that Spanish missionary and imperial agents played in the history of modern science at large. The general neglect of the Iberian and Catholic world in the modern historiography of science has also resulted in the obfuscation of the transcultural and hybrid origin of modern Western science. Recent scholarship about the history of early modern science suggests that along with Copernicus's heliocentrism, one of the most important epistemological developments of the early modern period was the gradual fusion of natural philosophy and natural history.[20] This is an intellectual process that cannot be understood apart from the Iberian colonization of the Americas, including processes of the cultural translation of Amerindian knowledge into European contexts. Beginning with the first return of Columbus to the Antilles in November 1493, European missionaries and men of science in the service of the emerging Spanish Empire began a systematic study not only of the natural environment but also of Amerindian histories, religious beliefs, and cultural and scientific practices. Although the scientific discipline of "ethnography" and even the word did not originate until the nineteenth century, Spanish *letrados'* curiosity about Amerindian cultures gave rise to what we might call today "ethnographic history," developed in histories written by Ramón Pané, Toribio de Benavente (also known as Motolinía), Bernadino de Sahagún, and José de Acosta, among others. Many of these histories were explicitly written to aid the missionaries in their effort to extirpate lingering native "idolatries" by detecting while partially comprehending non-Christian religious rites. At the same time, the mendicants and Jesuits understood that the success of conversion and the establishment of economically and politically viable new kingdoms and provinces in the the Americas crucially depended on an understanding and readaptation of native beliefs, knowledge, and practices. The ethnographic naturalism in the early Americas thus remained a constant component in the experience-based description and classification of the world's natural history and pharmacopeia.[21]

The restructuring of natural history into the pragmatic foundation of natural-philosophical authority is in fundamental ways also a history of the translation of Amerindian traditions and knowledge about America's flora, fauna, and climates into Western contexts. This protoethnographic process, while conditioned by its varied colonial contexts, was eminently collaborative and transcultural in nature. Yet, our understanding of its history remains partial and fragmented. Our second objective in this volume is therefore to highlight the seminal role that Amerindian naturalist knowledge played in the gradual transformation of natural philosophy and natural history into modern natural science. Although we cannot do justice to the epistemic richness and diversity of the pre-Columbian Americas—which had their own traditions of cultural translation and conducted their own translations of European knowledge—it is important to recall some of its components. In the paradigmatic case of Mexico, since the zenith of Teotihuacan in the fifth century (and beyond), the tradition of the *calmecacs* (priestly schools) ran uninterrupted until the dramatic cataclysm of the conquest and even then provided the model for the colleges established by the Franciscans for the education of the Nahua elite in the sixteenth century, such as the famous Colegio de Santa Cruz de Tlatelolco, officially opened in 1536.[22] In the *calmecac*, future priests learned the metaphysical tenets of Mesoamerican philosophy that posited a "world in motion" composed of opposing elements, all of them emanating from feminine and masculine principle based on a primordial dual deity, Ometeotl.[23] Apparently, many pre-Columbian cultures in the Americas recognized a dual primordial divinity from which emanated a universe composed of visible and invisible elements in continuous processes of coordination and discoordination, of life and death. Through ritual and poetry, humans were able to experiment in themselves the complex and fleeting harmony of *teotl* (divinity). Mesoamericans thus made use of poetry, music, graphic art, astronomy, astrology, and their vast knowledge of their natural environment to participate in the constant re-creation of a universe in harmony and chaos. Furthermore, Mesoamerican priests and *tlacuiloques* (writers-painters) were used to translate and syncretize knowledge and art from different cultural traditions. For them, language itself encompassed—in ways akin to the European humanist and Hermetic traditions—the precarious harmony of the universe, best revealed through poetic, musical language.[24]

Given the richness and complexity of Amerindian epistemologies and structures of feeling, it is hardly surprising that they permeated all New World scientific knowledge both in Europe and in the Americas, as several chapters in this collection show. In the wake of the Columbian encounters, European translations of Amerindian knowledge were highly dependent on sophisticated networks of knowledge established by metropolitan political and religious authorities in the Americas. Traditionally studied solely as enclaves and methods for the establishment of European authority and hegemony, these knowledge networks established in Amerindian places and territories throughout the early modern period were also indispensable sources of information and knowledge for most colonial endeavors. Its most productive centers were the convents, schools, and hospitals established by the metropolitan religious and political authorities of the colonies in Native Americans lands. The colonial character of cultural translation in the early Americas partially explains why the original native sources of knowledge were often suppressed or veiled under a single and mostly European author's name. Yet, early modern Europeans turned to Native American informants to inquire about the names of things, their uses, as well as traditions. Much of the knowledge that Europeans brought back from the Americas was therefore not the pure product of empirical observation and discovery; it was instead the transcultural product of complex processes of linguistic and cultural translations from Amerindian and African traditions. These translations were conducted in what has been called the "contact zones" or "cultural borders" of America, where knowledge exchanges between subjects of different cultures and civilizations were often fluid while remaining strongly mediated by the multiple demands of imperial power.[25]

The scientific importance of these cultural borders brings us back to our earlier discussion concerning the early modern European discourse of "discovery." As Juan Pimentel shows in his contribution to this volume, when early modern Europeans wrote about "discovering" new lands and seas in the Americas, their writings often suppressed the collective, social, and transcultural features on which their acquisition of knowledge crucially depended. After all, he reminds us, in the sixteenth century, "to discover" often meant the unveiling of something whose existence was already known, even if such knowledge was solely based on premonition. Focusing on the "discovery" of the Pacific Ocean by Vasco Núñez de Balboa in 1513, which opened the door to early modern globalization, Pimentel turns to the early Spanish sources to reconstruct the important role played by native informants in European geographic discoveries.

We consider the term "transculturation" to be the most appropriate concept to characterize these exchanges. The term was originally proposed in 1940 by anthropologist Fernando Ortiz, partially in counterdistinction to the concept of acculturation, which was dominant in mid-twentieth-century Anglo-American anthropology. Unlike acculturation (which was predicated on one-way models of cultural change), transculturation, Ortiz proposed, "carries with it the consequent creation of new cultural phenomena" through a dual process of acquisition and retention.[26] In other words, the notion of transculturation assumes that cultural changes accompanying massive migration processes are understood not as a gradual imposition of hegemonic cultural practices and ideas on subjugated or disempowered peoples (acculturation) but instead as open and conflicting processes of negotiation across cultures. For us, the term also emphasizes personal agency in all knowledge and cultural translations as well as a tendency to produce transient forms of cultural synthesis in heterogeneous social structures. In his contribution to this volume, Jaime Marroquín Arredondo fruitfully uses the concept of transculturation to explore the methodological and conceptual evolution of protoethnography as it was emerging during the sixteenth century in the works of Hernández and the Franciscan missionaries writing in New Spain. Similarly, Ruth Hill employs the concept of transculturation to demonstrate how Murillo Velarde's geographical work about the eighteenth-century Philippines synthesized both European and indigenous gazes and epistemes, also using his work as an example of how similar processes "marked the global Enlightenment as a whole."

Other critical concepts that are usefully employed by our contributors for the description of the intercultural nature of early modern scientific knowledge include the terms *mestizaje* and "hybridity." Whereas the former concept—derived from colonial Latin American history to denote cultural and (later) racial mixture—has recently been influentially developed by Serge Gruzinski to describe the often unpredictable, violent, and continuously incomplete processes of early modern cultural exchanges between indigenous and European people in colonial Latin America, the latter derives from Anglophone postcolonial theory (particularly as elaborated by Homi Bhabha) to describe the latent capacity of the colonial text to "reverse[] the effects of the colonialist disavowal, so that other 'denied' knowledges enter upon the dominant discourse and estrange the basis of its authority" to the effect of destabilizing hegemonic power.[27] Thus, Marcy Norton, using a microhistorical approach, considers the tradition of knowledge that originated with Mesoamerican ideas about the natural world and made its way into John Ray and Francis Willughby's *The Ornithology of Francis Willughby* (1676, 1678) via Sahagún's and Hernández's works. Similarly, Sarah Rivett discusses the "hybrid cosmology" emerging from the sustained language encounter between indigenous and Christian interlocutors in the missionary literature of New England and French Canada at the turn of the eighteenth century. Finally, Christopher Parsons explores the hybrid nature of early eighteenth-century French botanical treatises about what today is Nova Scotia, which, he shows, were utterly dependent on the expertise of local indigenous informants for the descriptions of maritime and coastal plants.

The term "history" (*historia*) and its different subgenres (chronicles, antiquities, and relations or narrations) were the preeminent generic vehicles for the translation of Amerindian knowledge to its new transcultural forms.[28] Although early modern titles such as "History of Animals" and "History of Plants" may seem strange to us today, *historia* was, as Gianna Pomata and Nancy G. Siraisi have noted, rather ubiquitous in early modern learning. Following Arno Seifert, they show that Renaissance humanists rediscovered the pre-Aristotelian usage of *historia* as *vera narratio*, associating the term with descriptive knowledge—knowledge that is based on sensorial experience, is nonlogically demonstrative and concerned with knowledge in general, and is not only limited to *res gestae* (things done) but also fully includes nature.[29] *Historia*—originally a branch of rhetoric—hereby became the generic vehicle for the search, investigation, and eloquent transmission of experience-based truths. The study of grammar and rhetoric was thus at the core of these epistemic developments. Language translation and narrative appropriation circumscribe and precondition what is known and how it is known as well as what remains unknown or hidden.

Sixteenth-century humanists rediscovered the value of grammar and rhetoric as the foundational disciplines for all knowledge. Like their Franciscan nominalist intellectual ancestors during the fourteenth century, they challenged Scholastic *logic* as the most important discipline of the Scholastic trivium. Before any logic could be successfully applied to human words, they argued, verbal expressions should be iterated with order and concert. It was mainly through *historia* that humanists attempted to update all knowledge inherited from antiquity by not only purifying ancient sources but also empirically verifying their validity, thus becoming, in the words of Arno Seifert, the "godmother[s]" of early modern empiricism.[30] Historians did so through the gathering of increasingly well-delimited *relaciones* (accounts or narrations) from reliable witnesses. These *relaciones*, collected through the systematic and judicial-like interrogation of "experts" or witnesses, were crucial in the development of new practices of information gathering, observation, and description that are considered key for the development of early modern empiricism due to their increasing matter-of-fact character.[31] Thus, Sara Miglietti aptly notes that these *relaciones* were at the core of most of the official scientific endeavors during the early modern period, including not only those conducted under the auspices of the Casa de Contratación in Seville but also those of the Society of Jesus and the Royal Society, among other institutions. These *relaciones* were the most visible part of the new ethnographic turn of most of the known sciences during the early modern period. The interrogations and dialogue-like practices conducted for the gathering of *relaciones* were the most effective when both questioners and respondents possessed an advanced mastery of each other's language and culture.

Amerindian languages, symbols, images, and systems of knowledge went through a complex, partly spontaneous, and highly rationalized process of translation and transmission. Paradigmatic is, again, the case of Francisco Hernández's *Historia de las plantas de Nueva España* (ca. 1577), which collected an enormous amount of Amerindian natural knowledge and materia medica through the systematic gathering of *relaciones*, as the chapter by Jaime Marroquín Arredondo demonstrates. Hernández's work also unveils how the new forms of *historia* evolved well before Bacon's "instauration" in interrelated ways on both sides of the Atlantic Ocean and were fundamental for the emergence of early modern natural and even human sciences.[32] The "godmother of empiricism" thus crucially depended on these colonial, unequal "dialogues" that ranged from the simple imitation and experience of the natives' uses of their natural resources to rigorous ethnographic interviewing techniques and systematic experimental practices to corroborate the accuracy of new knowledge. Bicultural rhetorical mastery permitted the most sophisticated epistemological exchanges among European, Amerindian, and mestizo scholars. Verification of knowledge's veracity departed from the rhetorical transformation of "experience" into well-delimited narrative "facts" usually transmitted through *relaciones*. These "facts" were often experiential testimonies gathered from authorized witnesses and later translated, verified, and *reduced* to European contexts through common legal, rhetorical, and scientific practices of the time.

Perhaps not surprisingly, the erasure of indigenous subjects in the translation of early modern natural knowledge on the part of many Spanish natural historians would eventually find its counterpart in the erasure of Iberian subjects by competing imperial agents, such as those of the Dutch West India Company and the Royal Society of London.[33] These erasures and misrepresentations of other cultures' knowledge constitute a fundamental yet poorly acknowledged aspect in the history of early modern science. On the one hand, a history of early modern science as global *translatio* narrates an astonishing process of systematic accumulation and verification of matter-of-fact knowledge about nature—a process that undoubtedly led to the rise of modern sciences and with it a new epistemology that would come to dominate our modern worldview. On the other hand, such a history also unveils how these early modern translations of knowledge always implied omissions, mistranslations, reformulations, erasures, and a surprising degree of blindness, voluntary and otherwise, toward vast parts of other cultures' knowledge.

Translating Nature in the Early Modern Atlantic World

Collectively, the chapters gathered here address the question of what role translation across cultures played in the history of science in the context of Europe's early modern colonial encounters. We present the chapters in four parts. The chapters in Part I, "Amerindian Knowledge and Spain's New World," focus on the translation of Amerindian knowledge into a Spanish imperial context. Beginning with geographic knowledge, Juan Pimentel, in "Sighting and Haunting of the South Sea: On Ponquiaco, Balboa, and What Maps Conceal," interrogates the collective and social features of transcultural translation in the so-called European discovery of America, specifically the discovery of the Pacific by Balboa in 1513. Pimentel turns to the early Spanish sources to analyze the representation of what was first a figurative region marked by historical distance as well as entangled information and misinformation and was subject to varied efforts aimed at establishing reliable knowledge. He particularly focuses on the role played by the native informant Ponquiaco in the Spanish accounts of Balboa's "discovery." However, Pimentel also demonstrates that to recover the role that indigenous actors and knowledge played in the European age of discovery, it is often necessary to attend to the spaces between what is explicit and what is passed over in silence in the European discovery account—the ellipses and omissions in the first reports and cartographic representations of the South Sea. This hermeneutical problem is especially acute in light of the fact that many of the native actors collaborating in the making of this heterogeneous geography as well as their descendants have disappeared, fallen victim to the violence of conquest or to disease. Pimentel asks, "How can we look into a culture that had disappeared, leaving hardly a trace? What can we know of their geographical knowledge and, more specifically, of the existence of the South Sea?" His discussion thus brings into focus the methodological challenges of adequately understanding the European colonial text and of separating European colonialist ventriloquism from the textual traces of native agency.

Two of the best corpuses that we have for the recovery of Amerindian agency and knowledge are the missionary ethnographies and the Crown-sponsored natural histories written in the sixteenth century—even though they were written so as to radically change the cultures whose knowledge they described. In "The Method of Francisco Hernández: Early Modern Science and the Translation of Mesoamerica's Natural History," Jaime Marroquín Arredondo investigates the official translation of Mexico's Amerindian naturalist scientific knowledge through an analysis of Hernández's empirical and rhetorical methodologies employed for the composition of his famous *Historia de las plantas de Nueva España*, a prime example of the global and transcultural character of Renaissance natural history. An analysis of the methodologies of Hernández's natural history reveals their reliance on the systematic gathering of *relaciones* and their relationship with an emerging historiographical genre, the *historias de indios*, or ethnographic histories, a fact that Marroquín Arredondo uses to highlight the common epistemological origins of the early modern natural and social sciences. In Hernández's and Sahagún's works, Marroquín Arredondo adds, it is evident how the medieval European traditions of *translatio studiorum* (the translation and Christianization of knowledge from one culture to another) were adapted to the radical epistemic novelty of the Indias Occidentales (Spanish possessions in the Americas) through a skilled manipulation of *historia*. For both Hernández and Sahagún, humanist expertise in grammar and rhetoric, their participation in the development of new procedures—borrowed from the judicial tradition—for the systematic verification of experience-based information through *relaciones*, and their involvement and knowledge about the rapidly evolving empirical practices make their works pioneer examples of the transformation of Renaissance *historia* into a new methodological and rhetorical framework for the acquisition, verification, translation, and "reduction" of witness-based (autoptic) knowledge acquired through incipient global networks of knowledge.

As noted above, besides the Franciscans, the most prolific gatherers and translators of ethnological knowledge in the early modern period were the Jesuits. And not coincidentally, the vigorous religious, political, ethnographic, naturalistic, and pedagogical activities of the Jesuits greatly contributed to the new rationalization and empirical understanding of the sciences while also attesting to the transcultural character of the gradual transformation of natural history and natural philosophy. In "Bernabé Cobo's Inquiries in the Natural World and Native Knowledge," Luis Millones Figueroa focuses on one of the most important sources for the colonial Andes, the Andalusian Jesuit Bernabé Cobo, who immigrated to the New World as a young man, became a member of the Society of Jesus, and spent over forty years in a number of locations in both South and North America. In 1653 he finished the manuscript of his *Historia del Nuevo Mundo*, an ambitious work whose first and most original part was devoted to nature in the New World. Although Cobo's life was centered on his duties with the Jesuit order, he was a naturalist at heart and took every opportunity to learn about the natural world. The part of his work devoted to nature has been praised ever since it came to light in the late nineteenth century. Millones Figueroa's chapter examines Cobo's interactions with native knowledge as part of the investigations leading to the composition of this natural history. He argues that Cobo's relationship with native knowledge was ambivalent: on the one hand, Cobo had no doubt about the superiority of the Western tradition of knowledge he had learned as a Jesuit, to the point of making fun of the presumed ignorance of the natives; on the other hand, the familiarity he had acquired over the years with certain aspects of native knowledge made him appreciate its value in more than one way. As Millones Figueroa shows, Cobo's experience in the New World convinced him of the limitations of traditional Western knowledge and revealed to him the Eurocentricity of many time-honored scientific certainties. Instead, it was increasingly native knowledge that became indispensable for solving some questions of his investigations. As a result, he prided himself on his understanding of native knowledge, which, he claimed, distinguished him as a naturalist from others who had written on the subject before him. In this, Millones Figueroa concludes, Cobo's example illustrates the reason why the Jesuits played such a leading role in the transmission of indigenous medicinal knowledge to European society.

While the chapters by Pimentel, Marroquín Arredondo, and Millones Figueroa focus on the translation of Amerindian natural knowledge mainly into Spanish context, the chapters in Part II, "Amerindian Knowledge in the Atlantic World," extend the investigation of the mobility of Amerindian knowledge beyond the Spanish Empire. Thus, in "Pictorial Knowledge on the Move: The Translations of the *Codex Mendoza*," Daniela Bleichmar examines an early phase in the relationship between the discovery of advanced Amerindian knowledge and its necessary translation through a study of the famous *Codex Mendoza*, a pictorial manuscript created in Mexico City in the 1540s. Bleichmar explores the role that translation played in the production and transmission of the *Codex Mendoza* in both senses discussed above: translation as a movement from one language into another and as a movement through space. On the one hand, despite its postconquest origins, the *Codex Mendoza* is less an example of hybridization, or *mestizaje*, she argues, than it is "an instance of translation, suggesting the constant movement, adjustments, and transformations involved in negotiating differences between languages, writing systems, and cultures." Indeed, as Bleichmar shows, the production of the codex involved multiple acts of translation: from Nahuatl to Spanish, from images to words, and from indigenous to Spanish versions of the content and its interpretation. Knowledge was made and transformed in the process. On the other hand, no sooner was the ink dry than the codex entered a second kind of translation: its physical transferal from place to place as it moved from Mexico to Paris, London, and Oxford, meanwhile being widely disseminated in publications such as Samuel Purchas's immensely popular *Hakluytus posthumus: Or Purchas his pilgrimes* (1625). As Bleichmar observes, "Thanks to Purchas, the *Mendoza* may well be the single most reproduced non-Western manuscript in early modern publications." As noted, it was through Purchas's publication, for example, that the *Codex Mendoza* reached the Jesuit polymath Athanasius Kircher (1602–1680), who used it for comparative material in his *Oedipus Aegyptiacus* (1652–1654), one of the most important works in seventeenth-century Egyptology inspired by Renaissance Hermeticism. But the *Codex Mendoza* was not alone in its travels: numerous other codices as well as all kinds of New World artifacts circulated through European collections. Thus, Bleichmar examines the *Codex Mendoza*'s translation across media, from manuscript to print, and discusses the ways in which various publications produced not only different interpretations but also multiple versions of the codex based on the pages they reproduced, the varying relations they articulated between images and text, and the conclusions they drew about Amerindian culture.

If the Franciscan and Jesuit Orders were the most important religious networks in the translation of Amerindian knowledge, equally important was the imperial machinery of knowledge production centered in the House of Trade and the Council of the Indies in Seville as well as the royal court in Madrid, including Philip II's monastic refuge outside Madrid, the Escorial. The courtly curiosity about the New World led to one of the most extensive and influential scientific expeditions of the sixteenth century under Philip II's *protomédico*, Francisco Hernández, who arrived in New Spain in 1570 to conduct the systematic study of American flora and fauna as well as materia medica, including Amerindian natural knowledge, to date. In "The Quetzal Takes Flight: Microhistory, Mesoamerican Knowledge, and Early Modern Natural History," Marcy Norton investigates the transmission of Amerindian ideas about nature throughout the early modern Atlantic world via Sahagún's and Hernández's works. In particular she focuses on Francis Willughby's *Ornithology* (1678), which was revised and published by Willughby's fellow member of the Royal Society of London John Ray and has become a canonical text in the history of the biological sciences, conventionally being associated with a view of the scientific revolution based in northern Europe. Norton argues that the *Ornithology*'s intellectual debt to the works of Hernández and his Nahua informants is one of the central features of the text and that by foregrounding this aspect of Willughby and Ray's project, we can see more broadly that early modern natural history cannot be understood independently of Native American agents, knowledge, and cultural systems. Thus, Norton argues, early modern European scientific writing about the New World should be understood in the context of an intercultural milieu that is at once European and indigenous and/or African. On the one hand, natural histories such as those of Sahagún and Hernández (as well as other sources used by Willughby and Ray) were informed by European practices of "natural history"; and on the other hand, they were thoroughly marked by the indigenous world in which they originated.

The section's third chapter, Sarah Rivett's "Local Linguistics and Indigenous Cosmologies of the Early Eighteenth-Century Atlantic World," juxtaposes Reformed British American and French Jesuit ethnographic practices within a circum-Atlantic context during the early eighteenth century, when the shattering of biblical linguistics made it increasingly difficult to map human diversity. In parallel, language philosophers turned to the specificity of place to reconfigure language as part of a national rather than biblical genealogy. Thus, Rivett focuses on the breakdown of Atlantic networks of philological study around the turn of the eighteenth century. Whereas only a generation earlier Royal Society members displayed keen interest in the mystical potential of North American languages, post-Lockean philosophers all but abandoned earlier interests in missionary linguistics. Philology thrived as a field of study in the British Isles under the direction of such influential figures as Edward Lhwyd, keeper of the Ashmolean Museum in Oxford from 1691 until 1709. Lhwyd designed a comprehensive study of British languages and their etymologies, customs, and traditions but as a nativist project, decoupled from the peoples, languages, and histories to be discovered in North America. Rivett sets Lhwyd and his philosophical coterie in contrast to Lafitau's attempts to explain to a European audience the genetic relevance of the peopling and languages of North America. While missionary knowledge of North American languages faded into the background of Anglo philosophical interest, Rivett argues, French natural philosophers such as Lafitau continued to value linguistic knowledge and remained engaged with the ethnological data produced therein. While North American missionary linguistics disappeared from by then global networks of information exchange during the eighteenth century, Rivett's chapter shows that this breakdown of Atlantic networks yielded some surprising and fruitful results: once unmoored from the need to fit indigenous words back into a Christian cosmology, missionaries began to learn from so-called indigenous language philosophers. Together, they arrived at unprecedented insights into North American linguistics. Among the Wampanoags in Plymouth and Martha's Vineyard and the Abenakis in Maine, Experience Mayhew, Josiah Cotton, and Sebastian Rale compiled records that remain the most lasting evidence we have of these languages today. Moreover, this sustained language encounter led these missionaries to insights that were astonishingly commensurate to indigenous cosmologies, thus veering toward what Rivett calls a "hybrid cosmology" that is both indigenous and Christian.

If we insist on the crucial role that cross-cultural translation played in the history of early modern science, it is not to suggest that such translations were the happy product of multicultural cooperation conducted for the benefit of humanity at large. Rather, they were deeply enmeshed in early modern geopolitics and sociopolitics of conquest, imperial rivalry, and pro-tonationalism. The chapters in Part III, "American Nature and the Politics of Translation," focus on the geopolitics of the translation of knowledge about the Americas from the Spanish context into other European contexts. Thus, Ralph Bauer in "The Crucible of the Tropics: Alchemy, Translation, and the English Discovery of America" focuses on the translation from Spanish to English contexts. Bauer's example here is Richard Eden's English presentation and reorganization of the natural histories of Oviedo, which appeared in Eden's volume together with a number of other texts relating to the discovery of America as well as with an early modern alchemical text, namely Vannoccio Biringuccio's *De la pirotechnia*. Bauer argues that Eden conceived of the European discovery of the New World and the alchemists' forays into the microcosmic occult in analogous terms by synthesizing classical naturalism with the Christian model of the martyr and the ethos of Christ's passion of the cross (from which the alchemical word "crucible" derives). Both early modern geographic discovery and alchemical experimentation are predicated on an esoteric construction of the occult that is reconciled with the Christian (i.e., Augustinian) interdiction on "vain curiosity" through its messianic and salvific reason. Thus, the religious underwriting of both alchemy and New World discovery legitimizes the modern materialist quest and the naturalist "discovery" of the secrets of nature. Moreover, the patent intellectual debt that Eden and later English men of science writing in the seventeenth century owe to the sixteenth-century Spanish natural historians of America such as Oviedo, Hernández, and Acosta through translation exposes not only the modern legacy of the Black Legend, according to which Spanish (Catholic) science was viewed as "old" science, but also the White Legend, according to which English knowledge about the Americas was a "new science" that resulted not from a conquest or from translation but instead from an empirical "discovery" of a virginal terra incognita.

If the narrative of discovery is thus often predicated on a geopolitics of appropriation and erasure of the knowledge of "others," these geopolitics of appropriation also frequently generated their own sites of resistance. Thus, in his chapter "Flora's Fate: Spanish Materia Medica in Manuscript," John Slater investigates sites of resistance by Spanish natural historians to the translation, appropriation, and recontextualization of their natural histories by Northern European popularizers, such as the famous Flemish botanist Carolus Clusius, writing in Antwerp, in the context of national and imperial rivalries. As Slater explains, the rise of Spain as an imperial superpower of global dimension in the course of the sixteenth century resulted in a reorientation of Spanish scientific humanism—"a turning away from Venice and the East toward the West of New Spain." One aspect of this reorientation entailed the language and the medium of the book itself by which Spanish natural knowledge about the New World was presented, disseminated, and communicated. Specifically, Slater examines the move in Spain away from imitations of printed Aldine Latin editions—which were still the model for the early works written by the famous physician Nicolás Monardes—and toward the use of the Spanish vernacular in natural histories written to remain in manuscript. Focusing on the later natural histories written by Monardes as well as those written by Juan Fragoso and Bernardo de Cienfuegos, Slater's chapter helps explain why, in the realm of medicine and natural history, a vernacular culture based on manuscript transmission came to thrive in Spain, while elsewhere in Europe we see a trend toward print. Most important, Slater argues, these shifts signal a change in the community that scientific writing presupposes, a Republic of Letters based on patriotic national linguistic and relational networks defined by imperial political boundaries rather than transnational distinctions in social status and education.

But despite this general vernacular turn of European science in the latter part of the sixteenth century, the Spanish natural histories written about the Americas continued to be disseminated throughout Europe, albeit now more often translated into other European vernaculars rather than into the lingua franca of Latin. The works of Oviedo and Monardes are cases in point, both being translated into Italian, French, and English. The scientific paradigm of natural history itself—encompassing the study of the entire Aristotelian sublunar world, including minerals, flora, fauna, and human cultures—was hereby intimately bound up with early modern theories about climate. In "New Worlds, Ancient Theories: Reshaping Climate Theory in the Early Colonial Atlantic," Sara Miglietti analyzes how Europeans negotiated the health challenges posed by overseas travel during the age of discovery, using Spain's exploration and settlement of the Americas as a case study. Focusing on travel accounts and experimental science during the seventeenth century—a period that has largely been overlooked by historians of climate theory—she considers the often contradictory ideologies that underpinned European overseas expansion and investigates how ideas about climate influenced European responses to the new foods and peoples they encountered in their travels around the globe. In so doing, she finds two major shifts in thinking about climate during the course of the seventeenth century: on the one hand, a shift from a "cosmological" to a "chorological" model, and on the other, a shift from the traditional notion of fixed climates toward an anthropogenic understanding of climate change. These shifts, she argues, can be traced through multiple processes of translation—across languages, investigative methodologies, disciplines and genres, geographical spaces, and institutional sites of knowledge production—and had far-reaching implications for the scientific terms in which the very concept of climate was construed as well as for ideas about its ethical and political effects on human beings.

The chapters in Part IV, "Translation in the Transoceanic Enlightenment," focus on the role that translation played in the transoceanic history of science during the eighteenth century, often seen as the century in which a strong turn toward scientific rationalism and the building of taxonomic systems mitigated interest in the collection of local particulars and indigenous knowledge. Thus, in "Columbian Circulations in the North Atlantic World: François-Madeleine Vallée in Eighteenth-Century Île Royale," Christopher Parsons investigates the eighteenth-century translations of local knowledge in the northern French colonial possession in the early Americas, particularly at the littoral ecosystems near the fortress of Louisbourg at Île Royale (today Cape Breton Island). As did the rest of the continent, this region bore witness not only to the circulation and translation of knowledge but also to the creation of entangled landscapes that blurred distinctions between colonial and indigenous natures. Parsons shows how in or around 1725, at the beginnings of a new "enlightened" science, François-Madeleine Vallé sent a fourteen-page text titled the *Mémoire sur les plantes qui sont dans la caise B* that sought to discursively and materially transport these fluid ecologies across the Atlantic. Vallée, like many who sought the support of Paris's Académie Royale des Sciences, used botany to prove his use to would-be Parisian patrons. Yet, alone among texts that embraced Latin names and standardized descriptions, Vallée's *Mémoire* frequently focused attention on the expertise of local indigenous peoples (likely Mi'kmaq) and acknowledged the contributions that they had made to colonial knowledges and ecosystems alike. In its descriptions of maritime and coastal plants—ranging from Kokocar to the herbe á jean hebert—the *Mémoire* therefore also highlighted the fluid boundaries between indigenous and colonial knowledge in early eighteenth-century North America. The text's subsequent Atlantic history also illustrated the selective erasure of indigenous contributions to European science, for when the *Mémoire* arrived in Paris, its remarkable content was dismissed. Instead, it was valued primarily for the dried plants pressed between its pages and archived in the Jardin du Roi's herbarium, where it survives to this day.

Parsons's chapter aptly illustrates our volume's attempt to conceptualize the entangled and mutual translations of metropolitan, colonial, and indigenous knowledges in an increasingly cosmopolitan early modern Atlantic world. While Parsons's examples are derived from the French Enlightenment, Ruth Hill, in "Native Engravings on the Global Enlightenment: Pedro Murillo Velarde's Sea Map and Historical Geography of the Spanish Philippines," proposes that the Spanish Enlightenment, framed as a process rather than as an event, was overall even more cosmopolitan or global than the French, English, and German Enlightenments. This was so in part, she argues, because of the growing Northern European perception that Spain was backward, compelling Spanish *novatores* to devour the scientific cultures of other countries and regions (knowledge economies that had earlier relied to varying degrees on the Spanish world for their own scientific modernity), and in part because Spanish culture, folk and learned, was variously informed by the imperatives and contingencies of a transatlantic and transpacific empire. Focusing on the vast corpus produced by Murillo Velarde—historian, geographer, jurist, catechist, and cartographer—Hill's chapter outlines the heuristic, epistemic, and ideological principles at work in Spanish Enlightenment construction of nature. She argues that Velarde's taxonomic gaze, manifest in his remarkably accurate maps of the Philippines (1734, 1744), was forged from a variety of native and European knowledge cultures he had come into contact with as a missionary in the Philippines and as a distinguished professor of law at the University of Manila. Having also spent time in Mexico, especially Acapulco and Mexico City, he published his *Curso de derecho canónico hispano e indiano* (*Cursus Iuris Canonici Hispani et Indici*, 1743), which secured his status as the decisive textual authority on canon, Spanish, and Indies law well into the nineteenth century. Murillo Velarde's construction of nature attests to the fact that the "new philosophy," or modern science, relied on the patronage of the wealthy and the powerful at the same time that it naturalized and systematized the hierarchies that enabled it. Significantly, Hill shows, many of Murillo Velarde's taxonomic criteria for classifying plants, animals, and humans in Spanish America and Spanish Asia were derived from native gazes and epistemes. Thus, asymmetrical relationships between estates, different human groups, and metropolitan and Atlantic and Pacific economies are redoubled when Murillo Velarde builds taxa using the language of atomists and corpuscularians.

Collectively, the chapters assembled here explore the crucial role that the translation of philosophical and epistemological ideas played in European scientific exchanges with the American (and Asian) Indians; the ethnographic practices and methods that facilitated the efficient appropriation of Amerindian knowledge; the rhetorical and historiographical ideas and practices used to record, organize, translate, and conceptualize Amerindian naturalist knowledge; and the persistent presence and influence of Amerindian and Iberian naturalist and medical knowledge in the development of early modern natural history. The history of early modern natural science, we insist, is multicentered, transcultural, and transoceanic in character and born from an age of translation.

Part I

Amerindian Knowledge
and Spain's New World

Chapter 1

Sighting and Haunting of the South Sea:
On Ponquiaco, Balboa, and What Maps Conceal

Juan Pimentel

On September 27, 1513, Vasco Núñez de Balboa, accompanied by 67 of his men and an indeterminate number of natives, climbed a promontory in the mountain range of the Chucunaque River and at last sighted open sea. Two days later, together with 26 of his men and another indeterminate number of natives, he reached the sea at a place that he baptized as the Gulf of San Miguel because it was the feast day of the archangel. Balboa thus realized the goal he had set for himself twenty-two days earlier when he began the trek with an army of 190 Spaniards and about 600 natives from Santa María de la Antigua, the Spanish enclave in the region of Darién (on the other side of the isthmus) on the Gulf of Urabá.[1]

The chronicler Gonzalo Fernández de Oviedo y Valdés recounts how that morning (it must have been about midday) the *adelantado* had to postpone his long-awaited meeting with the waters, for although he had everything prepared (arms, the royal standards, his speech), the tide was out, and the sea was some leagues away. Between Balboa and the sea there lay an impenetrable quagmire of mud and scrub, a place full of debris from the nearby mangrove swamps and unsuitable for the solemn scene he wanted. He then decided to sit on the sand and wait for the tide to come in, doubling the dramatic effect. "As he sat thus," says Oviedo, "the sea rose before all their eyes, rapidly and forcefully" until the captain allowed himself to be—how can we put it?—embraced? bathed? baptized by the ocean?

When the sea reached Balboa, he stood up, took a royal banner bearing the image of the Virgin and Child, flourished his naked sword, and "walked into the water of the salty sea until it reached his knees." Walking in this way along the shore, waving his weapons, Balboa pronounced the solemn declaration taking possession of the South Sea, as recorded by Oviedo in Book 19 of his *Historia general y natural de las Indias*. In the name of Don Fernando and Doña Juana, the sovereigns of Castile and Aragon, respectively, the captain proclaimed the "real and corporal possession of these seas and lands and coasts and ports and islands of the south, with all their adjacent kingdoms and provinces . . . both discovered and yet to be discovered."[2] This was a somewhat lengthy proclamation, probably prepared and also likely to have been quite accurately noted. Oviedo reached Tierra Firme (the Spanish Main) the following year, in 1514, with the expedition of Pedro Arias de Ávila (often known as Pedrarias), Balboa's great rival and eventually his father-in-law as well as his executioner. The chronicler met the protagonists of that day personally and collected and read their documents, and in this case it is likely that he reflected the wording left by the scribe Andrés de Valderrábano, a witness to the events, undoubtedly dictated by Balboa himself.

Thus began the earliest sequence of the account of one of the most important geographic discoveries in the history of the expansion of the Western world, the first contact of European man with the South Sea, years later recognized as the same ocean that Ferdinand Magellan sailed, the Pacific Ocean. With some variations, this version of events passed into the writings of Mártir de Anglería and Bartolomé de Las Casas, the other two principal sources on the early colonization of the Caribbean and Tierra Firme; in addition, we have the chronicle of Pascual de Andagoya, a witness very close if not in person, who also landed in Tierra Firme in 1514.[3]

There are many questions that a historian could and should ask about this account. We have to ask ourselves about the nature of the events recounted: their plausibility and intention as well as omissions or ellipses. Texts say many things and suppress others, but between what is explicit and what is suppressed there is, let us say, a *contact zone* in which the majority of events of the past lie. There are things that are half said, or half hidden: omissions, ellipses, things at once said and hidden. I am going to follow two of these ellipses, or clues, that will lead us to the two subjects I wish to comment on and that I shall in turn base on two images.

The first clue comes from the contrast between the precision when enumerating the Spanish contingent (Oviedo took the trouble to take down the names of Balboa's sixty-seven companions) and the vagueness when counting and identifying the native presence at the moment of the discovery. Of course, the Amerindians are not totally absent from this extract from Oviedo or from any of the chronicles recounting the arrival of the Spaniards to the other side of the isthmus. They are not totally deleted. They simply appear blurred and are depicted according to the cultural stereotypes of their observers.[4]

In this chapter, I want to explore the role of the indigenous peoples in this *discovery* and in general terms the role of native knowledge in the preparation of maps, descriptions, and other European devices at the heart of so-called modern science. From David Turnbull and Helen Watson-Verran's cross-cultural comparisons of knowledge to the studies of Barbara Mundy and Alessandra Russo on mestizo cartography, the histories of science and colonial studies have concerned themselves with the geographical knowledge of the indigenous peoples, the processes of cultural hybridization, and how space is represented in the contact zones.[5] Bruno Latour dedicated the famous episode of the encounter between the Chinese and Jean François de Galaup, comte de Lapérouse, on the beach of Sakhalin to this subject of cross-cultural cartographic comparison.[6] The Europeans wanted to know if it was an island or formed part of a continent (the classic question, the same as Balboa posed). To Lapérouse's astonishment, a local elder began to draw a map of the island in the sand while a younger resident of the island, aware that the tide would erase the sketch in a few hours, copied it into one of Lapérouse's notebooks. The fundamental difference between the geographical knowledge and maps of one or another, Latour reasoned, does not lie in their accuracy, their reliability, or the type of projection used but instead in a point related to communication: Lapérouse would return with these observations and markings to Versailles, where they would be recorded and engraved on maps. While some forms of representation are circulated and reproduced, the native map on the beach is washed away by the tide and disappears.

In our case, what disappeared were not just the maps (the cartographic devices if there were any) but also the actual natives in question. The inhabitants of Darién and Veragua, known as the people of the Cueva language, suffered the biological impact of the first contact and became extinct in a few decades. Smallpox and other infectious diseases finished off the devastating effect of the Spaniards. Experts have quantified this demographic disaster: in 1500 there were between 125,000 and 500,000 inhabitants on the isthmus.[7] By 1550 there was not a single survivor of the Cuevas. They were succeeded by the Cunas and other ethnic groups, but as Kathleen Romoli showed, the

Cuevas belonged to another ethnic group, linguistically different, that was wiped out forever.[8] How can we look into a culture that had disappeared, leaving hardly a trace? What can we know of their geographical knowledge and, more specifically, of the existence of the South Sea?

Archaeologists and ethnographers agree that the peoples of the Caribbean and lowland South America (Tierra Firme) lacked any writing or graphic system to depict the territory, let alone on paper. This does not mean that they had no idea of space and ways to memorize, indicate, or communicate the territory. Generally, says Neil L. Whitehead, an expert anthropologist of the Caribbean and Central America who is well versed in indigenous cartography, "the earth and sky were actively mapped through a wide variety of mediums including rock carving and painting, basketry, woodworking, dance, chant, personal adornment, and architecture."[9]

The chronicler Oviedo described the *areytos*, ceremonies involving song and dance, and had the perspicacity to compare them with the letters and accounts of the Spanish.[10] In other words, the Cuevas lacked what Balboa had at his disposal: notaries, scribes, and ways to write down events, positions, and the profiles of the topology. But the Cuevas had other unwritten systems for recording events, which in many indigenous cultures are associated with places. The different Cueva groups dressed and painted themselves in different ways, although they used the same language or dialects, particularly in the Darién area. They were hunter-gatherers. They traded, communicated, and fought wars among themselves. They calculated distances in days of travel, which the Spaniards quickly translated into leagues. The movement of Cueva ceramics and metalwork shows contacts to the north and south of the Pacific. In a word, the people Balboa contacted were in control of their environment and knew its geography. And without a shadow of a doubt, they knew of the existence of a sea on the other side of the mountain range and the dense jungle, although they surely considered that the information the Spaniards demanded was superfluous: we need no maps to move around our town, and we do not find it particularly amazing that the sun rises every morning in the same place. Simply put, the sea was where it has always been.

Between 1510 and 1513, Balboa was collecting evidence of his presence. Meanwhile, his enclave of Santa María de la Antigua was suffering regular shortages of supplies. His authority was in question in Hispaniola and at the Spanish court. Some of his emissaries had become lost in the Caribbean, and others were busy agitating against him (among these was Fernández de Enciso, author of the well-known *Suma de Geografía*). A master of the art of surviving in adverse conditions, Balboa strengthened his position on the ground between the two groups of people with whom he needed to fight: his army and the Indians. By turn popular and hated, Balboa was a cruel leader in battle and generous in victory. His policy of alliances with the indigenous groups was a success and inspired Hernán Cortés and those who followed him in colonization, showing the way to imposing themselves in the *Indias Occidentales*: versatile diplomacy aimed at taking advantage of conflicts between the native groups.[11] Balboa established alliances with several indigenous groups from Darién and Veragua, notably with the caciques Careta and Comogre, whom he named Fernando and Carlos, respectively. Balboa punished others, such as Ponca and Torecha, but normally used the double treatment of punishing them first and then offering them protection, a tactic that proved to be most effective.

From all of them he obtained valuable information about the two subjects that obsessed him: the existence of gold and that of a sea beyond the mountains of Darién. These two great geographic obsessions, inherited directly from Christopher Columbus, guided the first steps of the Spaniards in Tierra Firme (soon to be known as Castilla del Oro—Golden Castile—a clear advertising ploy) and indeed were to define the first globalization, marked by transoceanic voyages and the circulation of precious metals. Balboa interrogated all the people with whom he had contact about these two subjects, and almost all of them told him what he was hoping to hear and what was best for them: both water and gold were to be found in abundance but farther on, much farther on. *Coiba* is the word, according to the chronicles, that the Indians repeated, literally "farther away." The Spaniards, naturally enough, confused this with Quibó, Cibao, and other gold-bearing fantasies, for in this search—as in every discovery, in any exploration—the facts of experience had to be adapted to expectations just before the latter were radically changed by the former. While for the Spaniards this could be a *plus ultra*, the natives perhaps only hoped that the foreigners would pass them by and go and harass someone else, preferably their enemies. At first Balboa conjured up the existence of Dabaibe, a forerunner of El Dorado, up the Atrato River (San Juan for the Spanish). The following year he decided to undertake the discovery of the South Sea just after Pedrarias had been appointed governor and Balboa's own authority was threatened. At the worst season of the year, without the 1,000 men he had asked the Crown for but with about six hundred natives to act as guides, diplomats, porters, emissaries, translators, experts in crossing and fording rivers, nurses, cooks, and suppliers of food, Balboa set off to play his last trump card.[12] He spent some time gathering information from the interpreters, spies, and undercover agents, those figures known in recent historiography as *passeurs culturels* (go-betweens) and what the Spaniards called *lenguas* or *medianeros* and the natives of the region called *yurás* or *jurás*. There were Spaniards such as Juan Alonso, a soldier who had spent some time among the Indians and had been found and then reassimilated, and natives such as the princess Anayansi, the daughter of the cacique Careta and whom Balboa, anticipating Cortés, took as his wife and thanks to whom he was able to thwart a conspiracy of tribes against him.[13]

And, of course, we have Ponquiaco, the son of the cacique of Comogre, at whom we should look a little more closely. Anglería and Las Casas show Ponquiaco as an outstanding protagonist in this story. Oviedo, however, gives this role to the cacique of Ponca. This discrepancy once again highlights the indeterminate, anonymous, or blurred character with which the natives appear in the chronicles. To mix up foreigners, to see them as all the same, is something familiar elsewhere, as when one sees microscopic cells for the first time. So, let us take him as an allegorical figure, a symbolic person. It was Ponquiaco who assured Balboa that at the other side of the mountain, several days' march away, there was a *pechry*, a sea. Las Casas describes Ponquiaco as *un mozo prudente* (careful and wise lad).[14] Anglería goes further and says that Ponquiaco was a "discreet" man and possessed of a "marvellous natural wisdom,"[15] two striking epithets. Ponquiaco was a well-informed individual, an expert or wise man, someone who had mastered the secrets of nature, another common expression in the chronicles: "he revealed to them the natural secrets these lands held."[16] Other passages mention certain natives, expert in roaming the rivers, and herbalists who knew and applied remedies of amazing effectiveness (antipyretics, antiseptics, purgatives). The natives taught them what woods were immune to the teredo worm as well their agricultural practices and the pattern of sowing and harvesting for different types of maize, a fundamental point since subsistence in the region was always very precarious. Although from there they could see "land with more gold than iron ore in Biscay" or "rivers in which gold was fished in nets," we know of the shortages and terrible hunger that the Spaniards suffered. As one of them so rightly said, "we had more hunger than gold." Ricardo Piqueras titled his book on the subject *Entre el hambre y El Dorado: Mito y contacto alimentario en las huestes de conquista (s. XVI)* (*Between Hunger and El Dorado: Myths and Food Contact in the Armies of the Conquista*).[17] Abundance and scarcity: these are the two poles around which the discourse on the New World revolved that are already clearly visible in the life of Santa María de la Antigua, the first city founded by the Spaniards on the new continent. Instead of the supposed abundance of natural resources (particularly in the mines), we find scarcity, the principal concept of political economy, and one of the great contributions of Latin America to the social sciences, dependency theory, as Pablo Sánchez León recalls in a short work significantly titled *Abundancia y frustración* (Abundance and Frustration).[18]

Figure 1.1, which shows Ponquiaco as rendered by the publisher, engraver, and goldsmith Theodor de Bry, gives a visual account of an episode narrated by Las Casas and Anglería to illustrate the cultural interchange between Balboa's army and the people of Comogre. It is a much later image, a copperplate engraving, included in the volume *Americae pars quarta* (Frankfurt, 1594), dedicated to the voyage of Girolamo Benzoni, in the series *Great Voyages*. This picture was included in an iconographic collection that was one of the most efficient propaganda weapons against Spanish domination, one of the pillars of the Black Legend.[19] Apparently and following his usual custom, Balboa accepted the habitual tribute in Comogre in the form of jewels and ornaments, offered without resistance by the natives. And as he had recently begun to do in this kind of meeting, he prepared to distribute the spoils among his army there and then, keeping aside the *quinto real* (king's fifth) but rewarding his soldiers straight away, a method of satisfying them immediately. As we have said before, the captain had learned how to operate and negotiate between the Indians and his men. At that moment a dispute arose among the soldiers over the sharing of the spoils. And it was then that young Ponquiaco, that cautious and wise young man, rebuked them for their behavior: "If you are so hungry for gold that you disturb so many peace-loving people, suffering so much misery and discomfort, exiled from your country by the whole world, I shall show you a region rich in gold where you can slake that thirst."[20]

Beyond the valley and the mountains—a six-day march away, he assured them—was the lord of Tubanamá, who possessed more gold than them, not far from where there was an open sea: "The whole side that faces south from the watershed of the mountains produces gold in abundance." After crossing several mountain ranges, they would see "a broad sea on which sailed craft with oars and with sails, and beyond they would find a place with a great quantity of gold where its people ate and drank from great gold vessels."[21] While in the humanist Anglería's version Ponquiaco appears to embody the *virtus* of the ancient Romans and the cunning of someone trying to escape from his troublesome visitors, Las Casa's version is even more interesting,

Figure 1.1. Johann Feyerabend and Theodor de Bry, "Indi cuiusdam Gnomologia insignis de Christianorum avaritia," in *Americae pars quarta: Sive, Insignis & admiranda historia de reperta primum occidentali India à Christophoro Columbo anno M. CCCXCII, Francofurtensi* [The Remarkable Gnomology (Wisdom) of an Indian Regarding the Christians' Greed] ([Frankfurt am Main], 1594). Courtesy of the John Carter Brown Library at Brown University.

claiming that Balboa ordered them to melt down the works of art immediately; in other words, the booty was to be shared out after the pieces were melted down.[22] Indeed, we have several testimonies that Balboa traveled with the necessary technical equipment for melting the precious metal in his forays before Pedrarias erected the first permanent foundry in La Antigua, shortly replaced by another in Acla.[23] This little device enabled Balboa to share out the gold on the spot without waiting to return to his base camp. If this was the case, Ponquiaco's interruption may well have been motivated by seeing how the invaders were destroying the accumulated wealth incorporated in these delicate pieces of handiwork, "very rich in craft," perhaps figures of the local fauna, eagles, frogs, bats, or jaguars. According to the ethnographers, the value that the natives accorded to these jewels was not in their gold content, in carats, but instead in the ritual and semiotic meaning of a finished and transformed object. Balboa used the portable tools for melting gold as an instrument for sharing profits among his men and build their loyalty; at the same time, this was a technology that destroyed the technology of the Indians, transforming their accumulated wealth, their labor, and converting it into a monetary item, what economists call a liquid asset. Herein lies the powerful symbolic value of the device and of the scene at the center of the picture, while on either side are two parallel conversions: that of the natives on the right (through baptism) and at last the sighting of the ocean, announced and revealed by Ponquiaco, on the left. The beach next to the mangroves, the familiar sea where the people of Chiapes live, a natural and perfectly normal presence for the Indians of the region, is transformed into the Gulf of San Miguel, the place where Balboa, guided by the Indians, sights the South Sea, wades into its waters, and takes possession of it.

The indigenous contribution to the discovery of the South Sea reminds us of the collective nature of scientific practice and helps us to tone down the epic approach with which the traditional history of science—and more particularly the history of geographic discoveries—was usually presented (and still is; one only has to look at the commemorations held in 2013 on the occasion of the anniversary of this historic deed). The sociology of science has for years been explaining why we assign individual merit to discoveries, when in reality they are normally social negotiation processes.[24] In this sense, the concealment or marginalization of the natives in the account of the discovery of the South Sea obeys the fondness of the old narrative of science for those heroic scenarios accomplished by individuals: reinforced in this case by the supreme Eurocentrism of the history of geographic discovery, whose central argument, obviously, is European expansion.

As a matter of fact, we could question the use of the term "discovery" in its most traditional sense, as a concept evoking the unique, heroic, mental, and pioneering action that is revealed at the magical moment of the eureka. Balboa was guided by the Indians, who led him toward a place they knew well, and let him view a sea that was not unknown but quite the opposite: it was perfectly obvious and for them quite prosaic. Following this argument, we could question the discovery of all the oceans and continents. Nor would rivers, mountains, or lakes be discovered: they have all been there for thousands of years, they have all been known to some human communities. Nevertheless, some years ago Augustine Brannigan in his book *The Social Basis of Scientific Discoveries* explained why we should consider geographical discoveries as scientific discoveries (just as we discover planets or new natural species). In fact, Brannigan chose the significant example of why we should consider Columbus as the discoverer of America, in the same way that we consider Herschel as the discoverer of Uranus, despite the fact that Columbus was not the first European to reach American shores and never stopped believing that he had reached a land adjoining the Orient.[25] Perspective, viewpoints, and tradition make up our way of seeing the past. We explore and relate the past both retrospectively and prospectively. Just as Columbus's voyages produced a disclosure in our tradition, just as they launch a new era in our ideas of geography, by starting a public and social process, so too did Balboa, for he led the expedition that unleashed the knowledge of the Pacific Ocean, indeed, the construction of the Pacific Ocean as such, because every ocean—as has been said—is no more than a "figment of the cartographer's imagination."[26] In other words, the Western geographical tradition that has been responsible for distributing land into five continents and five oceans as well as distributing and organizing the past—the history of geographical discoveries—places Balboa at the origin of all the stories, descriptions, and maps that make up that tradition. It must be stressed that like Lapérouse, Balboa took notaries, clerks, and reliable witnesses able to record, in some way, the geographical position and the profile of that coast. Some of these inscriptions survived and were subsequently elaborated and put into a connected meaningful sequence. Soon would come Magellan, and the amazing extent of the ocean would be revealed. Then Andrés de Urdaneta would follow, finding the way to sail from Manila to Acapulco. More than the "Spanish Lake" (which was neither a lake nor ever Spanish, as Ricardo Padrón has written), it was the beginning of the age of the Pacific Rim.[27]

So, what kind of discovery was it? What sort of sea did Balboa discover? As well as analyzing the indigenous contribution, we must look into what Balboa was seeking and what he found before tradition gave meaning to his discovery, stressing his role and minimizing that of the natives. Or to put it another way, after reviewing how Balboa reached that point and before the invention of the Pacific got under way, with its priorities and its concealments, we have to ask ourselves what Balboa hoped to find there, what he saw, and how he depicted it.

We said at the beginning that we would make use of two elliptical clues, two half-said or half-hidden things in Oviedo's account. If in the first case it was the vagueness about the number and identity of the natives in the Gulf of San Miguel, we can now look at another detail, apparently trivial, that the chronicler lets slip: Balboa found himself obliged to postpone his encounter with the sea. The tide was out, extraordinarily far out. He was very likely calculating the high and low tides using the Caribbean tide tables. He did not expect—nor could he know—that in that place the tides would rise and fall so far. While in the Gulf of Urabá the tidal range was of no more than thirty centimeters, in the Gulf of San Miguel it could be of up to six meters. In other words, Balboa was totally unaware of the colossal size of the ocean and the range of its tides in this place.[28] This fact was no doubt the first sign that showed him that he had before him a very large sea, although he could not suspect just how large. Indeed, once the water reached them the soldiers tasted the water to see if it was salty. They were not sure whether it was a sea or a lake.

Balboa's knowledge of the region was full of doubts and uncertainties but was nonetheless very effective. Balboa was not a humanist like Cortés or a cosmographer like Enciso but rather a man of action, practical and expert in fieldwork. Historiography has normally depicted him as a tropical leader avant la lettre, a frontier captain, a man who could take care of himself among the jungle, his rivals, his soldiers, and the Indians.[29] He knew how to obtain information and what to do with it, but he also made use of disinformation: Bethany Aram, the author of a comparative study of Balboa and Pedrarias, has precisely pointed out the role played by disinformation in the exploration and conquest of the region.[30] The slowness of communications, the lack of information, and the difficulty of checking it were exploited by the natives, the court, and Balboa, each in pursuance of their own interests. In Balboa's case he devoted himself to spreading his hopes of finding gold going down the San Juan River and a sea on the other side of the mountain ranges, in both cases toward the south. These were, as we have said, his two geographical obsessions. And they were both linked: they were linked in the news provided by the natives because they were connected in his system of expectations, and thus they appear mixed in the letters he wrote to the king. They had been the same for Columbus, who sailed southward, as Nicolás Wey-Gómez brilliantly showed in his monumental *Tropics of Empire*.[31] We may say that three of Columbus's most important preconceptions or geographical concepts made footfall and began to grow in Tierra Firme: first, that the Torrid Zone was more habitable than some believed; second, that where the sun shone, gold was produced in greater quantities than in temperate zones; and third, that the newly discovered lands were the Indies—in other words, that in some way or other the Antilles and Tierra Firme led to Cathay and India—and that the New World was not really so new, only in part. The continental nature of the New World, its independent and separate character, could obviously only be proved once the Pacific Ocean had been revealed: this was done by one of the most famous and at the same time most mysterious maps of all time, Waldseemüller's mappa mundi.[32] As is well known, this map named America for the first time, drawing a nameless space between Asia and America in 1507, before any European had reached the west coast of the New World. An ocean foretold? In a way.

Ricardo Padrón, the author of several outstanding works on this subject, has pointed out that Balboa was indebted to the idea reflected in the image that Bartolomé Colón and A. Zorzi had outlined, where the southern New World was connected to Asia by a sort of isthmus or land bridge.[33] Although some maps, such as that of Waldseemüller, omit this isthmus, it was usual to think that the New World was joined to Asia by a narrow strip of land at the other side of which was a sea, perhaps Ptolemy's Sinus Magnus.

So, what sea did Balboa sight? No doubt it was one that in some way he expected to find, for the indications of the Indians seemed to corroborate the cosmographic forecasts that were being used by various Iberian navigators and cosmographers: an ocean foretold but as yet indefinite. In a classic of Portuguese historiography, Armando Cortesão recalled that the word *descubrimiento* at that time did not mean to reveal something for the first time but rather to recognize it, to bring to light something whose existence was in a sense already known.[34] Thus, princes sent pilots and navigators to *discover* lands of whose existence they had some information. The Canaries were known before they were discovered in 1336, Madeira before 1420, and the Azores before 1427.

Before Balboa caught sight of it, the South Sea was thus a foreseen or foretold ocean: a geographical supposition ranking with the strait that, farther north or farther south or better still both, must join the Atlantic with the route to the Indies. So, while America made an unexpected appearance, the South Sea was a necessary sea, a cosmographic rumor, an imaginary presence, perhaps shapeless but well supported. Perhaps now there would emerge for once and for all the *Quarta Pars*, the southern continent suspected by the ancients. We know about the importance of suspicions and projections in the process of discovery: Juan Gil dedicated a successful trilogy to the myths and utopias of the *descubrimiento*.[35] Another historian long before him, when dealing with the most noted of these myths, used an interesting term: *El Dorado fantasma*, the ghostly El Dorado.[36]

Here would be a good moment to talk of the *specter* of the South Sea, a presence detected with no empirical evidence, a presumed entity. Balboa's discovery is that of an expected ghost. On the promontory in the Darién Mountains there took place a sighting, a vision, an apparition, an epiphany or revelation, the first visual contact by a European with a foreshadowed phenomenon.

What is left of that vision? Unfortunately, Balboa too suffered from concealment, marginalization, and other vicissitudes of history. Important documentation about his figure has been lost, including his first *juicio de residencia* (trial of residence) and several of the letters he sent to the king, including the figures—the maps—that he drew of the Gulf of San Miguel.[37]

We do, however, still have one map, as far as we know the first map showing the Pacific coast on the Isthmus of Panama.[38] It is a portolan chart measuring sixty-eight by ninety centimeters (Figure 1.2). It is anonymous and undated, but evidence points to the Casa de Contratación (House of Trade) and the reform of the *Padrón Real* (Royal Register) in about 1518. The map is kept in the Herzog August Bibliothek in Wolfenbüttel, where it arrived within the collection of the humanist Konrad Peutinger. In the same collection are other famous portolan charts by such cartographers as Jorge Reinel and Diego Ribero. Balboa's map was studied several years ago by Richard Uhden and more recently by Maria Luisa Martín Merás, Jose María Sanz, and Antonio Sánchez.[39]

This is a portolan chart, that is, the classic sort of navigational chart representing the Mediterranean. We can see the central wind rose surrounded by the usual sixteen roses, from which are drawn the thirty-two conventional rhumb lines, drawn according to tradition in black, red, and green. Portolans are nautical charts, designed for sailing from one port to another. In addition to the typical rhumb lines, this chart includes another distinctive feature, the succession of place-names perpendicular to the coast.[40] Unlike the portolans of the Mediterranean, where the main or reference place-names are picked out in red (according to other interpretations, those whose location was certain), here they are all written in black ink: the New World was too recent, and the position of places (Indian villages, capes, inlets, and other features) was still uncertain. The place-names show the discoveries contained in the information available to its authors. There are the details of Amerigo Vespucci's surveys as far as latitude 30° South, at the level of Cabo Frío near present-day Rio de Janeiro. The chart includes the latest movements in Florida and also the discoveries in the areas that interest us: Tierra Firme, the Darién, and Veragua as far as Yucatán, which is still drawn as an island. The uncertainty of these outlines is significant, one of those "eloquent silences" of which Brian

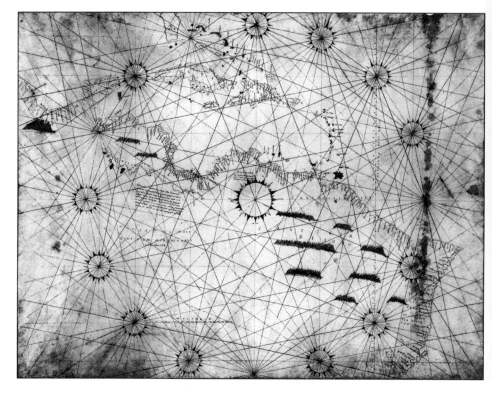

Figure 1.2. Portolan map. Courtesy of the Herzog August Bibliothek, Wolfenbüttel (Cod. Guelf. 103 Aug. 2°).

Harley spoke.[41] This is the result of lack of knowledge, but some of them are intentional: the names of the native towns are not shown inland; they do not occupy the territory but instead hang from the shore, since their function is purely orientative like the capes and gulfs, marked on the coast so they could be found on the coast and reached from there.

The chronicler Pascual de Andagoya wrote in his account that the Castilians called the province of the interior of Darién the "Behetrías,"[42] a medieval term designating a settlement where the inhabitants could choose their overlord: in other words, a land with no recognized authority, or not subject to the authority of anyone who might seize it. There was a shoreline drawn according to the conventions of the nautical cartography of the Mediterranean to reach its coasts, and a qualification of the interior was adopted from medieval

Castile to declare it juridically open to conquest: if every map implies a specific vision of the territory, this one is a hymn to access and possession.

In the middle of the map is the name of Dabaiba, the great gold-bearing fantasy of the moment, just on the equator, which is some 8° above its real position.[43] Immediately below the equator the name of Castiglia del Oro stands out, the recent designation for a territory that concealed other great treasures and at the time comprised what was later known as Nueva Andalucía. There we can see the mountains, crowned with golden peaks, that dominate the unknown territory, hope, the future, the imaginary geography. "Castiglia del Oro": this is not the only Italianism. Among the 289 place-names there is an abundance of Italian and Portuguese terms alternating interchangeably with Spanish, indicating the numerous Italian and Portuguese pilots and cartographers who worked for the Crown of Castile and also the collective nature of the map itself. Any map, even if it is signed, is the result of a collective effort. This one is no exception. Behind it lie the knowledge and contributions of many actors, from Ponquiaco and the Cueva Indians to Bastida, Balboa, Nicuesa, and the pilots, traders, and cosmographers of Seville. The map must have been made in the Casa de Contratación and appears to be one of the fragments of the *Padrón Real* or a copy of it: if there was ever a phantom map in the history of mankind it was the *Padrón Real*, whose very existence has even been questioned.[44] If the Iberian cartography of the New World was a "secret science,"[45] the *Padrón Real* was perhaps its most elusive, most clandestine treasure. The pace of the discoveries was so fast that it was difficult for the newfound knowledge to find its way to a map. Year after year what was known became obsolete. The *Padrón Real*, then, was something like the perfect secret, for it was never fully declared.

The Wolfenbüttel map, in addition to representing the first surviving cartographic depiction of the South Sea, possesses two other characteristics that make it even more valuable. In the first place, it seems to be the first portolan chart showing a scale of latitude, next to two of the wind roses on the right-hand side of the map, here labeled "Altitudo Poli Artici."[46] This is a considerably modern feature. The medieval portolans of the Mediterranean had no latitude scale; they only had the usual bar showing leagues, a scale of distances. If the Mediterranean was the nursery where Europe learned to sail, as Joseph Conrad wrote, and the Caribbean still allowed coastal sailing, within limits, the dimensions of the oceans would call for new methods and new nautical practices. The Atlantic and above all the Pacific Ocean, whose first corner is seen in this anonymous map, would oblige Europeans to develop astronomical navigation. The exact positions, first of latitude and later of longitude, would be the two fundamental conquests in a history that opened with the voyages of Columbus and ended with the great explorations of the Pacific during the Enlightenment. This scale of latitude written on one side of the map, and perhaps added later, is a small detail that cannot be overlooked. It is a nod toward the future written on a medieval tool, yet another example of how traditional technologies have had to incorporate innovations in order to survive change and also of how through minor modifications traditional technologies have been able to survive and in what way: the portolans reached the eighteenth century and in many cases depicted the territory with an accuracy that was difficult to surpass.[47]

Yet another peculiarity of the portolan chart is that neither Europe nor Africa appears. Its center of gravity is Tierra Firme, and its heart lies in the equatorial zone, where nature offers gold in abundance in a fictitious region, the Dabaibe. So, it is an emancipated image of the Old World, autonomous and decentralized: the periphery is the center. The territories of the New World, hardly recognized or dreamed of, are disconnected, cast away from the Old World.

But let us look at the legend that includes the discovery of the South Sea. It is in Latin and says that

> When King Ferdinand of Spain wanted to know more about this land, he sent about five hundred experts and specialists in military law to the lands so they could carefully investigate everything, and when they had gone in about sixty miles they found another immense wild sea, the current of whose waves rolled toward the shore from the south. Hence, it is clear that this land is not a continent as many cosmographers would have wished.[48]

Two things surprise us, both equally noteworthy. Again there is a striking omission: Balboa is not even mentioned, surely due to the persecution he suffered at the hands of the authorities. The king had sent Pedrarias in 1514 to seize power from him in the region. In 1519 Balboa was beheaded in a public square in the town of Acla (a native name, by the way, meaning "bones of men," for in the surrounding area there are many skeletal remains—according to legend—of two native brothers who fought over the leadership). Fratricidal struggles make Castilians and Indians alike. They are both the same when they suffer the violence of their enemies: real or symbolic, like the case of the disappearance of Balboa in the legend. The traces of enemies or traitors (the radical "other") are erased from the maps. Like Ponquiaco, Balboa is hidden from the discovery.

The second fact we should note is the conclusion that the author of the map reaches: the discovery of the South Sea shows that this land is not a continent, "as many cosmographers would have wished." This may seem surprising: the sighting and finding of the geographical fact that reveals the continentality of America, its independence from Asia, shows just the opposite. But this is not so. What is surprising is that we do not more often consider the retrospective nature of such a deduction. The obvious may not be so; maybe it is not obvious at all.

"This land is not a continent": the sentence is always (and also retrospectively, of course) reminiscent of Michel Foucault's famous essay on René Magritte's painting *The Treachery of Images* (*Ceci n'est pas une pipe*). Images are treacherous, and so are maps. "The word is not the thing," "the map is not the territory," said Korzybski, the creator of general semantics. Indeed, any map is an artifact that generates the illusion of knowledge and at the same time distorts, highlights, darkens, and silences facts as a function of the interests of those whose interests it serves, the technologies it uses, and the ideology it proclaims.

The Wolfenbüttel chart is one of the few portolans to have survived. It is estimated that only a tiny percentage of those that existed formerly are still in existence.[49] (Some) European cartographic instruments have also suffered from the tides of time. (Some) European explorers also suffered partial or temporary eclipses. But it is nothing in comparison with the phantasmification suffered by individuals such as Ponquiaco or the geographical devices of the Cueva Indians.

Below in the chart there is another revealing caption: "the Western Sea, which connects with the Southern."[50] The connection between the two oceans, the existence of a passage or strait leading to the Orient, is still alive in the imagination of the cartographer. The New World must be an island. Seen in this way, the snapshot of this discovery once again highlights the impact of presupposition on the data collected, the tenacity with which what is found must adapt to what is imagined. Ricardo Padrón very rightly commented that the invention of the Pacific was the result of the interchange between the observed facts of experience and the cultural expectations held by the explorers.[51] This case affords a good example of it as well as of the successive concealments, silences, and ellipses produced by discoveries: those empty spaces reflected by the texts and images and that, besides, are never definite but partial and temporary. While it is true that any discovery sheds light on certain facts at the cost of casting shadows on others, it is also the case that history, like cartography, is an unstable discipline, always on the move.

Chapter 2

The Method of Francisco Hernández: Early Modern Science and the Translation of Mesoamerica's Natural History

Jaime Marroquín Arredondo

Every scholar who studies Francisco Hernández's *Historia natural de las plantas de Nueva España* (ca. 1576) is used to telling the story of the tragic loss of the most complete, illustrated version of Mexico's most famous natural history during the 1671 fire in the Royal Library of El Escorial. One rendering of this story might begin with Hernández's return to Madrid in the early months of 1577, ill after six years of intense labor in Mexico overseeing the efforts of his many collaborators and writing a natural history that roughly quadrupled the number of known plants in Europe.[1] As careful and methodical as he was, he had ordered his scribes in New Spain to copy the four volumes that composed the written part of his natural history. There could be no copy, however, of the eleven volumes that contained the nearly 4,000 colored illustrations of Mexican plants, animals, and Mesoamerican gods and rituals.[2] Upon his return, Hernández urged the king to help him print and disseminate a work that accomplished the incredible feat of uniting the natural history of the two worlds. Hernández warned Spanish authorities that he was old and sick, that the printing process of his *historia* would be long, that only he had the ability to "put it in reason and make it useful," and, moreover, that his work was unrepeatable, since many of the Indian doctors and painters who had helped him died during the plague that devastated Mexico in 1576.[3] He would spend the last ten years of his life working on his natural history and trying to have it published, to no avail. The number of illustrations likely made the price prohibitive for an empire in constant financial trouble.[4]

Hernández's natural history would nevertheless have considerable influence in the development of early modern natural history.[5] As is well known, Nardo Antonio Recchi's abbreviated version of Hernández's natural history would be the basis for the *Rerum medicarum Novae Hispaniae Thesaurus* (1628), the most influential of all the works published by the Academia dei Lincei, often regarded as the first modern scientific academy, whose bicultural content dissemination in northern Europe is evocatively tackled by Marcy Norton in her chapter in this volume.[6] As is also well known, a copy of Recchi's short version of Hernández's Mexican natural history would be the basis for Francisco Ximénez's *Quatro libros de la naturaleza* (1615), which was published in Mexico and made part of Hernández's work accessible on the other side of the Atlantic.[7]

The *Historia de las plantas de Nueva España* has achieved in the last thirty years the recognition, study, and praise its author hoped it would attain during his lifetime. Studies about it have been fundamental to the ongoing incorporation of Iberian and Amerindian sciences and empirical practices into a more global history of modern science. These studies, however, have devoted little attention to the analysis of Hernández's (and most historians' of the Indies) epistemological ideas, methodologies, and rhetorical practices employed while translating, validating, and corroborating early American naturalist knowledge.[8] Historians of science have embraced the notion that local time, space, and culture always conditions the production and circulation of knowledge, yet very little attention has been devoted to transcultural linguistic and rhetorical practices, which remain the most visible "place" where one can partially analyze how local knowledges become "early modern science." Thus, this chapter outlines a history of the translation and appropriation of Mesoamerica's naturalist knowledge as a key component of the evolution of early modern natural history's information-gathering methodologies, rhetorical practices, and epistemological ideas. Through a detailed examination of Hernández's research methodologies, I highlight the parallel and interrelated evolution of Renaissance natural history with the emergence of a new and heterogeneous historiographical genre, often referred to as ethnographic history.[9] I claim that this ethnographic turn is one of the most salient aspects of the transformation of classical natural history into an early modern scientific genre. This turn can be apprehended through a careful study of the several narrative and methodological layers involved in the composition of Francisco Hernández's *Historia de las plantas de Nueva España*.

Key to this argument about the mostly overlooked ethnographic component of early modern science is an analysis of the development and evolution of the narrative genre that united most forms of scientific knowledge in the sixteenth and seventeenth centuries: the *relación*, considered by Francis Bacon in *The Advancement of Learning* (1605) as the most truthful kind of *historia*.[10] The analysis of the *relación* as a genre and as it relates to the emergence of early modern scientific disciplines sheds new light on our understanding of Renaissance *historia*, since *relaciones* were systematically involved in the description of particulars based on sensorial perception, a process that very often was transcultural and protoethnographic.[11]

With a long tradition of use in judicial affairs, the *relación*—a short witness-based account of events, often based on standardized questions—permitted the massive accumulation of matter-of-fact information from the Indies, precisely the kind deemed necessary for adequate imperial rule. The framing of the questions to be answered by qualified witnesses determined not only the kind of information desired but also how deep and thorough the translator's knowledge about indigenous languages and cultures needed to be. In a quite literal way, these ethnographic *relaciones* helped change the structure and language of history.

Although it is by no means ideal to use nineteenth-century terminology to name Renaissance variants of *historia*, the term "ethnographic history" makes explicit that the systematic study of a different culture—what anthropologists would come to define as the description and analysis of "cultural *alterity*"—was indeed a common and rather systematic component of sixteenth-century histories composed in the Iberian Americas.[12] Moreover, sixteenth-century Iberian narrations about Native Americans' customs, religion, past, and knowledge were a rather identifiable historical genre. Their authors used different names for them, such as "antiquities" of Indians, "general histories" of Indians, "commentaries" of Indians, and "histories" of Indians.[13] Most of them were based on *relaciones*, gathered through the systematic interviewing and translation of qualified indigenous witnesses.

During this process *historia*, as a genre, became not only a new narrative form but, crucially, also provided a well-established epistemological, methodological, and rhetorical framework for the translation of indigenous knowledges. This process is well known with regard to Europe, as one of *historia*'s branches, natural history, gradually became a fundamental genre for many scientific studies during the sixteenth century. Its rise led to Francis Bacon's famous dictum regarding natural history as the very foundation of a "new science." As he wrote in *The Advancement of Learning*, "So of natural philosophy, the basis is natural history; the stage next the basis is physic; the stage next the vertical point is metaphysic."[14] This chapter revisits some of these pivotal epistemological processes as they happened in sixteenth-century Mexico, one of the several epistemological global centers involved in the renewal of natural history and natural philosophy.[15]

The "translation of Indies" was both haphazard and systematic. With varied degrees of complexity and success, it often followed the centuries-old tradition of *translatio studiorum*. Indeed, *translatio* was the privileged vehicle for ensuring the passage of textual and material culture from Egypt to Greece, from Greece to Rome, from Byzantine to Arabic culture, and from Greek and Arabic languages to Latin, Italian, and Spanish. An idea of cultural translation and transmission had its most explicit origins with the *translatio imperii* of the Christian empire from Byzantium to Rome under Charlemagne's rule. Classical pagan culture was "reduced" or Christianized to the seven liberal arts of the medieval trivium and quadrivium. The idea of *translatio imperii*, or translation and transfer of power, included a larger sense of *translatio studiorum*: the translation of a knowledge patrimony to another cultural context.[16] *Translatio studiorum* implied the necessary transformation and appropriation of knowledge to new historical and cultural contexts, tolerating neologic invention and abundant neosemy and providing detailed commentary and clarification of obscure passages or texts. These accompanying forms of incorporating pagan knowledge to Christianity were called *reductio artium*.[17]

As recent scholarship has shown, most of the new ways of understanding a suddenly global nature were dependent on emerging transoceanic networks of knowledge established by imperial authorities with the aid of men of religion, science, letters, and crafts.[18] The history of early modern science is gradually turning its attention to the complex material and epistemological processes involved during the translation of other civilizations' knowledge during the early modern/colonial period.[19] In this sense, a structural analysis of Hernández's influential natural history makes it possible to study the emergence of some of the constitutive parts of early modern science in its colonial settings, at the foundational and deadly borders of colonial empires.[20] Moreover, the evolution of the aims, methodologies, and standards for judging their efficacy, as well as the rhetorical practices employed for the composition of Hernández's natural history, reveal that the *historias de Indias*

(East and West) ought to be incorporated into Arno Seifert's famous characterization of *historia* as the "godmother of empiricism."[21]

While reconstructing Hernández's methodological and rhetorical practices, I point out and briefly summarize key contributions from precursors of his ethnographic work in Mexico. The chapter proper begins by briefly placing Hernández's work in the context of early modern natural history. This is followed by a thick historical description of the methodological and rhetorical processes that Spanish and Amerindian authorities employed to translate vast fragments of Mesoamerica's knowledge into historiographical words and images. I illustrate the evolution of Hernández's methodologies by outlining their progression in three sections: collection and corroboration; experience and experimentation; and rhetoric and narration. I also demonstrate that Hernández's work was dependent on the gathering and composition of *relaciones* from qualified indigenous informants, many of which were empirically verified through the use and readaptation of common European forms of medical experimentation. The chapter concludes with a reflection about the relevance of this kind of work not only for the history of science but also for our understanding of Iberian American colonial knowledge production.

Francisco Hernández and Early Modern Natural History

Francisco Hernández was born in Puebla de Montalbán, in the province of Toledo, between 1515 and 1520, the years of the coronation of Charles as king of Spain and Emperor of the Holy Roman Empire of the German Nation.[22] Iberia was then a key contributor in the production of scientific knowledge.[23] In the field of natural history, Iberian humanists contributed to the process of commenting and updating Pliny's *Libri naturalis historiae*, which had been reassembled into a coherent text late in the fifteenth century.[24] Moreover, one of the first two books to be named as a natural history during the Renaissance was Gonzalo Fernández de Oviedo y Valdés's influential *Sumario de la natural historia de las Indias* (1526), some of whose aims, dissemination, and influence in northern Europe and particularly in England are traced and analyzed by Ralph Bauer's chapter for this volume.[25] In medicine, several Spanish universities and hospitals were active agents in the European rediscovery of Dioscorides and Hippocrates as well as in the Vesalian reform and the incorporation of Amerindian and African materia medica to the renewed and multifaceted genre of natural history.[26]

A young Hernández decided to study medicine, most likely in the prestigious University of Alcalá de Henares. After some years of practice in central Spain, he moved to Seville around the year 1550, where he alternated his medicinal practice with herborizing expeditions aimed at the composition of a local herbal of Andalusia.[27] By the late 1550s he began working at the prestigious Monastery of Guadalupe, in Extremadura, whose hospital was open to botanical and medical innovations in Europe and possessed the best medical library and botanical garden in Spain. Hernández practiced there as a physician, conducted human dissections, worked in the botanical garden, collaborated with the apothecary, and herborized in the surrounding fields. He also did work in the monastery's library, writing his now lost critical comments about Galenism and beginning a commentated translation of Pliny that he would finish while working in Mexico.[28]

At the time, the study of nature was conceptualized from the precepts of natural philosophy, one of the three branches of speculative (or theoretical) philosophy along with mathematics and metaphysics.[29] Natural philosophy had its origins in Aristotelian physics (*physike*), which established the principles of change that govern all natural entities through the study of the form and movement of matter.[30] In the particular genre of natural history, the overarching theory was the *scala naturae*. The great chain of being, created by God, began with Heaven's angels, had its middle step in humanity, and ended with the inanimate things of nature.[31] Celestial radiation communicated part of its nature, or essence, to every element of Earth.[32] The physical world was considered reducible to four fundamental properties: heat, cold, dryness, and humidity. Natural histories, a quite heterogeneous genre, often contained a mixture of philological, medicinal, botanical, and cosmological information.[33]

Medicine and natural history were perhaps the two most important scientific disciplines of the early modern period, generously sponsored and financed by European monarchies.[34] This led to the evolution of Renaissance gardens into laboratories for the acclimation and cultivation of medicinal, ornate, and rare plants that could become valuable state commodities.[35] The most sought-after plants—pepper, ginger, cinnamon, and cloves—all came from Southeast Asia.[36] During the sixteenth century, Spaniards attempted unsuccessfully to establish a similarly lucrative exchange in the Atlantic.

When Hernández returned to Toledo by the middle of the 1560s, the Spanish court was increasingly interested in the commercial possibilities of Mexican medicinal plants.[37] A few years later while already working as a physician at the court nearby Madrid, he collaborated in the development and improvement of the royal botanical garden of Aranjuez.[38] The Spanish Crown's interest in the commercial exploitation of Mexican plants became strong enough to organize an exclusively scientific expedition to the Americas.[39] On January 11, 1570, Hernández received from the king his appointment as protophysician-general of the Indies. The main aim of his mission was, famously, to "gather information generally about herbs, trees and medicinal plants" from New Spain.[40] He also understood his work as an opportunity to begin writing a new global kind of natural history.[41] This would accomplish, as he wrote in the dedication of his translation of Pliny, "the modern perfection of Spain and of the rest of its kingdoms, which, if the remaining princes did [the same] in theirs, would [make] our age enjoy what those who preceded us did not."[42]

Collecting and Corroborating *Relaciones* about Mexico's Plants and Medicine

At the time of Hernández's appointment as protophysician, the Crown was aware that there were "more plants, herbs and medicinal seeds [in New Spain] than elsewhere."[43] There were already well-established networks of knowledge production and dissemination in Mexico, coordinated by the political and religious authorities of New Spain. In every place he visited, Hernández and his assistants were to be referred by Spanish and Indian authorities to "the doctors, medicine men, herbalists, Indians and other persons with knowledge in such matters."[44] A similar chain of information was available to Francisco Domínguez, the cosmographer appointed by Philip II to accompany Hernández to Mexico, where he conducted a mostly unsuccessful land survey of the viceroyalty.[45]

Hernández's informants were contacted through the political pyramid of the viceroyalty, including *corregidores*, medical doctors, friars, mayors, Indian principals, Indian translators, and Indian doctors. His main sources were Spanish doctors and, above all, Mesoamerican *ticiti* (physicians) from Mexico City and the different regions he explored.[46] Hernández conducted some of his naturalist and medicinal investigations at the University of Mexico, the Hospital Real de San José de los Naturales (where he established his more permanent working place), the Hospital de Santa Cruz de Oaxtepec, and other hospitals established by religious orders all over New Spain.[47] He greatly benefited from his own expertise doing fieldwork and took particular advantage of the remains of ancient pre-Hispanic gardens from Texcoco and Oaxtepec.[48]

Knowledge production in the Iberian Americas followed increasingly bureaucratic and legalistic methods, all based on the gathering of *relaciones*.[49] Oviedo famously wrote in the prologue of his *Sumario de la natural historia de las Indias* that he had relied on *relaciones* collected from "truthful people" when dealing with matters not personally experienced. The Crown had in fact provided Oviedo with "orders and warrants" to this effect, specifying that all "governors, magistrates and officers of the Indies" were supposed to provide him with "notice and truthful *relación* of everything worth of history, through authentic testimonies, signed with their names [in presence] of public clerks."[50]

In Mexico, these methods had their most significant beginnings in the commission of 1525, given to the judge Juan Ponce de León, which included a proposed method for collecting cosmographic, topographic, commercial, and ethnographic information.[51] According to this commission, New Spain's authorities were supposed to consult with people who possessed adequate experience and training, making them answer a questionnaire.[52] The *Descripción de Nueva España*, now lost, was dispatched to Madrid on July 5.[53] This work, a pioneer approach at the official translation of indigenous knowledge from Mexico, was coordinated by the *oidores*, or judges of the Audiencia of New Spain, the ruling colonial institution, along with the provincials of the religious orders, all under the leadership of Sebastián Ramírez de Fuenleal, former bishop of Santo Domingo and president of the Mexican Audiencia.[54] Throughout most of the colonial period, the Spanish Crown's and the religious orders' "epistemological settings" and aims in Mexico would remain entangled, most particularly during the seminal presidency of Ramírez de Fuenleal.[55]

On April 30, 1532, seven months after disembarking in Veracruz, the newly appointed president of the Audiencia informed the emperor that he had already started gathering the necessary information to compose the requested *Descripción de Nueva España*.[56] Fuenleal, a humanist who studied canon and civil law at the Colegio Mayor de Santa Cruz in Valladolid,[57] explained in his letter the methodology he had followed to describe the territories' extension and names; the natives' political organization, rites, customs, tribute-collection mechanisms, and common forms of land distribution; and even the animals that inhabited the lands.[58] Following the Crown's instructions, the Audiencia of New Spain had instructed the tribute collectors of all known towns—the *visitadores* or *calpisques*—to write a *relación* of the diverse lands they commonly worked on. He had then instructed all *corregidores*, monasteries' guardians, *encomenderos*, and Spanish towns' mayors to write a more detailed *relación* of their particular land. Indian principals had been ordered to compose "paintings" of their own lands and towns.[59]

From these pioneer efforts, Spanish colonial authorities would keep developing more detailed geographical, ethnographical, and naturalist questionnaires to be sent to all American possessions at different moments during the sixteenth century.[60] At the time of Hernández's expedition, the Consejo de Indias (Council of the Indies), under the presidency of Juan de Ovando, was attempting to perfect its knowledge and control of the Indias Occidentales (Spanish possessions in America). The famous *Relaciones Geográficas de Indias*, a direct result of Ovando's presidency, was among the most powerful tools for the Spanish Crown's growing political control and economic organization of its American territories. The earliest answers to the questionnaire elaborated for the *Relaciones Geográficas* came in 1571, placing the expedition of Hernández as part of Juan de Ovando's information-gathering project.[61] The ethnographic character of all these *relaciones*, as Sara Miglietti notes in this volume, would help transform the previous cosmographic paradigm of knowledge into a new one, dependent on the newly developed ethnographic methodologies and networks.[62]

The study of sixteenth-century Iberian "ethnography" thus provides one of the earliest examples of the epistemological blending between judicial and historiographical practices, a well-known catalyst for the emergence of modern science. The concept of fact (*fait*), a key conceptual link between natural and human sciences, needs to be understood in its colonial dimensions.[63] Early modern facts were often testimonial reports of particular forms of experience. They were aimed at establishing reliable narrative forms and experience-based methodologies for the validation of a rapidly expanding accumulation of information from a suddenly global world. These new "matters of fact" soon became commodities as valuable as the ones extracted from nature.[64]

The beginnings of the systematic study of Amerindian cultures can be dated roughly forty years before Hernández's arrival in Mexico, in 1533, when President Ramírez de Fuenleal ordered Franciscan friar Andrés de Olmos, former student of canon law at the University of Valladolid, to study and compose a book about the "antiquities of this native Indians," particularly those of Mexico, Texcoco, and Tlaxcala. This would allow the preservation of some "memory" of the Indians' past and would better refute the erroneous parts of their beliefs. Crucially, Fuenleal added in his instructions to Olmos that "if something good were to be found, it [then] could be noted, as many things of other gentiles are noted and kept in memory."[65] Evidently, the protoethnographic project of the humanist mendicant friars in Mexico was not only a tool for the religious conversion of the Indians. The establishment of official policies for the *translatio studiorum* of Mesoamerican cultural heritage also aimed for the preservation of Nahua history and knowledge and its translation into Europe's intellectual tradition through *historia*.[66]

Both Sebastián Ramírez de Fuenleal and Andrés de Olmos were familiar with judicial processes. The president of the Mexican Audiencia had worked as an inquisitor in Seville before being appointed president of the Consejo de la Mesta in 1526.[67] For his part, Olmos had worked with Juan de Zumárraga while investigating witchcraft cases as an inquisitor in the Basque province of Zagarramurdi.[68] Sixteenth-century inquisitorial processes differed from late medieval ones in that they made the judge more participative in all stages. The inquisitor had to take statements and interrogate witnesses personally.[69] Olmos's ethnographic histories would inherit some of the methods of information gathering and corroboration from these inquisitorial processes as well as from the already well-established methodologies for the gathering of *relaciones*, developed by the Spanish Crown and the authorities of the Consejo de Indias.[70]

The first ethnographic *relaciones* gathered by Olmos were responses from expert informants about ancient Mexico's religion and cosmology. He relied on the transcultural rhetorical expertise of young Nahua scholars, knowledgeable of the oral and pictographic texts (*amoxtli*) of ancient Mexico and also of Spanish and Latin grammar and rhetoric.[71] In his *Historia de los mexicanos por sus pinturas*, written between 1533 and 1536, Olmos described his own research methodology. His sources were "the characters and writings they [natives] use," the narratives "of the elders and of those who were priests," and the testimonies of the "lords and principals, to whom the law was taught and [who] were raised in the temples."[72] Olmos interrogated principals and priests from the ancient cities of Tlatelolco, Huejotzingo, Cholula, Tepeaca, and Tlamanalco. His work is almost fully descriptive and nonexplanatory, suggesting his dependence on *relaciones* composed through standardized questionnaires.

The work of Bernardino de Sahagún, a disciple of Olmos, signals the sixteenth-century epistemological culmination of European and Mesoamerican transcultural translations. Along with four Nahua scholars from the Colegio de Tlatelolco—Antonio Valeriano, Martín de Jacobita, Alonso Vegerano, and Pedro de San Buenaventura—Sahagún traveled in 1547 to the town of Tepepulco, in the ancient *altepetl* of Texcoco. Sahagún and his Nahua scholars had prepared a series of questionnaires designed to gather specific information about ancient Nahua cosmology, religion, politics, history, and naturalist knowledge. As is well known, for about two years Sahagún interviewed extensively ten or twelve elders knowledgeable about the priestly teachings at the Texcoco *calmecac*.[73] The Nahua scholars from Tlatelolco declared, translated, and transcribed visual and written texts into *relaciones* in Nahuatl.

Ten years later, in 1557, Sahagún had the opportunity to verify and complete the facts of his ethnographic history. Along with the same group of Nahua scholars, he interviewed around ten elderly people as well as several specialists of diverse trades, all from the barrio of Santiago de Tlatelolco, the former city and *altepetl* of Mexico Tlatelolco. Sahagún and his students compared there the *relaciones* from Tepepulco and Tlatelolco and developed a master historical narrative in Nahuatl. Indian painters (*tlacuiloque*) trained in European artistic techniques illustrated it. Around 1565, Sahagún coordinated the writing of a clean version of his twelve books of history at the convent of San Francisco el Grande. He then wrote in a different column a paraphrase or free translation of these books in Spanish. Under pressure from the Crown, he had to finish and submit to Madrid his famous *Historia general de las cosas de Nueva España* in 1577.[74]

The knowledge-gathering methods developed by the Crown and the authorities of New Spain would be at the base of Hernández's own research methodology, along with common European botanical practices. The *protomédico* skillfully used Franciscan proto-ethnographic methodologies along with European natural history's own evolving techniques for the gathering of expert testimonies, often collected through systematic note taking.[75] For Renaissance natural history, taking notes of a particular object of nature implied fixing it in the observer's gaze, excluding its surroundings, describing and often sketching it, and then reading and comparing one's notes with all other available information.[76] These notes and drafts were not made to survive the passage of time; hence, hypothesizing from finished works is often necessary to learn about their authors' particular methods of note taking or gathering of *relaciones*.[77]

Fortunately, we do have enough direct and indirect information to outline Hernández's two main information-gathering and corroboration methodologies. The first and most direct one was itinerant, as Hernández stayed at different monasteries and hospitals while herborizing and interviewing informants from towns and fields near each convent.[78] In 1573 and 1574 he apparently traveled the area surrounding Mexico City and Puebla as well as today's states of Guerrero, Oaxaca, Michoacán, and Veracruz.[79] He had a rather long retinue, including his son, one or more Indian guides,[80] two or three plant gatherers,[81] at least one Indian interpreter,[82] two or three *tlacuilo-que*,[83] and at least one scribe.[84] He also traveled with an unspecified number of slaves and servants.[85] Perhaps he also was accompanied by some Nahua *ticiti*, although this is not clear.[86]

Hernandez's ethnobotanic fieldwork most likely started by interviewing Spanish and Indian doctors at the Hospital Real de Naturales and the surviving *ticiti* from Tlatelolco who had already given medical information to Sahagún.[87] Hernández obtained the names, general description, and most relevant properties of several plants shown to him in situ or brought to him by an Indian doctor (*ticitl*), an Indian expert on the properties of the plants (*tepatiani*), or a plant vendor (*panamacani*), who knew the location and Mesoamerican techniques for plant collection.[88] Hernández partially followed the Franciscan friars' verification methods, as he obtained an initial *relación* of every plant and proceeded to verify his information, plant by plant, "observing it at least ten times in different seasons" and asking "at least 20 Indian doctors" about it, adding to and correcting his original *relación*.[89] Hernández had access to such abundance of qualified informants to verify his findings thanks to the large network of hospitals built by the religious orders. Most if not all doctors in these hospitals were Indians. They had been evangelized and partially adapted their medical practice to Western conventions.[90]

Hernández also employed a more sedentary method, rarely acknowledged in contemporary studies. Helped by a royal bill, he received in the Hospital de San José de los Naturales or in another central location dried and live plants as well as *relaciones* about plants and animals and even plant sketches, all collected through the information networks of the viceroyalty.[91] He also collaborated with Spanish and Creole physicians in the theoretical and experimental investigation of the medicinal properties of several of these plants, aiming to compose a book of "substitutes": a comparative study of medicines from Europe and Mexico.[92] Also revealing of his strong reliance on the systematic gathering of *relaciones* through official information networks is his suggestion to the Crown to provide him with notes and sketches of all the natural things of the Canary Islands, Hispaniola, and the Philippines.[93] As he indicated to the court, it was necessary that "their virtues and temperaments be described from the accounts and experiences of the natives, and that they [should] be sent to me so that I may make the style consistent and have it drawn my way, and add it to the rest."[94]

Hernández's ethnobotanic questionnaires probably were similar to the model provided by Sahagún.[95] According to López Austin, Sahagún's questions for his medicinal and botanical *relaciones* were something like the following: (a) What is the name of the plant? (b) What kind of plant is it? (c) What does it look like? (d) What parts of it are useful? (e) for what illnesses? (f) How is the medicine prepared? (g) How is it administered? (h) Where is it found?[96] Hernández probably used similar questions, adding more specific categories of inquiry. He divided his questions into three categories. The first one was taxonomical: (a) What is the name of the plant? The second was morphological. He would have asked his informants to get him the following information about live or dried specimens: (b) Which kind of plant is it (shrub, herb, or tree)? (c) What is the shape of its root? (d) What is the shape of its leaves? (e) How do its branches look? (f) Does it have flowers? How do they look? (g) Does it have fruits? How do they look? How do they taste? (h) How do its seeds look? (i) Where does the plant grow? The last category was related to the uses of the plant, emphasizing its therapeutic values. His final questions were utilitarian: (j) Are parts of this plant edible? What parts? (k) What are the uses of this plant? (l) How is its taste? (m) How is the medicine from this plant prepared?[97]

Central to Hernández's naturalist efforts was the adequate illustration of most of the plants for proper identification. As he himself wrote to humanist Benito Arias Montano, these illustrations were "the greatest part of my care, so that nothing, from the point of view of a thumb would be different from what was being copied, but instead all would be as it was in reality."[98] He trained his painters for the sketching of each plant studied in situ and also received different sketches, or *esquizos*, from *tlacuiloque* living in different regions of ancient Mexico. When he was certain about the name, parts, and properties of a plant, Hernández instructed his *tlacuilo* to make a perfect copy of it and took care to eliminate most of Mesoamerican pictographic style and symbols by training his painters to follow a more naturalistic approach. As he wrote to Philip II on December 1571, he had already depicted eight hundred plants "with large figures on large papers . . . all true to life and representing all the parts and proportions with greater and fresher exactness than ever before."[99]

Having lost Hernández's natural history illustrations has made it challenging to determine their visual characteristics as compared to similar examples of the time. What seems more plausible, as José F. Ramírez noted at the closing of the nineteenth century, is that these illustrations followed in general terms contemporary European models while sometimes allowing certain Mesoamerican elements to remain present. His two examples are the illustrations of the *atatapalacatl* and the "*tenochtli*," as depicted in Juan Eusebio Nieremberg's *Historia naturae, maxime peregrinae*, published in Antwerp in 1635. In both images, Mesoamerican symbolism provides distinct information about the soil where the plants usually grow. Further strengthening of this hypothesis is the engraving of the Mexican *mecapatli*, part of Francisco Bravo's *Opera Medicinalia*, published in Mexico in 1570, whose woodcut would be used in the *Rerum medicarum Novae Hispaniae Thesaurus* (Figures 2.1, 2.2, and 2.3).[100]

A T A T A P A L A C A T L.

Figure 2.1. Atatapalacatl, Juan E. Nieremberg's *Historia naturae, maxime peregrinae* (1635). The name of the plant, according to José F. Ramírez, roughly translates as "plant of wide leaves that grows in meek or stagnant waters." Courtesy of the John Carter Brown Library at Brown University.

TVNA, SIVE NOPALLI SAXIS INNASCENS.

Figure 2.2. *Tuna*, in Nieremberg's *Historia naturae*. Ramírez noted that the original name of this species of prickly pear, as recorded by Hernández, is *tenochtli*, or "nopal that grows in rocky soil." Courtesy of the John Carter Brown Library at Brown University.

Experiencing and Experimenting with Mesoamerican Information

Unlike any of his predecessors in Mexico, Francisco Hernández conducted systematic experiments for the empirical verification of his newly acquired medicinal knowledge. His instructions clearly stated that he was supposed to "experience and test at first hand" the medicinal and practical uses of Mexican plants.[101] Hernández's empirical work shows not only the increasing value

Figure 2.3. "Mexican Çarçaparrilla," in Francisco Bravo's Opera *Medicinalia* (Ciudad de México, 1570). Courtesy of Biblioteca Histórica José María Lafragua at the Benemérita Universidad Autónoma de Puebla.

placed on experience-based knowledge but also the difficulties of harmonizing such knowledge with the dominant epistemological theories of the time.

Early modern practices regarding the observation and testing of nature came from the medieval practices designated by *experientia* (cumulative knowledge) and *experimentum* (a trial or test of knowledge). These two words were often used as synonyms, since they both referred to knowledge that could not be deduced from philosophical first principles or rationalist systems.[102] The *experimentum* was also a common medieval scientific genre. In medicine, collections of *experimenta* were composed of successful remedies "derived from and tested by experience" that were unjustifiable on doctrinal grounds.[103] Sixteenth-century humanist doctors and naturalists perfected the study of living organisms and their interactions with the environment through systematic forms of experience-based knowledge developed in the emergent colonial world.[104]

A pioneer of empiricism in the early Americas was, once again, Oviedo, who explicitly defended experience as the epistemological foundation of his work.[105] As he wrote in his *Sumario de la natural historia de las Indias*, "what for would I want to bring the ancients' authority to the things that I have seen or to the ones that Nature teaches everyone?"[106] He noted that Pliny had gathered most of his information from 2 million volumes, while he had gathered his own from the "two thousand million works, needs and dangers" he had "seen and experimented" himself for more than twenty-two years.[107] Oviedo took ample advantage of Amerindian empirical naturalist knowledge to compose his work.[108] His naturalist studies were greatly dependent on the informal gathering of Taino naturalist knowledge, redefined through his own knowledge, sensory experience, and rhetorical competence. Oviedo openly recognized that Indians were great herbalists, experts in plants' virtues and medicinal properties. Indian priests in particular had a vast medicinal knowledge of "trees, plants and herbs," and "since they healed many with such art, they had great veneration and obedience towards them."[109]

Similarly, the naturalist work of Sahagún often validated information by claiming recourse to personal experience. Obsidian, or *itzetl*, for example, was helpful for rheumatism and improved the voice's sonority; he knew such things by "many days experience."[110] More important, part of the rationale that justified the foundation of the Colegio de Santa Cruz de Tlatelolco in January 1536 was the need to prove or disprove, empirically, the intellectual capacity of Mexican Indians.[111] According to Sahagún, the Colegio de Santa Cruz de Tlatelolco would permit Spanish religious and political authorities to measure the Indians' intellectual capacity "by experience."[112] Moreover, the Colegio de Tlatelolco was in itself a social experiment, providing ample empirical proof of the equal intellectual capacities of Mesoamericans and Europeans. As Sahagún wrote in the prologue of his *Historia general*: "we see now from experience that they are skillful in all mechanical arts, and practice them; they are also competent at learning all the liberal arts, and the saintly Theology, as has been seen from experience in those who have been taught these sciences."[113]

By the time Hernández began his natural history, early modern methods of empirical verification of knowledge were already under development in the Indias Occidentales by Spanish religious and political authorities. Hernández's methodologies for experiencing and experimenting with central Mexico's flora and fauna were dependent on local practices as well as on experimental ones developed by European doctors and naturalists. He created a herbarium at the Hospital Real de Naturales in Mexico City, where he studied several plants in more detail, and classified them based on his Galenic training, where illnesses were conceived as an imbalance between the four fundamental humors: blood, phlegm, and yellow and black biles.[114] Galenists also believed that medicines had their own intrinsic powers (*dynamis*) and four degrees of heat, humidity, dryness, and coldness.[115] Properties from first-degree medicines could barely be perceived by the senses, while those from fourth-degree medicines could be destructive.

Hernández worked alongside Indian doctors, learning their approaches for treating illness and testing the therapeutic properties of most of the collected plants by performing experimental work at the different Indian hospitals and particularly at the Hospital Real de Naturales. There, he also conducted clinical experiments on Indian patients and on himself.[116] His experimental work led to interesting syntheses and conflicts between two medical philosophies and worldviews. As Hernández noted in his *Historia de las plantas de Nueva España*, Nahua *ticiti* believed in using medicines of a similar nature and temperature to the illness being treated.[117] Mesoamerican colonial therapeutics also understood medicines in terms of hot-cold and dry-humid dichotomies. The *tonalli*, one of the three invisible entities that composed the human body, was responsible for the body's temperature. A person's *tonalli* came from the sun and therefore was of a hot nature. Tiredness and pain, for example, were often attributed to a cooling of the *tonalli*. An excess of heat by the physical abuse of the body's capacities was also dangerous.[118] Hernández mostly dismissed these ideas as empirically based, devoid of method and theory, and generally inconsequential.[119] Indian doctors, he wrote, prescribed medicines "without knowing the reason, cause or accident of the disease"; they did not "follow any method in the diseases they are to cure." They were, in short, "mere empiricists and only use for any disease those herbs, minerals or parts of animals that, as if passed from hand to hand, they have received as some hereditary right from their elders."[120]

Nevertheless, Hernández recognized that this experience-based knowledge contradicted Galenism in important ways. *Ticiti* repeatedly demonstrated that it was possible to cure heat with heat and cold with cold. When writing about the bark of the tree called *quauxíotl*, Hernández stated that its juice, despite being cold, dry, and astringent, cured cold illnesses such as cough and hoarseness. He speculated that perhaps it cured by mitigating heat. At the end of this entrance he stated that "is it strange that the Indian doctors had discovered by *experience* that it happens in this way, when I myself have confirmed that very astringent plants mixed with *metl* wine admirably cause urination, and other similar facts that appear false at first glance, but that more attentively considered and examined seem not to occur without a reason. But of all these things we will speak, God permitting, in its own places."[121] While writing about the *zacayauhtli*, Hernández openly expressed doubts about the complete validity of Galenism. He wrote that *zacayauhtli* was a bush, "warm in third grade, bitter, smelly, and somewhat glutinous. They say that it is effective against diarrheas and fevers of kids, perhaps somehow evacuating the cause or taking the cold away, although I very well know that it is a deeply rooted opinion among the Indian doctors that heat fights heat, which perhaps is not completely wrong nor is it completely devoid of truth."[122]

Hernandez's empirical investigations allowed him to contrast the effectiveness of the medical practices of both cultures. Throughout his works, Hernández frequently impugned Galenic medical ideas without ever rejecting them as a complete system.[123] Had he published all of his work, particularly his Mexican natural history in the unknown form he envisioned but also the medicinal treatise he apparently had in mind, his lost (or perhaps never written) treatise on how to study the plants of the world, and his earlier critical comments about Galenism, he would have contributed to the reform of Galenic medical theory.

Rhetoric and Ethnographic History

Michel Foucault famously stated in 1966 that the beginnings of a modern worldview are perhaps best understood as the collapsing of an analogical view of the universe. Analogy can be defined as an infinite chain of correspondences and similarities between all things, a philosophical and poetic principle that permits conceiving all things, including words, as related and united. According to this view, human language is what best exemplifies the existence of a *logos*, a principle of order that coordinates (and discoordinates) all things material and ideational. The analogical view of language during the Spanish Renaissance was clearly expressed by the Spanish humanist friar and poet Luis de León, who wrote in *De los nombres de Cristo* (1587) that the unity of the universe was best perceived in language. Thanks to words, things could become "spiritual and delicate . . . images of truth." To speak of the world with proper, beautiful words meant reducing it to a temporary unity, which also permitted an admittedly limited access to the secret rhythm of the correspondences between all parts of the cosmos.[124] According to Foucault, modernity is best understood as a new understanding of language, one that conceives language as an arbitrary system for the representation of a reality ultimately alien to the words that describe it.[125] As several chapters in this volume note, Christian missionaries believed in the analogical unity of all languages, a biblical and classical notion that informed their efforts at Christianizing Amerindian cultural and religious traditions in their own languages.

Analyzing the ethnographic histories written in the sixteenth-century Americas, one could argue, echoing Michel de Montaigne, that the beginnings of the split between words and things studied by Foucault was a more mundane matter: the result of a growing awareness of the apparently infinite variety and diversity of nature, impossible to be reduce to a coherent unity.[126] At the waning of the Renaissance, Iberian chroniclers of the Indias Occidentales did begin to distance themselves from the unifying codes of classical rhetoric, which proved insufficient to assimilate the massive amount of information being collected. This shift was not one that the new historians ever aimed for. From Andrés de Olmos to Francisco Hernández, there is a recurrent preoccupation with accomplishing beauty of expression and imitating the appropriate historiographical form while translating Mesoamerican knowledge. Nevertheless, the ethnographic methodologies used for the composition of their *historias* made them rhetorically dependent on the concise matter-of-fact-based genre of the *relación*.

The transition from a scientific language rooted in humanist philological and rhetorical studies to a new scientific language based on experience-based matter-of-fact information was thus related to the ethnographic practices required for the composition of all the natural histories from the Indies.[127] The case of Hernández is paradigmatic. Trained in the Spanish humanist traditions of learning, he shared common beliefs about the mastery of classical rhetoric as necessary for the advancement of human knowledge. One can even find a compendium of humanist rhetorical ideals in the dedication to Philip II preceding Hernández's translation of Pliny. Hernández wrote there that the great Roman naturalist historian had accomplished the incredible feat of giving *novelty* to ancient things, *authority* to new ones, *luster* to those unusual, *grace* to the cumbersome, and *credit* to the doubtful ones.[128] Hernández was proud of having transmitted "perhaps with no less felicity, the richness that he left varnished in Roman language to our Spanish talk."[129] Similarly, in his December 1571 letter to Philip II from Mexico, Hernández told the monarch that there were many things in the New World with wonderful virtues, all of which "I describe clearly and precisely in Spanish [and] in a not unpleasing style."[130] Likewise, after completing his work in Mexico, Hernández wrote to Arias Montano that he had been careful to write "whatever would be relevant to human health, or whatever else this natural narration of things would demand in language as appropriate as I could manage, and with due brevity."[131]

Like all humanists, Hernández admired the richness and precision of Greek and Latin and extended this admiration to Mesoamerican languages. In his translation of Pliny, Hernández asserted that Mexican Indian languages could be as "perfect and copious" as any of the languages of the Old World if there were wise Indians charged with knowing and imposing names on things.[132] Hernández even compared Nahuatl to Greek. As he wrote in his *Antigüedades de la Nueva España* (ca. 1576), Mexican was a language that possessed "happy and fecund composition of its dictions and in this it does not cede to Greek language."[133] When writing about the *axixtlácotl* (diuretic stick), he commented on how Nahuatl names commonly identified the plant's "principal and most excellent" property.[134] He found Nahuatl taxonomy to be close to Neoplatonic ideas about an ideal language, where each word was supposed to describe an essential part of what was named. As Luis de León asserted, "the name . . . should put in the senses of whoever hears it the image of that particular property, this is for the name to have in its meaning part of the essence of what is named."[135] Nahuatl classifies plant species by genre, adding determinative prefixes or suffixes to nouns that usually referred to the plants' properties of use. Hernández understood, admired, and was compelled to use this taxonomy.[136] He referred to it when he explained the generic names of fruits. He wrote that "Mexicans, among whom the language of this New Spain flourishes in all its propriety and elegance, used to call with certain universal denomination, *tzápotl*, all fruits with sweet flavor, as well as *xócotl* to all those with sour flavor. A genre of those is called *atzápotl*, that is, aquatic *tzápotl* because its tree grows near to the water and aqueous places."[137] For his study of Nahuatl vocabulary and grammar, he relied on skilled translators and on the vocabularies and grammar books developed and compiled throughout half a century of linguistic and philological research by Spanish mendicant friars and their native students.[138]

Rhetoric, the art of attaining and disseminating a persuasive truth, was considered an indispensable tool for all sciences during the Renaissance.[139] The first *artes historicae*, written in the middle of the sixteenth century, reinforced the rhetorical model of history.[140] Luis Vives, Erasmus's follower and friend, best formulated early sixteenth-century historiographical ideals. History, truthful narration, was part of rhetoric and therefore should be well ordered, capable of communicating truth with clarity.[141] Queen Isabella and Cardinal Cisneros's attempt to reform the Spanish Church had among its aims the promotion of rhetorical studies, considered indispensable for grooming effective and influential preachers and counselors.[142] These efforts were carried on to the Americas, where the art of persuasion provided the very possibility of achieving meaningful transcultural intellectual recognition. Rhetoric became "a cognitive strategy, a shared experience, a grasp of another's grasp," as is evidenced in President Ramírez de Fuenleal's letter to Charles V on November 1532.[143] Indian principals from Michoacán had visited him in Mexico City to complain about the constant abuses perpetrated by Spanish colonizers. Fuenleal noted that their speech had been "long and well ordered, and so judiciously said and of things so good," that it demonstrated by itself that the natives could be good Christians and as faithful and beneficial subjects as any others.[144]

The peak of Mexico's *studia humanitatis* is Bernardino de Sahagún's *Historia general de las cosas de Nueva España* (ca. 1577). As Jesús Bustamante noticed, humanist influence in Sahagún's historical endeavors is evident in his attempt to compose a Nahuatl *calepino*. Ambroggio Calepino's *Cornucopiae* (1502) was an encyclopedic dictionary that aimed to register Latin words at their moment of greatest cultural splendor in a typical humanist attempt to return vigor, precision, and beauty to Roman language.[145] Likewise, Sahagún's *Historia general* sought to register and re-create the Nahua religious, literary, political, and scientific "classical texts."[146] Sahagún explained that Calepino had gathered "the words and their meanings, and their mistakes and metaphors, from the lesson obtained from poets and speakers and the other authors of Latin language."[147] Since the Nahuas had no phonetic writing, he had to begin by learning how to get and record the lesson from ancient Nahua poets and speakers.[148] Sahagún tried to register all Nahua words and their uses in their most sophisticated and beautiful forms, so he began his work by gathering Nahua "literature" to then translate and "reduce" it to Spanish.

In Books 10 and 11 of his *Historia general*, Sahagún compiled the results of his medicinal and naturalist research. His research questions carefully separated naturalist knowledge from most of its religious, magical, and cultural components. He made this aim explicit in the same prologue to Book 11, where he wrote that his work should be useful to make ancient Mexicans stop attributing divinity to all creatures.[149] His work thus also signals of the emergence of a new historiographical language, designed for the systematic separation of natural things from superstition, art, and religion.

Upon Hernández's arrival to Mexico, he obtained almost immediate access to the transcultural intellectual tradition and resources of the Colegio de Santa Cruz de Tlatelolco and the several schools within the monasteries. He read and utilized for his natural history the ethnographic histories of Bernardino de Sahagún, Toribio de Benavente (also known as Motolinía), and most likely Diego Durán.[150] Unlike his predecessors in Mexico, Hernández belonged to a reduced group of Renaissance naturalists who began incorporating analytical elements into their botanic descriptions, adding more distinctive morphological categories.[151] While in Mexico he established every plant's kind and morphology, following Mesoamerican languages' own taxonomies and a classificatory system based on the plants' properties.[152] He then sought possible similarities or analogous characteristics with Western or other American species as well as the plant's Galenic characterization and its specific therapeutic or utilitarian values. Personal comments follow some of the entries, and they remain a vastly understudied aspect of Hernández's *Natural History*. For example, regarding the *cocoztámatl*, Hernández noted that it had potent diuretic properties and was used in catheterization procedures to unblock the urethra with a rush's stem. He then commented how the king's confessor, Franciscan Bernardo de Fresneda, the bishop of Córdoba, had suffered at the court "a serious suppression of urine." His illness was cured "as if by a miracle" due to the careful introduction into the urethra of a catheter covered with American medicines.[153] The Spanish physician, who was amply rewarded, confessed that such remedy came from a "certain Indian doctor that kept his secrets" and had cured many people in Spain, including himself.[154] Hernández added that some Spanish doctors argued that the cure was due to the medicinal properties of the *tlacuatzin*'s tail but that his investigations had proved that it was due to the *cocoztámatl* root's medicinal properties.[155]

It is impossible for us to know what the final version of Hernández's natural history was supposed to look like. Therefore, and as José Pardo-Tomás has noted, an adequate understanding of the *Historia de las plantas de Nueva España* needs to address its quality as an unfinished work in progress, which Hernández still needed to rework while incorporating visual, geographical, medicinal, ethnobotanical, and ethnographic information. Hernández was evidently concerned with the rhetorical aspects of his work and consciously attempted to give variety and amenity to his natural history. Upon his return to Spain, he intended to write a natural history that would serve as a model for the adequate composition of a natural history of all the Indias Occidentales.

Hernández had long wanted to write a syncretic natural history of the Old World and the New World following the example of Pliny, from whom he had learned the rhetorical tools needed for his universal natural history, or, as Hernández put it, the necessary "eloquence and harness."[156] Still, while working in Mexico he soon recognized that his life would not be long enough to accurately describe all the unknown plants from Mexico. As he wrote in his *Antigüedades de la Nueva España*, it was impossible for him to adequately write of the admirable natures of so many plants, animals, and minerals or of the many language differences in very small territories and the many customs and rites among peoples, which were so varied that the human mind could barely follow them no matter how skillful the representation. He confessed that a truthful image could only be understood by experience and not through language.[157] Significantly, in all the manuscripts of Hernández's natural history that have reached to us, the persuasive and literary aspects of natural history, present in Pliny's work, appear greatly reduced, favoring a more objective, useful, empirical, and descriptive discourse, apparently following the standardized rhetorical structure of Hernández's own *relaciones*.

Conclusion

Growing awareness of the heterogeneous individual and collective agencies present during the development of early modern ethnographic and natural history does not, of course, erase or soften the painful and conflicting legacies of European colonialism. Ethnographic histories were composed as utopian instrumental tools to impose desired and planned religious and cultural transformations in the Indies. Furthermore, the processes of translation of Amerindian knowledge were often accompanied by a repression of indigenous forms of writing and transmitting knowledge.[158] As Tzvetan Todorov aptly synthesized more than thirty-five years ago, Europe's victory over Mexico greatly diminished human integration with the natural world.[159]

At the same time, the global shift in structures of meaning brought by the colonization of the Indies cannot be understood in terms of assumed homogeneous and hegemonic European epistemologies, which in reality were heterogeneous and transient. Knowledge exchanges in sixteenth-century Mexico were dominated by the writing conventions of early modern Europe but allowed for constant negotiations of meaning.[160] In the seminal ethnographic histories of sixteenth-century Mexico, the words of non-European subjects were not erased or grossly falsified but instead were hidden in translation. As seen in several chapters in this volume, a similar faith bequeathed many Iberian voices in seventeenth-century Northern European imperial and scientific accounts of early America's natural and cultural worlds.

A comparative and transcultural history of the material and intellectual processes that accompanied the transformation of early modern systems of knowledge, at the cultural borders of the early modern colonial empires, provides a more nuanced understanding of the early globalization of rationalist-empirical knowledge that today rules the world's official epistemic exchanges. The methodological and rhetorical evolution of early modern ethnographic history in Mexico also provides a glimpse of the first modern utopia in the making: a complex system of material and symbolic exchanges in the borderlands that cannot be conceived in simple binary oppositions. A historical analysis of localized knowledge exchanges in colonial Americas uncovers corpses but also seeds and fossils of political and epistemological possibilities that should enlighten today's searches for local and global meanings.[161]

Chapter 3

Bernabé Cobo's Inquiries in the Natural World and Native Knowledge

Luis Millones Figueroa

One day in the early half of the seventeenth century while out on a walk through the Andean countryside, the Jesuit priest Bernabé Cobo (1580–1657) came upon a group of native peasants and asked them to fetch some branches so he could make a fire. Having secured the branches, the Jesuit turned his back to the peasants in order to hide what he was doing; in just a few moments he produced a small fire. As soon as they saw smoke beginning to rise, the Amerindians expressed great surprise and confusion. Their own method of starting a fire would have taken much longer, and the only European method they knew of involved striking metal against rock, yet this priest had created fire silently and apparently out of branches alone. This incident was not the first time Cobo had played a trick of this kind; he apparently found great enjoyment in astonishing the indigenous peoples of the New World with such displays, which to him clearly demonstrated the superiority of European knowledge.[1]

Of course, Cobo was not alone in finding great pleasure and advantage in the indigenous "naïveté." The chroniclers recorded a good number of such stories, telling of the delight of Europeans who displayed methods of Western knowledge and technology in order to disparage the native people. In one noteworthy example from his *Comentarios reales*, the Inca Garcilaso de la Vega narrates a tale of some native porters who were transporting melons for a Spanish merchant. The merchant apparently entrusted the porters with a written note for the melons' buyer, warning them that the note would inform the buyer if anything happened to any of the melons along the way. At a certain point in their journey the porters gave in to temptation and broke open some melons to taste, but to hide their actions from the note, they took the precaution of placing it momentarily behind a wall. Obviously, upon arriving at the destination the buyer looked at the note and immediately knew of the missing melons.[2] As was the case in Cobo's text, this kind of story created laughter and complicity in the European reader, reactions that derived from a sense of cultural superiority.

While still a young man, Cobo left his town in Andalusia and immigrated to the New World, where he would live for nearly sixty years. His imagination had apparently been stirred by the visions of wealth and grandeur promised by the organizers of expeditions to the Indies. However, upon arriving in Lima (after a brief stay in the Caribbean region), Cobo decided to continue his education and study with the Jesuits; eventually he chose to become a priest himself and a member of the Society of Jesus. Father Cobo enjoyed the journeys around the countryside that his missionary work demanded and also took a keen interest in getting to know and learn about the native peoples, cultures, and natural environments of the New World. He traveled extensively throughout the Peruvian viceroyalty and also spent about thirteen years in Mexico. The fruit of his travels, supplemented by years of archival research, individual interviews, and personal observations, was the long work he finished in 1653 titled *Historia del Nuevo Mundo*.

Cobo's text, the culmination of forty years of dedicated work, remained unpublished in the author's own day and has only survived in incomplete form. Even so, ever since its first publication in the late nineteenth century, many scholars have recognized the value of the work.[3] In his prologue, Cobo explains that his motive for writing the book sprang from a desire to discover and expose the truth regarding the conflicting information that was circulating about the New World and to point out and correct the errors he had found in the chronicles. The first part of *Historia del Nuevo Mundo*, which will provide the basis for the argument of the present chapter, is made up of fourteen books (or sections), each divided into numerous chapters. The first of these books deals with the world in general, beginning with a description of the universe and leading eventually to a description of the dominions of Spain. The eight books that follow focus on the New World, covering such topics as its climate, mineral wealth, and flora and fauna. The tenth book discusses the many plants and animals that Spaniards brought to the New World from Spain and other regions of the world. The last four books present a history of the Incas and descriptions of Incan society, focusing in particular on its form of government, its religious practices, and its customs.

Although the entire *Historia del Nuevo Mundo* is of great value, what is particularly noteworthy is Cobo's presentation of the New World's nature. And there is little doubt that when researching the environment, he became a learned and passionate naturalist. What role did Amerindian knowledge play in his research? The question is especially interesting given Cobo's prolonged and profound exposure to Andean and Mesoamerican cultures; that is, he undoubtedly had the opportunity to observe and appreciate how these non-European cultures understood and interacted with their natural surroundings. But was Cobo truly interested in native knowledge; did he believe that he could learn from it? Or was it the case, as his anecdote about the magnifying glass and the fire seems to suggest, that Cobo viewed European knowledge as so vastly superior to that of the ignorant and naive Indians that any consideration of their understanding of the natural world would be pointless? To even attempt a response to this question, it is first vital to examine the different epistemic traditions that Cobo had at his disposal and then try to understand how each could have influenced his understanding of the New World.

European Epistemic Traditions

There are at least four different European epistemic traditions that informed Cobo's *Historia del Nuevo Mundo*, and it makes sense to identify each of these individually. Although all four traditions make their presence felt throughout the work, there are certain sections in which one or another of them have a greater level of presence than the others. In no particular order of importance, then, the four epistemic traditions are hexaemeral literature, Western scientific thought, European natural history, and the Jesuit global network of knowledge.

Hexaemeral Literature

Although one can identify various sources of knowledge that inform Cobo's naturalist ideas in *Historia del Nuevo Mundo*, it is clear that he relied primarily on the tenets of Catholic dogma. Cobo concurred with the metaphor of nature as God's book of creations whose order and perfection was to be admired by all. In the opening chapters of *Historia del Nuevo Mundo*, he explicitly states that his explanation for the origin and order of things in the natural world is derived from the first chapters of the book of Genesis. By incorporating the Genesis narrative, Cobo was contributing to the hermeneutic tradition of hexaemeral literature, so called because it re-creates and elaborates on the biblical narrative of the six days of creation. The very structure of his narrative, Cobo points out, follows the same order that God imposed on nature and that is mirrored in Genesis. In other words, the organization of *Historia del Nuevo Mundo* was based on the idea—in its Christian formulation—of *the great chain of being*, which proceeds from the imperfect to the perfect. A faithful reflection of this principle, Cobo's work deals first with minerals, then plants, then animals, and finally the peoples of Peru, the subject of the final four books. The same organizing principle is applied to each section of the text: in one section he begins with herbs and then proceeds to bushes and finally to trees; in another section, using the same principle, he proceeds from fish to birds.

What is most interesting to observe in Cobo is the way he allows his acquired knowledge about the nature of the New World to coexist in complex ways with Catholic dogma. Indeed, he used his new knowledge to help resolve questions that the most learned Christian scholars had been debating for years. In cases where theologians and biblical scholars were arguing over the meaning of the Sacred Scriptures, Cobo was at times able to offer resolutions based on his experiences and observations in the New World. This happened, for example, in regard to the debate about the cyclical timing of God's creation of the world, on which opinions were sharply divided. The controversy largely centered on whether God had created the world in autumn or springtime, with proponents arguing that one or the other of these seasons was more vital in guaranteeing the continuity of the life cycle. However, based on his experiences with the American natural world, Cobo was able to intervene in the debate and propose a clear and simple solution. He criticized the ethnocentrism of the European debate, suggesting that the entire premise of the argumentation made no sense from the perspective of the New World. Cobo explained that in the New World plants and fruits were often found in different stages of the life cycle in one and the same season, depending on the particularities of their ecological contexts.[4] This is but one example of how he resolved a debate within hexaemeral literature based on the realities he observed in the New World.

That said, there were other times when Cobo's observations of the American natural world reignited or further complicated long-standing debates in Europe between learned interpreters of the book of Genesis. One such debate centered on explanations for the diversity and distribution of the many plant and animal species that existed in different parts of the world. The "discovery" of the New World, with its innumerable species of flora and fauna, many of which could only be found in very particular places, posed new challenges for those seeking to reconcile the natural world of the Indies with their knowledge of the Sacred Scriptures. It is important to keep in mind here that the biblical explanation for the origin and dispersion of species is based on the creation story and the story of the universal flood and Noah's ark. Debates on this topic ranged from arguments about the immutability or mutability of the natural world to disagreements on the dimensions of the ark.[5] Once again, Cobo's solution to these debates was clear and simple, criticizing overly complex interpretations and instead reaffirming Catholic dogma while elaborating that reaffirmation in an original way. Cobo argued that God first created each species of flora and fauna in the environment most propitious for its growth and then, through divine miracle, gathered all the species together and later returned them to their respective places. That miracle had taken place twice: once when all the species appeared in the Garden of Eden so Adam could name them and a second time when all species were transported back to their places of origin after having been saved from the flood in Noah's ark.

As these examples show, Cobo's newly acquired knowledge of the American natural world influenced his understanding and interpretations of the hexaemeral literature tradition. His own hermeneutical work never questioned the veracity of Catholic dogma; however, because his observations of the American natural world apparently clashed with traditional readings of the Sacred Scriptures, Cobo often found himself having to elaborate strategies of reconciliation with that same Catholic dogma.

Western Scientific Thought

A second epistemic tradition that influenced Cobo's naturalist ideas was embedded in the tradition of European scientific discourse. There is no question that the foundation for Cobo's entire presentation of American natural history was based on the scientific knowledge derived from a Western tradition of natural philosophy steeped in Aristotelian principles. Thus, for example, in the first chapter of Book 3, Cobo not only assumes the principle that all matter is composed of four fundamental elements but also explicitly ascribes to the categorization, established within Western philosophy, of all bodies composed of these four elements. Likewise, he reiterates the principle that the particular combination and proportion of these elements, in conjunction with the influence of the celestial bodies, created and determined the form of the bodies found in nature. Cobo also supports the theory of the four humors, or temperaments, as the key to understanding the human body. Clearly, then, Cobo's conception of the world was framed in terms inherited from the tradition of Western scientific thought. Moreover, on more than one occasion he notes that in the realm of the natural sciences, the native peoples of the New World had not yet "reached" this level of understanding.

At the same time, however, Cobo's observations on the American natural world convinced him of the limitations of traditional Western knowledge. His critique in this regard went beyond merely proving the human habitability of Torrid Zones, which many authors before him had already done. Cobo's experiences also led him to argue that European natural science was ethnocentric, based as it was on only a partial knowledge of reality, and that this ethnocentrism had led to errors that only a knowledge of the American world could correct. Such a revision, he insisted, would involve more than simply introducing into European knowledge an enormous variety of new flora and fauna from the New World. Cobo instead argued that the knowledge garnered from the American natural world would require an entire revision of some underlying principles of Western natural philosophy. One of those principles concerned the composition of one of the four elements of matter:

Conforme a la opinión referida . . . todo el espacio que hay desde nosotros hasta el cielo ocupa el elemento aire, al cual atribuyen los más de los filósofos estas dos primeras cualidades: calor y humedad. . . . Mas si he de decir mi sentimiento, movido de las experiencias que percibimos en este Nuevo Mundo, es que todos los que en Europa han escrito de esta materia, tratan de ella tan asidos a lo que en su hemisferio y clima experimentan, como si aquello fuera el modelo y regla que hubiera de guardar el cielo y clima de lo restante del mundo . . . siendo así que pasa tan al contrario en este Nuevo Mundo de lo que ellos escriben, que se pudiera sacar otra nueva filosofía, si con curiosidad y estudio se especularan y controvirtieran las experiencias que acá hallamos. . . . Volviendo, pues, al elemento del aire, lo que yo siento con los que más acertadamente tratan esta materia es que de su naturaleza es seco y frío, como experimentamos cuando está más puro y sereno; las cuales cualidades tiene tanto más intensas cuanto está más alto y cercano del cielo.[6]

In support of the aforementioned opinion . . . the entire space between ourselves and the heavens is occupied by the element of air, to which most philosophers attribute these first two qualities: warmth and humidity. . . . But if I were to present my view, brought on by the experiences that we perceive in this New World, it would be that all those who have written about this topic in Europe have dealt with it through strict adherence to the experience of their own hemisphere and climate, as if that were the model and rule that the skies and climates of the rest of the world must follow. . . . [W]ith that in mind, what occurs in this New World is so different from [the experience] that they describe, that if one were to analyze and argue on the bases of the experiences we find here, he could then derive a new philosophy. . . . Returning, in this sense, to the element of air, it is my belief, in accordance with those who have most carefully studied this topic, that [air] is by nature dry and cold, as we observe when it is in its purest and most dormant state; and these qualities become even more evident the higher and closer the air is to the heavens.

It is his experience in the New World that enables Cobo to distance himself from the enshrined wisdom of Western tradition. And although he supports his argument through reference to other philosophers who had already questioned the inherited notions about the properties of air, his own argument is both solid and daring in terms of its suggestion that a knowledge of the New World could generate a "new philosophy" of nature.[7] In short, one does not find in Cobo's work the same attempt to completely accommodate New World realities within the Western scientific tradition that was evident in relation to Catholic dogma; instead, what one finds is the conviction that knowledge of the New World was transforming European knowledge into something new.

European Natural History

Among the other epistemic traditions available to Cobo was the European tradition of natural history, keeping in mind, of course, that approaches to understanding and organizing nature varied widely and were in a key stage of transformation in the seventeenth century. On the one hand, Cobo could be seen as continuing the kind of encyclopedic natural history going back to Pliny the Elder and his *Naturalis Historia* and later represented by Renaissance naturalists such as Ulisse Aldrovandi and Conrad Gesner. On the other hand, as William Ashworth has noted, the New World natural histories were different in that they didn't incorporate an emblematic view of nature because the new fauna and flora had no known similitudes in the European tradition.[8] Cobo's *Historia del Nuevo Mundo* embraces the encyclopedic ambition even though he recognizes it is a goal beyond his reach. And despite the absence of an emblematic worldview, its influence can still be traced in some passages. Yet Cobo adopted a critical stance vis-à-vis classical natural history and a number of naturalist passages from the chronicles of the Indies; neither source, he believed, offered much insight into the true nature of the New World. Cobo's approach was that of a modern naturalist who valued experience and a descriptive method capable of representing nature effectively. Cobo criticized canonical authors such as Pliny and Dioscorides not only for the incomplete description of the world's territory but also for presenting descriptions that were too deficient to allow readers to identity which plants and animals were being referenced. For these reasons, he believed it best to completely forgo their texts.[9] Cobo was equally critical of the chronicles or natural histories of the New World that had been published up to that point. In fact, in the prologue to his work, he wrote that it was the great diversity of opinions and the many mistakes he had found in the chronicles that had convinced him of the need to write his own history. In terms of a descriptive method, Cobo tried to be as comprehensive as possible in each case, focusing on the physical characteristics (exterior and sometime interior), behavior, habitat, usages, and his personal experience with flora and fauna from everywhere he visited or was able to collect information. His disregard for both ancient knowledge and the existing publications on the New World must have also provided him with at least one motive for deciding to explore and incorporate into his narrative all the knowledge he could garner from the native people.

Like the European naturalists of the Renaissance and the later modern period, Cobo believed that experience was the key to understanding nature but also recognized that a familiarity with local languages and a careful descriptive methodology were both key elements in the ability to effectively describe the natural world. The six decades that he had spent in the New World equipped him with much more knowledge and experience than most of the other naturalists who had written about the New World. In addition to the direct contact he had with the native languages of Quechua and Aymara, his educational formation with the Jesuits had included the study of native languages along with classes on rhetoric. Language in general and competency in several tongues were without a doubt instruments of knowledge that served Cobo very well. This was especially the case because it was through language that he attempted to both resolve the issue of the many names that existed in nature for the same elements and differentiate those elements native to the New World from those that had arrived from Europe.[10]

Also in line with his contemporaries, Cobo had to consider whether to include illustrations in his work. To begin with, it probably would have been very difficult for him to produce illustrations himself; certainly he makes no mention of his own ability to draw or of the availability of illustrators, engravers, or other specialists. Moreover, ever since the Renaissance, the question of whether illustrations were necessary in naturalist texts had become a matter of debate. Some naturalists saw evident advantages in using illustrations to either replace or complement descriptions of natural elements; others, however, found the reliance on illustrations to be problematic, pointing to many examples of illustrated works that had contributed nothing to the greater knowledge of the natural world.[11] Cobo apparently supported the latter opinion, arguing that the very same plant could be illustrated in any number of ways and that the particular conditions of an ecological zone made it possible for the same plant, at any given moment, to be either flowering or not. Would an illustration or a textual description be more effective in making that plant identifiable? Although the tendency to include illustrations was on the rise in Europe when Cobo was writing his natural history, he would privilege words over illustrations in his work, declaring "describiré cada planta conforme a la más común disposición que tiene en este reino del Perú" ("I will describe each plant according to its most common appearance in this kingdom of Peru").[12] He was confident above all that his keen powers of observation, his capacity to incorporate key elements of botanical and zoological description, and his ability to manipulate language would together be sufficient to faithfully represent the natural elements. So sure was Cobo of his descriptive methodology that he readily invited readers to compare his work to those of the classical naturalists and judge it accordingly.[13] Antonio José Cavanilles, the renowned naturalist and director of Madrid's Royal Botanical Garden in the early nineteenth century, did just that in one of his reflections on Spanish botany during the colonial period. With great admiration he singled out Cobo for his descriptive accuracy, affirming that botanists of any era could identify which plants Cobo was referencing.[14] In recognition of this talent, Cavanilles gave the name *Cobaea* to a newly classified genus of plant.

It is quite clear that as a naturalist, Cobo wanted to avoid the significant shortcomings he identified in classical European natural history and the abundant mistakes in the chronicles of de New World. And although he did share some of the same aspirations of the epistemic tradition as his contemporary European naturalists, he rejected the emergent tendency to include illustrations, centering his own approach to knowledge instead on observation, methodology, and the descriptive power of language.

Jesuit Global Network of Knowledge

Another source of knowledge for Cobo was the one he found as a member of the Society of Jesus. On the basis of their activities in the New World, Jesuits were known not only for widespread missionary work but also for developing a prestigious educational tradition in which its priests produced great works in both the arts and the sciences. By the time Cobo arrived in Lima, sometime around 1599, the Jesuits were already well established in the Viceroyalty of Peru, having been there for some thirty-one years. Their members in Peru numbered nearly three hundred at that time, and various schools, rectories, and parishes had been established. Cobo enrolled in the Royal Academy of San Martin, which was a lay academy run by the Jesuits, and subsequently decided to join the Society of Jesus as an ordained priest. Over the course of his career as a Jesuit, he performed missionary and administrative work in various places in Peru in the mountain villages and coastal communities. And during the time he spent in Mexico he continued with his interest in nature and the natives. As many Jesuits before and after him, Cobo pursued his interest with intellectual rigor, seeking to become familiar with the Amerindians' cultures and disseminating what he learned in the Jesuit global network of knowledge.

Through cultural, intellectual, and material interchanges between its member priests and institutions, the Jesuits were able to develop an effective global network for the dissemination of knowledge. From the most remote communities targeted by missionaries to the provincial seats of Jesuit administration and the centers of Jesuit rule in Europe, all members of the Society of Jesus collaborated in the transmission of local knowledges as they traveled throughout the world, thereby constructing what Steven Harris has referred to as a corporation of extensive reach.[15] This process of knowledge dissemination enabled some provincial seats to become important centers of research and knowledge production, generating texts, artifacts, medicines, and other creations, all of which enhanced the overall economic and cultural capital of the Society of Jesus. This was certainly true in the case of the Superior College of San Pablo in Lima, whose library and pharmacy became a paradigm of Jesuit achievement in the New World.[16] The Jesuits' familiarity with and research into the American natural world bequeathed the most important corpus of naturalist works of its time, in great measure due to the dedication of its member priests and their network of knowledge dissemination.

Cobo was both a beneficiary of and a contributor to the Jesuit forms of knowledge. Although he was a great traveler, convinced that personal experience and eyewitness testimony were the keys to effective descriptions of nature, he also recognized the limits of his research. He also knew, however, that he could rely on the Jesuit network to expand those limits. This reliance is discernible in his history through his incorporation of observations and accounts received from other Jesuit sources, information that allowed him to fill in argumentative blanks or offer points of contrast and comparison with information he himself had gathered. For his part, Cobo did not hesitate to share the information he had learned with other Jesuits, thus participating in the transference and dissemination of knowledge about the natural world and about many other subjects.[17] Notwithstanding this mutual and effective dissemination of knowledge, there could still be significant differences among Jesuit authors in terms of their approaches or perspectives on topics great and small. Cobo's approach and perspective on natural history, for example, differed notably from those of José de Acosta, the most well-known Jesuit naturalist in sixteenth-century Peru and author of the 1590 *Historia natural y moral de las Indias*.[18] While Acosta dedicated his work to resolving the question of natural philosophy through reference to the particularity of the New World, Cobo was more interested in presenting a historical and broad-ranged exposition of the New World's natural elements.

Jesuit forms of knowledge were indispensable to Cobo's work. And while there is no doubt that Acosta's prestigious example was a powerful influence in Cobo's work, it seems to the present author at least that given the differences in their goals, Acosta's influence acted more as a catalyst for Cobo to explore and define his own views than as a model to carefully emulate. While Cobo shared and participated in the forms of Jesuit knowledge, he also at the same time was able to produce a history of great magnitude and originality, a history deserving of much more recognition than scholars to this day have granted it as a monumental work within the Jesuit intellectual tradition.

Native Knowledge

Beginning in his prologue, Cobo recognized that his work would take into account, even if only sporadically, the indigenous knowledge of the natural world and the uses of nature that indigenous peoples had developed. His work would mention those things the Spaniards had learned from indigenous peoples about the American natural world, particularly in terms of its nutritional and medicinal elements.[19] Although the references to this topic are brief, a careful reading of Cobo's *Historia del Nuevo Mundo* reveals that the author systematically incorporated his research of indigenous knowledge and culture throughout his history. And even though his references to indigenous knowledge often appear as a negative counterpoint—that is, to underscore from a European perspective the shortcomings of indigenous peoples' knowledge—it is clear that indigenous knowledge and culture informed Cobo's history in an essential yet seldom acknowledged way.

Ethnolinguistic Knowledge

In addition to his personal contact with native speakers, Cobo studied Quechua and Aymara during his time in the Jesuit colleges of Lima and Juli. Given the importance of this linguistic command within his history, he clearly was able to attain a relatively high level of fluency in these native languages. At various moments, Cobo affirms that he asked questions to indigenous informants "in their own language," and he even devotes an entire chapter to explaining the linguistic characteristics of Quechua. Cobo clearly believed that a knowledge of native languages was indispensable for a naturalist seeking to avoid the many mistakes and misrepresentations found in the existing chronicles. According to Roland Hamilton, who has examined Cobo's use of indigenous vocabularies, the greatest contribution made by the Jesuit naturalist was his identification of more than four hundred Quechua words and more than one hundred Aymara words, all referring to the natural and cultural worlds of ancient Peru.[20] Hamilton was also able to document Cobo's reliance on other sources dealing with these indigenous languages. At the time when Cobo was writing, for example, Domingo de Santo Tomás's 1560 study of Quechua grammar and vocabulary had already been published, as had two works by fellow Jesuits with whom Cobo most likely communicated on the topic of their shared linguistic interest. These works were Diego Gonzales Holguin's *Vocabulario de la lengua general de todo el Perú, llamada lengua quichua*

(1608) and Ludovico Bertonio's *Vocabulario de la lengua aymara* (1612). On the topic of the importance of native languages, Cobo was clear in his belief that a knowledge of Quechua provided privileged access to knowledge about the natural world, explaining that

> Investigando su etimología y origen, hallamos haber sido puestos sus vocablos o por alguna semejanza tomada de la cosa significada por ellos . . . o para denotar alguna propiedad de la cosa que significan; y éstos de ordinario son compuestos, cuyas partes de por sí son significativas. Del primer orden son los más de los nombres de animales, los cuales se asimilan al sonido de la voz de los dichos animales, canto, gritos o gemidos, en esta manera: a los pájaros pequeños llaman *pisco* por su delicado y sutil canto; a la perdiz, remedando su voz, *yutu*; a la bandurria, *caquingora*, por la misma razón; al *guanaco* lo llaman así por un relincho que tiene, con que parece dice su nombre; y asimismo al *cuy* y a otros muchos animales. Pero donde más a la clara esto se prueba es en la *vizcacha*, por un chillido que da este animalejo tan parecido a su nombre que parece que él mismo lo pronuncia. Del segundo orden son los más de los nombres de lugares, pueblos, campos, ríos montes y de otras cosas inanimadas, dándoselos conforme a las propiedades, señales y calidades que tienen: como "provincia de piedras," "pueblo del andén," "tierra de sal," "sitio de fortaleza," "lugar de oro, de plata, de agua," "río de la sal, río del *ají*," "tierra cenagosa," "lugar nuevo," "sitio de quebradas," "vega de oro, de hinojos," "campo de la batalla," "lugar ahumado"; y así por ese orden los demás.[21]

> In researching [Quechua's] etymology and origin, we find that words have been assigned either on the basis of some similarity noted between the thing signified and the words assigned . . . or in order to denote some property of the thing signified, and in this case, the [words] are usually compound with each part being a signifier. Of the former kind are the majority of animal names, which assimilate to the sound of the voice of a particular animal, whether it be its song, call, or moan, and so for example: the little birds are called *pisco* because of their delicate and subtle song; the partridge is *yutu*, in imitation of its voice; the black-faced ibis, *caquingora*, for the same reason; the *guanaco* is so named because of the snorting it seems to utter; and in like

manner for the *cuy* and other animals. However the evidence is most clear in the *vizcacha*, for the shriek that this animal emits is so similar to its name that it seems [the animal] itself pronounces [the name]. Of the latter kind [of words] are the majority of the names of places, communities, fields, rivers, mountains and other inanimate things, having been assigned [names] that conform to their properties, features and qualities, for example: "province of rocks," "community of terraces," "land of salt," "place of the fortress," "place of gold, of silver, of water," "river of salt, river of *aji*," "marshy land," "new place," "site of gorges," "meadow of gold, of fennel," "field of battle," "smoky place"; and in like manner the other [names].

This etymological analysis explains why a great number of Cobo's descriptions of plants, animals, and places of the New World included their Amerindian names—mostly Quechua and Aymara but also Nahuatl—that he had learned from native informants over the course of his travels and study.

One of the naturalist objectives of Cobo's work was to distinguish the native species of the New World from those transplanted from Europe. By the time of Cobo's writing, the biological exchanges under way since Christopher Columbus's first landing in the Caribbean had already brought—and were continuing to bring—numerous changes to the American natural world. Even so, Cobo believed that it was not too late to elucidate the ecological bases of the New World and that toward this end, a familiarity with the native languages constituted an essential form of knowledge. To begin with, it allowed for the possibility of interviewing indigenous elders who could recall the state of the natural world prior to the Spaniards' arrival and had witnessed the changes in the environment since that time. Moreover, the starting point in the process of identifying a species of New World origin was to discern if that species had a name in an indigenous language. In order for this process to be effective, however, Cobo knew very well that one's knowledge of native languages had to be both broad and deep, for the criteria of using language to identify the origin of a species presented various difficulties. One problem was that some native words had already emerged to refer to objects of European origin, as was the case with the Quechua words *quispi* and *quelcani*, which referred to writing and mirror, respectively. And one had to consider that the same kind of naming might have occurred with European species brought to the American natural world. When a species had a single indigenous name that was used commonly across an extensive linguistic territory,

Cobo suspected that the species was of recent arrival and that an indigenous name had been assigned to it at some point and later exported to other communities. As Cobo explained, there were an infinite number of indigenous languages in the New World, and a more effective way of proving the American origin of a species would be to establish the fact that different native languages referred to that same species using different naming words. Following this same logic, one had to be careful about a species whose indigenous name did not correspond to the linguistic community where the species was found, for such incongruence could signal a species originating in another region of the New World that had been transplanted along with its original indigenous name into a new ecological context.[22]

Agricultural and Medicinal Knowledge

As one would expect, Cobo firmly believed European culture to be superior to the Amerindian cultures. In his final analysis of the cultural encounter, he argued that Europeans offered more to the native peoples than vice versa. However, despite the general conclusion that Europeans had little to learn from the native peoples of the New World, there were some moments when Cobo did recognize the virtue and knowledge of Amerindian cultures. In those instances, he not only appreciated the detailed knowledge that native peoples had of their natural world and how to utilize and benefit from its resources but also recognized aspects of native knowledge that Spaniards had benefited from as a whole. Perhaps because of the close relationship between food and health in the early modern period and the importance of agricultural and medicinal products for the lives of Europeans in the New World, Cobo singled out native agriculture and medicine in particular as two areas where Spaniards had come to admire and utilize aspects of native knowledge.

According to Cobo, among all the arts necessary for human survival, the natives of Peru were especially skilled in agriculture. He noted that while the contact with Spaniards had brought about improvements in other practices in which natives engaged, agricultural practices had changed little. Even though in some places native farmers had adopted such European instruments as the oxen-driven plow and iron tools, these only facilitated the work to be done and did not fundamentally alter the native people's understanding of agriculture or their agricultural practices as a whole. Cobo summed up his appreciation for native knowledge of agriculture as follows:

En suma, ellos eran tan excelentes labradores de sus legumbres y plantas, y con la larga experiencia habían alcanzado tanta inteligencia de la agricultura, que nosotros habemos aprendido de ellos todo el modo de sembrar y beneficiar sus semillas, y mucho para el buen beneficio de las nuestras; como es la manera de . . . estercolar los sembrados en algunas partes, que es muy particular y diferente de como se hace en España.[23]

In short, they were such excellent producers of legumes and plants, and their long years of experience had provided them with such intelligence about agriculture, that they have taught us all the methods of planting and reaping benefits from their crops as well as many things about getting the most benefit from our own crops; for example, how to . . . spread manure on the plantings in some areas, which is very particular and different from what is done in Spain.

Cobo's passage emphasizes that Spaniards not only learned native methods of cultivating American crops but also adopted native knowledge to improve the cultivation and harvesting of European seeds.

Another aspect of the native knowledge of agriculture that Cobo admired was the way farmers were able to increase the area of arable land along Peru's arid coastal plain. With the growth of Spanish cities adding to an already numerous native population in the coastal areas, there was a great need for increased crop production. Cobo marveled in particular at two native techniques for expanding the area of cultivable land. One consisted in digging holes until they filled up with groundwater; the other took advantage of humid zones along the coast, utilizing the slopes of small coastal hills where there was no actual rain but enough humidity accumulated to sustain plant cultivation.[24]

While Cobo focused above all on those aspects of native knowledge needed to prepare fields and cultivate seeds, he also took note of the positive attitude that natives displayed while performing their work in the fields. Instead of viewing the cultivation of their fields as an onerous if necessary task, they actually enjoyed the work. Cobo observed with admiration how the native peoples had managed to transform arduous agricultural work into labor performed in a communal way and into rituals where an atmosphere of recreation and celebration prevailed.[25] In other words, Cobo recognized that native knowledge about agriculture transcended the practical and was embedded in their cultural values.

In regard to the principles of medicine, Cobo found the native peoples to be totally ignorant; that is, he found that they knew nothing of the notion of the four humors or temperaments, they could not explain the causes or effects of illnesses, and they did not know about reading urine or the use of compound medicines. Nonetheless, among their elderly and experienced healers, Cobo noted, there were "algunos grandes herbolarios" (some great herbalists) through whom "habemos nosotros venido a conocer las virtudes de muchas plantas que usamos ya en nuestras curas" (we came to know the virtues of many plants that we now use in our own remedies).[26] And while Cobo only explicitly credited these few "great herbalists," a careful reading of *Historia del Nuevo Mundo* suggests that his silence on his sources masked the fact that the Jesuit naturalist had systematically sought out and obtained an enormous amount of indigenous knowledge on medicine and other topics. In the more than five hundred descriptions of New World plants, animals, and minerals presented in his work, Cobo included whenever possible the food and medicinal uses of each one, usually beginning or ending the description of a particular element with its indigenous name in Quechua and Aymara or in Nahuatl or another indigenous language. There is no doubt that this incorporation of indigenous knowledge from mostly unnamed sources formed a key component of Cobo's work.

Indeed, the Jesuits as a whole played a lead role in the transmission of indigenous medicinal knowledge to European society. Their incorporation into Western medicine of knowledge about particular remedies originating in the New World was so influential that two such remedies even became known as "Jesuit powders" and "Jesuit tea." In this sense, Cobo's work surely benefited from the accumulated knowledge already stored in the pharmacies of the Jesuit schools, and at the same time his research must have contributed greatly to that same body of knowledge.[27] In addition to his many notes regarding both the usage and the specific method of administrating particular remedies, Cobo included stories based on personal experience. He recounted one time when he heard the dying confession of a man wounded in a stabbing, only to see that man subsequently cured with the sap of a tree.[28] On another occasion having to do with his own health, Cobo recalled having a molar that was loose and painful. On the way to see the barber to have the tooth removed, one of Cobo's priest friends recommended that he instead chew coca leaves for several days in a row; after doing so, the molar stopped being loose and no longer hurt.[29]

Hidden Knowledge

Cobo devoted himself in an exemplary way to the work of deciphering the nature of the New World and was able to achieve a vast and sophisticated understanding of many aspects of the natural world. But the natural world was also sometimes difficult to grasp, because the native peoples were not always willing to reveal what knowledge they had of curious phenomena, the place of origin of natural products, or even the names and ways to identify a natural element. In the difficult historical context of the encounter of cultures, the native peoples soon realized the value of their knowledge of nature and, not surprisingly, choose whenever possible to keep it hidden from Europeans.

There is no doubt that Cobo was able to access a huge amount of native knowledge for his work, but he was not only silent about his native informants but also avoided any discussion of the tensions and conflicts that undoubtedly were generated by the Europeans' desire to use native knowledge to appropriate and exploit the region's natural resources. While Cobo records the transformation of the New World's landscape with the expansion of European towns and their way of life, he does not dwell on the effects it produced for the native population. But some passages clearly suggest that the natives were not always willing to reveal their knowledge and that obtaining such knowledge was no easy task.

In one passage, Cobo tells the story of an accident suffered by the son of a local chieftain, or cacique, who was subject to the *encomienda* of Spanish overlord Don Diego de Ávalos. The boy had broken his leg, and the local Spanish physicians recommended amputation. The boy's father, however, sent for an indigenous physician, who was able to use a particular plant to mend the break and restore the boy's health. The Spanish *encomendero* was so impressed that he offered a large sum of money to the indigenous healer to find out which plant he had used for the cure. The healer, however, despite promising to show the plant to the Spaniard, kept postponing the moment with excuses and evasiveness and in the end never did comply with the Spaniard's wish.[30] In another passage, Cobo tells of some yellow powders called *siaya* that the Andean peasants offered to sell to the Spaniards in small tubes. The powders had a subtle yet pleasant odor and could be used for medicinal and hygienic purposes, specifically to alleviate heart problems and eliminate bad breath, but they also could be stored alongside clothing to provide a fresh scent and prevent moth infestation. Cobo referred to the tree from which these powders originated as the *siaya* tree, for he was sure that the Spaniards had never encountered this tree before or knew of its existence. Although Cobo did not explicitly say that the indigenous people kept this tree hidden from the Spaniards, he does insinuate that the natives kept these trees at a distance from Spanish settlements in order to preserve for themselves the knowledge of its powers.[31]

Another interesting case of hidden native knowledge has to do with the so-called bezoar stone. This name refers to a calcification that can form in the intestines of various ruminant animals, and these stones are particularly common in the camelids of the Andes. The bezoar stone has a long and complex history, one that explains its importance to Cobo and his interest in researching its presence and powers in the New World.[32] He was particularly interested in verifying claims that had been made from the early medieval period to his own day about the bezoar stone being the most effective antidote against all kinds of poison. Many authors in Europe as well as in the East and West Indies had written about the bezoar stone, analyzing this marvel of nature and all its possible attributes. At the same time, there was a great deal of debate over the exact circumstances and processes through which the stone acquired its curative powers. Cobo dedicated particular attention to this topic and these debates. He claimed to have found out from the indigenous people that the medicinal power of the bezoar stone originated in a plant known as *tola* in Quechua and *sopo* in Aymara. The Andean camelids that grazed on fields where this medicinal plant was found were the ones who produced and carried those bezoar stones of such amazing powers. It is important to note that Cobo was the only historian or naturalist of the New World to divulge this information, a fact that points to both his perseverance and the access to native knowledge that he had managed to gain. And in this case, unlike in the rest of the book, Cobo directly credits his native informants for the knowledge he has attained, even reproducing, albeit indirectly, the words they used to express that knowledge. At the same time, Cobo was careful not to affirm or deny the validity of their claims—that is, whether the herb in question was indeed the origin of the curative powers of the bezoar stone. The bezoar stone at that time had enormous value in the social imaginary and in the markets of medicinal products, and as such, an affirmation of the native claims would have been extremely controversial. In any case, the importance of native knowledge to Cobo's history is clearly discernable here, especially since he claimed that his experiences in regard to the bezoar stone led him to look favorably on the veracity of the particulars he was able to gather from the native informants.[33]

Mestizo Knowledge

Cobo's extended residence in the New World and his observations of the interactions between different communities and the natural world enabled him to appreciate the many kinds of knowledge interchange that had occurred between the Spaniards and the native peoples. Just as the encounter between different cultures was forging new cultures within the New World, so too was the interchange of knowledge resulting in new mestizo practices and forms of understanding.

This knowledge interchange took several shapes. Although a good number of Cobo's descriptions presupposed a native knowledge, in many cases he explicitly translated that knowledge into a European cultural context. Here is what Cobo wrote about the plant *acana*:

> La *acana* crece un codo de alto, en las ramas y hojas es muy parecida a la alfalfa; tiene flor amarilla del talle de la de la manzanilla, nace entre peñas y es hierba pectoral más amarga al gusto que la acíbar; es caliente y seca en el segundo grado. Comen los indios con ella la coca. Su cocimiento con un poco de alumbre es bueno para las llagas de la boca; y tomado caliente en ayunas con alfeñique aprovecha contra la tos y asma, y ablanda y limpia el pecho y el estómago. Allende de esto, aplicado su cocimiento al rostro quita las pecas de él y, si se hace con vino, quita las nubes de los ojos.[34]

> The *acana* reaches a cubit in height, its branches and leaves are very similar to those of alfalfa; it sprouts a yellow flower about the size of the chamomile flower, it grows between rocks and is a pectoral herb more bitter than aloe; it is hot and dry to the second degree. The Indians eat it with coconut. When cooked with a bit of alum, it is good for all mouth sores; and when consumed hot on an empty stomach with a bit of caramel, it wards off coughs and asthma, loosening and clearing up the chest and stomach. Add to this, that when the cooked substance is applied to the face, it removes freckles; and if it is cooked with wine, it disperses cloudiness in the eyes.

In addition to drawing comparisons familiar to the Spaniards in order to help his readers imagine the American plant, Cobo used European medical terminology to describe the plant's attributes, noting that the *acana* was "hot and dry in the second degree." Similarly, the medicinal prescriptions that he described incorporate such European elements as caramel and wine (alum was an element native to both Europe and the New World). Thus, Cobo perfectly accommodated his definition of the *acana* within a European medical context in terms of both how the plant should be used and against which maladies it would be most useful. And although his description included an explicit reference to how indigenous people used the plant, making it clear that he was proposing very different uses by Europeans, there is no question that the result would contribute to a mestizo system of knowledge.

In other examples involving knowledge interchange, Cobo simply pointed to the way different communities used new elements to most effectively address a particular need. For example, Cobo expressed surprise upon seeing indigenous peasants using bulls to transport firewood, something Spaniards had never done; he also noted how Spaniards used the native shrub called *yareta* for firewood, something the indigenous people had never done. Other instances Cobo mentioned centered on the important sharing of specific knowledge regarding agricultural practices. The Spaniards, he wrote, had learned a new way to gather the wheat harvest from the indigenous people, imitating the way the natives harvested their corn so as to best protect it during storage.[35] And for their part, the indigenous people learned the Spanish method of grafting fruit trees so as to obtain better varieties of fruit.[36]

One area where the knowledge interchange occurred quite naturally was in the preparation of meals, although admittedly this alimentary encounter between the different cultures was a complex and controversial process, given its importance to questions of identity and the social imaginary.[37] Notwithstanding the cultural and economic ramifications of this alimentary encounter, what is important to emphasize here is that Cobo, writing in the middle of the seventeenth century, observed how indigenous people had learned to cultivate European legumes and noted the particular adoption of and appreciation for garlic that highland natives demonstrated.[38] At the same time, he observed how Spaniards were utilizing potato flour to make delicious candies and cakes.[39] Cobo described these particular practices because he was conscious of witnessing the emergence of a mestizo culinary tradition grounded in a sharing of knowledge about the natural world.

Coda

Just as Cobo enjoyed surprising Amerindians with the trick of starting a fire using a magnifying glass, so too did he like to surprise Spaniards with aspects of the New World about which they knew nothing. So, for example, on a return trip by ship to Peru, he confounded those traveling companions coming to the region for the first time by predicting, correctly, that they would experience cold temperatures as they neared the equator (he knew from experience how that region was affected by cold winds from the south). What these anecdotes illustrate is that Bernabé Cobo recognized the advantages of having access to knowledge of different worlds. And if his *Historia del Nuevo Mundo* continues to be a valuable work today, it is precisely because it offers a privileged gaze into the encounter of European epistemic traditions with a new natural world and native knowledge during a special moment of history.

Part II

Amerindian Knowledge
in the Atlantic World

Chapter 4

Pictorial Knowledge on the Move:
The Translations of the *Codex Mendoza*

Daniela Bleichmar

Mesoamerican peoples such as the Nahuas, Mixtecs, and Mayas possessed sophisticated traditions of pictorial writing, which they used to produce records with multiple functions—historical, calendrical, divinatory, and so forth. The "painted books" created by indigenous painter-scribes (Nahuatl *tlacuilo*, pl. *tlacuiloque*) fascinated Europeans. But while collectors in the Old World valued them as rare examples of exotic writing, early missionaries in New Spain destroyed the vast majority of pre-Columbian pictorial manuscripts because of their "idolatrous"—that is, sacred or ritual—content. Nevertheless, painter-scribes continued to make codices long after the conquest, adapting their craft and incorporating both native and European traditions.[1]

In Mexico City, in the 1540s, artists and scribes created the pictorial manuscript we know as the *Codex Mendoza* (Figures 4.1 and 4.2).[2] To make it, indigenous artists painted colorful figures that recorded information about Aztec history, tributary practices, and social life.[3] Some of the drawings adhere to pre-Hispanic pictorial conventions, while others show their Europeanization.[4] Following indigenous custom, these figures provided the basis for an oral account in Nahuatl, speech that an interpreter then rendered into Spanish. In a final step, Spanish scribes wrote down a Spanish-language text that presented the information and decoded Nahua pictorial writing. Thus, this codex emerged from a complex and multistep process that engaged American and European makers and traditions. Amerindian aspects include the pictographic writing and oral account, the artists and interpreter (and perhaps a

Figure 4.1. *Codex Mendoza*, ca. 1540s, Mexico City, folio 1v, Mexico City, folio 1v. Bodleian Library, Oxford, Ms. Arch. Selden A. 1. By kind permission of the Bodleian Libraries.

Figure 4.2. Codex Mendoza, 1540s, Mexico City, folio 2r, Bodleian Library, Oxford, Ms. Arch. Selden A. 1. By kind permission of the Bodleian Libraries.

scribe), some of the pigments used in the figures, and the information that the document contains. European aspects include the paper, ink, and some pigments; the book format and adherence to pages as the narrative unit rather than the pre-Columbian screenfold, scroll, or cloth; the alphabetic writing; the scribes; and the intended audience, as it was made for export to Spain.

From its arrival in Europe in the sixteenth century, this codex has been celebrated as a key document for the study of Mesoamerica. The codex has received more sustained attention than any other Mexican manuscript, particularly in the early modern period. Authors in the seventeenth and eighteenth centuries referred to it as "a Mexican picture historie," "Mexican hieroglyphs," and "Mexican painted annals." In 1780, the Mexican Jesuit Francisco Javier Clavijero, writing in exile in Italy, suggested that the first viceroy of New Spain, Antonio de Mendoza (1495–1552, r. 1535–1550), commissioned the codex. Although that provenance is uncertain at best, it has since that moment provided a name for the document.[5] Today, scholars cherish the *Codex Mendoza* for the detailed information it provides about Nahua history, economy, and culture only two decades after the conquest of the Aztec Empire in 1521. It is also of remarkable artistic quality and historical importance. Finally, the document is unique in providing an alphabetic gloss to every single pictograph, which has positioned it as a sort of Rosetta stone or primer for the study of Nahua glyphs both in the early modern period and more recently. The Bodleian Library at Oxford, which owns it, exhibits it as a "treasure."

Scholarship on the *Codex Mendoza* has tended to focus on interpreting the pictographs, mining the document for empirical data about Aztec society, and using it as evidence of indigenous practices and agency. This chapter builds on existing studies by considering the manuscript as an object in motion, following its trajectories and transformations across language, cultural differences, space, media, and interpretations. The chapter begins with the codex's manufacture in New Spain in the mid-sixteenth century and traces its physical travels and printed reproductions in the seventeenth and eighteenth centuries. I am as interested in the document's production as in its circulation, reception, and reproduction and consider it as a source for the study of both sixteenth-century New Spain and early modern Europe.

Central to this study of the *Codex Mendoza*'s trajectories and transformations is an attention to processes of translation. Scholarship on early Spanish American visual and material culture has tended to parse indigenous and European elements, describing works that show traits from both traditions as examples of a unique "hybrid" or "mestizo" mixture characteristic of the region.[6] However, although the *Codex Mendoza* presents both European and American elements, its makers for the most part did not combine them. Quite to the contrary, the codex carefully juxtaposes image and text, Nahua and Spanish elements, presenting them as related but separate and distinct. It is less an example of hybridization or *mestizaje* than an instance of translation, suggesting the constant movement, adjustments, and transformations involved in negotiating differences between languages, writing systems, and cultures.[7] This chapter underscores the importance of situating translation culturally and historically, paying close attention to the nuances and specificities of a particular case, rather than as a broad but vague conceptual category.

The *Codex Mendoza* was created at a time when practices of linguistic and cultural translation were critical to almost every aspect of public and private life in New Spain. Postconquest codices often display the figure of the interpreter in a prominent position, featuring in particular the best known and most infamous of colonial go-betweens: Hernán Cortés's aide and lover Malintzin, who both translated for the Spaniards and underwent translation herself, as she was also known as Malinche, the Hispanicized version of her Nahuatl name, and as Doña Marina, her baptismal name.[8] Early missionaries faced the challenges posed by linguistic barriers by learning indigenous languages and creating a copious literature that included dictionaries, grammars, catechisms, collections of sermons, and *confesionarios*. The first printed Nahuatl-Spanish dictionary, *Vocabulario en la lengua castellana y mexicana* (Vocabulary in the Castillian and Mexican Languages), was compiled by the Franciscan Alonso de Molina and published in Mexico City in 1555. It offered an impressive 520 pages of paired entries; it was widely used and repeatedly emulated and expanded upon. The Franciscans also undertook the education of elite Nahuatl-speaking boys at the Colegio de Santa Cruz de Tlatelolco, providing a humanistic and religious education in Spanish and Latin.[9] The college's library, whose collection of printed books provided models of European texts and images, is linked to two important colonial manuscripts that are roughly contemporary with the *Codex Mendoza*: the *Codex de la Cruz-Badiano* or *Libellus de medicinalibus indorum herbis* (Little Book of the Medicinal Herbs of the Indies), composed in 1552 in Latin and Nahuatl, and the *Florentine Codex* (ca. 1555–1577), written in Nahuatl and Spanish. To live in Mexico City in the mid-sixteenth century meant to constantly engage in acts of linguistic and cultural translation.

In the early modern period, the word "translation" had two meanings. Sebastián de Covarrubias's *Tesoro de la lengua castellana o española* (Treasure of the Castilian or Spanish language), published in Madrid in 1611 and the first dictionary of any European vernacular, defines *traduzir* (to translate) as "to take one thing from one place to another" and "to turn a statement from one language into another."[10] Translation could refer to physical or linguistic movement, making the concept particularly well suited to the *Codex Mendoza*, a document produced through processes of linguistic and cultural translation, set in physical motion across space, and then repeatedly transformed in printed versions that constituted new acts of interpretive translation. This chapter's sections—or rather movements—follow the codex through these three types of translation, bringing into question the very notion that there is a singular object, the *Codex Mendoza*. Mobility, I argue, led to mutation and multiplication.

First Movement: Colonial Translation and the Making of the *Codex Mendoza*

The *Codex Mendoza* is an illustrated manuscript in book format, composed of seventy-one folios of European paper measuring roughly 30 x 21 cm (12 x 8¼ in). It consists of seventy-two pages of pictorial content annotated with Spanish glosses and sixty-three pages of textual commentary in Spanish, with pages of text and image interpolated (see Figures 4.1 and 4.2). The codex is divided into three sections. The first, in sixteen folios, presents a history of the Aztecs from the founding of the capital city of Tenochtitlan in 1325 to its fall in 1521. This is a political and military history organized chronologically according to the reign of each emperor, or *tlatoani*, providing the dates of his rule through blue-colored year glyphs and the names of the towns he brought into the imperial fold as tributaries (Figure 4.3).[11]

The second and longest section, in thirty-nine folios, relates Aztec imperial geography to economics. This part details the tributary obligations of towns subject to Mexica control, organized by region and specifying such items as fine feathers, animal skins, precious stones, gold, mantles, liquidambar, and cacao beans, among others (Figure 4.4). As in the first section, the content, format, and style are highly regimented. Towns are listed on the margin, starting at the top left and moving counterclockwise around the page. Tribute items occupy the majority of the page, accompanied by glyphs indicating quantities and organized in horizontal registers, with clothing always at the top of the page, military insignia such as warriors' uniforms and shields at the center, and foodstuffs and other items at the bottom.[12]

Figure 4.3. Codex Mendoza, 1540s, Mexico City, folio 15v, Bodleian Library, Oxford, Ms. Arch. Selden A. 1. By kind permission of the Bodleian Libraries.

Figure 4.4. Codex Mendoza, ca. 1540s, Mexico City, folio 46r, Bodleian Library, Oxford, Ms. Arch. Selden A. 1. By kind permission of the Bodleian Libraries.

Whereas the first two sections follow pre-Columbian traditions, the third represents a colonial innovation.[13] In sixteen folios, this portion of the manuscript describes Aztec social life: the upbringing of boys and girls from birth until age fifteen, when girls should be married and boys enter a trade or specialized schooling; various occupations, including detailed depictions of military orders and their uniforms; information about governance; and old age and death (Figure 4.5). In this portion there is a unique glimpse of "their private and public rites from the grave of the womb to the womb of the grave"—to use the evocative words of a seventeenth-century commentator—just as they were being thoroughly transformed in the new viceregal society.[14]

Making the codex involved various steps and types of translation. First, indigenous artists working in the Mesoamerican tradition recorded information about Mexica history, culture, religion, and tributary practices pictorially, leaving blank pages in between their paintings. In a second step, a narrator provided an oral account of what the drawings represented in Nahuatl, rendering images into spoken words. Then, a Spanish interpreter fluent in Nahuatl (*nahuatlato*) provided a Spanish translation of the indigenous speech. In a fourth step, a Spanish scribe wrote down the text and annotated every single figure with an explanatory gloss. The name of each ruler or town appears next to the appropriate figure; the banner (*pantli*) is always annotated as "twenty," the mountain glyph representing a town as *pueblo* (town), and so on (see Figures 4.2–4.5). Finally, the manuscript appears to have been reviewed by a person who corrected errors in the Spanish text and appended a concluding commentary about the document's production.

The relation between text and image is not one of primary content and secondary illustration. Rather, the text translates the image; each presents information according to one of two separate registers, a Mexica pictorial one and a Spanish alphabetic one. The text has a dual function: first, to translate the content itself—that is, to convey in words the information that the images present—and second, to translate the way in which the system of pictorial writing works. For instance, at the bottom of the first textual portion (see Figure 4.1) there is an explanation of a blue strip of year glyphs whose meaning is deciphered through inscriptions in both Nahuatl and Spanish, with the Nahuatl in red ink above the images and the Spanish in black ink below them.[15] Throughout the codex, the text thus provides information and also an introduction to Nahua pictographic writing. There is a constant back-and-forth between these two functions throughout the codex: the Spanish

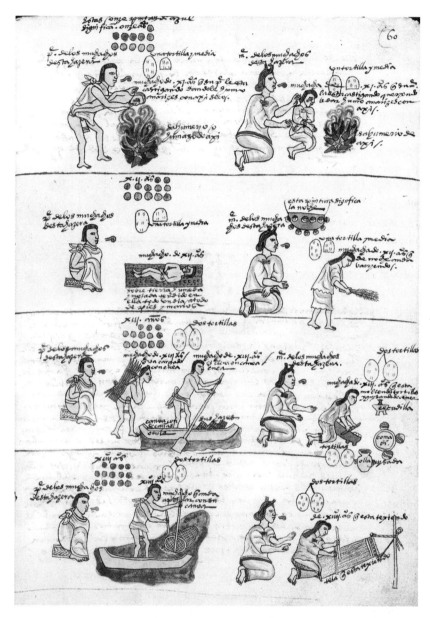

Figure 4.5. Codex Mendoza, 1540s, Mexico City, folio 60r, Bodleian Library, Oxford, Ms. Arch. Selden A. 1. By kind permission of the Bodleian Libraries.

writing will give a textual rendition of the content of an image, noting, for instance, that a ruler reigned for so many years, and then explain that the blue squares provide dates, that burning temples signify conquest, and so on.

The translation is insistent, indeed incessant. Glosses repeatedly offer the meaning of every single glyph even if they recur throughout the manuscript or within a single folio. It is never assumed that a reader already knows that the banner stands for "twenty" or that it is unnecessary to provide the individual translation for every single glyph, given that the accompanying text on the facing page details every item. In effect, each figure is translated twice, once next to the image and again in the textual version.

The codex also shows acts of cultural translation or interpretation, framing Mexica history and culture in the postconquest context and for European audiences. The first section of the codex, for instance, ends with the reign of Moctezuma Xocoyotzin (see Figure 4.3). The choice of Moctezuma as the "last" Aztec emperor omits his successors Cuitláhuac and Cuauhtemoc, who ruled between Moctezuma's death in late June 1520 and the surrender of the Aztec capital to Cortés and his allies in mid-August 1521. At the bottom of the page, the presence of uncolored year glyphs in pen and ink indicates a telling editorial intervention. The original chronology painted by the artists (in blue squares, each representing one year) ends in 1518, but the scribe appears to have extended this year count by adding three lines to the Roman numeral XV to transform it into XVIII and by drawing three year glyphs. The penultimate glyph is annotated "end and death of Moctezuma," and the last one is labeled "*pacificación* (pacification) and conquest of New Spain." Thus, the Spanish scribe not only rendered images into words but in this case also presented a particular account of history, showing how translation also involved revision and transformation.

Another example of cultural translation involves the celebrated depiction of the palace of Moctezuma (Figure 4.6). It includes on the left a "Council Hall of War" and on the right a "Council Hall" for the hearing of legal cases and the passing of judgment, both of them labeled. This page is well known as the only image to use a perspective view in the codex, a Europeanized vision of Aztec rule. Equally important is the fact that both image and text describe the Aztecs as an example of a civilized people by celebrating what the narrative terms their "order" and "good governance" (*orden, buen gobierno, buen regimiento*). These are crucial terms, as they connoted *civitas*, a critical category for Spanish and indeed European political philosophy that would clearly communicate to a European reader that the Mexicas were highly civilized people.[16]

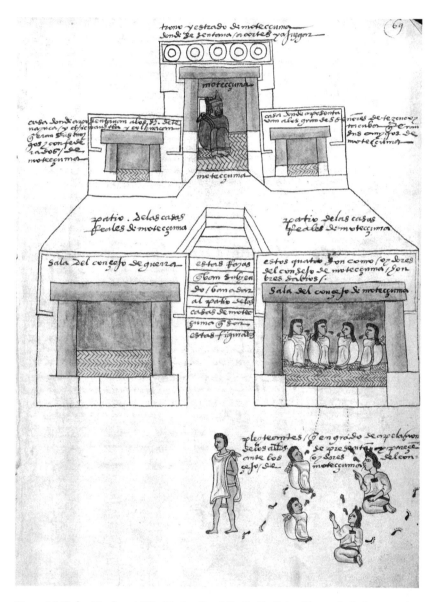

Figure 4.6. *Codex Mendoza*, 1540s, Mexico City, folio 69r, Bodleian Library, Oxford, Ms. Arch. Selden A. 1. By kind permission of the Bodleian Libraries.

The codex concludes with a page of text that directly addresses translation practices. The scribe begs for the reader's leniency with "the rough style in the interpretation of the drawings," explaining that indigenous artists provided the material to the interpreter only ten days before the ship that would take the codex to Spain was scheduled to sail. With such little time to work, the scribe explains, the translation was done *a uso de proceso*, that is, following legal conventions.[17] This is a most interesting revelation, as it indicates that the procedure used to make this important codex—transforming Nahua pictorial writing and oral testimony into Spanish prose—came directly out of the court system, where indigenous litigants routinely presented pictorial statements as evidence.[18] Thus, the codex's very last statement indicates that its makers viewed it precisely as evidence produced through translation.[19]

The *Codex Mendoza*, I have suggested, is the product of a series of translations or movements: rendering Nahuatl into Spanish, images into words, and oral interpretation into alphabetic writing as well as a hermeneutic movement in the interpretation of Mexica information for European eyes. After this, language translations gave way to physical ones. Apparently completed in haste, the codex traveled by land from Mexico City to the gulf port of Veracruz and there went aboard a ship that carried it across the Atlantic. Once set in motion, it continued to move for the next hundred years to destinations its makers never imagined.

Second Movement: Physical Translations, or Travels in Space

The *Codex Mendoza* led an eventful biography, which left its physical mark in the object in the form of multiple annotations.[20] It is unclear whether it ever reached Spain and also unclear how it ended up in the hands of its first recorded owner, André Thevet (1516–1590). Thevet was a French writer who traveled to Brazil, became an authority on the Americas, and served as royal cosmographer to the Valois court. He signed the manuscript in five separate places (see Figure 4.2, top left), and briefly discussed Mexican pictographic writing in his *Cosmographie universelle* (*Universal cosmography*, Paris, 1575) and *Les vrais pourtraits et vies des hommes illustres* (*The True Portraits and Lives of Famous Men*, Paris, 1584).

By 1587, it appears, the codex belonged to Richard Hakluyt (1552?–1616), an active promoter of English settlement in North America and the author of two important compilations that approached geography and travel from the perspective of English political aspirations toward the New World. The date is provided by a somewhat cryptic English annotation that was written in an early blank folio in the codex.[21] After Hakluyt's death in 1616, the manuscript went to Samuel Purchas (1577?–1626), an English cleric and the author of an immensely popular travel compilation that, as I will discuss, was of great importance to the codex's early modern reception. After Purchas's death ten years later, John Selden (1584–1654), the English jurist, politician, Orientalist, and author, acquired the manuscript and inscribed his motto on the first folio of the text. In 1659, five years after Selden's death, the Bodleian Library at Oxford received his extensive collection of books and manuscripts, which in addition to the *Codex Mendoza* included two other Mexican pictorial manuscripts, the *Selden Codex* and the *Selden Roll*.[22] This marks the end of the *Codex Mendoza*'s physical translations, with the Bodleian as a final resting place.

For about a hundred years after it was first made, the *Codex Mendoza* lived a life of constant travel. It changed hands at least five times and was a prized possession of some of the most noted European collectors and writers on the topic of travel and the New World. These highly contingent physical translations indicate the great interest that this kind of manuscript awoke among early modern European collectors and authors, who literally left their mark on the codex through various inscriptions.

The *Codex Mendoza* was not alone in its physical travels. Over the course of the early modern period, Mexican pictorial manuscripts—pre-Columbian and colonial—could be found in collections in Madrid, Rome, Florence, Bologna, London, Oxford, Reims, Paris, and many other cities.[23] European scholars were fascinated and mystified by what they termed "Mexican hieroglyphs," which they avidly reproduced in their publications as examples of exotic non-European writing.[24] However, they found Mesoamerican pictorial writing impossible to decipher. The catalog of Ferdinando Cospi's Bolognese *Wunderkammer*, published in 1667, describes the pre-Columbian *Codex Cospi* as a book of "Mexican hieroglyphs, which are most extravagant figures and for the most part depict men and animals that are strangely monstrous."[25] The publication reproduced some of the figures (Figure 4.7), but the author had no idea of what to make of them. "What these [symbols] mean," he noted, "I do not know, nor do I know of others in Europe who know it." He considered these "hieroglyphs" both fascinating and inscrutable, a "literary mystery, not yet explained," and their eventual decipherment "a beautiful and curious undertaking."[26]

The inability of early modern Europeans to make sense of pre-Columbian codices, which did not include alphabetic writing, helps to explain why the

Ne' margini poi delle fudette undici pagine egli fegnò alcuni Geroglifici Mini-
mi, che parimente fembrano fpiegazione de'Geroglifici
Maffimi, a' quali fanno corona. Ad ognuno de' quali
Geroglifici Maffimi fottofcritti fi mirano alcuni caratteri
neri rotondi, che fembrano zeri,
divifi a due a due, riga per riga con
una linea fola; e condue, quando
fono ad uno ad uno, come quì fi vede.

17 Che cofa fignifichino, non m'è noto, nè sò che
fia noto ad altri nell' Europa: non havendo per anco
trovato chi li mentovi, e ne dia lume alcuno: e poffo
dirne con l'eruditiffimo Vormio, il quale nel fuo Mu-
feo publicò, mà non ifpiegò (e così pure haveva fatto il *de Laët*) una Tavola di
fimil Caratteri *HIEROGLYPHICA MEXICANA*, *miris conftantia figuris vario
colorum genere depictis*, *ex quibus vix quifpiam quidquam collegerit*. Sò che s'accingerebbe ad una bella, e curiofa impreia, chi prendeffe ad illuftrare le tenebre di quefti mifterii letterarii, non per anco fpiegati nell' Europa.

18 Serbafi quefto fingulariffimo libro in una caffa quadrata di nobile artifi-
zio, con il coperchio di criftallo, effendone li XVI. Decembre del MDCLXV.
ftato fatto un rega'o al Mufeo dalla mano cortefe del virtuofiffimo Sig. Co. Va-
lerio Zani, Nipote di Monfignor Coftanzo Zani Vefcovo d'Imola, e Riftorato-
re dell'Accademia de'Gelat (di cui ne raccolfe, e publicò le Memorie, & un
Volume di Profe, mentre n'era Principe gli anni MDCLXX. e LXXI.) il quale
donò poi al Mufeo dell' Aldrovandi quella Verga di legno, che vi fi vede con la
fuperfizie tutta figurata di fimili geroglifici con particolare induftria intagliati-
vi, in ogni fua parte indorata.

19 VOLVME di SCORZA INTERIORE d'ALBERO, forfi di Tiglia,
fcritto con caratteri Barbari, di notabile antichità, i quali però tengono qual-
che fimiglianza co' Latini. Si diftende a pochi palmi, mancandoli il fine. Per
effere fatto di quella materia, che diceffimo chiamarfi da Latini propriamente
Liber, poteva, con molto maggior ragione, che i noftrali, chiamarfi *Libro*.
Con tuttociò non è per lui nome improprio quello di *Volume*, che li conviene
aflai

*Io de Laët.
l.5 c 10 de
feript. Ind.
Occident.
Vorm. l 4.
Muf. c. 12
p. 383. 384.*

Figure 4.7. Lorenzo Legati, *Museo Cospiano* (Bologna, 1677), 192. Getty Research Institute.

Codex Mendoza gained such a privileged and unique place in the European study of Mesoamerica. It was the only known codex that offered a translation of both Nahua pictorial writing and Nahua history, economics, and cultural information into alphabetic glosses in Spanish, which could in turn be translated into other European languages. The final section of this chapter turns to the *Codex Mendoza*'s paper travels, tracking its various translations and interpretations in early modern publications.

Third Movement: Paper Translations, or Travels in Print

Although the *Codex Mendoza* ended its physical travels when it entered the Bodleian Library in 1659, it continued to move through publication, with physical translations giving way to media translations. Its paper travels began with the publication of Samuel Purchas's widely read *Hakluytus posthumus: Or Purchas his pilgrimes*, 4 vols. (London, 1625). The third volume includes a fifty-two-page chapter with woodcuts reproducing almost the entire pictorial content of the *Codex Mendoza* as well as an English translation of the Spanish text, with additional commentary (Figure 4.8).[27] Purchas explained that although his book introduced the letters of other modern and ancient nations, including Chinese, Japanese, Indian, Arabic, and Persian, as well as Egyptian and Ethiopian hieroglyphs, this precious Mexican manuscript was the only known full-fledged history of and by a foreign nation, addressing their rulers, economics, religion, and customs.[28] For him, the *Codex Mendoza* represented much more than a collectible example of exotic writing: it constituted a unique indigenous source about the Aztec world. The fact that the manuscript was a history—a highly regarded genre at the time—mattered greatly to Purchas's assessment of the codex, helping to prove Aztec governance and civility and to establish the Aztecs as a sophisticated civilization rather than "barbarians" or "savages."[29]

Purchas memorably called the codex "the choicest of my jewels," musing that "perhaps, there is not any one History of this kind in the world comparable to this, so fully expressing so much without letters, hardly gotten, and easily lost."[30] Purchas's high esteem for the manuscript is evidenced by the decision to reproduce it almost in its entirety, which involved having the Spanish text translated into English and also commissioning a large number of woodcut reproductions of the figures, a laborious and costly choice. No other document in the four volumes of the text received comparable treatment in length or illustrations.

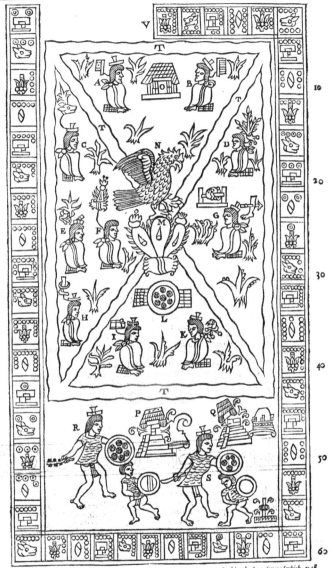

This Picture presents the number of 51. yeares : that is, the time of Tenuchs reigne : in this wheele or square (which, as all the like representing yeares, are in the originall picture coloured blew) the pictures of men signifie the ten Lords or Gouernours before mentioned ; their names are inscribed in the originall pictures, which here wee haue by the letters annexed directly to a following glosse. A. Acatuli. B Quapan. C Ocelopan. D Aguexotl. E Tecineuh. F Tenucb. G Xomimitl. H Xocoyol. I Xiuh- caqui.

Figure 4.8. Samuel Purchas, *Hakluytus posthumus: Or Purchas his pilgrimes*, 4 vols. (London, 1625), 3:1068. Library of Congress.

Table 4.1. Publications presenting material from the *Codex Mendoza*, 1625–1813

1. Samuel Purchas, *Hakluytus posthumus: Or Purchas his pilgrimes* (London, [1625]).
2. Johannes de Laet, *Nieuwe Wereldt ofte Beschrijvinghe van West-Indien* [1625], 2nd ed. (Leiden, 1630).
3. Johannes de Laet, *Novus Orbis seu descriptionis Indiae Occidentalis* (Amsterdam, 1633).
4. Johannes de Laet, *L'Histoire du Nouveau Monde ou description des Indes* (Leiden, 1640).
5. Athanasius Kircher, *Oedipus Aegyptiacus* (Rome, 1652–1654).
6. Melchisédech Thévenot, *Relations des divers voyages curieux* (Paris, 1663–1696).
7. William Warburton, *The Divine Legation of Moses Demonstrated* (London, 1738–1741).
8. William Warburton, *Essai sur les hieroglyphes des Egyptiens* (Paris, 1744).
9. Francisco Javier Clavijero, *Storia antica del Messico* (Cesena, 1780–1781).
10. Alexander von Humboldt, *Vues des Cordillères, et monumens des peuples indigènes de l'Amérique* (Paris, 1810–1813).

Purchas's version of the *Codex Mendoza* had enormous impact, as it was the only version produced from the manuscript until the publication of Lord Kingsborough's monumental nine-volume *Antiquities of Mexico* (London: Robert Havell; Colnaghi, Son, and Co., 1831–1848).[31] Between 1625 and 1831, Purchas's print translation provided the source material for no fewer than six other titles in eleven different editions, many of them influential and widely read works (table 4.1). For two centuries, the numerous authors who wrote about the *Codex Mendoza* based their information and images on Purchas's edition and to a lesser degree on later versions based on it. This meant that they knew the pictographs as black-and-white woodcuts rather than as vividly colored drawings and that they did not fully understand the Spanish textual presence. Thanks to Purchas, the *Codex Mendoza* may well be the single most reproduced non-Western manuscript in early modern publications.

Print not only gave the *Codex Mendoza* legs but also made it malleable. Authors' particular interpretations of the material and its significance created multiple versions of the codex as they used it to pursue interests in history, religion, pictographic writing, the civility of New World populations, the history of languages, and other topics. While a full analysis of the multiple versions of the *Codex Mendoza* that its printed travels produced is beyond the scope of this chapter, some examples will illustrate the interpretive mobility that publication yielded.

Purchas's most significant intervention was to alter the relationship between image and text in the manuscript. In his publication, the Spanish glosses that appear next to each single image in the manuscript vanished. The woodcuts replaced these annotations with uppercase letters in alphabetical order, keyed to a textual commentary set in italics below or next to the image (see Figure 4.8). While this was a standard mechanism for linking image to text in European publications of the time, in this particular case image became distanced from text, obscuring the Spanish presence within the manuscript itself. This separation of the pictorial and textual elements is emphasized by the running header for the chapter, in which Purchas portrays the *Codex Mendoza* as a "Mexican picture historie" and a "Chronicle without writing," despite the abundant presence of words throughout the codex.[32] Purchas's editorial interventions yielded a new version of the manuscript, one that emphasized image over word and the notion of a "pure" precontact indigenous culture over the mixing and transformation of the colonial era. This was not a facsimile; it was a translation or even a remake.

Indeed, Purchas was keenly aware of the centrality of translation to his work, as the title for his lengthy chapter on the codex indicates: "The History of the Mexican Nation, Described in Pictures by the Mexican Author Explained in the Mexican Language, Which Exposition Translated into Spanish, and Thence into English, Together with the Said Picture-Historie, Are Here Presented." The title presents the codex as the product of multiple translations, from pictures to words, from oral narrative to written prose, and from Nahuatl to Spanish to English.

Throughout the chapter, Purchas often refers to the difficulties of translation. In one passage, he reveals that the woodcutter used a letter to label a figure for which there was no Spanish text, forcing him to provide his own tentative interpretation of what that image might mean.[33] Elsewhere, he appears completely at a loss as to what to make of the pictographs that provide the names of rulers and towns, not realizing that the proper name in alphabetic writing is a translation of those images—that is, that the combined glyphs of a stone (*tetl*) and a prickly pear cactus (*nochtli*) signify the name "Tenoch," much like alphabetic writing does (see Figure 4.2, the ruler depicted immediately to the left of the name glyph for the city of Tenochtitlan). Purchas imagines that these figures must function in the manner of

European arms and leaves the task of making sense of them entirely up to the reader. "You see this king and every other both king and town distinguished by special arms or escutcheons, with other particulars, which here and in all the rest I leave to each reader's own industry and search."[34] No early modern European reader, however industrious, could access Mesoamerican images if they had not been translated into written words in a European language. Even text could pose difficulties, and Purchas's translator failed to provide English versions for some words in both Nahuatl and Spanish, leaving his readers to their own devices when faced with terms such as *xícara* (a mug or cup), *copal* (a Mesoamerican aromatic tree resin), *frijoles* (beans), *huipiles* (Mesoamerican tunics), and *naguas* (*enaguas*, or petticoats, surely also a translation of indigenous garb into European categories).

Later authors used Purchas's rendering of the *Codex Mendoza* to create new versions through processes of translation, interpretation, and selection. Johannes de Laet (1581–1649), the Dutch geographer, author, and founding member of the Dutch West India Company, drew on Purchas for the second and subsequent editions of his widely read *Nieuwe Wereldt ofte Beschrijvinghe van West-Indien* (*New World, or Description of the West Indies*, Dutch ed., Leiden, 1st. ed. 1625, 2nd. ed. 1630; Latin ed., Amsterdam, 1633; French ed., Leiden, 1640). De Laet selected portions of the manuscript for use in two chapters (out of thirty total) in the fifth book, which discusses New Spain. Chapter 10 focuses on language, counting, timekeeping, and the recording of history. It begins with a vocabulary offering Nahuatl terms for parts of the human body, colors, various "natural things," familiar relations, and numbers along with their equivalents in a European language, reiterating the primacy of translation for the study of the New World.

Unlike Purchas's great attention to Nahua pictographs, however, de Laet privileged words over images. He noted that Aztecs lacked "the art of writing," though they managed to record their history "by certain pictures, which are like hieroglyphs," and as an example he reproduced five small woodcuts representing dates and quantities—just five small figures out of the hundreds in Purchas.[35] Giving only a cursory glance to pictorial writing, de Laet focused instead on the information that the codex provided about Nahua dynastic history. His thirteenth chapter addressed "The succession of Mexican kings, according to their painted annals."[36] Here, de Laet carefully compared the text and images in Purchas's *Codex Mendoza*, noting discrepancies among them. De Laet then contrasted the chronology of rulers offered by the "painted annals" with those offered in two important publications by Spanish authors,

Francisco López de Gómara's *Historia general de las Indias* (*General History of the Indies*, Zaragoza, 1552) and José de Acosta's *Historia natural y moral de las Indias* (*Natural and Moral History of the Indies*, Seville, 1590). Thus, de Laet shared Purchas's interest in the manuscript as a historical source and credited it with the same authority as Spanish published accounts. However, de Laet's selective use of material from Purchas's *Codex Mendoza* as information spread through various chapters lost the sense of the codex as a document. For de Laet, it was one more source for the study of Nahua rule rather than a unique indigenous document, as Purchas had considered it.

The French Orientalist Melchisédech Thévenot (ca. 1620–1692) followed a rather different strategy when he used Purchas as the source for a "Histoire de l'empire Mexicain, representée par figures" ("History of the Mexican Empire Represented in Pictures"), a fascicle in his *Relations des divers voyages curieux* (*Reports of Various Curious Voyages*, Paris, 1663–1696).[37] Thévenot commissioned copies of every single one of Purchas's numerous woodcuts, and his chapter opens with forty-seven pages of printed images without any words. Only after the full suite of woodcuts does the text commence—a French translation of Purchas's English translation of the original Spanish interpretation of the Nahua oral and pictorial account. In Thévenot's version the image receives primacy and is also presented as formally dissociated from the text, giving the impression of two separate documents, one pictorial and one textual, as opposed to a single manuscript that brings image and word into dialogue on every single page. It is also worth noting that Thévenot promoted the view of Moctezuma's palace to the position of frontispiece (Figure 4.9) rather than the historical view of Tenochtitlan (see Figure 4.2 and 4.8) that Purchas made iconic—it was this woodcut more than any other that later authors reproduced. By focusing on the depiction of royal authority as a representation of Aztec imperial history rather than on the calendrical or numerical glyphs that so interested other interpreters as instances of hieroglyphic writing, Thévenot's frontispiece suggested greater similitude between European and Mexica traditions.

A third example is provided by the Jesuit polymath Athanasius Kircher (1602–1680), who in his *Oedipus Aegyptiacus* (Rome, 1652–1654) turned to Purchas's *Codex Mendoza* for comparative material. In his characteristically complex work, Kircher attempted to recover the secrets of ancient Egyptian religion and science by deciphering their hieroglyphic writing. To that end, he examined almost all hieroglyphic inscriptions known to Europeans at that time as well as comparative material from around the globe. Kircher took the

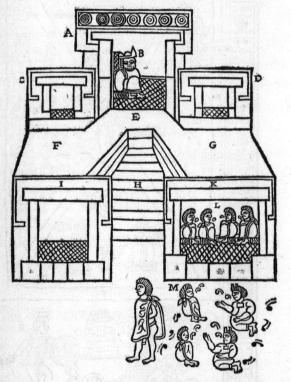

HISTOIRE
DE L'EMPIRE MEXICAIN·
reprefentée par figures·
RELATION
DV MEXIQUE, OV DE LA NOUVELLE ESPAGNE,'
Par Thomas Gages.

A PARIS,'
Chez ANDRE' CRAMOISY, ruë de la vieille Boucleric , au Sacrifice
d'Abraham.

Figure 4.9. Melchisedec Thévenot, frontispiece to "Histoire de l'empire Mexicain, representée par figures," in *Relations des diverses voyages* . . . (Paris, 1696). Boston Public Library.

widespread European notion that Mexican pictographs were hieroglyphs—another act of cultural translation—to its extreme conclusion, considering them a testament to the spread of Egyptian culture throughout the world.[38]

Detained in the library, the *Codex Mendoza* continued to move in print. It was included in travel collections as a source on Amerindian civilization. It provided material for the comparative study of cultures, religions, languages, and writing systems. It was recruited into discussions surrounding European colonial and commercial expansion and competition. It served antiquarians and collectors. It allowed for evolutionary arguments about the relative civility or primitivism of various cultures. And so on and on, multiplying with astonishing interpretive malleability. For almost two hundred years, the codex's printed translations produced numerous distinct versions, multiplying the object through interpretations while the manuscript itself remained for the most part out of sight, detained in the library.

Conclusion: Mobility and Translation

This chapter has examined the *Codex Mendoza* as an object in motion, from its production in early postconquest Mexico through its physical travels in space and its media voyages in print. Like many other rarities and curiosities from distant lands, the codex was valued both in its place of origin and in many other locations, and this interest is reflected in its multiple owners and many travels from Mexico City across the Atlantic to Europe and then to Paris, London, and Oxford—and it continues to travel today as a regular presence in high-profile exhibitions.[39] But while many if not most early modern objects that moved across distances and cultures left tenuous traces in the documentary record, making it hard for scholars who value them today to reconstruct what historical actors made of them in the period, the *Codex Mendoza* produced a stunning wealth of documented reactions. From the mid-sixteenth century to the late eighteenth century (and beyond), the codex evoked descriptions, comments, questions, and numerous reproductions that in their selective rendition of material created different versions of the document itself. The *Codex Mendoza* thus moved across languages, cultural categories, space, media, time, and interpretive horizons.

Translation was the one constant in the codex's life. It was created through processes of linguistic and cultural translation, "translated"—that is, moved—across space and media, and then translated over and over through interpretations. Translation was a process of creating versions, impressions, approximations, and rough equivalences rather than copies. Translation did not duplicate or reproduce but instead multiplied and *re*-produced. It implied above all transformation.

Tracing the codex's trajectories and transformations brings into question its ontological stability. Mobility was not a physical accident that befell an object that remained stable and immutable despite its travels. Instead, mobility was a series of transformative and constitutive acts of translation, selection, and interpretation that produced multiple versions of the object itself. Mobility made the *Codex Mendoza* flexible, unstable, and prone to mutability—as was the case with other early modern objects that moved across space and culture.[40] This changeling object could be used to ask numerous different questions and to provide numerous different answers. In various places and moments, viewers turned the pages and pored over the images and the words, creating their own *Codex Mendoza*.

Chapter 5

The Quetzal Takes Flight: Microhistory, Mesoamerican Knowledge, and Early Modern Natural History

Marcy Norton

John Ray, a founding member of London's Royal Society, wrote in the preface of *The Ornithology of Francis Willughby* (1676, 1678) that it was a singular and unprecedented work of natural history.[1] Ray emphasized that it rejected "fabulous" stories, eschewed "Fables, Presages, or ought else appertaining to Divinity, Ethics, Grammar or any sort of Humane Learning," and depended on firsthand observation ("from the view and inspection of it lying before us").[2] Modern scholars have largely agreed that this work—along with the others that Ray coauthored with Francis Willughby concerning insects and fish—marks a turning point in the history of science. Some view the *Ornithology* as the "first scientific classification" organized around morphological traits, anticipating Carolus Linnaeus's taxonomies and key features of modern zoology.[3] Even scholars who have rejected a positivist view of the history of science have continued to view Willughby's and Ray's works as marking an epistemological turning point. Their works are taken to exemplify the shift from the "episteme" of the Renaissance to that of the classical age (or the Enlightenment).[4]

There is another feature of the *Ornithology* that deserves attention: its dependence on natural histories based on indigenous knowledge. While this crucial aspect is often overlooked in much of the scholarship that concerns Willughby and Ray, historians focused on the science produced in the Iberian world have considered their use of American natural histories. José López Piñero and José Pardo-Tomás have demonstrated how Francisco Hernández's

"Historia natural de plantas" (ca. 1576–1577) was a major source for John Ray's botanical compendium, the *Historia plantarum* (1686–1704).[5] And Miguel de Asúa and Roger French have called attention to Ray and Willughby's extensive use of American natural histories, pointing out that in their work on fishes "almost the whole" of the section on fish in Georg Marggraf and Willem Piso's *Historia naturalis brasiliae* (Amsterdam, 1648) found its way into Willughby and Ray's *Historia piscium*.[6]

In this chapter, I likewise investigate the *Ornithology*'s reliance on natural histories of the Americas and, more particularly, argue that it was profoundly dependent on the labor, knowledge, and ontologies of indigenous people and communities. I do so by way of microhistory, a methodology uniquely suited to showing the precise nature of the entanglement of indigenous and European knowledge and its implications for transformations in European epistemology. By following the petite but magnificent shimmering green quetzal bird as it traveled from postclassic Mesoamerica and colonial New Spain to sixteenth- and seventeenth-century Europe, one can illuminate how Native Americans and Europeans coproduced early modern science. Beginning with his paradigmatic microhistory of Menocchio, a sixteenth-century miller, Carlo Ginzburg developed microhistory in order to illuminate the often purposefully effaced lives of subaltern actors and cultures, and microhistory has since been profitably employed to write global history[7] and the history of science.[8] Building on my earlier work on tobacco and chocolate, I seek to show how microhistory can be a powerful tool for writing the history of science that foregrounds the perspectives of subaltern actors and perspectives.[9] Microhistory can reveal aspects of the entanglement of indigenous and European technologies, epistemologies, and even ontologies that otherwise remain undetectable. Given that the Iberian naturalists producing scientific texts often "disavowed" indigenous contributions—and later Northern European naturalists disavowed their use of Iberian-world authors—it is often *only* on the microlevel in which their actual dependence is laid bare.[10] Though studies of epistemology—or the conditions of knowledge production—often focus on macrolevel phenomena such as taxonomy and classification, a microhistory is a valuable tool for understanding mechanisms of epistemological change. It is also on the microlevel that we are able to see the diverse ways that early modern science appropriated indigenous labor and knowledge: for example, though Mesoamerican knowledge about both the quetzal and the hummingbird infiltrated European natural history, their paths and effects were distinct, as a comparison of this study with that of Iris Montero Sobrevilla will demonstrate.[11]

* * *

The quetzal (also known as the resplendent trogon and *Pharomachrus mocinno*) was among the most important birds for Mesoamericans throughout centuries, if not millennia. Quetzal iconography abounds across time and space in Mesoamerica, including the murals at Bonampak and Teotihuacan that depict deities and powerful lords in blue-green quetzal headdresses. Classic Mayan representations abound of a floral paradise inhabited by quetzals and other brilliantly plumaged birds.[12] The people who lived in postclassic (1300–1500 CE) central Mexico were heirs to these traditions. Their sacred screenfold books attest to the continuing ritual and symbolic importance of quetzal birds.

One context for appearances of the quetzal in the screenfold books was that of sacred geography. The *Codex Fejéváry-Mayer* features on its first page an image that, according to Elizabeth Hill Boone, is "both a cosmogram of the central Mexican world and a 260-day almanac." Four flowering plants—or "cosmic trees"—of the cosmogram represent a cardinal direction, and on each tree is a bird. Perched on the flowers of the eastern tree (emerging from a solar disk) is a quetzal bird (Figure 5.1).[13] In other screenfold books of this type, this sacred geography is represented not in a single cosmogram but instead in a series of scenes associated with each cardinal direction.[14] In the *Codex Borgia* the quetzal appears twice: one sits a top the "eastern" tree and another atop the "cosmic tree"—here a maize plant—situated in the center of Earth (Figure 5.2).[15] The quetzal's connection with the east had both ecological and cultural resonance for central Mexicans. Ecologically, the habitat of the quetzal is the lush tropical regions, which lay to the east and south of the communities that produced these books. Yet the quetzal's relationship to the east was cultural as well. The inhabitants of the high-altitude plateaus in central Mexico viewed themselves as heirs to two equally important but divergent cultural traditions: the north belonged to Chichimec ancestors, a high-desert ecology, and a hunting ethos, and the south and the east belonged to Toltec ancestors, associated with settled agricultural society and such materials as cotton, cacao, jade, and precious feathers, above all those of the quetzal. The quetzal's ecological and cultural association with the east was such that when the rulers

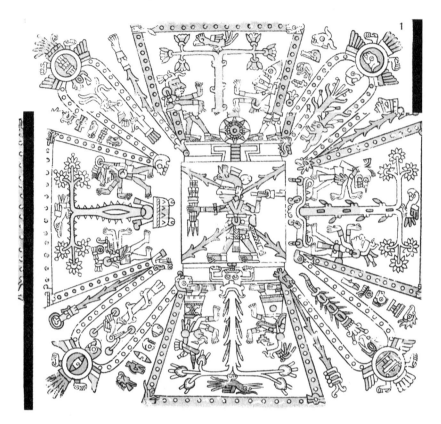

Figure 5.1. The first page of a postclassic screenfold book depicts the four world directions. A quetzal bird sits atop a flowering tree of the East (facing upward) emerging from a solar disk. *Codex Fejérváry-Mayer*, p. 1. *Codex Fejérváry-Mayer: An Old Mexican Picture Manuscript in the Liverpool Free Public Museums* (12014/M), ed. Eduard Seler (Edinburgh, UK: Printed by T. and A. Constable . . . at the Edinburgh University Press, 1901).

of the Aztec Empire, the Mexicas, conquered communities in these eastern regions, the feathers of quetzal and other tropical birds figured prominently in tribute requirements (Figure 5.3).[16] In these codices the quetzal was situated on a vertical as well as a horizontal axis, as indicated by its placement on the tops of trees and maize plants. In Mesoamerican sacred geography there was a notion of a sensuous and sensory realm that existed in the upper reaches of the multilayered cosmos—in the tops of the cosmic tree—the habitat of rain and fertility deities and fallen warriors transformed into birds or butterflies.

Quetzal birds—or more often their feathers—were also a ubiquitous presence in the adornments of deities depicted in the screenfold books. For

Figure 5.2. A quetzal bird sits atop a cosmic "tree"—here a maize plant—in this postclassic screenfold. *Codex Borgia*, plate 53. J. F. Loubat, ed., *Il manoscritto messicano borgiano* (Rome: Danesi, 1898).

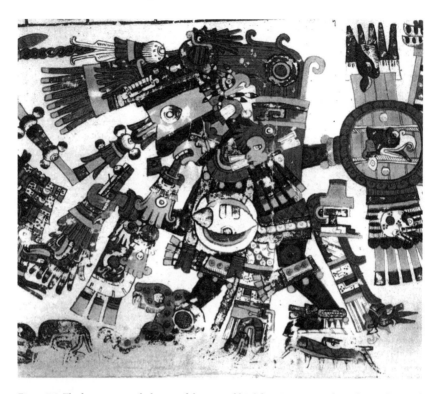

Figure 5.3. The long green tail plumes of the quetzal bird figure prominently in the attributes of the deity Tezcaltipoca; here his body contains all thirteen of the day signs. *Codex Borgia*, plate 17. J. F. Loubat, ed., *Il manoscritto messicano borgiano* (Rome: Danesi, 1898).

instance, in a section of the *Codex Borgia* explicating the 260-day ritual calendar and the deities governing thirteen-day segments (*tonalpohualli*), there are depictions of thirty-two deities, of which twenty-nine include quetzal feathers on their vestments or accessories, most often on headdresses (Figure 5.4).[17] The presence of these feathers reflects Mesoamerican practice and belief that sacred, precious properties inhered within feathers, especially those of the quetzal bird.[18] Though it is common to refer to Aztec or Mesoamerican "gods," Mesoamerican deities were ontologically distinct from those of the Judeo-Christian tradition. As explained by Boone, "Aztec deity names are simply cultic terms denoting the persons and objects central to the ritual activities. . . . [O]ne can say that individual Aztec gods do not exist ontologically, endowed with visual appearances and physical attributes that they may or may not assume at any given time. Rather, sacred power, mana,

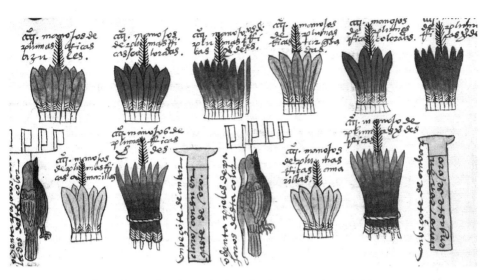

Figure 5.4. The *Codex Mendoza* depicted tribute that the Mexicas demanded from conquered communities. Bundles of quetzal feathers (annotated as "plumas ricas"), along with other "precious" birds and their feathers, featured prominently in the tribute required of Xoconochco (Soconusco), a region of the "East." *Codex Mendoza*, ca. 1540s, Mexico City, folio 47r (detail), Shelfmark: ms Arch. Selden A. 1. Bodleian Library, Oxford, Ms. Arch. Selden A. 1. By kind permission of the Bodleian Libraries.

or *teotl* (divinity) is called forth by the creation of a *teixiptla*. . . . The physical form, costume, and accouterments that comprise the *teixiptla* define the deity and even create it."[19] In other words, what we might call "costume" or "adornment" was essential to the deity's very being; outer display was identical to essence itself.

No element was more important for the creation of a deity's *teixiptla* than that of feathers. In the words of Alessandra Russo, "feathers are not the sole property of any one specific deity, but rather a kind of common denominator for the entire Mexican pantheon of deities."[20] The descriptions of deities and religious festivals in the *Florentine Codex* describing pre-Hispanic festivals demonstrate the particular potency of feathers in instantiations of divinity. With few exceptions, the deities described in text or image included feathers in his or her adornment, most often as part of a headpiece but also on sandals, shoulders, and shields.[21] Feathers from herons and eagles and from birds of "precious feathers" such as parrots, hummingbirds, and roseate spoonbills, among others, commonly featured in the *teixiptla* of deities, but none were featured as consistently as the quetzal bird: of the seven feather works that survive from pre-Hispanic "Aztec" style, the largest and most extravagant one—once known as the "headdress of Moctezuma" and now thought to be used in enthronement ceremonies or perhaps as part of a *teixiptla*—features lengthy quetzal feathers on more than three-quarters of its surface.[22]

Because of their potency, quetzal feathers were indispensable for displays of social and political power.[23] When indigenous nobles were asked about their customs before the Spanish invasions, they spoke about the "ways of adornment of the rulers when they danced" and included a list of thirteen necessary items, of which the first is a *quetzalalpiloni* (a crown of quetzal feathers) in addition to bracelets, headdresses, and fans made of the plumes.[24] Other elders interviewed told of an accessory made of a whole quetzal body.[25] When we consider the generative power of the quetzal bird and its feathers as well as its concomitant indispensability for religious and political ritual, it is no surprise that quetzal feathers linguistically evoked preciousness. It was explained to the Franciscan friar Bernardino de Sahagún that "Quetzalli" not only meant a "very broad and very green quetzal plumage" but was also "said of the king, or noble, or a royal orator."[26] The preciousness of the quetzal feathers in religious and social contexts manifested not only in their prominence in trade and tribute systems but also in the high prestige afforded to the skilled artists (*amanteca*) capable of fashioning the intricate feather works.[27]

The epoch of colonialism that began with the fall of Tenochtitlan in 1521 disrupted but also allowed for significant continuities in Mesoamerican traditions. The Nahua songs known as the *Cantares mexicanos* show how the "flowery world" exemplified by the quetzal bird seated atop cosmic and eastern trees in postclassic screenfold books endured in the colonial period. Written down in the sixteenth century and commingling traditional Mesoamerican and Christian imagery, the lyrics paint an image of a flowery world in which rapturous gods live in sensuous bliss, delighting in foaming cacao beverages, fragrant flowers, and iridescent birds, among which the quetzal is ubiquitous.[28] Louise Burkhart writes that for Nahuas "to sing of brilliant flowers calls into being this sacred iridescent paradisical place infused with creative animating power." She adds that the "terminology of blossoming and flaming is closely related to concepts of soul and the heart and of coming to life" that could be invoked by "colorful birds, stones and shells" as well as flowers.[29] Not only did the flowery world persist into the colonial period, but so did the quetzal's valences as the quintessential bird of the east and therefore a symbol of the Toltec inheritance.

The Christianization of Mesoamerica allowed and even facilitated the continued valuation of quetzal birds in material practice and symbolic imagery. The preconquest flowery world migrated to Christian paradise.[30] The Nahuatl *Psalmodia christiana*, composed by Sahagún and Nahua scholars around 1560–1580 and published in 1583, casts the archangel Gabriel as a quetzal bird in the Annunciation of Virgin Mary: "A heavenly quetzal bird was sent to God's mother. . . . The way its face case shimmering, it was like the sun, the way it came shining. Its wings, quetzal feathers are not so wide! They were quite pointed, quite green. They came shimmering brightly, they came glimmering brightly."[31] As suggested by this language, Christianity was not an obstacle but rather a vehicle for the quetzal's continued association with sacred brilliance, with its solar and specific green and iridescent qualities that made the quetzal so special and singular and the connoisseurship of the kinds of feathers needed to create sacred objects. Such imagery was made potent by the redeployment of feather works for communal celebrations and Christian devotion.[32] The supremely skilled *amanteca* continued to work their art and craft, and in the 1570s it was still commonplace to see feather workshops in Tenochtitlan[33] (Figure 5.5). The *amanteca* fashioned devotional objects out of feathers for Christian worship or made European-style coats of arms with quetzal feathers.[34] Precious ritual objects made of quetzal feathers—or the very feathers themselves—appear in the wills of native elites, and feather works with Christian imagery were sent back to Europe.[35]

* * *

As suggested by the continuity in the aesthetic, affective, and social role of the quetzal before and after the imposition of Spanish rule, central Mexico remained an indigenous space in sensory as well as political, social, and demographic terms.[36] This was the context in which Bernardino de Sahagún, Francisco Hernández, and their Nahua collaborators collected and documented knowledge about flora and fauna in New Spain. In 1558 Sahagún was commanded by his Franciscan superior "to write in Nahuatl what he thought to be of use for the doctrinal formation, the education, and the maintenance of Christianity of these natives of this New Spain, and for the aid of those workers and ministers that teach them."[37] To this end, Sahagún worked closely with a group of men he called the "grammarians."[38] These elite Nahua men, trilingual in Nahuatl, Spanish, and Latin, had been students of Sahagún at the Colegio de Santa Cruz in Tlatelolco. Over the course of two decades

Figure 5.5. Amanteca making feather works with long tail plumes of the quetzal as well as other birds of "precious feathers." Laur. Med. Palat. 219, Biblioteca Medicea Laurenziana, Florence. By permission of the Italian Ministry of Cultural Heritage and Activities. Any further reproduction for any purpose is forbidden.

Sahagún and his team of indigenous collaborators, who included not only the "grammarians" but also scribes, artists, and the "elders" they interviewed, created the "Historia universal de las cosas de la Nueva España repartida en doze libros" (Universal History of the Things of New Spain Divided into Twelve Books). The final iteration of the "Historia universal," known today as the *Florentine Codex*, is palimpsest of sorts, as its various components originated at different moments over the course of its production. The earliest Nahuatl text actually predates Toral's order, originating in the 1540s, when Sahagún was collecting oratorical formulations (such as expressions about the quetzal). Preliminary descriptions of deities and festivals date to the late 1550s, when Sahagún and the grammarians interviewed members of the indigenous nobility in Tepeapulco, who referred to pictorial books similar to the codices discussed above as well as their memories of festivals for their explanations about the deities and attendant rituals. Sahagún and his collaborators added to these drafts during the early 1560s in Tlaltelolco after conducting additional interviews with indigenous nobles from that city. In the late 1560s Sahagún worked on revisions in Mexico City, making organizational changes and beginning translations into Spanish, so that by 1569 there was a complete draft in Nahuatl of all twelve books. The final stage of work was conducted in the Colegio in Tlatelolco between 1575 and 1577, during which Sahagún and/or the grammarians translated—or rather adapted—the Nahuatl text into Spanish, and artists added copious illustrations.

As with the postclassic screenfolds, the quetzal made numerous appearances in the different books. Book 2 of the "Historia universal" provided a detailed textual analysis of the festivals associated with the ritual calendar and described with meticulous detail the *teixiptla* of different deities. These textual descriptions might be considered "translations" of the visual depictions of the deities found in the screenfold *tonalpohualli* and as such explicate the role of quetzal feathers in the *teixiptla*. During the festival of Izcalli a *teixiptla* of the fire deity Xiuhtecuhtli was constructed:

> They set up his image—only a framework of wood which they made. They gave it a mask, his face, made of precious green stone, horizontally striped with turquoise. . . . And they fitted upon it its quetzal feather crown, quite narrow at the bottom [but] large enough to fit around the head. The quetzal feathers spread out [above]. And two plumages stood one on each side, made like his horns. And the plumages both had quetzal feather cases. . . . And they laid over him a cape of quetzal feathers, made entirely of quetzal feathers, which hung long, trailing upon the ground. The wind penetrated it, [making it, as it were], stir upward [so that it glittered and gleamed].[39]

Descriptions such as these help us see the specific meanings associated with particular feathers as well as the general way in which materiality and divinity were interconnected. As the above description indicates, quetzal feathers were above all the quintessence of both feathers and the brilliant, "glittering" greenness that not only symbolized but also emanated generative fecund life. The careful arrangement of the feathers reinforced their association with wind (a vehicle for life-giving rains), movement (the essence of animation), and brilliance (the symbol of new growth). Likewise, Huixtocihuatl, a manifestation of the rain deity complex, had her face painted yellow like maize blossoms and wore "her paper cap with quetzal feathers in the form of a tassel of maize. It was of many quetzal feathers, full of quetzal feathers, so that it was covered with green, streaming down, glistening like precious green feathers."[40] In this *teixiptla*, there was a purposeful visual poetry that played on the resemblance between quetzal feathers and maize stalks.

The quetzal also appeared prominently in what became Book 11 of the "Historia universal." Modeled on European genres that concerned nature— above all Pliny's *Natural History* and the medieval encyclopedia *Hortus sanitatis*—Book 11 was organized into chapters about animals, plants, and minerals.[41] At the end of their stay at Tlatelolco circa 1564–1565, the gram- marians composed in Nahuatl the earliest extant draft of Book 11—now at the Real Academia de Historia (RAH)—to which Sahagún added Spanish headings and marginalia at a later date.[42] The Nahuatl text concerning the quetzal in the Tlatelolco draft and the "final" version of the "Historia univer- sal" (i.e., the *Florentine Codex*) are the same.[43]

At first glance, the entry on the quetzal in Book 11 seems to be a straight- forward physical description of the bird, denuded of cultural context (Figure 5.6). The Nahuatl text begins with the shape of the bill ("pointed"), followed by the color of the legs ("yellow"), its other body parts ("crest, wings, tail)," and its overall size (medium, likened to a *tzanatl*, a grackle). After these few lines, the rest of the entry was almost entirely devoted to a description of the quetzal's feathers. The description included names for different kinds: tail (*quetzalli*), crest neck and back (*tzitizcan*), belly (*olincayotl*), wing (*tzicoliuh- qui*), and four Nahuatl terms for those at the base of its flight feathers. The entry concluded with the information that the "breeding place of these birds is Tecolotlan" (Veracruz).[44] However, upon closer investigation, it becomes clear that the text signifies the supreme importance—the quintessence of preciousness—of the quetzal and the way that the distinctive aesthetic vir- tues of its feathers were inseparable from the ritual and social uses to which they put them, as described explicitly in all of the other parts of the "Historia universal" (e.g., in the books devoted to descriptions of the deities, festivals, traditional speech, and craftsmen).[45]

The signification of singular preciousness begins with the organization of the chapter on birds in Book 11. For starters, "quetzaltotol" appears first among all of the birds, reflecting the Mesoamerican valuation of its suprem- acy. It also appears within the subcategory of birds of "pluma rica." Common to earliest extant versions of Book 11 (RAH manuscript) and that of the latest

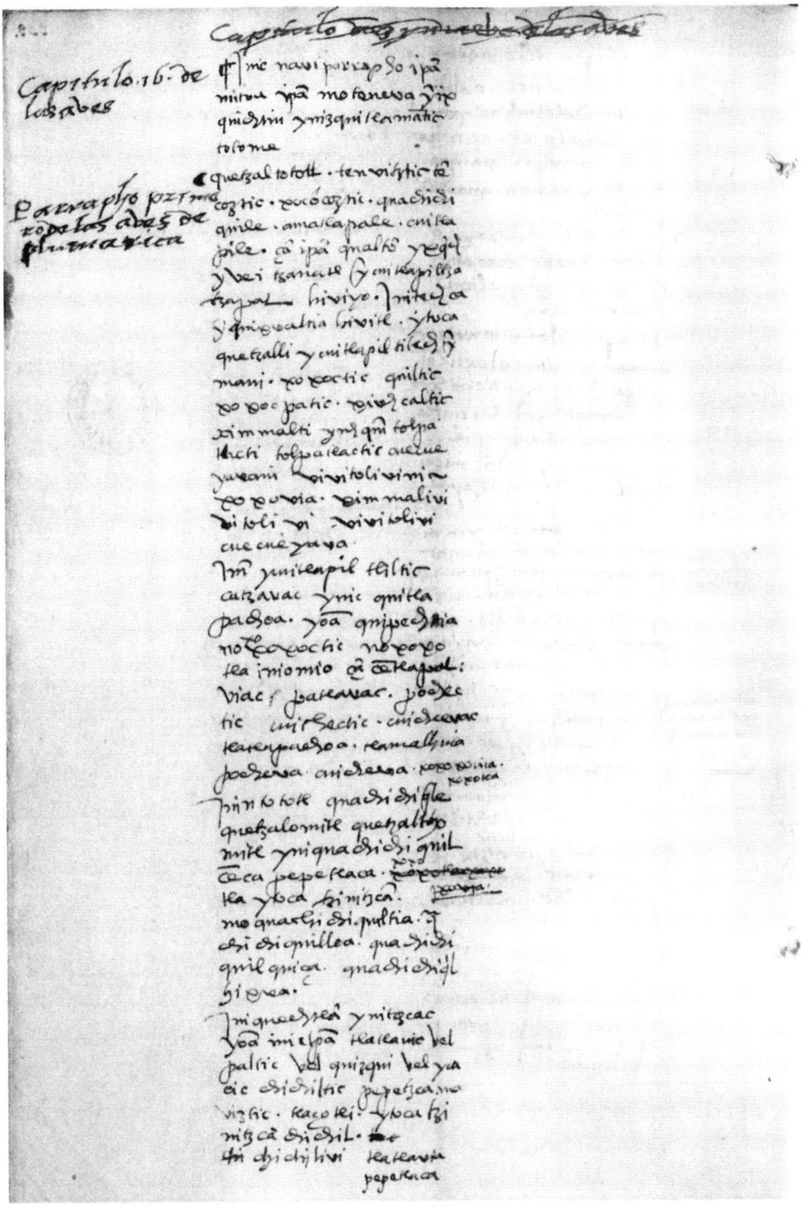

Figure 5.6. The quetzal was the first entry in the chapter on birds ("de los aves") in the draft of the *Historia universal* completed by Nahua humanists in Tlatelolco circa 1565. *Historia universal de las cosas de la Nueva España repartida en doze libros: En lengua mexicana y Española*, fol. 264r, Shelfmark: ms 9/5524[1], Real Academia de Historia (Madrid).

(the *Florentine Codex*) was the arrangement of birds into groups, or "paragraphs." The first and second "paragraph" in both versions are dedicated to birds of precious feathers, associated with the flowery world and prized for ritual feather works.[46]

The imagery and syntax found in the quetzal entry likewise indicate Mesoamerican concerns. The physical description is utterly entangled with the aesthetic qualities of the quetzal feathers and the ritual and social uses to which central Mexicans put them before and after the Spanish invasions. The language used to describe the quetzal evokes—and perhaps borrowed from— the song and poetry tradition that so often put into words and music the dazzling, shining beauty of the quetzal and other birds of "precious feather." When describing the most valued of all the quetzal bird's feathers, those of the tail, or *quetzalli*, Sahagún's informants explained that

> Those which are on its tail are green, herb-green, very green, fresh green, turquoise coloured. They are like slender reeds: the ones which glisten, which bend. They become green, they become turquoise. They bend, they constantly bend; they glisten.
>
> The tail of this one is black, dark. [These feathers] cover [and] underlie [the quetzalli feathers]. These are also green, glistening. [These feathers are] only on the interior side. They are [rather] long, side, smoky, blackish, sooty. They cover, they protect [the quetzalli] feathers.[47]

The rest of the entry repeats words related to the quetzal's greenness and iridescence (e.g., "very resplendent, very glistening," "green, herb-green, glistening green"). The imagery is that of the eastern flowery realm—a favored habitat of the quetzal bird and the birds described in subsequent paragraphs—found in postclassic screenfold books and colonial Nahuatl poetry alike. Greenness and feathers were both such essential attributes of the flowery world that it was variously referred to in songs as "in the plume water" (*quetzalatlitic*), "green places" (*xopan*), the "land of green places" (*xopantlalpan*), the "place of tassel plumes" (*quetzalmoyahuyocan*), and the "plume house" (*quetzalcalli*).[48] A "green location" could be a word meaning spring, summer, paradise, or ritual speech so that the insistence on greenness was also evoking the fecundity of the growing season, an association reinforced by the likeness drawn between green reeds, supple as they move.

Yet green is not the only color in the quetzal palette. Turquoise and black are also prominently featured; and the collective aggregation of these colors evokes Mesoamerican divinity. Jeanette Peterson explains that in Mesoamerican languages, "the sight of black (and notion of blackness) is enriched by a web of meaning associated with blue/green, metaphorically represented by turquoise, jadeite, and quetzal feathers, the most powerful signifiers in Mesoamerica for vegetation and water, indeed preciousness and life itself." And used by itself, blackness could denote "teotl" (sacred essence or deity), "linked to the very invisibility of gods,"[49] manifested by priests and lay penitents when they blackened their bodies during rites of passage. That this association between blackness and sacrality and divinity was likely intended by the authors of the Nahuatl *Florentine Codex* is suggested by the description of the bird that followed the quetzal: the bird was named "teotzinitzcan," or literally "divine tzinitizcan" (a word that could mean variously "precious feathers" or "head feathers"). The authors of the Nahuatl text explained the prefix "teo" because "its feathers are black, dark,"[50] in other words explaining the connection between divinity and blackness. Another way the language suggests the black feathers' inherent sacrality was to invest sacred agency in the capacity of the outer feathers to "cover" and "protect" the inner green feathers.

Another fundamental property of the quetzal's plumage evoked in the entry was iridescence. The feathers' brilliant shimmering surfaces were summoned by the words that connoted glistening, resplendent, shining, gleaming, and lustrous properties or, taken together, brilliance. Resplendence and iridescence were also conveyed in words by stringing together the color adjectives "green, herb-green, very green, fresh green, turquoise coloured," simulating the slight but detectable shift in hue as an iridescent surface moves or is viewed by one moving. Iridescence is itself a kind of visual movement; the association is made in text by an undulation between description of color hues and kinesthetic effects. And there is, of course, the repetition of "bending" in reference to the long plumes of the tail and, again, the comparison with reeds rustling. The kinesthetic qualities were likewise described in the "adornments" of the deities in Book 2 of the "Historia universal." This rustling and fluttering evokes birds in flight and movement of the wind, both of which are connecting mediums that link the earthly plane and the flowery plane above. Wind is what brings the fertilizing rains, while bird songs can move between the realms, descending, and song and music can move upward, ascending.

The shimmering turquoise-green feathers of the quetzal that bend in the wind, glide through the air, and sway like reeds create the beauty of the quetzal bird and summon, evoke, or create the life-giving rain, the transforming wind, and the transcendent beauty of the divine. The property of precious beauty, shimmeringness belonged to the quetzal in its feathers, and that property inhered in the feathers themselves. The demands of *teixiptla* lay at the bottom of the meticulously complete description of this splendid bird found in Book 11. That there could be no separation of materiality, affect, and ritual was embedded in vocabulary and syntax itself.

* * *

The Nahua grammarians' paragraph on the quetzal was copied not only into the *Florentine Codex* but also into Francisco Hernández's "Historia avium novae hispaniae" (History of Birds of New Spain, 1576–1577), one of the five treatises that comprised the "Historiae animalium novae hispaniae" (History of Animals of New Spain) (Figure 5.7).[51] Hernández's "Historiae animalium" originated from a royal decree that compelled Hernández, a physician, to "go to the Indies as its *protomédico general* and to make a history of those natural things"; however, the "instructions" he received from Philip II to interview "physicians, surgeons, herbalists, Indians and other *personas curiosas* who appear to you knowledgeable on these matters" only specified that Hernández collect information about botanical materia medica, but he took it upon himself to study animals as well.[52] Hernández arrived in Veracruz in 1571 and for the next three years traveled to numerous localities throughout New Spain. He and his largely indigenous entourage collected specimens and interviewed indigenous elders ("old Indians") and healers in a process that Jaime Marroquín Arredondo has described as "ethnographic history."[53] In addition to original research, Hernández also drew from the "Historia universal": Jesús Bustamante has shown that significant portions of Hernández's "History of Antiquities" were copied and translated from Book 2 of the "Historia universal" and hypothesizes that Hernández had access to the twelve books of a no longer extant draft of the "Historia universal."[54] A close analysis of the texts related to the quetzal reveals that he likewise drew from the "Historia universal" for his chapter on the quetzal as well as a number of other chapters in Book 11.[55] Nowhere in his writings does Hernández acknowledge his debt to Sahagún or the Nahua grammarians.

In translating and adapting the quetzal entry of the "Historia universal" for his "Historia avium," Hernández simultaneously removed essential Mesoamerican knowledge about the quetzal and offered context that ensured that its Mesoamerican origins did not disappear. He deleted certain Nahuatl

Cap. I.

De Hoaɛton Fœmina.

HOACTLI mare paulo maior eſt, ventre, colloque alba, ſed fulcis paſſim interſeɛtis pennis, reliquum corpus fuſcum interpoſitis albis, oculi magni nigrique, ſed iris pallens, cætera ſunt illi cum mare ſimilia. Ardeæ cinereæ videtur ſpecies; ſunt qui ſentiant generis eſſe ſui, nam magnitudine à cæteris ardeis duplo ferè vincitur,ſunt qui Xoxouh, qui Hoaɛtli vocēt.

De Quetzaltototl, ſeu Aue plumarum diuitum. Cap. II.

AVis eſt criſtata pauoninis magna ex parte ornata plumis, parcæ magnitu, dinis, roſtro acuto, luteoque, & pedibus pallidis, cauda Tzamatl plumis prælongis veſtita, atque virentibus, nitidis, & pauonini coloris Iridis folijs forma ſimilibus, opertiſquè ſupernè alijs nigricantibus, inſernè verò & qua parte pauoninas attingunt quæ in medio ſunt inclinantibus in virorem, quaſi cauente natura mediarum pulchritudini, criſta plumis conſtat ſplendentibus atque pulcherrimis, pectus, collumque inſernè rubris & micantibus, ac pauoninis ſupernè qualibus etiam dorſum tegitur, nec non eæ partes quæ ſubter alas ſunt, interque crura: ſed dilutis exilibus & mollibus, plumæ alaru ſunt prælongæ, virore tinɛtæ diluto, & in acumen deſinentes. Pennæ tegentes humeros vireſcunt, ſed ſubter ſunt nigræ,quæ vero alas interſtant non nihil incuruæ, ac vnguium colore. Plumæ huius Auis maximi æſtimantur apud Indigenas, ipſique auro quandoque præſeruntur, nempè longiores ad criſtas, & alia capitis ac vniuerſi corporis bellica, paciſque ornameɛta, cæteræ vero ad textilia opera, & rerum quarumuis, ſed præcipuè diuorum exprimendas formas. Cui rei pennas quoq; Auicularum (quas Hoitzitzillin vocant) permiſcere atque intexere ſolent. Viuunt in Prouincia Tecolotlani vltra Quauhtemallan tendentibus in vocatas honduras, vbi magna cura cauetur ne quiſquã eas occidat Aues, tantum licet eas plumis exuere, ac ſtatim dimittere, nec omnibus ſed ſolis Dominis: ſunt enim opimorum prædiorum loco, ac tranſeunt ad hæredes.

De Achalalaɛtli ſeu Piſcium Voratrice. Cap. III.

ACHalalaɛtli quam alij Michalalaɛtli vocant. Auis eſt Columbæ magnitudine, & forma ſimilis; roſtro acuminato, & nigro, tres digitos longo & proportione corporis craſſo, caput criſta ornatur è colore cyaneo in nigrum, tendente longaque, venter candidis tegitur plumis & collum torque eandent inſignitur. Alæ inſernè albeſcunt ſed poſtremis partibus videntur fuſcæ, & i

can-

Figure 5.7. The "History of Birds of New Spain" was copied from the manuscript that Francisco Hernández sent to Philip II in 1576. Chapter 1 is titled "De Hoacton Foemina" (Of the Female Heron), and chapter 2 is titled "De Quetzaltototl, seu Aue plumarum diuitum" (Of the Quetzal, or the Bird of Precious Feathers). Francisco Hernández, "Historiae animalium et mineralium novae hispaniae," in *Rerum medicarum Novae Hispaniae Thesaurus* (Rome, 1651), 13. Reproduced courtesy of the Library of Congress.

terminology, such as terms that referred to specific types of quetzal feathers (*quetzalli, tzinitzcan, tecpactic*, etc.). On the other hand, Hernández's entry is marked by the desire to transmit to a European audience the Mesoamerican cultural context for the quetzal. In the second part of his entry on the *quetzaltototl*, Hernández sought to convey the singular preciousness of the quetzal feathers by writing that the quetzal feathers are "highly esteemed among the Indians . . . preferred even before Gold itself." He conveyed the quetzal feathers' role as the quintessential material for the creation of ritual objects, for "headdresses and other ornaments both of the head and whole body, both for times of war and peace" and their use "to represent all kind of things, but above all divine things,[56] for which they tend to mix and interweave the feathers of little birds called *hoitzitzillin* [hummingbirds]."[57] By discussing the hummingbird in the same entry of the quetzal, he reinforced the notion of birds of "precious feathers" (already present in the title of his chapter) and the categorization of the quetzal in a class of birds indispensable for fundamental rituals. Hernández included other ethnographic information in his chapter on the quetzal not found anywhere in Book 11 of the "Historia universal." He wrote, for instance, that there "care is taken that no one kills these birds, only allowing them to pluck the feathers, leaving them afterwards in liberty, and this [privilege] not to everyone, but only to lords." He concluded the entry with the information that quetzal feathers "are considered one of the most coveted prizes and are transmitted from fathers to sons."

Hernández's translation of the passages he took from the "Historia universal" also suggests a process of transmission that allowed for affective qualities of feathers to be conveyed despite the abridgment from Nahuatl. A comparison of Hernández's adaptation and Sahagún's Spanish translation both reflect Hernández's (or more likely his native collaborators') familiarity with Nahuatl and bring into relief Hernández's desire to capture the affective qualities found in the original. In the original Nahuatl of the "Historia universal," the tail feathers are "green, herb-green, very green, fresh green, turquoise coloured. They are like slender reeds: the ones which glisten, which bend. They become green, they become turquoise. They bend, they constantly bend; they glisten."[58] In the Spanish translation they are "very green and resplendent; they are wide like bulrushes. They bend when touched by the wind; they shimmer very beautifully."[59] In Hernández's version they become "feathers [that are] very long, brilliant, peacock-colored in the shape of lily leaves."[60] Both Sahagún's and Hernández's translations into Spanish and Latin, respectively, convey the idea of brilliance (*resplandecientes* and *nitidis*) found in the original Nahuatl. However, Sahagún's translation emphasizes the feathers' qualities of being "very green" but not its "turquoise" qualities. Hernández used "Peacock-colored" (*pavonini coloris*), which conveys the green-blue—or turquoise—iridescent quality shared by quetzals and peacocks. Moreover, for a European audience, "peacock" was associated with regality, nobility, and preciousness—and resurrection—and so was an apt signifier of the symbolic as well as aesthetic aspects of the quetzal feathers.[61] Similarly, in choosing to translate "reed" as "leaves of the lily," Hernández eschewed the more literal translation found in Sahagún's Spanish translation ("hojas de espadaña," or bulrush). I hypothesize that reeds or bulrushes had pedestrian connotations for a European audience; they failed to suggest the great symbolic potency of reed in Mesoamerican contexts (such as the use of woven reed mats as a symbol of rulership, at least one of the uses that may account for the fact that "reed" was one of the twenty symbols used to signify calendar days). By choosing "leaves of the lily," Hernández not only selected a plant that had distinctive elongated green leaves—like reeds—but was also a signifier in Europe of singularity and sacredness and so captured some of the symbolic resonance of "reed" in a Mesoamerican context. Hernández eschewed a literal translation in favor of European idioms that connoted supreme value and preciousness, thereby translating figuratively the importance that Mesoamericans invested in quetzal feathers.

There are other examples of the entanglement between the physical description of the quetzal's body and its symbolic status in Hernández's text. Hernández's translation of the lines describing placement of the precious green tail feathers suggests direct familiarity with Nahuatl, which insisted on outer black feathers that "cover"; "they protect" the inner green ones. Hernández, following Nahuatl, wrote that the precious green feathers were "covered with others that were blackish on top but that go toward green where they touch the peacock-colored ones, as if nature took care to protect the beauty of the middle feathers."[62] In contrast, Sahagún's Spanish translation did not include this notion of protecting; in his version he wrote, more simply, that "this bird has some black feathers on its tail with which it covers these precious feathers" ("Tiene esta ave unas plumas negras en la cola con que cubre estas plumas ricas"). In the Nahuatl text of the "Historia universal"—and in Hernández's Latin—the physical description conveyed symbolic and even ontological meaning. Feathers, like all of the materials that could constitute a *teixiptla*, were invested with a kind of agency, and this ontology was reflected in the language of outer feathers "protecting" inner feathers.

As with the "Historia universal," information about the role of quetzal in Nahua—and Mesoamerican—cultures was signified directly in Hernández's work and also indirectly through metatextual features such as order and categorization. The quetzal's singular and supreme importance in Mesoamerican culture was conveyed by chapter placement. Here there is a revealing divergence between the surviving manuscript draft and the 1651 edition based on the Escorial manuscript that Hernández sent to the king. In the draft, the quetzal appears first among the birds, as it did in the Sahagún's manuscripts.[63] However, the quetzal chapter appears *second* in the "History of Birds of New Spain" (the second treatise in the "History of Animals"); the first chapter is that of the "Hoacton foemina" (female heron) (see Figure 5.7). Yet, the ordering of the heron first and the quetzal second no less reflects central Mexican priorities than the *Florentine Codex*'s placement of the quetzal first but privileges the particular history of the Aztecs and other peoples of the central Mexico plateau rather than the more Pan- and southern Mesoamerican importance of the quetzal. The juxtaposition of the heron and the quetzal relate to Aztec conceptions of the mythic-historical past. As Diana Magaloni-Kepler explains. "the association between the white heron feathers and the green quetzal feathers . . . must be based on the geographic-mythic site the birds represent." In Book 9 of the "Historia universal," feather-working informants explained that during early Chichimec times the heron feathers were in fact "*precious*" because for they "corresponded to those of the quetzal; with them they made the forked heron feather device in which the winding dance was performed."[64] During the later Mexica period, dignitaries replaced the white heron feathers with quetzal feathers. In other words, the placement of the quetzal after the heron in Hernández's "Historia avium" is suggestive of historical chronology for central Mexicans rather than its subordination to the heron and a particular Aztec conception of history that paid homage to both Chichimec and Toltec ancestors who were respectively responsible for heron and quetzal feathers.

* * *

Responding to royal orders in March 1576, Hernández shipped sixteen volumes filled with text and drawings, including the "Historiae animalium."[65] However, Philip II decided not to publish any of Hernández's manuscripts concerning American flora, fauna, and minerals. Instead, the king commissioned another physician, the Neapolitan Antonio Nardo Recchi, to copy the selections that were most medically useful. The copy of the "Historia natural" that Hernández sent to the king was eventually deposited in the Escorial palace but perished in a fire in 1671. However, because Hernández considered the version he sent to the king insufficiently "clean," "polished," and "ordered" to be published in that form,[66] he continued to revise and add material to the drafts that he kept in his possession; these drafts were eventually housed in the Jesuit Imperial College in Madrid.[67] Although Hernández did not live to see his "Historia natural" in print, it shaped the emergent disciplines of zoology as well as botany in early modern Europe.[68] Portions of his manuscripts were copied into influential publications in the late sixteenth and seventeenth centuries.[69]

In terms of the quetzal, Juan Eusebio Nieremberg's *Historia naturae* was the most important vehicle for Hernández's manuscripts.[70] Nieremberg, who held a chair in "sacred scripture" and natural history at the Jesuit Imperial College in Madrid, wrote natural history as theology.[71] According to Domingo Ledezma, Nieremberg particularly emphasized the most fantastic, marvelous, and exotic examples of flora and fauna because admiration itself was an important form of comprehension.[72] The Jesuit explained that "nature is a book of moral philosophy" and "shows all the virtues through animals," and he wrote in a later work that there are "so many things that without seeing them they would seem impossible, that nature claims credit for all the marvels." But the emphasis on the marvelous was not at odds with critical inquiry or, in his words, that "admiration should not impede affirming the veracity of the evidence and facts of nature" and that "veracity" was best achieved through consultation of books written by erudite men, such as Hernández and Carolus Clusius.[73] Given these priorities, it comes as no surprise that Nieremberg found a treasure trove in Hernández's works and carefully studied both versions of the "Historia natural": the manuscripts housed in the Escorial and the "originals" in the library at his College.

The quetzal appeared in chapter 65 of Book 10 of *Historia naturae*, which has a total of ninety-nine chapters devoted to birds (Figure 5.8). For the quetzal, Nieremberg hewed closely to Hernández's originals, and other than the title and the first sentence, the first paragraph is nearly a transcription of Hernández's text. The Jesuit also made editorial and translation decisions that had the effect of amplifying the emphasis on the quetzal's singular preciousness and its imbrication in religious and social ritual. While

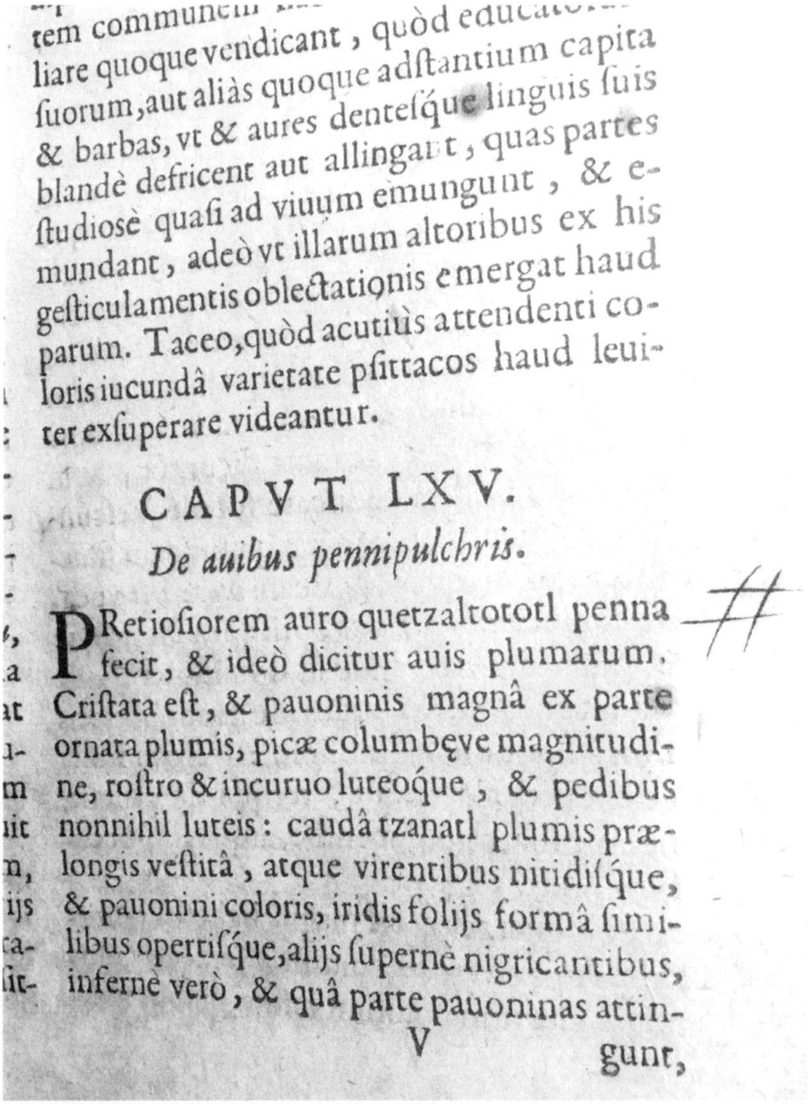

tem communem ....
liare quoque vendicant, quòd educato....
suorum, aut aliàs quoque adstantium capita
& barbas, vt & aures dentesque linguis suis
blandè defricent aut allingant, quas partes
studiosè quasi ad viuum emungunt, & e-
mundant, adeò vt illarum altoribus ex his
gesticulamentis oblectationis emergat haud
parum. Taceo, quòd acutiùs attendenti coloris iucundâ varietate psittacos haud leui-
ter exsuperare videantur.

CAPVT LXV.

De auibus pennipulchris.

PRetiosiorem auro quetzaltototl penna
fecit, & ideò dicitur auis plumarum.
Cristata est, & pauoninis magnâ ex parte
ornata plumis, picæ columbęve magnitudine, rostro & incuruo luteóque, & pedibus
nonnihil luteis: caudâ tzanatl plumis prælongis vestitâ, atque virentibus nitidisque,
& pauonini coloris, iridis folijs formâ simi-
libus opertisque, alijs supernè nigricantibus,
infernè verò, & quâ parte pauoninas attin-

V   gunt,

Figure 5.8. Nieremberg copied from Hernández's manuscripts for his chapter on the quetzal. Francis Willughby made the hash marks on those chapters that would appear in the appendix of his and Ray's *Ornithology*. Juan Eusebio Nieremberg, *Historia naturae, maxime peregrinae* (Antwerp, 1635), 229–230. Shelfmark Kislak QH41.N6 copy 2. Reproduced courtesy of the Library of Congress.

Nieremberg did not position the quetzal as the "first" bird as Sahagún and Hernández had done, he announced the quetzal's special status in other ways. He titled the quetzal chapter "The Bird of Beautiful Feathers" ("De avibus pennipulchris"), and his first sentence explains that "its feathers have made the Quetzaltototl more precious than gold," which also ensured the transmission of the Nahuatl name.[74]

In the rest of the entry, however, Nieremberg included text not found in either the Escorial or the draft versions of Hernández's chapter on the quetzal in the "Historia avium." Rather, as he wrote, he added material provided by "Fr. Hernández in some pretermitted annotations concerning the manner of taking these Birds some things worth the knowing." He offered details about the birds' behaviors in flocks as well their diet, their song, and the manner of their capture. The information is presented in such a way as to reinforce the notion of their singularity and spectacular beauty. After describing the way the birds "remain still and quiet, not struggling at all" after "sticking to the Birdlime," Nieremberg reproduced Hernández's annotations that told of "the beauty whereof they are so in love with, that they chuse rather to be taken and killed, than by endeavouring to get their liberty do any thing that may deface or prejudice [their feathers]." In these annotations Hernández also reported that the birds "love the open air, nor hath it been yet found, that ever they would be kept tame, or brought up in houses." And indeed, scientific studies from today have discovered that quetzals cannot survive in captivity because they rely on nutrients available only in the water of the place where they live.

Another way in which Nieremberg's quetzal chapter differs from the surviving versions in Hernández's work is by its inclusion of "the Tzinitzcan," which "next to the Quetzaltotl, the *Tzinitzcan* is most esteemed."[75] Following Hernández's text, Nieremberg wrote that these birds are "clothed with feathers of many colors, with which the Natives compose Images and Figures of wonderful subtilty and curiosity. They use and make show on Feast days, in War, in their Temples, and public Merriments and dancings."[76] Yet in his avian treatise Hernández placed the *tzinitzcan* in chapter 43 in the "draft" and chapter 54 in the Escorial copy.[77] However, by juxtaposing the *tzinitzcan* with the quetzal in the *Historiae naturae*[78]—a grouping also found in the "Historia universal"—Nieremberg ordered the birds in a way that precisely reflected the Mesoamerican category of birds of "precious" feathers. As a result, a 1635 book published in Spain contained more information about the quetzal than any of the surviving Hernández manuscripts or published works. The transmission and preservation of Mesoamerican knowledge was not a linear process.

* * *

To understand the place of the quetzal in Willughby and Ray's *Ornithololgy* requires looking at the circumstances around the production and publication of Willughby and Ray's ornithological project. Ray explained that the *Ornithology* was based on the "Manuscripts" of Willughby,[79] but after Willughby died in 1672, it was Ray who was responsible for compiling, annotating, revising, editing, and hiring engravers. He brought to press a Latin edition in 1676 and an English slightly enlarged and revised version in 1678. As discussed above, Ray celebrated the effort that Willughby expended in order to "himself accurately describe all the Animals he could find or procure either in *England* or beyond the Seas, making a voyage into forein Countries chiefly for that purpose, to search out, view and describe the several Species of Nature."[80] During those trips across England and later on the continent in the 1660s, they not only observed plants and animals in the wild and as used by locals but also studied specimens in museums and met with scholars.[81] Willughby had "designed a Voyage to the New World," wrote Ray, "but lived not to undertake it."[82]

Willughby and Ray considered the American natural histories as proxies for their own firsthand observation. Failing to view "species" firsthand, the American sources were necessary to fill the gap in both image and word and necessitated reading "what had been written by others."[83] Ray further noted that "Mr. Willughby (though sparing neither pains nor cost) could not procure, and consequently did not describe all sorts of Birds; to perfect the Work, I have added the Descriptions and Histories of those that were wanting, out of Gesner, Aldrovandus, Bellonius, Marggravius, Clusius, Hernández, Bontius, Wormius, and Piso; disposing each kind, as near as I could, in its proper place." The works of Marggraf, Piso, Clusius, and of course Hernández focused on animals of the Americas, and in addition to these, Willughby and Ray cited works by Gonzalo Fernández de Oviedo y Valdés, Andrés de Thevet, Jean de Léry, José de Acosta, and Johannes de Laet.[84]

It is important to note that Willughby and Ray's dependence on Hernández and other Spanish and Spanish American sources did not align with their political and religious commitments. Confessional and political divisions resulted in the English naturalists' having prejudicial views toward Spain and its intellectuals.[85] Willughby wrote of his impressions of Spain after touring through it for several months in 1664, describing its society as "very thin and desolate," ascribing to Spaniards laziness and other forms of wanton indulgence, and in typical seventeenth-century Protestant fashion blaming it on "A bad Religion" and "tyrannical Inquisition."[86] It is all the more notable, then, that Nieremberg, who as a Jesuit based in the Madrid college would have exemplified all that Willughby and Ray viewed as abhorrent in "bad religion," was such an important source. As a number of scholars have pointed out, Northern European scholars held an attitude toward Spanish sources that paralleled to a degree the one that Spanish authorities took toward indigenous informants.[87]

The *Ornithology*'s debt to the Hernández corpus can be seen in a number of ways. Nahuatl names are found in chapters about the toucan (*xochitenactl*), "tame poultry" (*tepetototl*), and pigeons or doves (*cocotzin*).[88] Most important, the *Ornithology* included an appendix of birds described in Nieremberg's *Historia naturae*, the majority of which were taken from Hernández's "Historia avium."[89] Of the forty-nine varieties of birds mentioned in the appendix, thirty-one can be traced back to chapters that Nieremberg transcribed and lightly edited from Hernández's manuscripts; the other appendix entries are derived from several authors, including Clusius. The full title in the English edition is "An Appendix of the History of Birds: Containing Such Birds As We Suspect for Fabulous, or Such As Are Too Briefly and Unaccurately Described to Give Us a Full and Sufficient Knowledge of Them, Taken Out of Fran. Hernández Especially." In the preface Ray further explained that "because I would not rely too much upon my own judgment, I have put in the *Appendix* the descriptions of some of that nature out of *Hernández*, which I refer to the Readers censure." From these passages it would be easy to conclude—as some scholars have[90]—that Ray dismissed Hernández's ornithological texts as a good source. Yet the truth is more complicated.

In fact, Ray singled out only five of the forty-nine entries in the appendix for containing "fabulous" information, and only two of these five (the *guitguit* and *momot*) were derived from Hernández/Nieremberg. When Ray found the information in the appendix false or "suspect for fabulous," he explicitly stated this in the annotations. For instance, he expressed incredulity at the notion that the small-size *guitguit* would attack ravens, writing that it was "feigned in imitation of what the Ancients have delivered concerning the wren."[91] Accordingly, the appendix chapters that *lack* such annotations reflect Willughby and Ray's judgment that they were good information. In other words, Ray believed most of the entries—forty-four—to be too valuable to not be included in their *Ornithology*.

Such an interpretation is supported by an examination of the copy of Nieremberg's *Historia naturae* that was annotated by Willughby and Ray.[92] Book 10—and no other section of this copy—was annotated by two hands. Dorothy B. Johnson, former archivist at the University of Nottingham (a main repository for Willughby's papers), has attributed the marginalia to John Ray and thinks that it likely that the hash marks were made by Francis Willughby (Figure 5.9; see also Figure 5.8).[93] John Ray's annotations regard the chapters dedicated to the *ave ovimagna* (bird of large eggs) or *daie* and the *momot*, and they appear close to verbatim in the commentary published in the Latin edition of 1676.[94] As translated in the English edition of 1678, he wrote in his commentary to "the Bird called Daie laying great Eggs" that he found "this History . . . altogether false and fabulous" because of the claim that the small birds laid numerous eggs "almost as broad as one's fist." In the commentary to the chapter on the *momot* (from Hernández), Ray doubted the claim that "it hath in its Tail one quil [*sic*] longer than the rest, and which is feathered only at the end," for "This is, I dare say, more strange than true: For the Tails of all Birds I ever yet saw have their feathers growing by pairs, that is, two of a sort, on each side one."[95] Read together, Willughby and Ray's marginalia and published annotations suggest that the majority of entries likely scored by Willughby—and all but two that originated in Hernández—were considered to be true if unverifiable, abbreviated, and difficult to fit into their classification scheme. The annotations on Willughby's copy of the *Historia naturae* do not suggest that either he or Ray doubted the veracity of the information about the quetzal: there is only a Willughby hash mark and no additional annotations from Ray (compare Figures 5.8 and 5.9).[96]

Filling almost an entire page, the chapter on the quetzal was the longest in the appendix (Figure 5.10). In the *Ornithologia libri tres* (1676), Nieremberg's chapter on the "avibus pennipulchris" is reproduced verbatim except for some changes in punctuation and orthography and two marginal notes where Ray explained unfamiliar terms. The English translation that appeared in the 1678 *Ornithology* does not differ greatly from modern critical translations of Nieremberg's chapter on the quetzal.[97] In one respect, however, Ray made alterations that reflected his confessional beliefs. In

IOANNIS EVSEBII NIEREMBERGII

scrobe collocare, & collocata citra incuban-
tis parentis opem atque reporem excludi, &
statim euolare pullos inde exclusos.

CAPVT VI.

De aue corrupeta.

Magnam audaciam exiguum capit cor-
pusculum. Minima auicula (*guirguit*
appellant Indi) regulo est similis , viridi
colore , & suaui nutrimento. Ea est naturæ
rerum vis, vt hæc tantula auis, ac fere nulla,
audeat persequi coruorum examina, eosque
cogat vbilibet latitare, & se aduertus illam
in arundinetis tueri.

CAPVT VII.

De maii.

Est & aliud auicularum genus
præcipue Cubæ gregatim volu
gentes prouentus atque visu) deua
lata, nomine *mais*, multo nutrimento,
que & facilis coctionis , coloniis
cui est in colli pollici parte capar
adminiculum , & nulli alii animali
cessum) ventriculus , primumque re
culum nutrimenti.

XOCHITENACATL.

Figure 5.9. John Ray made marginal note annotations on the *Historia naturae* when he thought
that the information might be "false" and reproduced many of these notes in the appendix
to the *Ornithology.* Juan Eusebio Nieremberg, *Historia naturae, maxime peregrinae* (Antwerp, 1635), 208. Shelfmark Kislak QH41.N6 copy 2. Reproduced courtesy of the Library of
Congress.

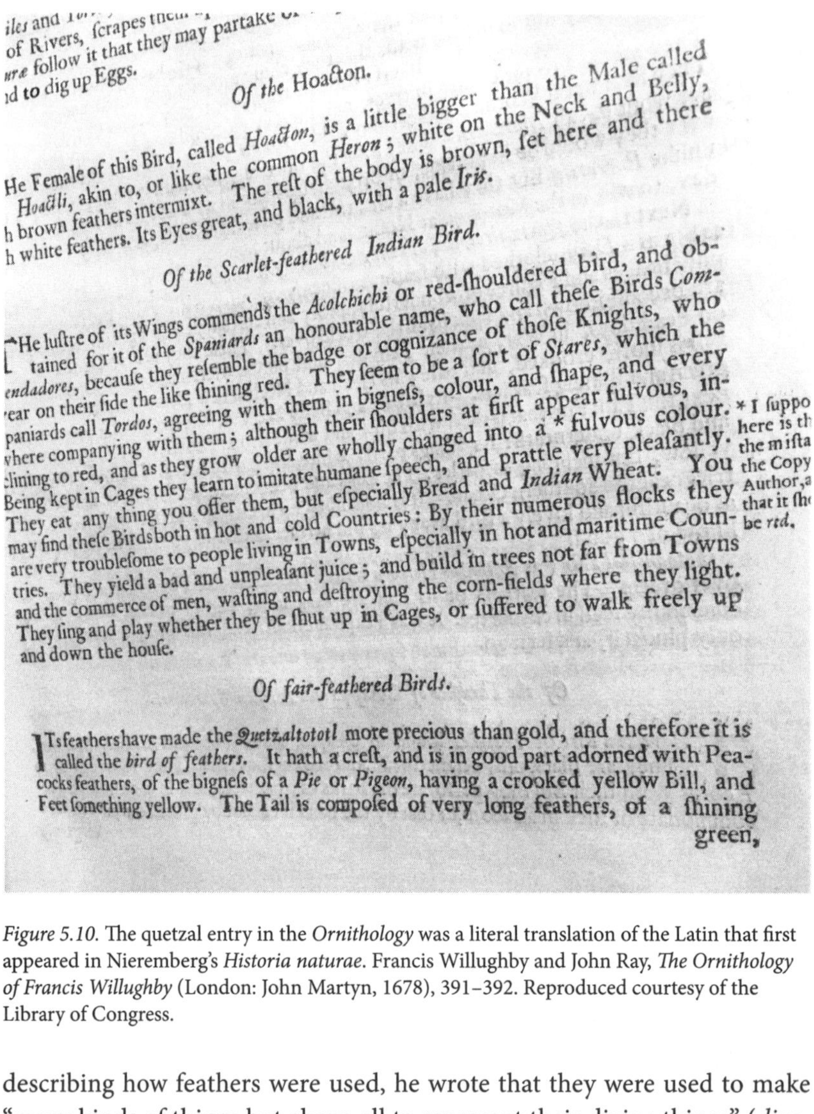

iles and *for...* fcrapes them ...
of Rivers, fcrapes them ...
ure follow it that they may partake of ...
id to dig up Eggs.

Of the Hoaˆon.

He Female of this Bird, called *Hoaˆon*, is a little bigger than the Male called
Hoaˆli, akin to, or like the common *Heron*; white on the Neck and Belly,
h brown feathers intermixt. The reft of the body is brown, fet here and there
h white feathers. Its Eyes great, and black, with a pale *Iris*.

Of the Scarlet-feathered Indian Bird.

He luftre of its Wings commends the *Acolchichi* or red-fhouldered bird, and obtained for it of the *Spaniards* an honourable name, who call thefe Birds *Com-
endadores*, becaufe they refemble the badge or cognizance of thofe Knights, who
ear on their fide the like fhining red. They feem to be a fort of *Stares*, which the
paniards call *Tordos*, agreeing with them in bignefs, colour, and fhape, and every
where companying with them; although their fhoulders at firft appear fulvous, in-
clining to red, and as they grow older are wholly changed into a * fulvous colour.
Being kept in Cages they learn to imitate humane fpeech, and prattle very pleafantly.
They eat any thing you offer them, but efpecially Bread and *Indian* Wheat. You
may find thefe Birds both in hot and cold Countries: By their numerous flocks they
are very troublefome to people living in Towns, efpecially in hot and maritime Countries. They yield a bad and unpleafant juice; and build in trees not far from Towns
and the commerce of men, wafting and deftroying the corn-fields where they light.
They fing and play whether they be fhut up in Cages, or fuffered to walk freely up
and down the houfe.

*(marginal note:) * I fuppo here is th the mifta the Copy Author,a that it fhe be red.*

Of fair-feathered Birds.

Ts feathers have made the *Quetzaltototl* more precious than gold, and therefore it is
called the *bird of feathers*. It hath a creft, and is in good part adorned with Peacocks feathers, of the bignefs of a *Pie* or *Pigeon*, having a crooked yellow Bill, and
Feet fomething yellow. The Tail is compofed of very long feathers, of a fhining
green,

Figure 5.10. The quetzal entry in the *Ornithology* was a literal translation of the Latin that first appeared in Nieremberg's *Historia naturae*. Francis Willughby and John Ray, *The Ornithology of Francis Willughby* (London: John Martyn, 1678), 391–392. Reproduced courtesy of the Library of Congress.

describing how feathers were used, he wrote that they were used to make "many kinds of things but above all to represent their divine things" (*divorum*), which Ray translated as "composing the figures of Saints and other things."98 In linking pagan gods to Catholic saints, Ray indulged his confessional antagonism. Other than this doctrinal barb, the entry on the quetzal is for the most part a translation of the text that can be found in the Nahuatl "Historia universal" of the mid-1560s. The original authors of the most important entry in the appendix of *The Ornithology of Francis Willughby*

were Nahua men living and working under Spanish colonial rule in the
mid-sixteenth century.

* * *

The first "modern" ornithology provided information about the quetzal built
on the knowledge and sensibilities of indigenous Mesoamericans in colonial
Mexico. A microhistory of the quetzal and its representations as they moved
from postclassic central Mexico to seventeenth-century England offers an
important perspective on early modern science. Though more removed spatially from Native America, *The Ornithology of Francis Willughby* was nonetheless an intercultural text such as the "Historia universal" and Hernández's
"Historia natural." Tracking the representations of the quetzal through texts
produced in the sixteenth and seventeenth centuries, one can see that the
transmission of knowledge was not a linear process or similar to the game
of telephone in which the transmission process is one of attenuation from
a primordial text. For instance, chapter 65 of Book 10 in Nieremberg's 1635
Historia naturae included quetzal-related information that was absent in
the "Historia avium" that Hernández sent to Philip II in 1576 and was later
copied for the Lincei Academy in 1628. And Hernández's translation of the
Nahuatl entry on the *quetzaltototl*, while less literal than the one made by
Sahagún, sought to convey symbolic and affective Mesoamerican meaning to
a European audience.

One way to make these linkages between "indigenous knowledge systems" and early modern science is to ask about all of the conditions of possibility that lay behind *The Ornithology of Francis Willughby*. The conditions
of possibility as revealed in this case study include the detailed anatomical,
ecological, and technological knowledge related to the quetzal bird possessed
by Mesoamerican hunters and feather workers that was itself a by-product of
the enormous ontological and ritual importance invested in the bird and its
feathers. These conditions include the modes of colonial inquiry that resulted
from evangelical and imperial-scientific priorities that were realized through
the particular projects of Sahagún, Hernández, and their native collaborators.
They also include the theological commitments of seventeenth-century Jesuits that embraced the transcription and explication of American intercultural
natural histories. In addition, they include the methods of the Royal Society
that recognized the singular value of Native American natural histories for
their zoological (and botanical) enterprises.

Chapter 6

Local Linguistics and Indigenous Cosmologies of the Early Eighteenth-Century Atlantic World

Sarah Rivett

Housed in the Watkinson Library is a 580-page tome measuring twenty-nine centimeters that is bound in marbled leather and contains over 22,000 Illinois-Algonquian words listed alphabetically. The dictionary is the work of Jesuit Jacques Gravier. His small penmanship economizes space. Words are crossed out and corrections made, sometimes in Gravier's hand and some-times in that of his successors. The result of two decades of work, the dictio-nary was most likely completed in the 1710s.[1] By the looks of this artifact, the Jesuits had made great strides in learning North American Indian languages since Father Paul Le Jeune declared in 1635 that he was making little progress and could only "learn a few stray words [in Montagnais] with a great deal of difficulty."[2] Learning indigenous languages was one of the most difficult chal-lenges that a missionary faced upon arrival in North America. Missionaries often had to abandon what they thought they knew about languages, which in the case of the Jesuits was a great deal, in order to parse through what sounded to them like unfamiliar savage sounds.

Gravier's dictionary bespeaks a colonial world in which this was no lon-ger the case. The manuscript volume reflects a vast amount of expertise that stands in striking contrast to records of fumbled linguistic efforts of earlier generations.[3] This dictionary and others like it suggest that the colonial lan-guage encounter was substantially different for third generation missionaries such as Anglo-Protestants Josiah Cotton and Experience Mayhew and French Jesuits Sebastian Rale, Jacques Gravier, and Antoine-Robert Le Boullenger. In contrast to their predecessors, these missionaries either had generations of knowledge at their disposal or learned American Indian languages as young children. Mayhew writes in his *Observations on the Indian Language* (1722) that "I learnt the Indian language by rote, as I did my mother tongue, and not by studying the rules of it as the Latin tongue is commonly learned."[4] The consequence of missionary practices of translation and transliteration, this heightened ethnolinguistic knowledge led to the emergence of unprecedented insights into indigenous linguistic structures and their accompanying cosmologies. Around the turn of the eighteenth century, a philosophy of language emerged in North America in contradistinction to philosophical advancements in Britain and on the continent. The manuscript archive from this period remains the most lasting evidence of indigenous languages that purportedly died around this same time, including Illinois, Wampanoag, Massachusett, eastern Abenaki, and Huron-Wendat.[5]

Linguistic knowledge developed out of a specific time and place to which its accuracy is indebted. In the early eighteenth century, American Indian languages outgrew their usefulness for both Christian cosmologies and Atlantic networks of philosophical exchange. The inutility of American Indian languages within broader religious and Enlightenment epistemologies permitted the dictionaries produced in this period to absorb and preserve an indigenous perspective on words. From this emerged an understanding of indigenous languages as syntactically autonomous, expressive of an entire cosmology, and aesthetically beautiful. This sense of indigenous languages stands in sharp contrast to contemporary European philosophical and political understandings of North American languages, most of which viewed them as deficient or irrelevant. Early eighteenth-century missionary linguistics made remarkable strides toward recognizing the cultural relativity of language at precisely the moment that the philosophical value of this knowledge decreased in Atlantic economies of exchange.

Anglo-Protestant missionaries defined their practices of Christian translation in direct opposition to the French Jesuits. Comparing third generation French Jesuits and Anglo-Protestants highlights an important facet of the colonial language encounter: despite their theological and imperial differences, both groups acquired insights into North American languages while also accumulating a vast paper and print trail of dictionaries, translated catechisms, and sermons written in Abenaki, Massachusett, and Wampanoag.[6] In their transcriptions and record keeping, French Jesuits and Anglo-Protestants came to disparate though simultaneous recognition of the semantic dimensions of the indigenous languages of North America. Such recognition happened through the active and integral presence of indigenous interlocutors in the production of these texts. A product of these interlocutors, American Indian language texts perpetuate indigenous language systems and enable language revitalization efforts today.

At the same time, the spatial split between localized knowledge of indigenous languages and more sweeping Atlantic epistemologies had consequences for long-standing divisions between indigenous and Atlantic history. A pivotal historical moment in which the division between localized indigenous knowledge in North America and broader Atlantic epistemologies began to take shape in the late seventeenth and early eighteenth centuries. Previous attempts to enfold American Indian languages into Christian cosmologies and scriptural history broke down irreparably. Biblical linguistics had long served as a compelling resource for understanding the dispersal of peoples and nations throughout the world. Yet the material realities of colonial encounters and concomitant advancements in natural philosophy that took place from 1680 to 1720 put increased pressure on scriptural history.[7] Philosophers, theologians, and missionaries confronted the enormous difficulty of constructing a coherent map of human origins and population dispersal out of the numerous "barbarous" languages of North America.[8] Indigenous tongues fell out of sync with modern time.[9] The observational capacities of missionaries changed when decoupled from a broader framework of population dispersal and nation. With the localization of indigenous linguistic knowledge, its relevance to Enlightenment epistemologies was dismissed.

Indigeneity in Anglo and French Language Philosophy

Central to the breakdown of biblical linguistics around the turn of the eighteenth century was the publication of John Locke's *Essay Concerning Human Understanding* (1689), which in Book 3 helpfully declared language as a social construct and made sense of the relationship between mind and nature but left unanswered the question of language's origins. Effectively, the *Essay* ruptured notions of language as evidence of the past unity of time and place. This profound disruption in the coherence of linguistic genealogy created a lacuna that seemingly every eighteenth-century European language philosopher would take a shot at resolving.[10] Post-Lockean linguistics played out in a particular way in North America. In previous generations, colonial language encounters often served as a kind of laboratory for European philosophy. Yet partly in response to Locke, early eighteenth-century philosophers on both sides of the Atlantic began to abandon the idea that there was a way of tracing what the "original language" of North America was. They asserted instead that there was no way of knowing how many tongues came out of Babylonian "disorder."[11]

Joseph-François Lafitau incorporates Locke's perspective on language as "necessary to form the bonds of society" and as "a purely arbitrary thing [composed of] signs adopted to represent the things to which they have been attached." And after five years spent in North America studying the Iroquois custom and language, he applies this Lockean insight to counteract biblical linguistics: "I do not know on what basis people have persuaded themselves that division was made into 72 original languages." Lafitau declares that speculation on the origin of North American languages was nothing more than "useless trouble."[12] Nonetheless, he wrote up much of what he did learn in his tome *Moeurs des Sauvages Ameriquains comparées aux moeurs des premiers temps* (1724). The study begins and ends with the claim about the futility of seeking "connections" between "the barbarous languages and the learned ones."[13] Despite the numerous "conjectures" that have been made, linguistic relations are too numerous to trace and too confusing to be used as a method of understanding genealogies of nations and civilizations or patterns of population dispersal.[14] Thus, while Lafitau takes the ample linguistic knowledge ascertained by his Jesuit brethren into account, he also eschews the possibility of using language as a heuristic for reconstructing the history of the world.

A chapter on language concludes Lafitau's two-volume work. Despite Lafitau's fairly substantial knowledge of Iroquoian grammatical and syntactical structure, he dwells in generalities in this chapter, invoking more questions than he answers. Toward the end of the chapter, Lafitau laments that he did not give a more thoroughgoing account of Iroquois structure, if only as a corrective to "travellers" who "have contented themselves with giving some imperfect vocabularies consisting of a few deformed words which are in most common use."[15] Proper treatment, Lafitau insists, would take too much narrative space, though it is hard to imagine this as a central concern when it comes at the end of a work over six hundred pages long. The "barbarous terms," Lafitau speculates, would be "disagreeable to the public." Perhaps most significant, "scholars themselves cannot gain much enlightenment" from these words other than to show how "very far from those known to us" these languages are.[16] Lafitau articulates a dynamic of philosophical exclusion that precludes eastern Algonquian and Iroquoian from early eighteenth-century networks of language-knowledge exchange. Despite his status as a competent Iroquoian and Huron linguist in his own right, despite the five years spent in North America where the Jesuits had accumulated vast knowledge of indigenous tongues, Lafitau dismisses the languages as too "barbarous," structurally different, and "deformed" through years of colonial interactions to be of much use to anyone, particularly scholars.

What is puzzling about this sentiment is that Lafitau knows better. Indeed, within this same passage he writes that Iroquois and Huron "are rich in spite of the poverty attributed to them. . . . [A]lthough they have a different structure from ours, they have great beauties."[17] In a pattern that we see with many Jesuit priests, once Lafitau knows Iroquois, it transforms from a "barbarous" compilation of deformed sounds to a pleasing system of beauty. Lafitau hints at an aesthetic potential for Huron and Iroquois, yet he fails to see any philosophical or scientific merit. His reflections add up to emphatic statements of fundamental difference: "Not only do the American languages have no analogy with the Hebraic language, the Oriental, Greek, and Latin languages, and all those which pass as learned, but neither do they have any with the modern European languages and the others known to us." Just as Lafitau's ethnographic descriptions ensconce the Indians within a primitive past, his remarks on language isolate this population from the rest of the world. Yet the contact that has taken place over the nearly three hundred years of American "discovery" has made communication a necessity, "forcing" the Iroquois and the French to speak in order to engage in trade or common defense.[18] Lamentably, according to Lafitau, this contact has led to the further degeneration of Iroquois tongues, producing "gestures" and "corrupt words" that do not belong to either language and "a speech without rhyme or reason."[19] There is nothing pure or original to be found in indigenous tongues. Instead, one finds barbarity unlike anything that the European ear is accustomed to, further degenerated through the force of contact.

At the same time that Lafitau dismissed the philosophical value of American languages, philology thrived as a field of study in the British Isles, though dismissive of North America. Edward Lhwyd, Welsh linguist and keeper of the Ashmolean Museum in Oxford from 1691 until his premature death in 1709, reframed prior beliefs in Adamic languages with a secular chronology of the nation in his *Archaeologia Britannica* (1707). A comprehensive study of British languages, including their etymologies, customs and traditions, preRoman monuments, and Roman and Welsh monuments with their inscriptions, the *Archaeologia Britannica* has very little to say about linguistic roots in

North America.[20] While Lhwyd acknowledged that the languages of America and Asia were interesting as points of intellectual comparison, of how name and sound are aligned in purportedly ancient tongues, they bore little relation to Briton's genealogy. Lhwyd and his coterie, including Richard Baxter, David Malcolm, Martin Lister, John Woodward, John Aubrey, and John Ray, parsed the script of ancient Celtic, read the Irish Bible, and measured inscriptions above church doors to discover the ancient roots of Britain's mother tongue. As they did so, North American missionary linguistics all but disappeared from the transatlantic network of information exchange that had character-ized Anglo-philosophical relations only a generation before.[21]

Lhwyd developed a method of studying words in relation to the speci-ficity of place, namely the landscape of the British Isles. In light of this new focus on the etymology of nation, missionary linguistics lost some of its momentum as an integral component of philological study in the Anglo-sphere. Lhwyd's approach posited word fragments as emerging from the earth and in certain corners of the British Isles, where they had remained untouched for centuries. Discoverable throughout the farthest reaches of Britain, ancient writing, in particular writing on stones, provided telling evidence of a language frozen in time. During his fieldwork, from 1697 to 1701, Lhwyd made numerous sketches of inscribed stones and stone sculp-tures in Wales and other Celtic areas. Frequently dating to the ninth century, such monuments served as material remains of ancient Britons.[22] A two-volume set of sketches of antiquities and inscriptions, believed to be copied directly from originals made by Lhwyd and his assistants by the British antiquary John Anstis, are housed in the British Library. The volumes cat-alog Druidical stone monuments from different regions in England, Wales, Scotland, and Ireland. Druidical spirituality and biblical time are recorded through these stones (Figure 6.1).[23] Old Testament patriarchs were believed to have erected such monuments. They were used to mark districts even through the early years of Christianity when they also became repurposed as objects of worship, with representations of Christ's crucifixion cut on them.[24] An index of time and place, the stones marked the landscape with Christian beginnings.[25] They were used by British antiquaries to make sense of the transition from the earliest fragments of Druid culture through early Christianity. Historical layers emerge across the landscape in palimpsestic synchronicity, as with the crosses that become repurposed from bound-ary markers to objects of worship. The stones often contained the earli-est records of writing through hieroglyphic figures believed to be of pagan

Figure 6.1. Sample word list from Edward Lhwyd, *A Design of a British Dictionary*, Bodleian Library, Oxford University.

origin. Lhywd thus posited that language was born out of a connection to the land, as immovable as ancient stones.

Lhywd's etymological work served as a new heuristic for the dispersal of people and the peopling of nations. His Scottish correspondent, Reverend David Malcolm, used this heuristic more emphatically than Lhywd as a way of rejoining biblical time and natural history. "Languages are in a great measure the keys of knowledge," Malcolm wrote.[26] By uncovering linguistic roots in their simple and unmixed form, one could treat words as fossils, applying the study of the ancient past to contemporary debates about world and biblical history. Malcolm proposed St. Kilda in the outer Hebrides, "the most remote" of all places "belonging to Great Britain," as the ideal place to do this. Describing the paucity of alphabetic letters and the simplicity of sound spoken there, Lhwyd asserts that the "simplest Shape of Language may be found in the remotest Places from the Center of the Dispersion of Mankind," thus making the island an apt laboratory for observation and study.[27] Words function on St. Kilda as a kind of time capsule, each one an encoded remnant of centuries past. To perceive this, the natural philologist had to begin to capture language in its simple and unmixed state, prior to linguistic relativism or separation from the natural world.

Stones engraved with hieroglyphs, fragmented words, and "primitive" tongues survived as the detritus of a post-Lockean world that beckoned new fantasies of prelapsarian synthetic wholeness through poetry and national affiliation. This was the past brought forward into the present.[28] Lhwyd's aim was to trace the legacies of the original Celtic tongue within modern British. The study of language and the study of nature went together in an effort to expand the "learning and promotion of Antiquity."[29] American Indian words, by contrast, became a source of differentiation as opposed to identification.

As British philological interests became more centered on the specificity of place and notions of Celtic as the primitive antecedent to modern English, missionary knowledge of North American languages faded into the background of Anglo philosophical interest. French natural philosophers, by contrast, remained more engaged with the linguistic discoveries of the Americas and particularly the ethnological data produced therein. The Society of Jesus continued to value linguistic knowledge. Consequently, third generation Jesuits demonstrate high levels of proficiency. A cohort of Jesuit missionaries, including Rale, Le Boullenger, Gravier, and Gabriel Marest, worked among the Abenakis and the Illinois from the 1690s to the 1720s. As self-described arduous students of native teachers, they developed an unprecedented level of linguistic expertise. In the Anglo context, despite Lhwyd's construction of a secular national genealogy of Briton and the simultaneous abandonment of wide-scale efforts to translate the gospel into indigenous tongues by early eighteenth-century missionary organizations, Anglo missionary linguistics persisted and even thrived.

Indian Teachers Among the Jesuits

Jesuits placed a primacy on learning native languages.[30] This ideal is woven throughout *Jesuit Relations and Allied Documents*, as in Julien Binneteau's letter of praise for Gabriel Marest. Binneteau describes Marest in terms idealized by the society. We learn that Marest has an innate talent for languages, such that he has learned Illinois in "four or five months," and a relentless work ethic: "he works excessively during the day, and he sits up at night to improve himself in the language. . . . [H]e lives only on a little boiled corn, which he sometimes mixes [with] a few small beans."[31] Zealous to the point of placing his own life in a precarious position, Marest exemplifies the ardor of language study as the first phase of the Jesuit's vocation in North America. This narrative motif, which derives from St. Ignatius's *Spiritual Exercises* (1548), recurs throughout *Jesuit Relations and Allied Documents*.[32]

Take Sebastian Rale's arrival in Quebec in 1689. Rale reported on his deep sense of isolation and alienation to the Society of Jesus. He describes New France as an Antipodean world full of animals rather than men. Yet he also understood his safe arrival in Quebec as divine dispensation, fastening him to his godly purpose. The first order of fulfilling his divine duty involved mastering the language of the Abenakis. In his letter, Rale explains that this is the only way to "teach them to pray." Learning requires immersion as the first order of Rale's vocation, for "there are not books, no grammars, no teachers but the Indians themselves. One must live with them, as they live, to succeed." Rale describes going to the wigwam every day, as a child would to school, sitting on the ground or on a mat and staying for "eight or nine hours." He explains that God has already "recompensed" him for this arduous labor, for he has been able to produce a "dictionary, which is quite thick and very useful." Based on the words recorded in this dictionary, Rale penned a catechism that, he reports, amply describes "the mysteries of our religion." He takes comfort in the fact that "there is nothing any longer that I cannot teach them."[33]

Rale spent thirty years in the village of Norridgewalk, on the outskirts of Quebec, working on his *Dictionary of the Abenaki Language in North America*. In a letter reflecting on his efforts, he comments on the specific manner in which one must learn the language: "it is not sufficient to study the words and their meaning, and to acquire a stock of words and phrases." Sufficient knowledge of Abenaki required a deep familiarity with the customs of the native speakers in order to acquaint oneself with the arrangement of words as well as the unique sounds of certain letters. During his residence in Norridgewalk,

Rale conceded that the French alphabet did not adequately represent the range of sounds in spoken Abenaki. In lieu of French letters, the "figure 8" is used to signify a certain sound that is made "wholly from the throat without any motion of the lips."[34] The pronunciation approximates the French word "huit" and represents the phonemes *o*, *oo*, and *w*. This orthographic variation reflects Rale's attempt to record the aural sound of Abenaki in his dictionary. His method of doing so involved a reverse scene of catechistical instruction. Rale reports spending hours "in [Abenaki] huts to hear them talk." He would then select some native speakers whom he felt had "the most intelligence and the best style of speaking." Before this group of assembled speakers, Rale would express some of the articles of the catechism in his own broken Abenaki and then hear their corrections. As a primary facet of both the "turn and genius of their language" and the way that it is "altogether different from the turn and genius of our European languages," Rale notes that some letters are "sounded wholly from the throat without any motion of the lips."[35] Listening carefully to the delicate expression, he would then record the sound immediately. The dictionary is entirely phonetic, an attempt to visually capture and accurately record a series of sounds.

While this method of learning from immersion and by correction from indigenous teachers is on the one hand a more salutary recognition of linguistic diversity than previous or contemporaneous understandings of the utterly savage sounds of native North Americans, linguistic mastery was also a means of cultural and religious control. Through language mastery, missionaries believed that they could more effectively penetrate the hearts and minds of their converts. Rale's sentiment that language mastery increases his pedagogical skill is a version of the famous quote by Antonio de Nebrija in his prologue to the *Gramática castellana* (1492) that "language was always the companion of empire."[36] This quote became famous through the historiography of colonial linguistics, which has pointed to the undeniably destructive elements of European encounters with indigenous tongues.[37] Other scholars have countered that this is only half of the story, that there were multiple avenues for acculturation and syncretism in Indian-language texts. David Silverman has written powerfully about the syncretic Christianity made possible by the "religious translations" that took place on Martha's Vineyard. Vineyard Wampanoag became "engaged and knowledgeable Christians," Silverman argues, while remaining wedded to their traditional faith. Language was a primary vehicle for this "dialogical process," for indigenous words "filtered Christian teachings" with Wampanoag religious ideas and terminology. The result was a form of indigenous faith that blended Christian teachings with Wampanoag beliefs in *manit*, the native concept of a spiritual power that animated the natural world.[38] This tension between a desire for control through linguistic mastery coupled with the subversions of authority that invariably happen through bidirectional knowledge flow and translational practices is replete throughout the archive of indigenous language texts and is particularly pronounced in relation to the early eighteenth-century dictionary projects.

Father Jacques Gravier enjoyed success as a missionary through his mastery of the Miami-Illinois language, for which he wrote his *Kaskaskia-to-French Dictionary* over a period of two decades. Encoded within the dictionary is Gravier's ethnography of Illinois practices of hunting, love, competition, and medicine. In his journal Gravier makes the point that such cultural knowledge is rare, commenting that the Illinois "are so secret regarding all the mysteries of their Religion that the Missionary can discover nothing about them." The letter continues to describe these mysteries unfolding through a young woman of seventeen who refused to marry and then became a spiritual exemplar and an instructor within the community. After experiencing the "displeasure" of her family over her decision not to marry, the young woman underwent a practice of intense mortification by wearing a "girdle of thorns . . . for two whole days." Gravier supposes that she might have crippled herself with this practice had he not been informed, whereupon he "compelled her to use it with more moderation." The colonial violence inscribed on the body of this young Illinois woman notwithstanding, the autonomy ascribed to her is striking. She veers from the path expected of her by her parents and her community by telling them that "she did not wish to marry; that she had already given all her heart to God." She then chooses the form of fleshly mortification appropriate for this action.[39] The severity of her self-flagellation is haunting. The girdle of thorns reflects a desire to confine her young still-developing body and sexuality. It also stands out as an intensified form of the already severe Jesuit asceticism recounted in the *Relations*. As a reward for surviving this display of austere piety, Gravier makes the young woman a translator and an instructor of Christianity. She demonstrates an intense desire to teach the children, spending hours listening to their catechisms and answering questions. The reward for such extreme asceticism is a greater degree of spiritual authority than this young woman might otherwise have enjoyed.

This incident suggests multiple levels of mediation operating through the translation of Christianity from one language to another and from one community of believers to another. The young girl embodies a certain spiritual ideal for Gravier and for her community. While obviously an asset to the fluency of catechistical instruction, once the young woman begins her instruction, meaning automatically becomes less fixed. The copperplate engravings that Gravier designed with the intent of imprinting a certain mental image on the Indian mind are replaced by a lively question-and-answer period, orchestrated by the young girl rather than Gravier. While third generation Jesuits gained more colonial control through higher degrees of linguistic and cultural knowledge, successful conversion and higher degrees of fluency among indigenous proselytes also decreased the fixity of meaning through which Christian truths were conveyed.

Le Boullenger, Gravier's successor, arrived at the Illinois mission in 1719, when the study of Miami-Illinois was already fairly advanced. When Le Boullenger began his *French and Miami-Illinois Dictionary* in 1719, he combined the genres of phrase book and hymnal. The lexical section consists of over 3,000 words. It is remarkable for the Illinois variants given under many of the French key words. For example, the verbs "voir" and "aller" contain multiple variants, many more than in Gravier's dictionary (Figure 6.2). This is likely due to the evolution in understanding of Illinois verb configuration. At the beginning of his dictionary, Le Boullenger lists all of the possible combinations of verb inflections. He also understood the importance of intonation in Illinois more thoroughly than his predecessors. Preaspiration is marked in Le Boullenger's dictionary such that the word for grandmother, *noohkoma*, was written as *nohc8ma* and *nocc8ma*, while Gravier transcribed it as *n8c8ma*.[40] Alongside the nuanced lexical portions of Le Boullenger's dictionary are multiple religious texts in Illinois, which are not translated. Hymns, sacraments, the Ten Commandments, and the history of Genesis all appear in Illinois with French titles. The contrast between these two sections reveals the discrepancy between an advanced level of linguistic expertise on the one hand and the creativity of the translator on the other. The number of variants offered for a simple verb such as "voir" reflect the impossibility of precise translation. Consequently, Le Boullenger does not aspire to create the appearance of transparency between Illinois and French. Rather, he permits the lexicon to embody the striking differences between each language. Yet in the ritual space of the hymn, or sacrament, or even in the narrative retelling of the fall of man, Le Boullenger drew upon his knowledge of Illinois phonetics to write an oral text designed to deliver an unequivocal spiritual message. In the oral ritual space, the religious text elided linguistic difference once words were lifted off of the page. Le Boullenger's devotional section suggests that when

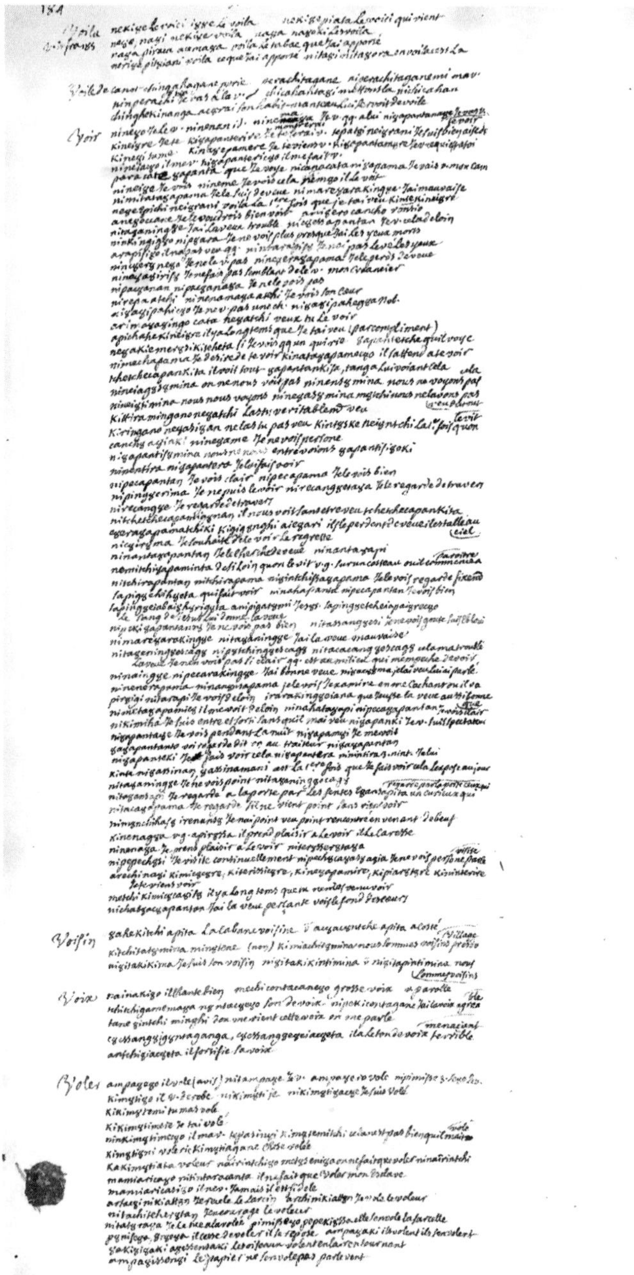

Figure 6.2. Antoine-Robert Le Boullenger, *French and Miami-Illinois Dictionary.* Courtesy of the John Carter Brown Library at Brown University.

enacted through a song or sacred text, the spirit infused the material word. The mysteries of Christianity could thus be conveyed across the cultural and linguistic divide.

Designed to produce more efficacious missions, dictionaries were produced by Jesuits around enhanced colonial control but also opened up lines of communication between Indians and priests. Both populations came to understand the flux of metaphysical meanings that resulted from the confluence of two distinct worldviews. Thus, while the Society of Jesus envisioned linguistic mastery as a means of more uniformly implementing Jesuitical doctrine, within the local communities themselves language often became generative rather than prescriptive. Hybrid forms of worship emerged out of the confluence of competing worldviews.[41] The practices of linguistic immersion that Jesuits had to undergo also often led to unanticipated forms of conversion, such as when Rale remarks that Abenaki "has its perfects," that it is a "grand" language, especially "when one considers its economy."[42] Giving an ample and unprecedented perspective on the subtleties of indigenous tongues, the dictionaries permitted the original Christian message to change in content as well as form through the process of translation. Yet the tensions traced in this section between the priests' efforts to maintain colonial control and local indigenous subversions of it were elided through a broader emergent discourse of language as a measure of savagery rather than the bidirectional exchange of concepts, as illustrated through Lafitau's writing. The Jesuit dictionaries, many of which existed only in manuscript form until the twentieth century's language revitalization efforts, record forms of knowledge that were rejected by a broader Enlightenment discourse that increasingly relegated Huron and Iroquian populations to not only a primitive past but also an untraceable past.

To Speak in Broken Indian

In contrast to the Jesuitical ideal of language learning, early eighteenth-century Protestant missionaries in North America began to soften their stance on the importance of the literate Christian encounter as the only true sign of evangelization. The Society for the Propagation of the Gospel (SPG) and the Society for the Propagation of Christian Knowledge (SPCK) increasingly took over from the Puritans as the engines of Protestant conversion.[43] In its initial 1701 proposal for "Propagating the Gospel in all Pagan Countries," the SPG began with the noble intention of "educating a competent number of young students of theology in those foreign Languages." However, this goal soon seemed impractical and inefficient. A proposal written the following year observed that the "multitude of pagan tongues" was a "Barr to the Propagation of the Gospel in any pagan country," but "particularly North America." The proposal imagined "removing that Barr by extirpating the various Dialects of the Indian Jargon, and establishing in its room the knowledge of the English Tongue." This "one Step," the proposal imagines, "would facilitate the great design of civilizing and converting that part of the Heathen world." And thus began a new era of Anglo-Protestant missionary progress, one characterized by a desire for uniformity through the growth of the English tongue rather than the translation of the word of God into a multiplicity of vernaculars.[44]

Even an organization such as the SPCK, which specialized in biblical translation, eschewed the significance of North American languages. Focusing on massive efforts to translate, print, and distribute copies of the bible in Welsh, Portuguese, Arabic, and Irish, members of the SPCK were dismissive of the value of conveying Christian truths in American Indian languages. Indeed, one letter addressed to a minister in New England supposed that even though Mayhew knew Massachusett, he instructed his proselytes "in English" on Martha's Vineyard since this "seems to be the shortest way of conveying divine Truths into the minds of a people whose native Language is barren of all polite Expressions." So impoverished was the Massachusett language, this letter claimed, that it was woefully inadequate to sustain "ordinary ocurrences [sic] of Life and Body" and therefore must be "infinitely defective for what relates to the Soul."[45]

Despite the SPG's and the SPCK's preference for Christian instruction in English, however, localized Anglo missionary efforts to learn indigenous languages certainly persisted well into the eighteenth century. The Dutch Reformed minister Bernardus Freeman, who was both a pastor in Schenectady and a missionary to the Indians in the Mohawk Valley, was the first Protestant to learn Mohawk and transcribe it into the Roman alphabet.[46] In a letter to the SPG, dated May 31, 1712, Freeman explains that his method involved working closely with an interpreter to discover the "16 Alphabetical Letters" applicable to this language. From this transcription, he translated the "Gospel of St. Matthew from the beginning to the End, and the 1,2,3, Chapters of Genesis." Additionally, Freeman translated several of the Psalms, the English Liturgy, and the Lord's Prayer. He claims to have "taught the Indian to read & write perfectly."[47] Freeman's linguistic work was necessary, for he discovered upon arriving in the Mohawk Valley that the Mohawks were completely opposed to learning English.[48] Freeman worked to translate and print Christian texts in Mohawk. His letters to the SPG suggest a high level of language proficiency and a concerted effort to translate the gospel into Mohawk such that standard Christian texts became integrated within the Mohawk community. Yet the goals of the SPG did not accord with Freeman's efforts, reflecting a high influx of English texts, including Bibles, versions of *The Book of Common Prayer*, and catechistical lectures, into the community. Within the Christian community, Mohawk survived despite efforts by the SPG to eradicate it.

Analogous to the Mohawk case, the Wampanoag spoken among Christian Indians on Martha's Vineyard and in Plymouth has been preserved through the localized efforts of early eighteenth-century missionaries, Experience Mayhew and Josiah Cotton, despite mounting pressure to instruct Indian proselytes in English.[49] Mayhew revealed his own particular expertise of the language spoken on Martha's Vineyard in a 1722 letter to Royal Society member Paul Dudley, who wrote a request for "accounts of the Peculiarities & Beauties of the Indian Language, and wherein they agree or differ from the Europeans." A response came in 1722. Mayhew reported that he was ill-equipped to answer this question, for he was "no Grammarian."[50] Cotton compiled an extensive manuscript vocabulary of the Massachusett language and composed several sermons in Massachusett while ministering in Plymouth. Like their French Jesuit counterparts whose linguistic knowledge spiked during this period, these missionaries acquired admirable linguistic skills by working in relative isolation. Missionary linguists of the Protestant persuasion were intellectually as well as physically isolated, cut off from broader networks of meaning, be they Christian or philosophical, such that their knowledge of indigenous tongues had no context in which it could be understood other than the local Christian community to whom they ministered.

Mayhew engaged in direct linguistic observation, in practice much like the Jesuit technique. Despite his evangelical investments, he was not compelled by an overweening need to reintegrate Massachusett into a coherent Christian cosmology. Rather, his letter to Dudley catalogs a sequence of linguistic anomalies in relation to European languages. Noun variations occur based on whether the word is "animate or inanimate" and whether "their magnitude" is "great or small." In contrast to English words, Mayhew tells us that "the names of persons and things" in Indian words is "very significant." Mayhew explains that word length often indicates the significance of a place. For example, a place called Nempanicklickanuk would be translated into English as "the place of Thunder-clefts."[51] He informs the reader that the place-name derives from the historical occurrence in this place of lightning striking a tree into pieces. Word length gives the word a more precise signification. Often this signification records the history of the land on which the natives dwell. Similar to Lhywd's insight into Celtic and Welsh, Mayhew records a deep connection between word and place as constitutive of Massachusett.

Even though missionary linguistics was all but entirely excluded from philological study in early eighteenth-century Britain and received a paucity of support from missionary organizations, a sustained language encounter not only flourished among Anglo-Protestant missionaries but also led these missionaries to insights that were astonishingly commensurate to indigenous cosmologies. Mayhew makes a case for language as constituted by time, place, and people. These observations are not only commensurate with Lhywd's but also veer toward a hybrid cosmology that is both indigenous and Christian. In learning Massachusett as he did his own mother tongue, Mayhew cannot help absorbing aspects of the worldview encoded in the structure of the words. Nouns are animate; therefore, nature is animate. Place-names wield a special significatory power that is often a record of the animate history of that land, of interactions between worldly and other-worldly forces such as lightning and a tree.[52]

Yet despite the specificity of time and place, Mayhew tells us that Indians from Canada to Virginia, consisting of vastly disparate populations, "speak what was *Originally* one and the same Language."[53] Condensed within this word "originally" is a recognition of the structural similarities governing languages within one family. It is also a subtle allusion to the lost language of Eden, referring to an ongoing belief in a biblical past. For Mayhew, Massachusett represents a hybrid cosmology that is at once associated with biblical accounts of disparate tongues and syntactically representative of indigenous cosmologies. Through this hybrid cosmology, Mayhew observed Massachusett words to be a rich source of aesthetic potential. The language is "good and regular," he tells his reader. While the "Terms of art" are not yet fixed, Massachusett is certainly "capable" of cultivating them. Additionally, Mayhew senses an opportunity for a uniquely American aesthetic because the "Indians" are not as beholden to other nations as the English are for borrowed words. Mayhew's observations foreshadow the Anglo-American literary fascination with the aesthetics of indigenous words to come.

Like Mayhew, Cotton built on the work of John Eliot, using both the Bible and the *Indian Primer* in an attempt to learn the rules of Indian orthography.[54] Yet Cotton also transformed Eliot's work through a more nuanced focus on Wampanoag's structural particularities. Also like Mayhew, Cotton was the descendant of three generations of missionaries. As the son of John Cotton Jr., who was himself a student of Wampanoag, Josiah Cotton grew up with a more subtle sense of the intricacies of the Indian tongue and the ways in which it differed from English. However, despite his native knowledge, Cotton encountered some difficulty in comprehension among his proselytes. A recorded dialogue vividly recounts the imperfections in the transmission of knowledge across missionary generations while also revealing the profundity of local variations of the Wampanoag tongue.

The dialogue begins simply. Cotton asks, "How shall I learn Indian?" The Praying Indian replies, "By talking with Indians, and minding their words, and manner of pronouncing." The dialogue begins by inverting linguistic authority. Rather than assuming the position of ministerial expertise, Cotton asks an Indian proselyte for advice. The indigenous perspective confirms his own suspicion that Indian is a "very difficult" language. Additionally, Cotton learns that one of the reasons he is having difficulty preaching in "Indian" is because his father, John Cotton Jr., learned the language on Martha's Vineyard, or "Nope" as the island is called in Wampanoag. The knowledge passed down from father to son is imperfect, according to this native informant, because the language spoken on Martha's Vineyard is in fact quite different from the language spoken within the Plymouth community. When Josiah Cotton asked his interlocutor to explain the difference between "the language of the Island, and the main," he could not do so entirely but explained that "these Indians [of Plymouth] don't understand every word of them Indians." Due to this apparent miscommunication between missionary generations, Cotton can only speak "broken Indian." While phonetically and orthographically similar, the intonation is quite different. Consequently, the Indian proselyte tells Cotton that in his sermons, he doesn't "put the tone in the right place." Because this leads to comprehension that is fragmentary at best, the Indian proselyte advises that it would be better to "preach to the Indians in English" than in "broken Indian."[55]

Significantly, the difference between the Wampanoag spoken in these two locales is a consequence of oral expression. Indigenous speakers highlight the integral aural quality of their language. Syntax and orthography might be uniform, but intonation makes all the difference in expression and comprehension. This indigenous perspective calls into question John Cotton Jr.'s linguistic expertise in a fashion that contradicts not only the testimonies of contemporary Puritan ministers but also the assumption among scholars that the languages spoken in Plymouth and Martha's Vineyard were mutually comprehensible.[56] Cotton Jr. did in fact learn Wampanoag on Martha's Vineyard in 1665, when he was sent there to redeem his name following a local scandal.[57] After an intensive year of linguistic study, he returned to a church of more than forty Praying Indians, gathered between Sandwich and Plymouth. Here he continued his study of Wampanoag, composing his own manuscript notebook of Indian vocabulary. Josiah Cotton inherited his father's linguistic work but also realized that he had to improve upon it, perhaps in light of the discoveries revealed in this dialogue. Poring over his father's records but also following the advice of the Indian proselyte that he "talk with the Indians," Cotton composed his own vocabulary list. In a small manuscript notebook, he transcribed about 3,000 translations of Massachusett words and phrases, producing what as far as I can tell is the only text in the early eighteenth-century Anglo-Protestant canon that comes close to mirroring the achievements of the French Jesuits, with their massive dictionary projects.

The vocabulary list shares with Mayhew's *Observations* a recognition of the autonomy and intrinsic beauty of Indian words. While Mayhew imagines the potential for developing terms of art for Wampanoag, Cotton does so, as he begins his list with a section on the arts that includes such phrases as "a comedy, or witty thing," "a tragedy, or sad thing," "an act," "a history," "melody," "a trumpet or music," and "inspiration." The list complements Mayhew's recognition of aesthetic potential encoded in Indian words. Conveying a hybrid cosmology such as Mayhew's *Observations*, Cotton's vocabulary is replete with Christian terms and concepts: "heavenly," "hell," "predestination," "psalmist," "idol," "state of innocency," "corruption of flesh," "incarnation," and "marrow of divinity."

This hybrid cosmology of Wampanoag Christian words survived the journey from Martha's Vineyard to Plymouth. The list of Christian concepts also has meanings that bespeak some aspect of the indigenous spirit world. According to James Hammond Trumbull's *Natick Dictionary*, "Kesuk," the translation for "heaven," means "the visible heavens, the sky," or "light" or in some dialects "the name of the sun as a source of heat."[58] The word for "hell," "chepiohkomuk," means "the inclosed place of separation, hades, hell."[59] "The misery of hell" translates as "Awakompanaouk," meaning "complaining, expressing of suffering, 'groaning.'"[60] A creative stretch at best, "predestination" translates into a phrase meaning something to the effect of thirsting after the "old, ancient and so first in the order of time."[61] The generic form of the vocabulary masks the thematic variation on theological terms by appearing to present a one-to-one correspondence between English and Wampanoag. This collaborative project among father, son, and indigenous teachers attains linguistic expertise through flexible forms of faith. In relinquishing the Protestant insistence on literal translation from the word of God to the vernacular, Cotton's vocabulary allows for a more fluid tool of cultural translation.

Epistemologies of Native Language Survival

Josiah Cotton's *Vocabulary of the Massachusetts (Or Natick) Indian Language*, Mayhew's *Observations on the Indian Language*, and the Jesuit dictionary projects that took place around the turn of the eighteenth century are storehouses of knowledge that would have otherwise been lost to history. The earliest written records of Miami-Illinois, a designation for a linguistic family once consisting of disparate tribal relations that are now untraceable, were by French Jesuits. The same European populations that worked to supplant tribal history with Christianity also left lasting written records of the languages of the regions they sought to colonize. The transcription of primarily oral languages into the Roman alphabet participated in the destruction of indigenous tongues while also preserving them. The missionary linguists examined in this chapter learned Illinois, Abenaki, and Wampanoag "by talking with Indians, and minding their words, and manner of pronouncing," as the Christian Indian in Plymouth encouraged Cotton to do.[62] Consequently, written records of native languages often convey an indigenous worldview. Through the missionaries' pen, combinations of Miami-Illinois verb inflections, aspirations of long and short vowels, and dialogues have been passed down as knowledge of a language that people stopped speaking by the early twentieth century.[63] Wampanoag, the ancient language of the Mashpee people, ceased to be a living language in the eighteenth century, just a few decades after Cotton and Experience Mayhew completed their studies. Descendants of the Aquinnah Wampanoag tribe are now reclaiming their language by using the colonial archive to reconstruct the pronunciation and morphological alterations of words.[64] Abenakis stopped speaking in their native tongue to their children in the 1950s when the Maine government purchased reservation lands and encouraged Abenaki children to be educated exclusively in white schools.[65] In each case, the missionary language record stands as a lasting remnant of an aspect of indigenous culture that it also helped to destroy.

Contradictory facets of preservation and erasure, translation and mistranslation, and syncretic and irreconcilable religious cultures are the inevitably entwined facets of missionary linguistics. Contemporary efforts to revitalize indigenous languages often replicate the desire for an ur-language that we see woven throughout biblical linguistics and eighteenth-century language philosophy. We have made the historical destruction of indigenous languages into a metonym for the destruction of identity, culture, and sovereignty. Yet, we forget that such classificatory linguistic associations themselves are built on Enlightenment assumptions.[66] Language is porous and malleable. It is a record of complex historical interactions rather than stasis. At the same time that it wants to resist the consequences of colonialism, language revitalization also risks essentialism. It risks replicating the false binary of modernity as it has been constructed throughout U.S. history as a series of ruptures and changes set against a static aboriginal culture encased within a primitive past.[67] It is my contention that the indigenous voice can only speak through the missionary text when we understand these histories as entwined, dialogical dynamics within a broader intellectual context.

Part III

American Nature and the Politics of Translation

Chapter 7

The Crucible of the Tropics: Alchemy, Translation, and the English Discovery of America

Ralph Bauer

Old Science/New Science

In his seminal 1970 study *Science in the British Colonies of America*, Raymond Stearns devoted his first chapter to what he called the "old science" in America—the sixteenth-century Spanish natural historians of the New World Gonzalo Fernández de Oviedo y Valdés, Nicolás Monardes, José de Acosta, and others—before turning to the actual topic of his book: science in the British colonies of America, which would presumably be the "new" (i.e., Baconian) science emerging during the seventeenth century.[1] The old/new binary in Stearns's organization of the history of science in the Americas was a common rhetorical feature among twentieth-century Anglophone and Northern European historians of science. This binary undergirded narratives of the so-called scientific revolution that depended on a quasi-religious observance of modern national, cultural, and linguistic boundaries that obscured the significant intellectual debt owed by seventeenth-century men of science to the sixteenth-century tradition of natural history about the New World.[2] This tradition manifested profound changes in scientific mentalities and epistemologies, brought about by the state-sponsored corporate networks of knowledge production rationalized by the imperial project and legitimated by its messianic apostolic mission. While the center of these epistemic transformations was located elsewhere during the sixteenth century—mainly in Spain and Spanish America—they were not lost on Englishmen, who busily translated scientific knowledge about the Americas into English and recontextualized it for England's own imperial enterprise.

With regard to the assessment of Spanish science as "old" science, Stearns's narrative had its most immediate ideological roots in the anti-Catholic sentiments of the French Enlightenment and ultimately in the sixteenth- and seventeenth-century Protestant Black Legend, according to which all things Spanish were backward and "medieval."[3] With regard to the narrative's invocation of the old in order to legitimate the new, it reproduced what Kellie Robertson, a historian of medieval literature, has called the "gap" narrative that has structured the historiography of (early) modern science, especially that of the scientific revolution of the seventeenth century. This gap narrative of old/new, or medieval/modern, is one of the manifestations of the "Great Divide" that, as Bruno Latour has argued, we moderns have invented to persuade ourselves of our modernity.[4] However, recovering the crucial role that transcultural and transnational translation played in the history of early modern science can help us see beyond this Great Divide and apprehend the history of science in terms not of a series of revolutionary ruptures of scientific traditions but instead of the fertile interplay between scientific tradition and innovation as well as in terms of the cross-fertilizations of scientific traditions becoming entangled in intercultural exchanges and contests. Attending to the role that translation played in the making of English knowledge about the Americas thus exposes the modern legacies of the Black Legend as well as the White Legend in the modern history of science, according to which English knowledge production about the Americas is the result not of conquest but instead of "discovery"—a discovery of virginal land yet unknown by either Amerindians or Catholic Iberians.

As a case in point, I will explore the disseminations and translations of the natural histories written by Oviedo throughout Europe while placing special emphasis on the English translations undertaken by the English alchemist Richard Eden. Indeed, I will use the example of Eden as an alchemist and translator in order to explore the historical connections between the resurgence of alchemy and the increasing scientific curiosity about the New World in early modern England. It is a connection, I will argue, that is crucial for understanding the rise of the experimental sciences in the seventeenth century. Despite their marginalization by modern historians of science such as Stearns (and too many historians of science after him), the works of Oviedo were the first point of reference for all subsequent writers about the New World generally and the Caribbean specifically. In particular, the transmission of his works into sixteenth- and seventeenth-century England provide a crucial link in the history of modern science and the scientific revolution. As I will suggest, sixteenth-century Spanish natural history about the New World fused a long classical pagan (especially Epicurean) tradition of inquiry and curiosity about the natural world with the Christian rhetorical model of the pilgrim and the eyewitness (especially the martyr), hereby laying the ideological groundwork for early modern state-sponsored imperialist and empiricist knowledge production and the scientific revolution of the seventeenth century.

Curiosity and Religion

One of the most influential modern philosophical expressions of Stearns's gap narrative can be found in Hans Blumenberg's *The Legitimacy of the Modern Age* (1966). There, Blumenberg presented his argument as a critique of the so-called secularization thesis of history philosopher Karl Löwith, who had seen the central concepts of scientific modernity—especially that of scientific "progress"—as but secularized versions of medieval ideas, especially Christian apocalyptic eschatology. Against Löwith, Blumenberg insisted on an essential discontinuity between the medieval and modern age (and thus on the legitimacy of the idea of a "modern" age) by focusing on the history of scientific mentalities, especially what he called "the preponderance of theoretical curiosity in the modern age." The "legitimation of theoretical curiosity" during the Renaissance, he argued, was the "basic feature of the history of the beginning of the modern age." During the Middle Ages, man's curiosity was circumscribed by theology, especially the Augustinian interdiction on "vain curiosity" (*vana curiositas*). As Augustine had explained in *The Confessions*, curiosity was one of the Christian vices, one of the three forms of concupiscence, namely that of the "lust of the eyes" (*concupiscentia oculorum*). Not only was curiosity a vice; it was the first step into the cardinal sin of pride. This negative evaluation of curiosity did not, of course, originate with Augustine but was already evident in the stoic tradition of Western philosophy at least since Cicero, especially in his portrayal of Ulysses as the quintessential "*curiosus*," as somebody vainly "longing to know everything." In the subsequent Christian tradition, the interdiction of curiosity was, according to Blumenberg, especially severe when it came to the realm of the occult, which was understood to be hidden from us by providential design. "In the hiddenness of the *res obscurae* [obscure subjects] from human understanding, there lies a sort of natural prescription of the region to which the cognitive will should remain restricted by practical reason."[5]

If medievalists have increasingly begun to subject Blumenberg's paradigm to critical scrutiny, they have also rejected Löwith's secularization thesis, which was predicated on an assumption of a categorically antagonistic relationship between science and religion in the Christian West. Heiko Oberman, for example, pointed out that while there were indeed areas in which medieval theologians such as Augustine saw Christianity as incompatible with curiosity (especially when it came to magic), the Christian tradition had not only a tradition of *vana curiositas* but also one of *iusta curiositas* (just curiosity)—a curiosity that is "not seen to be in contradiction with the faith, for it is a sort of curiosity that aims to further the faith."[6] Indeed, recent assessments of the history of modern scientific culture in the West have lent support to Oberman's critique by showing how scientific inquiry in the West was often explicitly underwritten by religion. Stephen Gaukroger, for example, has argued that the "reasons commonly adduced for the success of a scientific culture in the West in the wake of the scientific revolution—its use of adversarial non-dogmatic argument, its ability to disassociate itself from religion, its technological benefits—are mistaken and cannot explain this success."[7] Significantly, Gaukroger begins *The Emergence of a Scientific Culture* in the West not in the seventeenth century but rather in the thirteenth century, with a process that he calls the "Aristotelian amalgam"—the reintroduction of Aristotelian natural philosophy in the West. Even this thirteenth-century "Aristotelian amalgam" continued an earlier process of translation in which Christian theologians such as Augustine had appropriated Pagan (Greek) philosophy—in a process that Gaukroger calls the "Augustinian synthesis"—that presented Judeo-Christian (revealed) knowledge as the fulfillment and perfection of pagan Neoplatonism. If science and religion had nevertheless remained in tension in the aftermath of this "first" (thirteenth-century) scientific revolution, Gaukroger argues, one of the distinctive features of the early modern scientific revolution is that unlike other earlier scientific programs and cultures, it is driven, often explicitly, by religious considerations: Christianity set the agenda for natural philosophy in many respects and projected it forward in a way quite different from that of any other scientific culture.

Thus, it was the amalgamation rather than the separation of natural inquiry with religion that set the stage for what Gaukroger sees as the "anomalous" path that Western scientific culture has taken since the seventeenth century, when the "traditional balance of interests" between cognitive practices characterizing premodern and non-Western societies was "replaced by a dominance of scientific concerns, while science itself experiences a rate of growth that is pathological by the standards of earlier cultures, but is ultimately legitimated by the cognitive standing that it takes on" and is no longer open to "refutation from outside."[8] As we will see, the Spanish natural histories of the New World were a first step in this amalgamation between science and religion in an imperial context.

Gonzalo Fernández de Oviedo y Valdés and Cross-Cultural Transmission

Oviedo was born in Madrid in 1478. His interest in the Indies had first been sparked in 1493 when, at age fourteen, he was in the service of the Spanish infante, Don Juan, and witnessed Christopher Columbus's triumphant entry into the city of Barcelona after having returned from his first transatlantic voyage. Many years later, Oviedo remembered being awed as Columbus presented the Catholic monarchs with small quantities of gold as well as colorful arrays of exotic plants, animals, and even human beings never seen in Europe before. When in 1497 Crown Prince Don Juan unexpectedly died, Oviedo, now in his early twenties, left for Italy, where he spent his intellectually formative years at the Renaissance courts of the Italian aristocracy in cities such as Genoa, Milan, and Mantua, becoming deeply engrossed in a flowering humanist culture of classical learning. He returned to Spain in 1502, where he lived in relative obscurity for several years. Oviedo first embarked for the New World in 1514, traveling as the official *veedor de las fundaciones de oro de la Tierra Firme*, or the inspector of gold mines on the mainland, in the expedition of Pedro Arias de Ávila, often known as Pedrarias. In 1523, Oviedo briefly returned to Spain to file official charges against the tyrannical government of Pedrarias. While at the royal court, Oviedo received a request from King Charles, recently elected Holy Roman emperor, for a literary description of his overseas territories in the Indies. Oviedo had already begun such a work, but he had left the unfinished manuscript at his residence in Hispaniola. To oblige the king, Oviedo hastily composed a new book titled *Oviedo de la Natural hystoria de las Indias*, working largely from memory. Frequently referring the reader to the much larger and detailed work he had already begun, he called the present work a mere *sumario* (summary), which is the title under which this work has also become known by subsequent historians.

Published in 1526 in Toledo at Oviedo's private expense, the *Sumario* was the first book about the New World that offered not a narrative account of travel and conquest but instead a detailed and systematic description of the landscapes, flora, fauna, and human cultures of Hispaniola and Tierra Firme, the mainland of what is today known as the Isthmus of Panama.[9]

In 1530, Oviedo was appointed by Charles as the official royal chronicler of the Indies, relieving him of his duties as inspector of mines. As a result, Oviedo was able to complete his longer work, but only parts of it would be published during his lifetime. In 1535 the first part, containing the first nineteen books, was published in Seville by the Cromberger printing house under the title *Historia general de las indias*. It provided an account of the voyages of Columbus and a description of the Antilles, including also a chapter on shipwreck narratives (which would eventually become the fiftieth and final chapter of the complete manuscript).[10] Book 20, the first book of the second part, was not published until the year of his death, in 1557, in Córdoba. It treated Ferdinand Magellan's voyage to the Moluccas and the Southern Cone, Trinidad, Venezuela, and Colombia. The remaining books of the *Historia general* had to await publication until the nineteenth century, when the complete work of fifty books was edited for the first time by Amador de los Ríos for the Spanish Academy of History in 1851–1855. It included all the materials that had remained in manuscript, which deal with the explorations and conquests of Panama, Central America, the Yucatán, Mexico, parts of North America, and Peru and Chile.

Historians have speculated that one of the reasons why only a fraction of Oviedo's magnum opus was published during his lifetime—besides the prohibitive costs of publishing such as massive work—was the fierce opposition from the Dominican friar Bartolomé de Las Casas, who regarded Oviedo's work as unhelpful to his political cause as "defender of the Indians" and alleged that it contained "almost as many lies as it has pages."[11] It is true that Oviedo's portrayal of Native Americans and their cultures could be unflattering at times. For instance, in the *Sumario* he had attributed Indian knowledge and use of natural substances—such as the poison extracted from the raw Yucca juice—to demonic revelations. Also, he had claimed that the Indians were exceptionally hardheaded in their resistance to peaceful conversion—a point of particular contention for Las Casas. Thus, Oviedo had written that the Indians' "skulls are four times thicker than those of the Christians. And so when one wages war with them and comes to hand to hand fighting, one must be very careful not to hit them on the head with the sword, because I have seen many swords broken in this fashion."[12] Overall, however, it must be said that Oviedo was also critical of the Spanish conduct in the Indies, which had led to a severe depopulation of the islands. Thus, he wrote in the *Sumario* that

> there are very few [Indians] there [in Hispaniola] now, and not so many Christians as there should be, since many of those who once were on the island have gone to other islands or to Tierra Firme. Being men fond of adventure, those who go to the Indies for the most part are unmarried and therefore do not feel obliged to reside in any one place. Since new lands have been discovered and are being discovered every day, those men believe that they will swell their purses more quickly in new territory. Even though some may have been successful in this, most have been disillusioned, especially those who already have established homes and residences in Hispaniola.[13]

Perhaps due to the incomplete availability of the *Historia general* in its Spanish original until the nineteenth century, its wider dissemination throughout Europe remained somewhat limited during the early modern period. In 1556, Giovanni Battista Ramusio published a partial Italian translation as part of the third volume of his *Navigationi et viaggi* (1556), which included also a summary of the chapters on the discovery of the Marañon River that Oviedo had sent in manuscript to Pietro Bembo in 1543 but was excluded from the Spanish edition. Also, a French translation of the printed materials available in Spanish was published by Michel de Vascosan twice, in 1555 and 1556.

If the massive work for which Oviedo is best known today was thus available only in fragments in the early modern period, his shorter work, the *Sumario*, enjoyed a broad dissemination throughout Europe. A complete Italian translation of the *Sumario* by Andrea Navigero, the Venetian ambassador to Spain, was first published in Venice in 1534 as Part 2 of Ramusio's sequential *Summario de la generale historia de l'Indie Occidentali* and would be republished four more times in the next one hundred years, three times as part of Ramusio's *Navigationi et viaggi*. An English translation by Richard Eden was published twice during the sixteenth century and again (in extracts) during the seventeenth century in Samuel Purchas's monumental *Purchas his pilgrimes* (1625). A French translation (based on Navigero's Italian translation) by Jean Poleur was published in 1556. And it was even translated into Ottoman Turkish in the 1580s by Emir Mehmet ibn Emir Hasan el

Suudi, though this translation was not published in Istanbul until 1730, when it appeared together with Turkish translations from the New World histories written by Francisco López de Gómara and Agustín de Zárate.[14]

The great interest with which Oviedo's *Sumario* was greeted throughout Europe in the sixteenth century is not surprising, as it was the earliest natural history of the New World whose author could speak with the authority of an eyewitness when describing such exotic plants as the rubber tree, maize, tobacco, and cinnamon as well as animals never seen before by Europeans, such as the armadillo and the anteater. Unlike the earlier accounts by explorers and conquerors such as Columbus, Amerigo Vespucci, and Hernán Cortés, Oviedo did not organize his account chronologically as a narrative account but instead as a topically and systematically arranged catalog of nature. In his descriptions he drew from his classical training and taxonomic conventions that Italian Renaissance natural history had inherited from the Roman (and pagan) tradition of Pliny's *Historia naturalis*, which had divided up the natural world into general categories such as the elements, physical geography, man, animals, fishes, bird, insects, and the various types of plants, each category containing headers on the various subspecies. In the prologue to the *Sumario*, addressed to the emperor, Oviedo wrote that

> The wonders of nature are best preserved and kept in the memory of man by histories and books in which they are written by intelligent persons who have traveled over the world and who have observed at first hand the things they describe and who describe what they have observed and understood of such things. This was the opinion of Pliny. . . . A very accurate scholar, Pliny always cited his sources when he quoted a story which he had heard or read. He also included in this history many things which he had observed at first hand. In the manner of Pliny, then, in this short study I want to describe for your Majesty what I have seen in your Occidental Empire of the West Indies, Islands and Tierra Firme of the Ocean Sea.[15]

Nevertheless, Oviedo was also eager to distinguish himself from his classical pagan model, writing in his prologue to the *Historia general* that

> I have not culled them [these materials] from two hundred thousand volumes I might have read, as Pliny wrote . . . , where, it seems that he related what he had read. . . . I, however, compiled what I here

write from two hundred thousand hardships, privations, and dangers in the more than twenty-two years that I have personally witnessed and experienced these things. . . . In one way my book will differ from Pliny's model: this will be to relate something of the conquest of these Indies, and . . . justify the reason for their discovery.[16]

Unlike the classical pagan natural historian, who may have described the local plants by direct observation but relied on books regarding the exotic, remote ones, the natural historian of the New World has no books on which to rely and so must suffer the hardships of travel. And unlike his classical model, Oviedo argues, the reason why he wrote his natural history was his desire not merely to assuage his curiosity but also to further the conquest of the Indies for the sake of expanding Christendom and the territories of the Holy Roman emperor. Throughout his works, Oviedo therefore underwrites the language of Aristotelian and Plinean *scientia* and the curiosity about the secrets of the Indies with the Christian language of passion, pilgrimage, and martyrdom.

Christianity is, as Anthony Pagden has noted, a "religion of observance." The martyr (as Pagden notes, a word whose original Greek root means simply "witness") is a Christian hero who has "seen" but failed to persuade others of the unique authenticity of his or her vision, a pilgrim who has not returned.[17] The fusion between the Christian language of the witness and of classical science in the early modern period was the culmination of a long process that had given rise to the so-called thirteenth-century scientific revolution and had underwritten Aristotelian science with Christian messianism in the writings of such late medieval alchemists as Raymond Llull, Arnaldus of Villanova, and Roger Bacon. As a result, early modern European culture embraced, as Stuart Clark has explained, "A kind of ocularcentrism . . . in which the twin traditions stemming from the perceptual preferences of the Greeks and the religious teachings of St. Augustine combined to give the eyes priority over the other sense."[18] Whereas Saint Augustine had approved of a "just curiosity" (*iusta curiosidad*) about the marvels of nature only if it edifies man in the contemplation of God's creation, these late medieval alchemists pressed natural curiosity in the service not only of the contemplation of God but also of the expansion of Christendom in its struggle against the scientifically advanced culture of Islam and in preparation for its final struggle against the Antichrist. In effect, these late medieval Christian alchemists proposed that the Arabic science of Aristotelian alchemy (*al-kimia*) could legitimately be appropriated to beat the Arabs with their technology, as hundreds of Arabic treatises were being translated into Latin at recently reconquered south European cities such as Toledo. In this Christianized alchemical tradition, "discovery" meant the revelation of the secrets of a divine providential design that had remained hidden from the pagan philosophers and was inaccessible to the penetrating power of human reason. In other words, it was an idea of discovery not in the Scholastic sense of "making manifest" by demonstration but instead by experience through the empirical senses and, in its unpredictability, was akin to divine revelation. The Christian alchemists' empirical program, which had subsisted during the Middle Ages mainly as a "secret science" and often on the borders of religious orthodoxy, became the dominant model for the Spanish imperial production of knowledge about the New World during the course of the sixteenth century as it was adopted by early modern institutions of Spanish imperial power, such as the office of the royal chronicler of the Indies, the Casa de Contratación (House of Trade), and the Consejo de Indias (Council of the Indies). Thus, in the context of Spanish imperial expansionism in the New World, the medieval alchemists' "secrets of nature" became the imperial "secrets of state," and the medieval alchemist evolved into the (early) modern secretary.[19]

The redaction and publication of Oviedo's works were key events in this historical and generic transformation during the sixteenth century. Thus, there is in Oviedo's natural history not only an objective rhetoric of science derived from the classical authority of books but also a self-conscious emphasis on the subjective or empirical qualities in its composition. While each individual chapter in the *Sumario* focuses on a particular thing (*cosa*)—a particular plant, animal, or ethnographic fact—this taxonomic organization, especially in the early part, is compromised by and synthesized with the imposition of a narrative timeline that follows the trajectory of Oviedo's own travels. Thus, he begins with a chapter on the voyage—from the House of Trade in Seville down the Guadalquivir River to San Lúcar de Barrameda (Seville's seaport) and out into the Atlantic on the first leg of the journey, the ten-day trip to the Canary Islands; the second leg, the twenty-five-day journey to Hispaniola; and finally the seven-day trip to Tierra Firme. From there, chapters proceed from general geographical observations to descriptions of the cultural mores of the natives—their foodways of making bread made from maize and yucca—and then finally to the myriad plant and animal species. As several critics have noted, the subjectivism of this organization may have functioned as a sort of mnemonic device for Oviedo. Similar to Thomas

Aquinas's technique of memorizing a long sermon by imagining its progress in analogy to a movement through the rooms of a building, Oviedo memorizes the particulars about the plants and animals by literarily reenacting his journey through space.[20]

In his descriptions of plants and animals, Oviedo adopted Pliny's basic model of natural history, including the Roman's "popular zoology." In his discussion of birds, for example, Oviedo categorizes them into those species that are "similar to those in Spain" and those that are different, singling out for special emphasis exotic birds such as the turkey, the pelican, and the hummingbird. Yet if the Plinean tradition gave him a general taxonomic principle for organizing his materials, Oviedo soon realized the limits of its usefulness in approaching the nature of the New World. Recent critics such as Jeremy Paden and Andrés Prieto have investigated this "crisis in representation" in Oviedo's natural history, as it evidences the author's increasing realization of the relativity of Aristotelian descriptive categories once deemed to be universal. According to this Aristotelian system of classification, biological forms are categorized by way of mutually exclusive oppositions with regard to their natural habitat: "animals" live on land, "fish" in the sea, and "birds" in the air. The very basic terms of this taxonomy, they argue, break down in the description of such Caribbean animals as flying fish and the iguana.[21]

There is, however, also a rhetorical aspect in Oviedo's appeal to the senses. Thus, his natural history, while thoroughly steeped in an Aristotelian understanding of nature and versed in the generic and rhetorical tradition of Plinean natural history writing, enlists the Christian language of the pilgrimage and the eyewitness to engage in a critique of some of the fundamental assumptions of these traditions. Whereas Aristotle had held that the Torrid Zone is uninhabitable by human beings, Oviedo proves, by the authority of his own experience, that the West Indies, which lie in Aristotle's Torrid Zone, are fecund and temperate. It is by Christian pilgrimage alone that God's providential design of the world is revealed.

Oviedo's fusion of the language of Aristotelian and Plinean *scientia* with that of Christian pilgrimage will provide a model for other European natural historians about the New World throughout Europe. Nowhere would this synthesis be expressed more memorably than in the "House of Solomon," Francis Bacon's fabulous academy of science in his utopian treatise *New Atlantis* (1627). However, whereas the inhabitants of the original utopia in Thomas More's prototype, published a hundred years earlier, were still Greek-speaking pagan Epicureans, Bacon's inhabitants of "Bensalem" were

Spanish-speaking Christians, and their scientific Epicureanism was derived not from pagan philosophy or poetry (such as Lucretius's poem *De rerum natura*, rediscovered in 1417 by Poggio Bracciolini) but instead from Christian revelation, particularly the Apocalypse of John, a copy of which had miraculously found its way to Bensalem.[22] As more than one critic has noted, Bacon's "House of Solomon" was modeled on the Spanish House of Trade, the clearinghouse for all information about the New World established in Seville in 1505. To understand the relationship between Bacon's programmatic model of the modern research laboratory and the Spanish House of Trade in Seville, however, it is necessary to trace the dissemination of Oviedo's model of science into sixteenth-century England.

Richard Eden: Alchemist and Translator of New World Marvels

What's notable about the English reception of Oviedo's book in the early modern period is the interest it received from humanists with a dual interest in translation and alchemy. The book first appeared in English in a translation by Richard Eden, an alchemist and staunch promoter of English colonialism working under the reign of Mary I. Eden's interest in alchemy was apparently inspired by his tutor at Queen's College, Thomas Smith, who had harbored a lifelong passion for distilling herbal remedies. In 1547, Eden was offered the position of distiller of waters in the royal household of Henry VIII, succeeding Thomas Seex at an annual salary of forty pounds. The annotations of Eden's copy of the writings of the great thirteenth-century alchemist Roger Bacon betray a distinct interest in the alchemical distillation of gold. After Henry's death his successor, Edward VI, appointed someone else to the position, and Eden had to look around for gainful employment. He found a patron in Richard Whalley, a Notthinghamshire gentleman and receiver of the court of augmentations for Yorkshire, who employed Eden at his mansion so that he could devote himself to the search for the quintessence.[23]

In 1552, Eden became secretary to Sir William Cecil to publicize the voyages to China and the Far East, in which Cecil was invested. Eden had good credentials for this appointment. After having translated Vannoccio Biringuccio's alchemical and metallurgical work *De la pirotechnia*, Eden had begun to work on a translation of Book 5 of Sebastian Münster's monumental *Cosmographiae Universalis* (Basel, 1550), one of the earliest and most comprehensive cosmographies to incorporate all the empirical knowledge gained with the new voyages of discovery. Eden published his translation of Münster in 1553 under the title *A Treatyse of the Newe India, with Other New Founde Lands and Islandes, as Well Eastwarde as Westwarde*. This work provided accounts of India, China, and the Spice Islands as well as the voyages of Columbus and Vespucci to the West Indies. Eden's last chapter, titled "Whether Under the Aequinoctial Circle or Burning Lyne (Called Torrida Zona) Be Habitable Regions," is not derived from Münster but rather from Aeneas Silvius (Pope Pius II, 1404–1464), whose *Cosmographia Pii Papae* had played a formative role in Columbus's geographic ideas by arguing (following Albertus Magnus) that the habitable part of the globe extended beyond the Northern Hemisphere—in contradiction to Aristotle's theory of climactic zones.[24]

Eden apparently saw an analogy between the science of alchemy and that of modern cosmography. In his prefatory address to John Dudley, first duke of Northumberland, Eden placed Münster in the tradition of the great thirteenth-century German alchemist Albertus Magnus (1193–1280), whose occult knowledge was rumored not only to have made his garden bloom in the middle of winter but even to have constructed an artificial man, who was then allegedly destroyed by one of Albertus's most brilliant students, Thomas Aquinas, who warned his teacher against indulging in such "promethean ambitions."[25] Not only had Albertus already refuted Aristotle regarding the latter's claim of the uninhabitability of the equatorial regions of Earth, but his knowledge even exceeded that of St. Augustin, Eden argued, who fell into "erroure in the science of Astronomie in which he travayled but as a stranger."[26]

From the point of view of mid-sixteenth-century England, there were indeed a number of similarities between alchemy and cosmography. The early 1550s had been plagued by an economic crisis that resulted from the war with France (1552–1556), as specie had been leaving the country and creating a chronic shortage of bullion. Efforts were stepped up to exploit the silver mines within England, but Dudley (the addressee of Eden's preface) had concocted a bolder scheme with Sebastian Cabot: they would sail an army up the Amazon River in pinnaces and wrest Peru from Spain, which was extracting enormous sums of silver during the 1540s from the newly discovered silver mines at Potosí. While the harebrained scheme was prudently abandoned, both Dudley and Eden apparently thought of the nature of the New World as a sort of alchemical "crucible." In his preface to his translation of Münster, Eden attempts to prove that the biblical Ophir and Tharsis, to which Solomon's navies sailed from Ezion-Gebir, were not parts of Cilizia in Turkey but instead lay in the south parts of the world. . . . For not only olde and new Histories, dayly experience, and the principles of Natural Philosophie doe agree, that the places moste apte to bring forth gold, spices, and precious stones, are the Southe and Southeast partes of the world, but also our Saviour Christ approveth the same declaring that the Quene of the Southe (meaning the Quene of Saba) came from the utmost partes of the worlde to hear the wisdom of Solomon.[27]

In 1553 Mary the Catholic ascended to the English throne and the year after married Philip II of Spain, who promptly appointed Eden to a position in the treasury. When in 1555 Eden issued a new compilation about the New World, his choice of texts clearly reflected his accommodation to the new order: it included parts of the *Decades* by the Italian humanist and first official chronicler of the Indies, Peter Martyr; a Latin edition and English translation of Pope Alexander's bull *Inter caetera* (1493), which had divided the New World between Spain and Portugal; English translations of parts of Oviedo's *Natural hystoria* and various other texts, such as Antonio Pigafetta's account of Magellan's circumnavigation, a discourse by Francisco López de Gómara about the controversy caused by *Inter caetera*; accounts of South America by Vespucci and Andreas de Corsali; and accounts on Muscovy and Cathay. Also making a surprising reappearance in his compilation of travel histories is Biringuccio's work on alchemy and metallurgy in a chapter titled "Of the Generation of Metalles and Their Mynes with the Maner of Fyndinge the Same: Written in the Italian Tounge by Vannuccius Biringuczius in His Booke Cauled *Pyrotechnia*."[28]

These contexts shed light on Eden's presentation of Oviedo's natural history in English translation. In his preface to the reader, Eden writes that though Peter Martyr of Angleria is still unrivaled "in declarynge by philosophical discourses the secreate causes of naturall affectes bothe as touchynge the lande, the sea, the stares, and other straugne woorkes of nature. . . . *Gonzalus Ferndinandus Ouiedus*, (whom the lerned *Cardanus* compareth to the ancient writers) is doubtless the chiefe" among those who can speak from eyewitness experience. However, Eden entirely reorganized Oviedo's natural history, getting rid of most of the subject headers, to the effect of enhancing its appearance as a coherent account and almost entirely losing its taxonomic character as a catalog of nature. Eden's reordering of materials betrays his primary interest in Oviedo's text. After the introductory prologue to Charles V and the first chapter, which provides details about the voyage, Eden bypasses some eighty chapters that contain virtually all of Oviedo's naturalistic descriptions of the island of Hispaniola and Tierra Firme and their flora and fauna (including Oviedo's famous descriptions of New World animals and exotic fruits) as well as their native populations and their cultural practices—in effect everything that had identified Oviedo's text as a natural history. Instead, Eden proceeds to Oviedo's conclusion—which discusses the easy accessibility of the Caribbean from Europe—and then to chapter 82, which discusses the gold mines of Castilla de Oro in Tierra Firme. He omits Oviedo's chapter 83, on fish and fishing, and jumps to chapter 84, on pearl fishing. Then he returns to Oviedo's tenth chapter, "Indians of Tierra Firme, Their Customs, Rites, and Ceremonies," but omits everything except for Oviedo's discussion of the *tequina*—the Indian warlords—and retitles the chapter "Of the Familiarity Which Certeyne of the Indians Have with the Deuyll, and Howe They Receaue Answere of Hym of Thynges to Come."[29] In sum, it seems evident that Eden is primarily interested, as were the earliest Spaniards, in gold and conquest.

In addition, Eden seems interested in the philosophical questions that Oviedo's natural history had raised about the New World. Thus, Eden picks up from an earlier part of Oviedo's chapter on the customs of the Indians but gives it the title "Of the Temperature of the Regions Under or Neare to Be Burnt Lyne Cauled Torrida Zona or the Equinoctiall: And of the Dyvers Seasons of the Yeare." In this section Oviedo had presented his dispute with the ancients who had claimed that the Torrid Zone was noninhabitable. Eden here inserts a lengthy footnote in order to shed light on "the secreate woorke of nature," making it possible that the Torrid Zone should have temperate climates.[30] The reason for this, he explains, is the prevalence of water there, which has its "course toward the South as to the lowest part of the earth." In other words, the Southern Hemisphere has more water because water has a tendency to flow "downward" into its proper "lower" place (according to Aristotelian physics). As modern discoveries have revealed, the downward tendency of water is not just an accidental aspect of the order of nature; rather, it is part of a divine providential design that had been hidden from the ancients. He quotes from Gerolamo Cardano's "De Elementis" (possibly the *De subtilitate libri XXI*, 1550), who had written that the ancients' belief that the world was mostly made up of land, with only little terrain being covered by the ocean sea, held true only for the Northern Hemisphere. The reason why God had made it this way was that "water by his couldnesse might temperate and not destroy the lyfe of beastes."[31] The hot south has therefore much water, and the cold north has little. If it were any different, the Torrid Zone would indeed be uninhabitable, as Aristotle posited. The reason why the pagan philosopher was wrong about the climate of the Torrid Zone, despite his superior natural reason, was that he did not have the benefit of Christian revelation, the gradual unveiling of God's providential design that only modern discoveries had brought.

One of the consequences of these revelations is the realization that the conceptions of human reason, which were held to be universal and concordant with the world that was really out there, turn out to be relative. The defiance of West Indian climate to be reduced to European concepts of the seasons is a case in point. Whereas in Europe July is hot because it is in summer and January is cold because it is in winter,

> in golden Castile or *Beragua*, it is contrary. For the sommer and tyme of greatest drowght and withowt rayne, is at Chrystman and a moneth before and a moneth after. And the tyme when it rayneth most, is about midsummer and a moneth before and a moneth after. And this season whiche they caule winter, is not for that it is any coulder then, then at any other tyme of the yeare, or hotter at Christmas then at other seasons, the tyme in these regions being ever after one maner, but for that that in this tyme which they caule winter, the soonne is hyd from theyr syghtes by reason of cloudes and rayne more then at other tymes. Yet forasmuch as for the moste parte of the yeare they lyue in a cleare, open, and temperate ayer, they sumwhat shrynke and feele a little coulde durynge the tyme of the said moist and cloudy ayer, althowth it bee not coulde in deede, or at the least such coulde as hath any sensible sharpenes.[32]

Thus, the encounter with Caribbean climate turns presumably universal categories such as winter into relative categories: "winter."

When Eden does finally return to Oviedo's botanical and zoological headings, he offers a rather condensed translation of Oviedo's descriptions of the animal world of the West Indies, discussing all of the plants as well as animals, fish, and birds summarily in one chapter each. When Eden does finally turn to Oviedo's sections on Native American culture, he merely refers his reader to Peter Martyr's *Decades* (which preceded Oviedo's text in Eden's text). Eden closes with a few paragraphs from Oviedo's dealing with Bacalaos (Cape Cod) and assigns it its own chapter title: "Of the Lande of Bacoaleos Cauled Terra Baccalearum, Situate on the North Side of the Firme Lande."[33]

Thus, Eden's reorganization of Oviedo's natural history clearly betrays the promotional character of his translations. They were written with a curious eye less on the natural particulars and more on the mineral riches and their economic potential in order to entice English adventurers to invest in a lucrative colonial enterprise.

The intense interest that English translators and men of science had in the literature of the Spanish conquest of the New World generally and in New World natural history particularly shows that the sixteenth-century tradition in natural history writing of authors such as Oviedo (as well as Francisco Hernández, Monardes, and Acosta) was not "old science" from which the "new" sciences had to disassociate themselves (as Raymond Stearns once claimed); rather, they provided the models on which a "new" (Baconian) science would be built in England by synthesizing Aristotelian naturalism with the Christian rhetorical model of the eyewitness. The literature of the Spanish discovery and conquest of America and especially the writing of the natural history of the New World represents an important chapter in the story of this historical development. By amalgamating the traditions of Aristotelian (pagan) natural philosophy with the Augustinian theology of *iusta curiositas* and the Christian tradition of pilgrimage, these authors built on the rhetorical tradition of thirteenth-century alchemists such as Raymond Llull, Roger Bacon, and Albertus Magnus. But it was in the crucible of the tropics that the sixteenth-century natural Iberian natural historians laid the generic, rhetorical, and philosophical cornerstones for the seventeenth- and eighteenth-century emergence of modern science.

Chapter 8

Flora's Fate: Spanish Materia Medica in Manuscript

John Slater

Natural histories of exotic flora enjoyed a minor vogue in the presses of Iberian empires during the second half of the sixteenth century. The half dozen volumes published by Garcia de Orta, Cristóbal Acosta, and Nicolás Monardes—small-format, rustic works on materia medica written in the vernacular—sparked European imaginations for decades to come. By the 1580s, however, these authors' Iberian readerships had largely moved on. Spanish interest in exotic medicines could be fickle, and books often appeared in print well after demand for the drugs had dried up. Andreas Vesalius noted that there was "no end of praise for novel remedies" at the court of Charles V but that "guaiac wood [was] totally rejected in Spain" by 1546; this was nearly two decades before Monardes began publishing on exotic drug plants, including guaiacum, in 1565.[1] As José Pardo-Tomás notes, the publishing boomlet lasted fifteen years: there were no editions of Monardes's or Acosta's works published in their original Spanish after 1580 or during the entire seventeenth century.[2]

This brief moment in the history of Spanish scientific publication influenced the way modern historians came to understand the development of early modern natural history. A major goal of the history of Spanish science for much of the twentieth century was to reconstruct the influence of Spanish naturalists such as Monardes and Francisco Hernández on European natural history.[3] In the case of Monardes, this meant that historians generally started their narratives in Seville with Monardes's first work on exotic materia medica published in 1565 and followed the fortunes of this and his subsequent vernacular publications in the Latin translations of Carolus Clusius (Charles de l'Escluse) published by Christophe Plantin and his successors in Antwerp. The repackaging of Iberian works in presses in the Low Countries—and the movement from Spanish into Latin—is a classic chapter in traditional accounts of how natural knowledge was translated and disseminated. The vernacular Monardes was a significant but fleeting success; in the translations of Clusius and many others, Monardes became one of the most successful scientific authors of Spain's sixteenth century.[4]

The appeal of Clusius's books for historians is obvious: they are gorgeous examples of what is easily recognizable as a precursor to modern botany. If you open one of the rather unprepossessing editions of Monardes's work on exotic flora (1565, 1569, 1571, all published in Seville and all in diminutive octavo) and lay them next to Clusius's deluxe *Exoticorum* (published in folio at the Plantin press in Leiden, 1605), it is hard not to think that Monardes's workmanlike efforts have been elevated by Clusius to some more sublime and beautiful world.

There is a sensual temptation in that beauty: the temptation to luxuriate in the *Exoticorum*'s marvelous pages. There are social attractions to Clusius's world too. Clusius's life as revealed in his books seems to be an unfolding tale of friendships and shared enthusiasms, networks and nascent academies, domains of comity and cosmopolitanism. Clusius translated Monardes into Latin, for the benefit of "prelates, nobles and scholars."[5] Monardes, on the other hand, was something of a huckster, as Daniela Bleichmar recounts.[6] He was a slaver and a bankrupt who sought asylum in a church to avoid paying his debts. Why slum with Monardes when you can soar with Clusius?

The first reason to stay with Monardes and the Spanish natural historians is that if we follow the *Historia medicinal* into the *Exoticorum*—from Spanish into Latin, from Seville to the Low Countries—we perfectly invert Monardes's own publication trajectory.[7] Monardes published his books exclusively in Latin between 1539 and 1564—drawing on Venetian models—and switched definitively to Spanish fairly late in life. The Monardes of 1564 published in Latin and in Antwerp. Just a year later he would begin his famous run of Spanish-language works, published in Seville. This was in fact part of a general preference for the vernacular among Spanish naturalists that would persist for a century after Monardes's death. To study how Spanish natural history was Latinized is to miss, at least potentially, the importance of the vernacular herbal in Spain. To understand the broader currents within the natural history of Iberia's global empires, one must take into account Monardes's representative shift *away* from Latin-language books published in Antwerp and *toward* vernacular works published in Spain.

There is another reason to avoid making the leap to the Low Countries: naturalists in Spain kept on writing books of natural history but stopped publishing them. Throughout the seventeenth century, there are intriguing mentions of herbal manuscripts as well as chronicles abounding in natural knowledge circulating in Spanish. The contributions to this volume by Marroquín Arredondo, Millones Figueroa, Daniela Bleichmar, and Marcy Norton suggest the breadth and richness of American chronicles, *relaciones*, and manuscripts. But we will never know how many chronicles, such as Felipe de Pamanes's *Notables del Perú*, have been lost. Iberian herbal manuscripts such as Bernardo de Cienfuegos's *Historia de las plantas* have largely been ignored. It is not surprising that printed works fared better than manuscripts. The spectacular output of Plantin's Antwerp press brought to public attention marvelous works of exotic natural history by Clusius and others. However, focusing on works published in Antwerp, at the European limits of the Hapsburg Empire, can occlude the significance of manuscript works produced nearer the imperial metropolis and in Spain's colonies.

By the beginning of the seventeenth century many Spanish naturalists produced vernacular manuscripts, while at the same time richly illustrated herbal manuscripts printed in Latin became the building blocks of modern histories of botany. Modern historians' reliance on print works is understandable. Many more of them survived. However, printed herbals tend to reflect a particular set of what Brian Ogilvie has called "aesthetic impulses."[8] The selection bias for ideologically uniform printed herbals produced far from the Iberian Peninsula has inevitably skewed our understanding of Spanish natural history. Although it might be tempting to see the works of Garcia de Orta, Cristóbal de Acosta, and Monardes as the primitive antecedents that gained fuller realization outside of Spain and in Latin translation, this is, I believe, a mistake.

From the perspective of the history of Spanish science, it is more accurate to see the vernacular turn in the works of Iberian naturalists and physicians as a prologue to a Hispanic manuscript tradition. Ogilvie has demonstrated that the appreciation of nature and pleasure one took in it became part of the shared aesthetic of northern naturalists.[9] The tendency of northern naturalists to revel in the delights of nature, beautifully studied by Ogilvie, was not uncontroversial. Cienfuegos would distinguish between, on the one hand, the printed herbals of Clusius and other northerners that, Cienfuegos believed, were unreliable monuments to personal gratification and idleness and, on the other hand, manuscripts that faithfully preserved the painstaking observations of a skilled observer.

Examining three moments in the development of Spanish natural history—the works of Monardes, Juan Fragoso, and Cienfuegos—will show what it meant for Spanish authors to move away from Latin-language printed works toward vernacular manuscript works. When in 1565 Monardes abruptly switched from Latin to Spanish, he significantly altered the tone and significance of his works. Fragoso examined this shift in tone with philosophical cynicism in 1572; his *Discursos* contain a playful interrogation of the business of vernacular natural history. What was ambivalence in 1572 became vehement rejection by the 1620s when Cienfuegos cast a disparaging eye on Clusius, Monardes's translator, implicating publishing itself as the source of scientific error.

The works of Monardes, Fragoso, and Cienfuegos—spanning a critical period in Spanish natural history—suggest the ways in which Spanish natural history written on the Iberian Peninsula took on a different form and tone than the books published in Antwerp during the same period. As with the fortunes of Flora herself—simultaneously goddess and courtesan, exalted and common—early modern natural history long seemed to enjoy divergent fates: a sublime destiny in Flanders and a much humbler lot in Spain. But just as the last half century has taught us to reject the virgin/whore dichotomy, there is good reason to rethink the Spanish study of flora. The divergence of Madrid and Antwerp indicates the beginning of two distinct scientific cultures, each with its own practices and political ends, each with a different historiographic destiny. For their part, Spanish naturalists came to distrust printed works by Mattias L'Obel, Rembert Dodoens, and Clusius; print, according to Cienfuegos, was a medium apt only for frivolous works that were essentially ludic. By the seventeenth century, serious natural history was done in Spain by men who put pen to paper and controlled every aspect of the finished work.

Monardes and the Vernacular Turn

Monardes's protean life was spent at the intersection of two transformative phenomena, both related to trade. The first of these was Italy's dissemination of the mythology of its own Renaissance (as Lucia Binotti suggests, its most important export); early in life, for example, Monardes was taken with the humanism of Aldo Manuzio's publications in Venice.[10] The second was

European expansion and globalization. After a series of minor works that reflected his Aldine fascination, Monardes won fame by promoting exotic medicines, particularly from Spain's American territories.

To understand the significance of Monardes's works on American materia medica, it is necessary to compare them to his earlier books, published in Latin between 1539 and 1564. Monardes's early humanist enthusiasms are evident in a work such as *De Citriis*, a very brief treatise on citrus trees in Latin composed between 1536 and 1540.[11] The slight work was to have a very bright future. As Fernández and Ramón-Laca explain, the text was edited, cleaned up, and included in Clusius's *Exoticorum* (1605). From there, passages of *De Citriis* found their way into Gaspard Bauhin's 1651 *Historia plantarum* (the chapter titled "Poma Adami").

Written as a response to a letter from "Cuadra" (as Fernández and Ramón-Laca Hispanicize it), *De Citriis* begins with a pleasingly flowery salutation: "Quantum exhilaratus tuis literis fuerim non possum scribere" (I cannot express how your letter delighted me).[12] Because Cuadra was a surgeon, Monardes moves next to a discussion of surgery: it is ancient and noble, it forms a part of medicine, and in order to be a good surgeon, one must begin training young. These observations would seem to be out of place in a discussion of citrus trees, but Monardes is carefully cultivating his authority by basing the passages concerning surgery on Book 7 of Celsus's *De Medicina*.[13] Monardes is at one point candid enough to acknowledge that he is quoting Celsus verbatim, although this sort of respectful imitation would not have raised eyebrows among his contemporaries.

Like most medical texts of the period, *De Citriis* contains a familiar parade of classical and early modern authorities. Monardes cites Theophrastus, Pliny, and Virgil's second eclogue as well as an anecdote, recounted by Jean Ruel, from Athenaeus's *Deipnosophistae* (a third-century work that takes as its conceit the erudite conversation of a group of men gathered at banquets).[14] It is in the citation of the *Deipnosophistae* that Monardes tips his hand and reveals the extent of his ambition.

Important passages of the *De Citriis* are based on Manuzio's Latin preface to the 1514 Venice edition of the *Deipnosophistae*, whose text is in Greek.[15] Manuzio was one of the pivotal figures in sixteenth-century Venetian publishing, the "archetype of humanist publishers," and a monumental influence on Spanish authors.[16] The prefaces that Manuzio attached to many of his editions helped shape the identity of the Republic of Letters.[17] Monardes copies with a light touch; Manuzio's opening sentence, "Quantum gratuler . . . non facile dixerum," in Monardes's hands becomes "Quantum exhilaratus . . . non possum scribere."[18] These salutations sound as if they had been stripped from Erasmus's *De copia*: "The happiness occasioned by your communication is greater than I can describe," or "It is difficult to say how much happiness was occasioned in me by your letter."[19] However, the similarities run much deeper. Both Manuzio and Monardes go on to draw on Virgil's second Georgic in almost exactly the same way. More important, both cite Book 4 of Theophrastus's *Historia plantarum* and note that Theophrastus confuses the "malus persica" (*Prunus persica* L., or peach) and "malus medica" (*Citrus medica* L., or citron). As Manuzio notes but Monardes does not, this is one of the passages recounted in Book 3 of Athenaeus's *Deipnosophistae*, in which the mistake is noted and corrected by one of the banqueters.

Manuzio cites the passage from Theophrastus to underscore the importance of the *Deipnosophistae*, which was valuable to Renaissance scholars as a compendium of classical quotations. Manuzio points out that when Theodorus Gaza—an important early humanist—undertook his Latin translation of Theophrastus's *Historia plantarum*, the manuscript sources were so corrupt that Gaza had to consult the quotations of Theophrastus as they appear in Athenaeus. This is a complicated history of scrupulous textual reconstruction—from Theophrastus to Atheneaus to Gaza—that Manuzio deftly condenses. In his treatise on citrus trees, however, Monardes gives the impression that he, Monardes, is correcting Theophrastus (we are led to surmise for the first time). Taking a step back, we can see that what Manuzio does is cite a quotation (Gaza's) of a correction (Athenaeus's) of an error (Theophrastus's). What Monardes does in copying Manuzio is *plagiarize* a citation of a quotation of a correction of an error. But Monardes's audacity goes further: he credits neither Manuzio nor Gaza nor Atheneaus. The difference is striking: Manuzio establishes his authority by demonstrating effortless knowledge of humanist practices and mastery of original texts. Monardes, on the other hand, establishes his authority by claiming to correct Theophrastus's ancient mistake. (Never mind that Theophrastus's mistake was already identified by Atheneaus in the third century.)

It is easy to see why Monardes found Manuzio's preface so attractive. If Monardes did write *De Citriis* sometime after 1536, he would have been imitating Manuzio when the renown of the Aldine press was still at its height. Monardes took his models from the best sources, classical and contemporaneous: from the Roman Celsus to the Venetian Manuzio. Through this imitation, however, Monardes also reveals his scholarly limitations: he cites Ruel's Latin translation of Atheneaus, not the Greek edition to which Manuzio appended his Latin preface. Monardes was interested enough in Athenaeus, however, to hunt down both the Aldine edition and Ruel's recounting of the same episode.

Monardes's attempt to take on the codes and rhetoric of Manuzio's Venetian humanism indicates the radical nature of the shift he made in 1565 when he published his *Historia medicinal* in Spanish.[20] Monardes's use of the vernacular was part of a broader trend in Hispanic medical cultures; the influence and prestige of Spanish as a medical language was at its zenith during the sixteenth century.[21] But the suddenness of Monardes's switch from Latin to Spanish in 1564–1565 does reveal a new orientation in his work: a turning away from Venice and the East toward the West of New Spain. He exchanged verbal borrowing for material appropriation.[22]

The first chapter of the *Historia medicinal* of 1565, about gums and resins, characterizes American "copal" as a medicinal alternative to or substitute for incense: "Usamos acá dello [i.e., copal] . . . en lugar de Encienso" (Here we use copal in the place of incense).[23] Monardes notes in the preface that incense is only found on the Arabian Peninsula: "en sola la Región de Saba."[24] So, for Monardes, copal is a Western substitute for a highly valued Eastern product. Monardes wrote in Spanish about the vernacular medicines of the Hapsburgs' expanding empire.

In other instances, the Americas simply provided what Monardes believed to be a new source for a plant known since antiquity. He mistook the "higuera del infierno" of New Spain (*Jatropha curcas* L., or physic nut) for the castor oil plant (*Ricinus communis* L.).[25] Dioscorides, for example, had written about castor oil in the first century. Substitutes for and new sources of medicines known to the ancients are a major focus of Monardes's *Historia medicinal*. In Monardes's telling, the New World is often marvelous because it contains an abundance of new products that are just familiar enough to be easily assimilated into European medical practice. His rhetorical turning away from Italy is mirrored in his fascination with plants that are available within Spanish territories.

Although Monardes did not turn his back on Renaissance iconography when he wrote in Spanish, few traces of Manuzio's elegance remain.[26] Bleichmar emphasizes this new tone, calling Monardes's vernacular publications "sixteenth-century infomercial[s]" and explaining that "Monardes' text adopts the manic enthusiasm of the advertising pitch."[27] In seeking to explain why no new editions of the *Historia medicinal* were published in Spanish after 1580, Pardo-Tomás hypothesizes that Monardes's ebullience and enthusiasm for trade were quashed by the Crown following the dynastic union of Spain and Portugal in 1580.[28] I have proposed that Monardes's fervent tenor reflects his desperate recognition that Spanish markets for American medicinal plants were precarious.[29] Although there is currently no consensus regarding the abrupt end to the successes of the *Historia medicinal* in Spanish, nearly everyone agrees that Monardes wrote about exotic materia medica in an attempt to stimulate trade. If in hindsight it seems to modern readers that Monardes was manically beating a drum for imperial excess, we are not alone. That is exactly how Fragoso saw it in 1572.

Fragoso's Playful *Discursos*

The year 1570 was a watershed for the surgeon Juan Fragoso (1530–1597). He was called to court to be the personal surgeon to Anne of Austria just after she was married to her uncle, Philip II, and shortly thereafter Fragoso's influential surgical manual *Erotemas chirurgicos* went to press.[30] Fragoso had earned this recognition: he was sensible, neither cowed by classical authority nor overawed by novelty, and was as likely to write about materia medica or medical jurisprudence as surgery.[31] Despite engaging in medical debates that today smack of prurience—whether sex between women could lead to conception or whether medical examination could produce evidence of sodomy—he was cementing a reputation as a leading Spanish surgeon.[32]

Fragoso's next book, *Discursos de las cosas aromaticas*, was published in 1572. It was the year of the great supernova in Cassiopeia, which proved fitting because Fragoso was proving to be a new star in the courtly firmament.[33] The *Discursos* showed the signs of his increasing fame and esteem: it was dedicated to Juana of Austria, Philip II's sister and formerly queen regent of Spain.[34] The book, as Fragoso says in the dedicatory, was a study of the medicinal plants "que se traen de las unas Indias y de las otras" (brought from the East and West Indies). The *Discursos* was widely read in the original Spanish and reached an international readership when Israel Spach translated the book into Latin.[35] Drawing heavily on the works of others—including Monardes's *Historia medicinal*—Fragoso's book served to place the royal imprimatur on the natural historical information circulating in works by authors who lived far from court.[36]

It is thus surprising that having made his way to the center of imperial power and writing on exotic flora—a subject of intense interest to his contemporaries—Fragoso should begin the dedicatory by comparing himself to

Diogenes the Cynic, a philosopher remembered today as much for mastur-
bating in public as for making a fool of Plato.[37] Fragoso recounts the story
of Diogenes during the siege of Syracuse: while the inhabitants of the city
busily prepared to defend themselves from Philip II of Macedon, Diogenes
went about the streets noisily banging on his tub to avoid, he said, seeming
lazy in the midst of so much toil. The Cynic—Diogenes—imitates his coun-
trymen, mocking both them and himself and adding to the confusion but
not to the cause. For his part, the surgeon—Fragoso—compares the state of
thinking about the medicinal plants newly arrived from Asia and the Americas to the siege of Syracuse; materia medica, Fragoso says, is "combatida y
acossada de diversas opiniones" (attacked and assaulted by various opinions).
To avoid being left out, Fragroso, like Diogenes, decides to "rodear el vaso" of
his "entendimiento" (roll about the tub of his understanding).

In addition to imitating Diogenes, Fragoso was very literally copying
peers. He took their words verbatim.[38] Pardo-Tomás points out that Fragoso copies from Monardes but abandons the dialogue form of the *Historia medicinal*; this is fitting, because Fragoso silences all of his interlocutors,
hardly mentioning their names. As was common in works of the period, large
swaths of the *Discursos de las cosas aromáticas* are borrowed without attribution from the famous naturalists and historians of the day: Garcia da Orta,
Monardes, Clusius, Gonzalo Fernández de Oviedo y Valdés, Joan Plaça, and
so on.[39] The source of the anecdote about Diogenes—Lucian's famous *De Historia Conscribenda (How to Write History)*—lampoons historians who copy
others verbatim for their "servile imitation."[40] Publishing a book generally
composed of lifted passages, Fragoso shows almost shameless brio in alluding
to Lucian's *De Historia Conscribenda*.

Fragoso the surgeon looks around and, like Diogenes the Cynic, does
what others do and speaks as others speak. Through his reference to Diogenes, Fragoso hints at the fact that by the 1570s natural history could be
done convincingly or poorly but already possessed a style that could be aped
or affected. Like the preparations for war, the clanging of a tub, or the beating
of a drum, natural history had a *sound*.[41]

Likening his book to Diogenes's tub rolling gives the impression that Fragoso is making light of the changes in early modern pharmacopoeia caused by
the introduction of new medicines into Europe. But Fragoso's levity has political implications. The first real hint that politics are at stake in the *Discursos*
is the fact that Philip II of Macedon never conquered Syracuse and Diogenes
never lived there. The story, as Lucian recounted it in *De Historia Conscribenda*,

concerns the siege of Corinth, not Syracuse. Fragoso, however, changes the set-ting to Spanish Sicily—Syracuse, or "Siracusa," is frequently rendered "Zara-goza de Sicilia" during the period—which calls even more attention to possible parallels between Philip II of Macedon and Fragoso's future patron, Philip II of Spain.[42] In other words, Fragoso takes a story about Diogenes's absurd civic participation and only intensifies its possible political commentary by locating it within the limits of the sixteenth-century Spanish Empire. The Cynic rolled his tub because "he had nothing to do," but the surgeon sought to "aprovechar a la Republica Christana, para que sepa . . . los grandes secretos que ay en estas cosas naturales" (be of use to the Christian Republic so that the great secrets of nature contained in these plants might be known).[43] So, it is absolutely the case that Fragoso saw his book as a form of civic engagement.[44] Imitating Diogenes becomes a way of getting from natural history to politics through mimesis. At the same time, it is hard to avoid feeling that Fragoso is cynically rolling his tub while others make meaningful contributions to the Crown.

Particularly during the sixteenth century, Lucian was influential in Spain and, as Michael O. Zapalla notes, "an authority for historical writing."[45] Two important naturalists of the period—Juan de Jarava, the translator of Leon-hart Fuchs's *De historia stirpium*, and Andrés de Laguna, the translator of Dioscorides—translated Lucian.[46] Lucian was taught to first-year students of Greek at Alcalá de Henares, the university where Fragoso studied, so there are a variety of reasons to think that Fragoso would have been well acquainted with Lucian's works.[47]

Lucian's *How to Write History* was interpreted by Fragoso's contemporaries as an attack on historians "for their failure, evident in their use of poetic dic-tion, fantastic description and invention, to respect the distinction between poetic and historical writing."[48] The opposition that Lucian drew between poetry and history—between the language of fact and that of fiction—made his text of particular interest to everyone who struggled to write believable accounts about the New World, whether they were composing texts such as the *Discursos* or chronicles. Bartolomé de las Casas, for example, was partic-ularly fond of Lucian.[49] As Mary Malcolm Gaylord explains, the enthusiasm for Lucian's historiographic satire was "the period's way of turning a pervasive source of cultural anxiety—how to know the real truth about the newly dis-covered territories, how to gauge the truth-value of contemporary accounts, how to speak and write credibly about the world—into merriment."[50]

Through his allusion to Lucian's well-known anecdote about Diogenes, Fragoso announces from the outset that natural history, like cartography or colonial historiography, is an ordering system that responds as much to literary convention and political intent as to the particulars of a plant's life history. It is, at least partly, ludic. The playful humanism of Fragoso's easily recognizable (and playfully corrupt) allusion to Lucian at the very beginning of the *Discursos* and the placement of the work within Lucian's historiographic context is an acknowledgment of the tensions that Fragoso was negotiating among plants, politics, and play.

Ultimately, readers of Fragoso's dedicatory are struck by the author's ambivalence. It is not altogether clear whether writing about natural history is a sincere form of service to the Crown or merely a parody of such service. The shift is slight but significant: Monardes's drumbeating seems slightly silly in light of Fragoso's tub rolling. Publishing books about exotic materia medica might be little more than a game.

Cienfuegos, Clusius, and the Case Against Print

The shifts in the tone of and attitudes toward natural history that began with Monardes's mania and developed into Fragoso's cynical ambivalence became vehement protest in Bernardo de Cienfuegos's combative and beguiling *Historia de las plantas*.[51] It is a stunning manuscript of 5,000 pages divided into seven volumes and completed around 1630. It is one of the many natural history manuscripts produced in Spanish during the period by authors such as Álvaro de Castro, Pere Jaume Esteve, Bartolomé Marradón, Miguel Navarro, Diego de Calderón, and others. Many are manuscripts whose titles we know: Juan Gutiérrez de Santander's "Historia de las plantas," the "Tesoro de medicinas" by Gregorio López, the "Discursos medicinales" by Juan Méndez Nieto, the "Simples medicinales indianos" by Alonso de Robles Cornejo, Vicente de Burgos's "Historia Natural," Tomás Murillo y Velarde's "Tratado de raras y peregrinas yerbas halladas en Madrid," and the "Concordias medicinales de entrambos mundos" by Matías de Porres (ca. 1621).[52] Early modern bibliophiles such as Antonio de León Pinelo and Nicolás Antonio cataloged some of these manuscripts in encyclopedic works; other evidence of the early modern circulation of natural history manuscripts surfaces in offhanded mentions. In the dedicatory to his *Quid pro quo*, Fragoso praises Gutierrez de Santander's "Historia de las plantas."[53] Porres hints that Robles Cornejo's "Simples medicinales indianos" was well known.[54] Cienfuegos regarded Felipe de Pamanes's lost colonial chronicle "Notables del Perú" very highly for its descriptions of plants.[55] However, nearly all of these manuscripts are either irremediably lost or have yet to be studied in depth. As such, they represent a glaring lacuna in our knowledge of early modern Hispanic natural history.

The gap in our understanding of early modern Spanish natural history makes Cienfuegos's *Historia de las plantas* especially important. Cienfuegos's devastating critique of published naturalists' desire for fame illuminates the ways in which early modern translation and printing were themselves instruments used to constitute and shape scientific communities.

Cienfuegos did not merely write in the vernacular; he scrupulously avoided even the most basic Latin terms whenever possible. He is only interested in fixing Iberian vernacular terminology, which for him includes Spanish, Catalan, and Portuguese and the "aljamía" of Moriscos (well after their expulsion in 1615). In the case of lavender, for example, Cienfuegos notes terms in Spanish ("espliego o alburzema") in Catalan and Valenciano ("espigol") and "aljamía" ("kuzima").[56] He goes so far as to ask the reader's forgiveness for using any foreign terminology at all, explaining the need to collect vernacular terms in the wake of the expulsion of the Moriscos: Spain was "losing its knowledge of plants, which had been held by wise women and Moriscos or Africans who used them to cure and were expelled from these kingdoms" ("perdiendo su conocimiento en España que estava en mugercillas y muchos moriscos o Africanos que se curaban con ellas y fueron expelidos destos Reinos").[57] It is not simply that Cienfuegos is trying to standardize botanical terminology in Spanish; he is writing about vernacular culture in order to preserve it.

Scholars have begun to pay greater attention to the tendency of translations to eliminate or minimize the roles of native informants and women.[58] Florike Egmond also stresses that scientific plant descriptions in translation often omitted information that "belonged to local dialect, local knowledge and local situation, setting or habitat."[59] The translation of natural historical texts during the early modern period often involves reframing the national context of natural originals that have not only origins but also rich cultural traditions associated with them. It was common to recast the national, political, and cultural significance of exotic flora; this was almost always done through the strategic omission of human actors.

Although cultural reframings of the origins of natural historical knowledge have been noticed by many historians, it is still the case that modern readers tend to treat the elision or substitution of informants with less skepticism than Cienfuegos did. Both Ogilvie and Egmond see in Clusius's study of the clove an example of scrupulous natural history, which Clusius himself improved and corrected over time.[60] Things looked quite different from the vantage point of Spain.[61]

As a rule, Cienfuegos doubted that printed books could be trusted at all.[62] Of Pietro Andrea Mattioli's edition of Dioscorides, Cienfuegos says that there were so many dissimilar editions, each with its own illustrations, that even when one looks at the very same plant in two different books, it seems to be an altogether different thing: "Cada impression que se haze de las obras de Mathiolo tallando y retallando las estampas y variando el tamaño y grandeza, aunque es una misma planta, pareze diversa."[63] Cienfuegos reserved a special degree of disdain for Clusius. López Piñero and López Terrada pointed out decades ago that Cienfuegos believed that Clusius was a liar who passed off invention as fact; this only scratches the surface of Cienfuegos's incredulity.[64] According to Cienfuegos, Clusius writes about plants he has not seen, trusts the wrong people, and relies too much on authority.[65] Cienfuegos says that Clusius uses the wrong names for things: "no sé qué razón tenga Carlo Clusio en el lib. 1 de plantas raras para llamar a estas plantas espartos."[66] Clusius deludes himself and sees only what he wants to see: "Persuádese mucho Clusio."[67] Clusius cannot differentiate between natural variation (i.e., accidents) and different species.[68] The biggest problem, however, is that Clusius's books are unreliable.

On page after page of the *Historia de las plantas*, Cienfuegos pores over multiple descriptions of plants, comparing the works of Dodoens, Dalechamps (whom Cienfuegos can hardly bring himself to mention by name), Clusius, and others. In the case of Clusius's description of the *Lilium persicum* in the *Rariorum plantarum historia*, published by Plantin in 1601, Cienfuegos compares Clusius's work to Dodoens's description and illustration of the plant Dodoens calls "Corona imperialis" in his *Stirpium historiae pemptades sex*, published by Plantin in 1583 in Antwerp, as well as Dalechamps's description of the same plant in *Historia generalis plantarum*, published in two volumes in 1586 and 1587.[69] Cienfuegos points out that although the text and nomenclature vary wildly, the illustrations are nearly identical. Cienfuegos contends that Clusius, Dodoens, and Dalechamps are not representing nature; they are copying each other. Clusius's image of the "Tusai" or "Lilium persicum" is identical to Dodoens's "Corona imperialis," despite the fact that Clusius revises the history of the plant, suggests new nomenclature, and provides a new description. This seems to suggest that Clusius's image is not drawn from life but is instead drawn from his predecessor's book. By representing one another instead of nature, the works of Dodoens, Dalechamps, and Clusius reproduce cultural and ideological uniformity, then pass it off as natural history. In contesting what he perceives to be the erasures, shoddiness, and misrepresentations of reliable natural knowledge, especially knowledge about the vast Hapsburg territories, Cienfuegos signals, as Bauer and Marroquín Arredondo explain in their introduction to this volume, the processes of cultural translation that permitted the rise of early modern science.

Cienfuegos delights in insulting Clusius with epithets; for example, Cienfuegos calls him "a lover of impertinent novelties" ("amigo de novedades impertinentes").[70] But while Clusius may be a bumbling armchair naturalist, his politics, from Cienfuegos's point of view, are deadly serious. For Cienfuegos, there are very clearly two scientific cultures: one that exists in print (and is untrustworthy) and another that exists in manuscript (which the author controls). These different cultures are *antagonistic* to one another. This antagonism manifests in seemingly inconsequential matters, such as Clusius's description of the "Tulipa Hispanica."[71] After translating the entire passage from Latin into Spanish, Cienfuegos sarcastically summarizes Clusius's work: "Whenever foreigners (who are our very good friends) have the chance to steal Spain's honor, glory, reputation or fame, they do it."[72] The strategy of Clusius's natural history, according to Cienfuegos, is to rob Spain of its glory (which Bauer and Marroquín Arredondo call, in a different context in their introduction, the "geopolitics of appropriation"). The major tactic of this strategy is print. Cienfuegos suggests that the inverse, the refusal to print, is a testament to disinterestedness. What becomes clear in the *Historia de las plantas* is that trust is a function of disinterest. To print is to violate trust.

Conclusion

Cienfuegos did not simply prefer the vernacular herbal manuscript: he profoundly distrusted works of natural history printed in Latin. In light of Cienfuegos's rejection of the community of scholars that we have come to know as the Republic of Letters, Monardes's turn away from Manuzio's cosmopolitan humanism takes on a different hue. More than a stylistic change, Monardes's linguistic shift represents a change in the community that his writing presupposes. There is a movement away from abstract concerns and imagined communities and toward the specific needs of readers closer at hand. (Clusius begins his study of Iberian flora in the Canary Islands with the spectacular *Draco arbor*; Cienfuegos starts the *Historia de las plantas* with humble fodder crops, "the most common and widely used grains" ["los granos mas comunes y usuales"].)[73] Just as we have come to think of the Hapsburg Empire as a global entity and at the same time a polycentric monarchy, it is possible to situate the local significance of herbal manuscripts within the "polycentric and fluid networks of objects or processes in motion."[74] Cienfuegos also helps us understand Fragoso's playful natural history. Fragoso's *Discursos* is a kind of ludic exercise that illuminates the ways in which participation in a community of naturalists and in its work could be playfully simulated.

Cienfuegos saw enemies everywhere, but his suspicions are significant. We have not taken seriously enough the extent to which Spanish naturalists resisted the translation of their knowledge of American flora, fauna, and climate into a Northern or broadly European context. We also underestimate the extent to which early modern communities of scholarship created insiders and outsiders. The use of the vernacular natural history manuscript was one tool for the creation of communities. The cumulative effect of choices such as Cienfuegos's decision not to publish was to make Spanish natural history invisible to modern historians, as Mar Rey Bueno explains.[75] It is difficult for us now to assess the aggregate effect of Spanish natural history in manuscript—because so many of these manuscripts have been lost—or to map the contours of its implied communities.

Clearly, however, the natural history manuscript in the age of the printed herbal was a material argument about the proper locus of enunciation and consumption, a way to contest the implicit claims of universality and ubiquity that print culture made. A great deal of early modern Spanish natural history was a statement about the local utility of knowledge, the special power conferred by the possession of that knowledge, and a counternarrative of imperial universality based on "comercio" not as trade but instead as a process of cultural, ideological, and spiritual conversion. This is without a doubt a unidirectional process that locates Madrid and Seville at its center. It is also a refusal to subscribe to a supranational Republic of Letters. This knowledge allows us to see the rise of the vernacular herbal manuscript in early modern Spain as the result of conscious choices, informed by a particular understanding of how communities of scholarship should be configured.

Chapter 9

New Worlds, Ancient Theories: Reshaping Climate Theory in the Early Colonial Atlantic

Sara Miglietti

Several chapters in this volume have shed light on the crucial role that colonial geoethnography played in transforming early modern science. This chapter will move in a similar direction, delving deeper into the question of how the numerous *historiae* of American lands and peoples that were compiled by early modern travelers, settlers, and missionaries went on to stimulate further intellectual change in the Old World.[1] This chapter will focus on a particular type of geoethnographic inquiry, very popular in the early modern period and known today as "climate theory,"[2] that studied how geography and climate can influence the mode of existence of human societies. Inspired by a long tradition that dated back to the Hippocratic school of medicine (fifth century BCE), early modern climate theorists such as Levinus Lemnius (1505–1568), Juan Huarte (1529–1588), Jean Bodin (1529–1596), and Giovanni Botero (1544–1617), among many others, set out to identify the causal connections that allegedly tied the physical properties of a place to the "natural character" of its inhabitants, thus explaining, for instance, their moral and intellectual dispositions as well as their preference for particular political regimes (e.g., free republic versus despotic monarchy).[3]

For centuries after its birth in classical Greece, climate theory circulated extensively across the Western world, informing not only abstract speculation but also collective behavior in a number of ways (for instance, by orienting settlement patterns in the colonies)[4] and being constantly modified and "updated" in the process. In this sense, climate theory can be seen as a paradigmatic case of "traveling theory"—that is, in Edward Said's terms, a conceptual system that moves across time, space, and languages, changing shape each time it is received in a new cultural context.[5] The early modern period in particular was one of enhanced engagement with climate theory and thus also unsurprisingly one of accelerated change in this long-standing intellectual tradition. Precisely one of these spectacular changes will be the main focus of this chapter: namely, the shift from a "cosmological" to a "chorological" approach to the study of climate and its influence on mankind,[6] which took place between the sixteenth and seventeenth centuries for reasons not yet entirely clarified. As the chapter suggests, such a shift was not so much a direct consequence of European expansion in the New World (which according to many scholars spurred Europeans to rectify long-held geographical and climatological assumptions inherited from antiquity) but instead resulted from the implementation of new epistemic protocols for gathering, selecting, and organizing geoethnographic information. In Section 3 in particular we shall see how these new protocols informed the numerous instructions, questionnaires, and lists of queries produced at different times by four distinct institutions: the Spanish House of Trade (Casa de la Contratación, est. 1503) and the Council of the Indies (Consejo de Indias, est. 1524), both located in Seville with informants all over Spanish America; the Society of Jesus (est. 1540), based in Rome with important adjunct hubs in Lisbon and Seville and a number of colleges and missions scattered around the New World; and the Royal Society in London (est. 1662), whose wide-ranging network of correspondents included travelers to Canada, North America, and the West Indies as well as settlers residing in the American colonies. It is well known that these four institutions were all similarly invested in gathering useful knowledge from and about the colonies and that they each developed comparable strategies for collecting and managing information.[7] However, the exact extent to which these institutions communicated with and learned from one another remains open to further investigation, particularly for what concerns their geoethnographic pursuits.[8] This chapter will hopefully shed some new light in this sense. It will examine the instructions and questionnaires developed by these institutions alongside some of the accounts that they elicited in response, with the ultimate goal of explaining how these developments may have contributed to the chorological turn in early modern climate theory.

The Chorological Turn in Early Modern Climate Theory

Generally speaking, climate theories fall under two major models that could be called "cosmological" and "chorological" by way of analogy with the two main types of geographical description (cosmology and chorology) theorized in late antiquity by authors such as Ptolemy and still widely practiced in the Renaissance.[9] These two models of climate theory differ from each other in many important respects, including the way in which they each frame the very concept of climate. Cosmological climate theory primarily understands the climate of a place in terms of what we would now call its average temperature, whether hot, cold, or temperate; temperature itself, in this view, is considered to depend primarily on the place's location on the grid map of Earth, particularly with respect to its latitude (which determines the amount of solar heat that any given place receives throughout the year). A good example of this outlook can be found in the so-called Macrobian world map, reproduced here in an early sixteenth-century printed version closely modeled after medieval manuscripts (Figure 9.1). This map divides the world into five major zones: two cold zones, two temperate zones, and a Torrid Zone that stretches across the equator.[10] Cosmological climate theorists built on this rough subdivision to formulate assumptions about the human types inhabiting each of these zones: for instance, they argued that people living close to the Torrid Zone (the Torrid Zone itself was for a long time considered uninhabitable) had weak bodies and keen minds, while they assumed the reverse—that is, strong bodies and weak minds—of people living in cold regions. As for the inhabitants of temperate regions, they were thought to have a similarly temperate constitution, which made them much more likely to grow into well-rounded, civilized human beings.

The chorological model portrayed climate in quite different terms, namely as the result of complex interactions between a number of site-specific factors that were (rightly) thought to influence heat and rainfall distribution as well as other local meteorological phenomena. While cosmological climate theory revolved around broadly sketched climatic zones, chorological climate theory focused on much smaller regions and analyzed these regions in considerable detail. Moving from the empirical observation that places located in the same latitude often present striking differences in climate, chorological climate theorists explained such differences in light of specific landscape features such as the nature of the terrain (e.g., flat or hilly), the qualities of local bodies of

Figure 9.1. Zonal world map. Macrobius, *In somnium Scipionis libri duo* (Cologne: [Eucharius Hirtzhorn], 1521), sig. c4v.

water (e.g., running or standing), and the type of soil (e.g., sandy or rocky, fertile or barren). These and other features were held responsible for shaping local microclimates within the broader climatic regions defined by latitude. A good example of this perspective can be seen in a map of Rome drawn for Marsilio Cagnati's neo-Hippocratic treatise on the salubrity of Roman air, which was printed in Rome in 1599 (Figure 9.2). This medical-environmental map zooms in on specific geographical features—such as Rome's seven hills and the Tiber River—in order to explain why different parts of the city proved more or less conducive to physical and temperamental diseases among local inhabitants.[11] Like Cagnati, many other early modern climate theorists relied

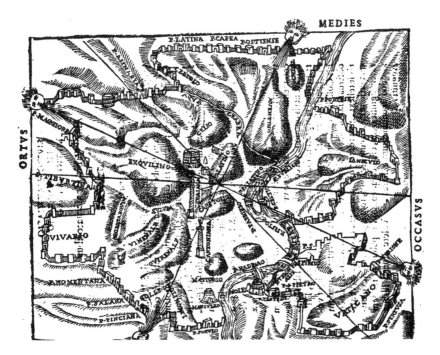

Figure 9.2. Map of Rome emphasizing landscape features. Marsilio Cagnati, *De Romani aëris salubritate* (Rome: Luigi Zanetti, 1599), 55.

on the site-specific nature of climate to explain the presence of different human types within the same band of latitude—an experiential truth that cosmological climate theory could not apparently account for.

Cosmological and chorological climate theories thus seem to differ from each other in crucial respects. While both models posit a direct causal correlation between climate and human nature, they disagree on matters of great importance, such as what climate is, what determines it, and the proper scale at which it should be analyzed, and also whether it is possible to ascertain the climate of a place—and therefore the natural character of its inhabitants—based simply on the place's geographical coordinates (primarily latitude, although some climate theorists, including Jean Bodin, ascribed a role to longitude as well). While cosmological climate theorists argued that latitude was a reasonably accurate predictor of climate and climatic influence, chorological climate theorists objected that specific landscape features ought to be taken into account as well. Consequently, cosmological climate theorists tended to operate primarily with the classic tools of mathematical cosmography, whereas chorological climate theorists often incorporated some degree of observational fieldwork into their procedures.[12] From the point of view of method, then, cosmological climate theory appears to be predominantly deductive and predictive, while chorological climate theory is fundamentally inductive and, at least to some extent, empirical.

These undeniable differences should not, however, be overstated. Surprising as it may seem in light of what has just been said, cosmological and chorological climate theories coexisted side by side with relative ease well into the Renaissance. The reason for this is that the two models were not perceived as mutually exclusive but instead as complementary. To be sure, theorists often had preferences for one or the other model: to take two famous examples from classical antiquity, Aristotle's approach in Book 7 of *Politics*[13] is predominantly cosmological, while the Hippocratic treatise *Airs, Waters, Places* leans decidedly toward the chorological model. Still, it was not rare for authors to experiment with both models, whether in different places in their corpus (Ptolemy, for example, alternated a chorological approach in his *Geography* with a cosmological approach in his *Tetrabiblos*) or within the very same work, apparently without any sense of self-contradiction. Good examples of this are the Spanish Dominican Bartolomé de Las Casas (1484–1566), who combined the two models to describe the climate of Hispaniola in his *Apologética historia sumaria* (largely composed around 1551–1552),[14] and the aforementioned Jean Bodin, whose systematic overview of climate theory in his *Methodus ad facilem historiarum cognitionem* (1566) begins at the general level of cosmology but subsequently moves down to the detailed level of chorology, in the top-down fashion typical of many early modern cosmographies.[15]

This dynamic coexistence of cosmological and chorological climate theories was still the norm in the second half of the sixteenth century, but things were bound to change dramatically in later periods. Over the course of the seventeenth century, a hiatus opened between cosmological and chorological climate theories. Attention now shifted to the latter, while the former fell out of favor and became increasingly marginal to the climatological debate, only to resurface again in the eighteenth century.[16] What triggered this shift is still unclear. A common explanation connects it to the geographical explorations, suggesting that empirical observation of unfamiliar climates led Europeans to reconsider their long-held assumption that latitude was the primary determinant of climate and thus to abandon cosmological climate theory in favor of its chorological counterpart.[17] European travelers to the New World specifically observed that places located in the same latitude were comparatively much colder in America than in Europe (largely as a result of the mitigating effect of the Gulf Stream in Europe, a phenomenon that early modern observers were not completely unaware of but failed to relate to the different climatic conditions in the two continents). American climates were perceived as overall more extreme than their European counterparts, with colder, longer winters and exceedingly hot summers. Yet European settlers also frequently remarked that the American climate was becoming more and more temperate as forests were cleared, agriculture was developed, and urban centers multiplied in the wake of European colonization.[18] Experience thus seemed to prove that landscape, not latitude, was the single most important factor in determining the climate of a place, so much so that the conscious or unconscious manipulation of particular landscape features—for instance, through changing patterns of land use—could go so far as to alter the climate of a whole country.[19]

If we trust this dominant narrative, the chorological turn in seventeenth-century climate theory should stand as a bright example of the revolutionary power of empirical observation, further confirming the crucial role that the great discoveries played in redefining early modern science. It seems, however, that such an account does not pay sufficient attention to the flexibility and resilience of ancient epistemic paradigms. Following Anthony Grafton, one could point out that for a good century after Christopher Columbus, the new empirical knowledge flowing in from the Americas was incorporated with surprising ease into the conceptual frameworks inherited from antiquity.[20] Even the most disruptive piece of evidence could be used to reinforce traditional doctrines rather than to challenge them. Thus, Bodin invoked the new geographical discoveries to buttress the established worldview based on Holy Writ and classical authorities,[21] while the Jesuit José de Acosta—a famously outspoken critic of Aristotle's meteorology, at least on the surface—structured his understanding of South American climates around the principles of Peripatetic natural philosophy.[22]

These and other examples seem to suggest that empirical evidence alone is not enough to cause the collapse of long-standing epistemic paradigms. What, then, is needed to generate deep conceptual change? The next section will sketch out an alternative answer, suggesting that the chorological turn in seventeenth-century climate theory owed less to the inflow of fresh geoethnographic information than to the new strategies that were being developed for soliciting, organizing, and validating such information; less to the *content* of knowledge than to its *forms* and *structures*—that is, to the ways in which knowledge was framed and communicated.

From Seville to Rome: The "Birth" of the Questionnaire

Around the middle of the sixteenth century, geoethnography was one of the fastest-developing fields of knowledge in the Latin West. The flood of incoming information about the so-called New World and its native inhabitants found a place in the growing body of natural-historical and ethnographic literature avant la lettre, including travel accounts, cosmographies, and natural-philosophical treatises that comprised anthropological sections.[23] While the Iberian Peninsula was one of the earliest and most important epicenters for the collection and systematization of geoethnographic knowledge in this period, the phenomenon quickly spread to other European regions, gaining particular momentum in countries such as France, England, the Low Countries, and some German-speaking territories that engaged more or less extensively in colonization efforts in the Americas and elsewhere.[24]

In a context of increased geopolitical competition, the acquisition and dissemination of information about the New World was caught in tensions between secrecy and transparency, rivalry and collaboration, as María Portuondo has stressed in her landmark study of cosmography and empire in the early Iberian Atlantic.[25] In Spain, two institutions were entrusted with the delicate task of storing geoethnographic information safely while also making it easily accessible and exploitable for actual governmental practice: these were the House of Trade and the Council of the Indies. Both institutions were based in Seville, both had been established in the early stages of Spanish colonial expansion in Central and South America, and both became instrumental for collecting and managing information of all kinds about the New World. To do so, these institutions developed new data-gathering strategies, which included the distribution of standardized questionnaires among travelers to or residents in the American colonies.[26] While this practice was first introduced by House of Trade pilots and cosmographers in the early decades of the sixteenth century, it was later brought to perfection by the Council of the Indies, particularly under the directorship of Juan de Ovando (1515–1575), who thoroughly reformed the council's administrative structure and made considerable efforts to establish more systematic mechanisms for collecting and managing various types of information of colonial interest.[27] Upon Ovando's initiative, a first questionnaire in thirty-seven chapters was circulated in 1569 among colonial officials and informants in the Indies. Other questionnaires followed in 1571 and 1573, and a final list of fifty queries, drafted shortly after Ovando's death, was sent to the presses in 1584. The focus in many of these questionnaires was first and foremost on the environmental properties of the site described and on the character of local native populations. Such an emphasis on geoethnographic material was not new: already in 1533, in a royal proclamation to the Audiencia of Mexico, Charles V had recommended the collection of data about "the qualities of the land and its wonders" and the "types of native people [who] are there."[28] But compared to these earlier and rather vague instructions, the later questionnaires were much more elaborate "tools of inquiry" that often included "precise specifications for how questions were to be answered."[29]

This is especially true of geoethnographic queries, which became increasingly detailed over the years. For instance, the *Memorial* of Alonso de Santa Cruz, composed in the mid-1550s, prompted travelers and explorers to provide thorough information about the environmental characteristics of each site ("whether it is mountainous or flat, whether it is full of wetlands and marshes") as well as about specific landscape features (rivers, mountains, lakes, springs), natural resources, and the character and customs of indigenous populations.[30] The questionnaires that were drafted in the 1570s and 1580s following Ovando's guidelines continued and strengthened this trend. For instance, the *Memorial* that the Council of the Indies issued in 1584 for Nueva Galicia included questions about the region's climate ("whether it is very cold or hot, humid or dry; whether it rains often or not and at what times rain is more or less frequent; and what are the strongest winds that blow there and from what direction they blow and in what periods of the year"), landscape features ("whether the land is even or rugged, flat or mountainous, abounding in rivers and springs or not, rich or poor of water, full or not of fertile meadows, fecund or barren of fruits and other sustenance"), and latitude ("the height or latitude of the pole . . . or, in which days of the year the sun does not project any shadow whatsoever at noon"), placed alongside queries about the number, character, and customs of local inhabitants ("whether there are many or few Indians, and if there were more or fewer before than now and if so why; if there are any, whether they are settled in fixed, nucleated settlements; and the size and nature of their mental skills, inclinations, and way of life").[31]

This combination of environmental analysis and ethnographic inquiry similarly characterizes the reports compiled in response to the council's questionnaires, generally by colonial officials. Later known as *Relaciones de Indias*, these reports usually took the form of itemized lists of answers, arranged in the same order as the queries in the questionnaire: they typically started with detailed descriptions of the environmental properties of the site at hand, followed by remarks about the physical and moral constitution of local indigenous populations. For instance, a 1586 *relación* about the Andine region of Vilcas Huamán, in modern-day Peru, started out by saying that most villages in the area were located in "healthy sites and climates" (*asiento y temple sano*) and went on to observe that native inhabitants tended to enjoy good health, aside from occasional bouts of scrofula (*lamparones*), fevers (*calenturas*), and abscesses (*apostemas*).[32] In the same year, the author of a *relación* on the *repartimiento* of San Francisco de Atunrucana y Laramati, in what is now the Huamanga region of Peru, reported that the inhabitants of La Concepción and Guanca, two low-lying sites, were often ill on account of the excessive heat, whereas those who lived in the "well-tempered" (*de buenos temples*) villages up in the sierra were free from disease.[33] In both cases, the juxtaposition of remarks about local environmental properties and about the complexion of indigenous populations invited the implicit conclusion that temperament and climate were intrinsically connected.

While Spanish colonial administrators played a fundamental role in promoting the questionnaire form in the sixteenth century, the use of questionnaires as information-gathering tools was not unparalleled at the time. Soon after its official establishment in 1540, the Society of Jesus began to use similar strategies to collect and manage information of various kinds, including geoethnographic data on foreign territories where the society had recently established colleges and missions for the propagation of the Christian faith.[34] Toward the end of the sixteenth century, these territories included Brazil (the first Jesuit mission in the Americas, founded in 1549), Peru, Paraguay, Florida, and New France (i.e., modern-day Quebec).[35]

Missionary concerns explain not only the centrality of geoethnographic knowledge to the Jesuit *ratio studiorum*[36] but also the special place that climate theory occupies in the works of Jesuit or Jesuit-educated writers such as the aforementioned José de Acosta, whose *Historia natural y moral de las Indias* is an important document of Jesuit climatological ideas,[37] and Giovanni Botero, whose *Relationi universali* (1591–1596)—an ambitious geopolitical description of the known world—is structured around the notion of environmental influence.[38] Further demonstration of Jesuit interest in climate theory comes from the *litterae annuae*, reports compiled once a year from the overseas provinces that contained various kinds of information about life in the missions.

Though initially meant for manuscript circulation within the Society of Jesus, these letters soon became so popular that they began to appear in print, either individually or as part of larger collections such as the best-selling *Lettres édifiantes et curieuses écrites des missions étrangères* (1703–1776). The engrossing descriptions of exotic lands and peoples contained in these letters certainly did much to captivate a much larger readership than originally intended.[39] But these descriptions were also meant to fulfill another, perhaps more fundamental, function: namely, to convey information of immediate operative value.[40] As early as 1554, the founder of the Society of Jesus, Ignatius of Loyola, had instructed missionaries to the overseas provinces to send detailed reports of the "cosmography of the regions to which they travel," the climate and wildlife found in those regions, and any "extraordinary" properties of the land.[41] Ignatius explained that such information was of crucial importance because "the state of the air" and "the nature of places" were known to have direct repercussions on "human mores."[42] From a missionary perspective, the value of climate theory rested primarily in the fact that it enabled one to understand the character of indigenous populations and thus devise effective strategies for evangelizing them.

Ignatius's instructions for missionary letter writing mainly revolved around content, but other Jesuits also took a keen interest in form and structure; indeed, precise guidelines in this sense were issued since the early days of the Society of Jesus.[43] The template of the *litterae annuae* in particular was formalized in 1547 by the society's secretary, Juan Alfonso de Polanco (1517–1576), in a short text that was subsequently included in the *Constitutions* of 1558.[44] While Polanco's instructions for letter writing (*Reglas que deven observar acerca del escribir*) contain no specific mention of geoethnographic information and no indication of how such information should be gained and organized, the recurring pattern visible in the geoethnographic sections of many Jesuit letters suggests the existence of separate guidelines, possibly in the form of questionnaires dictating patterns for the collection and communication of this type of data. More research in the Society of Jesus archives would be necessary to confirm this point, but recent studies on Jesuit information-management practices show that by the latter half of the sixteenth century, the society had developed a highly standardized questionnaire-based method of gathering knowledge on various matters. Particularly strong evidence in this sense comes from Marcus Friedrich's work on Jesuit *informationes*. These documents were used to collect information about the moral and intellectual qualities of individual Jesuits at crucial steps in their career so as to decide, for instance, "which type of religious vows should be taken by candidates, who was to govern, who was to be dismissed, who was to become a missionary," and so forth.[45] Friedrich has demonstrated that from the 1560s onward, questionnaires became the most commonly used means for gaining such information because of the "high degree of standardization" that they allowed. Since the *informationes* solicited personal assessments that could be tainted by subjective bias, "prefabricated questionnaires" based on a "standard evaluation template" were soon introduced to ensure objectivity and fairness. Each type of *informatio* (there were several: *ad gradum, ad gubernationem, ad dimittendum*, etc.) proposed the same set of twelve or so questions "about biographical detail, virtues, physical appearance, character, and behavior"; answers should follow in the same order as the questions and should never exceed the space allotted in the form.[46] These general principles remained fairly constant, but the actual way in which the questionnaires were filled out seems to have evolved over time. While the earliest known examples of compiled *informationes* (ca. 1595) feature short paragraphs of narrative prose, toward the end of the seventeenth century this discursive form was progressively abandoned in favor of greater concision, and answers were gradually reduced to "single qualifying words" inserted into "a pre-fabricated cloze."[47]

From Rome to London: The Royal Society's "Heads" and "Queries"

The trends documented for the Society of Jesus find some interesting parallels in other institutional contexts over the course of the seventeenth century. A case in point is that of the early Royal Society, yet another institution deeply invested in collecting "useful knowledge" about non-European countries and their inhabitants.[48] One of the first initiatives taken by the society shortly after its foundation in 1662 was to establish a worldwide network of correspondents to contribute toward the compilation of a "natural history of all countries." At the time, it must be noted, "natural history" encompassed not only the world of nature but also that of humans: in the case of the Royal Society, this inclusion of "the human world within the remit of the natural historian" was a direct consequence of the firm belief of many of its early fellows in the influence of environmental factors over human beings.[49] Henry Oldenburg (1619–1677), the society's long-term secretary, spelled out such a belief most explicitly in his preface to the March 1676 issue of the society's journal, the *Philosophical Transactions*. Here, Oldenburg called for an exhaustive and "methodical" natural history of "the great variety of soyls, fountains, rivers, lakes etc. in the several places of this globe; and of the manifold effects, productions and operations of the sun, and perhaps of other celestial influences, upon them all; or of subterranean steams, or peculiar winds, arising at state or uncertain times."[50] Oldenburg argued that such a history would clarify, among other things, why "the shapes, features, statures, and all outward appearances, and also the intrinsick mentals or intellectuals of mankind" varied so greatly in different parts of the world.[51] The New World occupied an especially important place in this grand scheme, for Oldenburg noted that the relatively pristine environments of "many parts of America, and of some countreys remote, and thinly inhabited in the North" could offer more accurate information about "the nature of the places" and its influence on living beings than the "richly cultivated and polite neighbourhood of France, Italy, Spain, Germany, etc.," where "culture, improvement and artificial ornaments" had deeply changed the land as well as its inhabitants.[52]

Just like Spanish colonial administrators and Jesuit superiors, Royal Society fellows turned to the questionnaire as an effective tool for collecting information.[53] This continuity in data-gathering strategies may be more than just coincidental, especially if seen in light of recent scholarship that has stressed the impact of Iberian and Jesuit science on the early Royal Society.[54] The numerous lists of "heads" or "queries" now preserved in the society's archives in London were for the most part drafted in the 1660s and early 1670s by a group of fellows that included Robert Boyle (1627–1691), Thomas Henshaw (1618–1700), John Hoskyns (1634–1705), Robert Moray (1609–1673), and Oldenburg himself. Some of these questionnaires were disseminated in manuscript form among selected correspondents: for instance, a list titled "Enquiries for Barbary" was sent to Sir Henry Howard, the English ambassador in Morocco, and to other contacts in the region in 1669;[55] another list of questions about Brazil, in Latin ("Inquirenda per Brasiliam"), was addressed in 1671 to Thomas Hill (possibly a younger brother of Abraham Hill, the society's treasurer), who promised to forward them to a Dutch Jesuit in Salvador de Bahia—"a very curious, ingenious and inquisitive man, and especially desirous to serve the Royal Society," who had lived in Brazil for several years and was said to know the country well.[56] Other questionnaires were printed in the *Philosophical Transactions*, thus reaching a wider public: in a single year (1667), the society's journal published lists of queries on Turkey, Persia, Surat and other East Indian regions; Virginia and the Bermudas; Guyana and Brazil; Hungary and Transylvania; Egypt, Guiney, and Greenland.

These questionnaires all shared a similar template: a series of numbered questions, following one another with no apparent order or connection (an order actually *did* exist,[57] but responders were not expected to grasp it; they were, in fact, actively discouraged from doing so, for reasons that will become clear later). The queries solicited information about aspects such as the "temperature of ye air," the "diseases ye inhabitants are most subject to," the "variations of ye weather" and the types of "meteors it is most wont to breed," "the nature of ye soyle" and other "observables" of the land (such as mountains, rivers, lakes, ponds, and springs), and finally "ye inhabitants, men and women, what are their inclinations, dyet, aeconomy, conveniences of living, their strength, agility, stature, shape, color."[58] This template had been set by Robert Boyle with his *General Heads for a Natural History of a Countrey, Great or Small*, written on Oldenburg's request in the spring of 1666 and published shortly afterward in the *Philosophical Transactions*.[59] The great majority of questionnaires on individual countries that were drafted after 1666 followed Boyle's model closely and departed from it only in requesting additional information about matters specific to a particular country. There is, however, one major difference between Boyle's *General Heads* and the later lists of queries compiled in its wake. While Boyle's list opens with questions about the "longitude and latitude of the place" (specifically insofar as these are "of moment in reference to the observations about the air") and the "fixt starrs" and "constellations" to which the place is "said to be subject to,"[60] later questionnaires usually leave out cosmographical and astrological considerations altogether and move straight into the second of Boyle's heads, concerning air and meteorological phenomena. In 1669 Oldenburg adopted this simplified format in his suggested restructuring of Boyle's *General Heads*, which is preserved in an autograph manuscript in the Royal Society archives (Figure 9.3).[61] Although Oldenburg's revised list of *General Heads of Inquiries for All Countries* was never printed and therefore enjoyed a more limited circulation than Boyle's original version,[62] it is an important document of wider trends within the early Royal Society. In particular, as the next section will show in further detail, Oldenburg's manuscript testifies to shifting notions of climate and climatic influence in this period and more specifically to the marginalization of cosmological factors in favor of chorological ones.

As we have already seen in the case of the Jesuit *informationes* studied by Friedrich, responders to Royal Society questionnaires were expected to answer each question concisely in the order provided and without adding

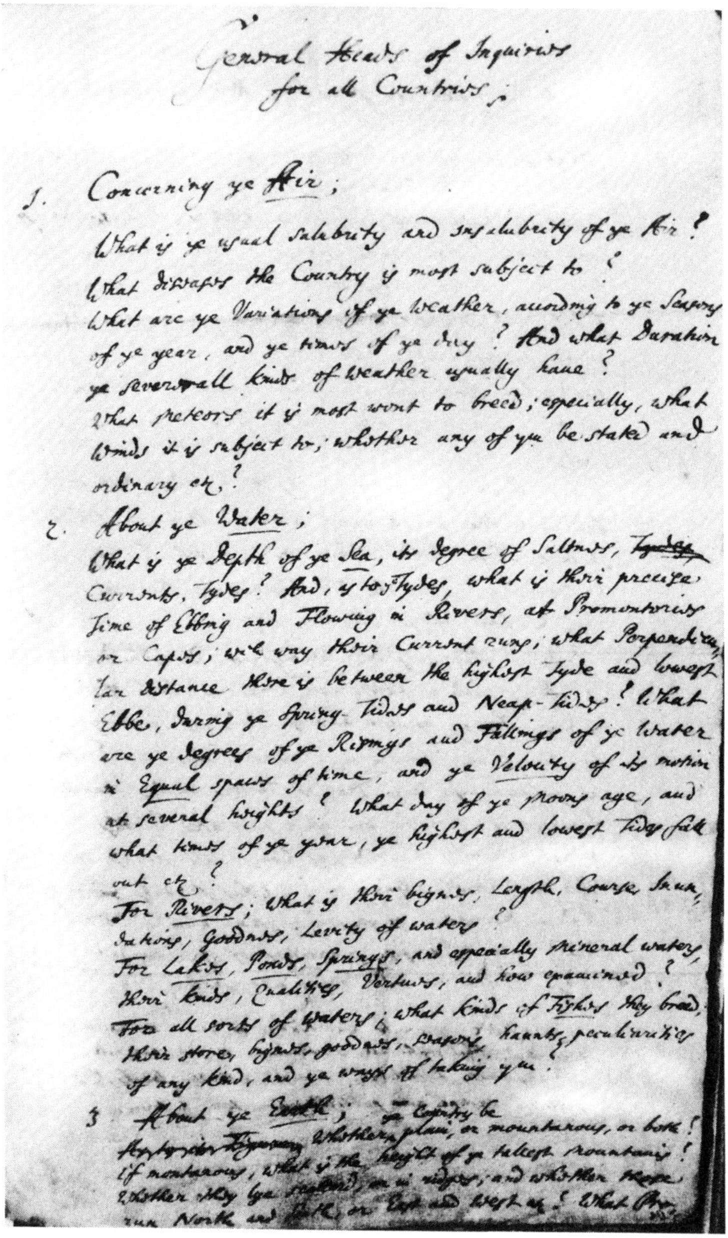

General Heads of Inquiries
for all Countries;

1. Concerning ye Air;

What is ye usual salubrity and insalubrity of ye Air?
What diseases the Country is most subject to?
What are ye Variations of ye Weather, according to ye Seasons of ye year, and ye times of ye day? And what Duration ye severall kind of weather usually have?
What meteors it is most wont to breed; especially, what winds it is subject to; whether any of ym be stated and ordinary etc?

2. About ye Water;

What is ye Depth of ye Sea, its Degree of Saltnes, ~~Tydes~~ Currents, Tydes? And, is to Tydes, what is their precise Time of Ebbing and Flowing in Rivers, at Promontories or Capes; wch way their Current runs; what Perpendicular distance there is between the highest Tyde and lowest Ebbe, during ye Spring-Tides and Neap-tides? What are ye degrees of ye Risings and ~~Fallings~~ Fallings of ye Water in Equal spaces of time, and ye Velocity of its motion at severall heights? What day of ye moons age, and what times of ye year, ye highest and lowest Tydes fall out etc?

For Rivers; What is their bignes, Length, Course, Shun, duration, Goodnes, Levity of waters?

For Lakes, Ponds, Springs, and especially mineral waters, their kinds, Qualities, Vertues, and how examined?

For all sorts of waters; what kinds of Fishes they breed, their stores, bignes, goodnes, seasons, haunts, peculiarities of any kind, and ye wayes of taking ym.

3. About ye ~~Earth~~; ... whether plain, or mountainous, or both? If mountainous, what is the height of ye tallest mountains; whether they lye ... in ridges, and whether they ... run North and ..., or East and west etc? What ...

Figure 9.3. Henry Oldenburg, "General Heads of Inquiries for All Countries" (October 6, 1669), London, Royal Society, Classified Papers, 19/43. Photo: Sara Miglietti. Courtesy of the Royal Society Library and Archives.

any extraneous material. Evidence from surviving sets of answers suggests that these instructions were taken very seriously.[63] Responders should also restrain from articulating transitions between the answers, as one would normally do in account or narrative; they were instead required to respect and replicate the fragmented nature of the questionnaire in their own responses by offering discrete facts in a disconnected fashion. As a result of this scattered appearance, when some of these texts were prepared for publication in the *Philosophical Transactions*, Oldenburg (in his capacity as editor in chief) occasionally intervened to modify them by, for instance, introducing connecting words or phrases that would improve readability.[64]

Textual dispersion, it would seem, was not an unintended by-product but rather a carefully crafted effect of the questionnaire form. Indeed, such textual dispersion was integral to the epistemic strategies that leading Royal Society fellows such as Boyle were eager to promote at the time. Harriet Knight has shown how Boyle deliberately cultivated textual incoherence as a way to collect vast amounts of "factual data" without running the risk of falling into "premature and fanciful systematization."[65] A similar (and equally Baconian) concern with pretheoretical "matters of fact" also inspired the society's geoethnographic questionnaires, which solicited raw data devoid of any narrative or argumentative arrangement in order to reduce the danger of theoretical or ideological bias.[66] The form of the questionnaire was, in other words, a rhetorical strategy in the service of a particular epistemology.

In this respect, the Royal Society's lists of "heads" and "queries" for the collection of geoethnographic knowledge continue a long trajectory that, as this chapter has shown, can be traced back to the introduction of questionnaires as an information-gathering technology in early sixteenth-century Spain and to their subsequent adoption by Jesuit missionaries around the globe. Along the way, the questionnaire form evolved in the sense of an increasing systematization and standardization, and important changes also occurred in the form and structure of the responses prompted by these questionnaires. While the *Relaciones de Indias* of the 1570s and 1580s were still predominantly narrative in character, the narrative component was gradually reduced in early seventeenth-century Jesuit *informationes* and virtually disappeared (at least in principle) in the responses that Royal Society correspondents returned to London throughout the last third of the seventeenth century. By encouraging the traveler-reporter to uncouple description from explanation and privilege the former over the latter, Royal Society questionnaires performed the crucial epistemic function of "teaching the eye to see" in a different way, beyond—and if necessary against—long-standing conceptual frameworks.[67]

Conclusion: The Questionnaire Form and the Chorological Turn

Among the long-standing conceptual frameworks that the questionnaire form contributed to unmaking and remaking was the age-old theory of climatic influence. As we have seen at the beginning of this chapter, climate theory underwent a deep transformation over the course of the seventeenth century, as the long-dominant cosmological model was gradually replaced by its chorological counterpart. The chorological turn in seventeenth-century climate theory has often been explained in light of the new empirical evidence that had become available in the aftermath of the great explorations. In this view, the discovery of the habitability of the Torrid Zone and the realization that vastly different climates coexisted within the same band of latitude contributed to discrediting cosmological conceptions of climate. This chapter has taken a different approach to the question, examining how changes in the form and structure of geoethnographic discourse may have contributed to reshaping climate as a scientific object by promoting a new way of gathering and communicating knowledge about it.[68] Particular attention has been given to the geoethnographic questionnaires that were issued by institutions such as the Council of the Indies, the Society of Jesus, and the Royal Society and then widely disseminated through extensive networks of correspondents around the globe. The adoption of questionnaires as a means of collecting geoethnographic information thoroughly modified the form of climatological discourse by replacing explanation with description and by reducing the narrative component traditionally prevalent in travel accounts. In so doing, questionnaires contributed to redirecting the traveler's gaze toward specific "matters of fact" and away from unwarranted generalizations, causal inferences, and premature systematizations. By forcing the traveler-reporter into an artificial, rhetorically induced condition of pretheoretical experience, questionnaires helped call into question (or at least suspend judgment on) long-standing epistemic paradigms, thus also paving the way for the gradual emergence of new ones.

In many ways, the story reconstructed in this chapter has been that of a fourfold process of translation: across languages, disciplines and genres, geographical spaces, and institutional sites of knowledge production. But it is also a story of epistemic change and a study in its dynamics. How do highly

resilient conceptual paradigms change and evolve? In the case of climate theory, it seems likely that the change took place, or at least became possible,
when the imposition of a new layout for the collection and communication of
geoethnographic information modified the ways in which early modern travelers encountered, experienced, and represented New World environments
and the people in them. When seen in this light, the chorological turn in
seventeenth-century conceptions of climate appears as a subparadigm shift
(from cosmological to chorological climate theory) that took place *within* the
overarching paradigm of climate theory—leaving the central notion of climate's influence of man unscathed but thoroughly transforming the terms in
which this notion was construed, with far-reaching implications for its theoretical and practical uses.

Clear indications of such a shift can be seen, for instance, in editions
and translations of sixteenth- and early seventeenth-century cosmographies
that were later reprinted without the introductory cosmological sections.[69]
Another telling sign comes from Oldenburg's revision of Boyle's *General
Heads* in 1669 (examined in the previous section), which similarly reflects a
departure from the cosmological and astrological components of traditional
climate theories in favor of a wholly meteorological and chorological outlook.
Overall, this chapter has argued that such changes were facilitated by the
widespread adoption of questionnaires as a means of soliciting information
from travelers. The revolutionary force of these questionnaires rests less in the
content of the information conveyed by those who responded to them than in
the particular *forms* in which both questions and answers were framed and
expressed. Initially introduced as a practical strategy for managing information flows, these questionnaires generated a chain of epistemic consequences
that reached the very core of European natural-philosophical thought, ultimately extending to the time-honored doctrine of climatic influence.

Part IV

Translation in the Transoceanic Enlightenment

Chapter 10

Columbian Circulations in the North Atlantic World:
François-Madeleine Vallée in Eighteenth-Century
Île Royale

Christopher Parsons

Pehr Kalm arrived in New France in 1749, taking advantage of the cessation of the War of the Austrian Succession to collect plants for his colleague and mentor, Carolus Linnaeus. In his account of his travel, Kalm wrote that "not a single botanist had yet researched or carefully described the plants that are found" in New France; he would be the first scientist to travel to the colony.[1] Kalm's *récit de voyage* was a heroic narrative par excellence where even the seas themselves seemed to conspire against his efforts to bring Enlightenment science to this distant colony.[2] To complete his expedition, he wrote, he principally had to rely on his own trained eye, translating colonial roads, forests, and fields into inches and miles. Plants he translated into discrete features, each measured with an exact attention that transformed Kalm into one observer in what was a veritable army of standardizing travelers whom Linnaeus sent worldwide.[3]

As the chapters of this collection amply demonstrate, by the eighteenth century the natural and human environments of the Americas had been transformed through centuries of contact, exchange, and study. We might push further, following the invitation of Ralph Bauer and Jaime Marroquín Arredondo in their introductory chapter to recall translation's signal of both spatial and linguistic movement and to understand early American environments as translated spaces. Cognitively and linguistically, centuries of cultural and ecological encounters had produced translated knowledges, botanical and zoological pidgins, and novel forms of knowledge production and dissemination.[4] Spatially, the well-documented Columbian Exchange and the neo-Columbian exchange translated plants and animals across great distances through commercial, imperial, and often informal networks of exchange.[5] An Atlantic history of science is a history of these movements: of texts, people, flora, and fauna.

Kalm, as much as he embraced a discourse of heroic discovery, was demonstrably aware of the centrality of these translations in forming and conceptualizing the American environments through which he traveled. Kalm was routinely careful to explain his reliance on local naturalists, aboriginal guides, colonists, and missionaries. Even if he claimed the privilege of being the first botanist in the region, he understood that this was a peopled landscape. His pursuit of useful and novel plants to bring back to Sweden and Linnaeus meant that Kalm became as much a collector of testimony as specimens.[6] He repeatedly showed himself to be particularly interested in collecting the knowledge of aboriginal communities, yet he most often gathered indigenous knowledge from colonists and missionaries he had the good fortune to have as guides.[7] A priest, for example, told Kalm that he himself had seen a *sauvage* use red osier dogwood to cure one of his friends of dysuria, or painful urination.[8] Likewise, Monsieur Cartier, one of Kalm's many local guides in the colony, told him that "goose tongue" was eaten by indigenous peoples farther to the north.[9]

It is because of Kalm's attention to this local knowledge that we know as much about it as we do. Kalm's text is remarkable as much for its capacious project and attention to detail as it is for its singularity in an era where little else was published about colonial Canada's natural environments that represented these colonial perspectives. While colonial authors such as Nicolas Denys and Pierre Boucher had written natural histories of Laurentian and Acadian settlements in the seventeenth century, there was little that could equal their ambition or skill produced by colonists or colonial promoters in the eighteenth century. By this time, metropolitan-trained naturalists Michel Sarrazin and Jean-François Gaultier had brought not only new techniques for observation and collection but also a scientific culture that accepted the authority of the Paris-based Académie Royale des Sciences. Much of their work languished in manuscript, unpublished in their day and often lost in the ensuing centuries. Whereas in the seventeenth century the history of science in New France maps readily onto familiar narratives of a growing confidence in explaining the New World to audiences in the Old World, by the eighteenth century this history might easily be framed as a footnote to a broader narrative of the centralization of the scientific culture of the French Atlantic world.[10]

My point of entry into this discussion is a document titled *Mémoire sur les plantes qui sont dans la caise B*, which was written by a colonial engineer, François-Madeleine Vallée, and sent from the fortified city of Louisbourg to Paris in or around 1725. The *Mémoire* is a short text with great ambition; it is a document unique in its attention to capturing the complexities of colonial ecosystems and knowledge. Composed of only fourteen handwritten pages, the *Mémoire* attempted to relate the littoral ecosystems of Île Royale (now Cape Breton Island) to a wider Atlantic—if ultimately Paris-based—audience. The focus of the text was eleven different plants presented in no discernible order, each of which, the author suggested, had been observed and collected in or around 1725. Five of these descriptions were complemented by physical leaves that were pressed between the pages.[11]

Yet alone among texts that embraced Latin names and standardized descriptions, the *Mémoire* frequently privileged the expertise of local indigenous peoples (likely Mi'kmaq). In his descriptions of maritime and coastal plants—ranging from "Kokocar" to the "herbe à jean hebert"—he also outlined the equally fluid boundaries between indigenous and colonial knowledge. The *Mémoire* therefore does not simply provide a glimpse into the botanical knowledge of the indigenous communities of Île Royale. Rather, the text provides evidence of extensive and multidirectional translation between aboriginal and colonial knowledge systems and between French and indigenous ecologies. When the *Mémoire* arrived in Paris, however, the content of the text was dismissed. Vallée's document was ultimately valued primarily for the dried plants pressed between its pages and was archived in the Royal Garden's herbarium, where it survives to this day. Illustrative of both the extent of cross-cultural communication and the selective erasure of indigenous contributions to European science, the production, circulation, and reception of this singular document therefore provides a rare insight into the complicated relationship between cultural and ecological exchanges in an age of translation.

François-Madeleine Vallée might at first glance seem like an unexpected figure through which to explore the history of cultural and ecological exchange in early America. The exact circumstances under which he and his family arrived in Louisbourg in 1723 remain uncertain. In a letter that he wrote in the first year after his arrival, Vallée referred to the cause of his transatlantic immigration obliquely, describing only a "lettre de cachet" that sent him to the colony and that excluded him from most work once he was there.[12] While the charges that led to his exile remained unspecified, Vallée wanted to prove himself useful to colonial officials to overcome any lingering doubts about his character.

Once in Louisbourg, Vallée inserted himself into the intellectual networks of the eighteenth-century French Atlantic world. He arrived at a moment when the entire region was in a state of considerable upheaval following the Treaty of Utrecht in 1713 and the cession of much of Acadia (in what is now Nova Scotia) to British control.[13] By the time Vallée arrived at Louisbourg, French colonists had been coming to terms with the local landscape for over a century. The marshland farming of the area is rightly famous because of scholars who have offered in-depth analysis of the specific techniques of drainage, diking, and cultivation that can be tied to specific regions of France.[14] Although small in number throughout the seventeenth century, natural increase allowed colonial expansion that targeted the salt marshes throughout the Bay of Fundy.[15] By the era of the Acadian deportation, colonists had reclaimed 13,000 acres of marshland while leaving a relatively light footprint on nearby forests.[16]

Although Île Royale had been singled out as a site for imperial expansion—colonial officials had seen it is a possible location for both an agricultural colony and an intermediary site for trade between Canada and the wider Atlantic—it was only following Utrecht that plans for settlement began in earnest.[17] Sites throughout Île Royale were remapped and readied for settlement by displaced colonists from Acadia and Placentia (in what is now Newfoundland) (Figure 10.1). Those with whom Vallée met would have arrived only recently, bringing with them a century worth of knowledge about local maritime environments.[18] Related plans to draw Native American allies to Île Royale seem to have been far less successful, as Mi'kmaw, Abenaki, and Malecite communities preferred to stay on ancestral territories now firmly within a British sphere of influence. Instead, native communities made annual trips to meet with French officials and receive diplomatic gifts.[19]

Vallée explicitly tied his prospects in the colony to his education and technical skills. Shortly after arriving, the exiled engineer completed an analysis of the recently completed fortifications of Louisbourg that could attest to his unique skills.[20] In 1723, he wrote to an unnamed benefactor that "I have written a little memoire on the most essential faults" of the fortress.[21] He hoped, he wrote, that both the *Mémoire* and an accompanying map would testify to

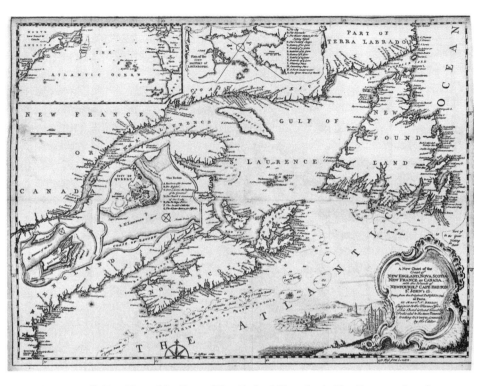

Figure 10.1. "A New Chart of the Coast of New England, Nova Scotia, New France or Canada, with the Islands of Newfoundland, Cape Breton, St. John's &c," in *The Great Importance of Cape Breton* (London, 1746). Courtesy of the John Carter Brown Library at Brown University.

the fact that "I am aware of how many blessings I have received" and attest equally to "the conduct that I hold to in this country."[22] His research, he added, would demonstrate his desire to "make myself useful."[23] In the years following his arrival in North America, it was his skill as a surveyor that secured the support of local officials such as the governor of Île Royale, Joseph de Monbeton de Brouillan, dit Sainte-Ovide.[24] Vallée's supporters sought to have him appointed to the post of royal surveyor and professor of mathematics, although they initially met with resistance from metropolitan authorities.[25] Vallée ultimately had to wait until 1731 to receive his surveying license, but he began surveying undeveloped lots and modifying the layout of the burgeoning community soon after.[26]

Vallée's foray into colonial botany was likely a similar attempt to prove that he could be useful to colonial authorities. Many local officials' libraries reveal a significant interest in the natural and mathematical sciences.[27] While travel accounts, administrative documents, and missionary relations had shown considerable attention to the diverse environments of the French Atlantic world in the seventeenth century, the period during which Vallée arrived witnessed a significant interest in botanical commodities that could enrich a mercantilist empire.[28] If in 1723 Vallée made use of his education in engineering to highlight flaws in the fortress at Louisbourg, his 1725 study of the flora of Île Royale therefore aimed to draw attention to the richness and promise of local ecosystems.

Vallée's ambitions for his 1725 *Mémoire* are unknown, but he became more explicit in subsequent efforts. In 1733 Vallée wrote to then minister of the marine Jean-Frédéric Phélypeaux, comte de Maurepas, to request transport "to go collect plants from the different ports of this island."[29] His interest in botanical exploration, he wrote, had been renewed by a recent *mémoire* that Maurepas had sent to Île Royale in which the minister requested that colonists "attach themselves to research anything that might be curious" and to "write detailed *memoires* [and] even send some specimens of each thing."[30] He promised his Parisian patrons that he would draw on his own research and information from local informants, explaining that they could expect a number of important discoveries from his study, including minerals, petrified plants, shells, and earth with which to produce paints and pottery.[31] His research would focus particular attention "on the botany of different plants used by the *sauvages* which have unique virtues . . . [including] plants, or simples, which are terrestrial as much as marine."[32]

Whereas Vallée once measured the distance between imperial plans and colonial deficiencies, he now emphasized the creative potential of these centrifugal forces and the emergence of new creolized ways of knowing. When he sought indigenous knowledge, he turned to the Acadian colonists who had interacted with these communities. Upon their arrival in the region in the early seventeenth century, French colonists observed trade networks that bound agricultural communities in New England and people such as the Mi'kmaq who relied more heavily on seasonally available food sources.[33] The colonist Marc Lescarbot, for example, had described encountering people who had come to trade "tobacco, some chains, necklaces and armlets made of periwinkle shells . . . held in great repute among them; also corn, beans, bows, arrows, quivers, and other such small wares."[34] This trade was an effort to profit from and overcome the limitations of major climatic transitions in the region; Algonquian communities to the south in regions where corns, beans, squash, and tobacco could reliably be grown traded to those farther north where such agricultural products could not be grown in abundance.[35] The trade in furs that grew in colonial Acadia grafted onto these networks and provided European goods and foods in exchange for locally caught furs and foods.[36] As William Wicken writes, where Acadians farmed and Mi'kmaq fished and hunted, "co-occupation remained possible."[37] Contact with indigenous peoples grew as the colony expanded from its roots at Port Royal and through practices such as trading and intermarriage.[38] The level of intermarriage remains debated, but close seasonal proximity—when Mi'kmaw communities traveled to the coast to occupy summer villages and take advantage of maritime resources—is undeniable.[39]

Accounts of early Acadian colonization suggest that the exchange of plants supported conversations about their use. After receiving grapes in trade with local Mi'kmaq, for example, Lescarbot recounted that "In pressing the raisin in the glass, we showed them in what fashion we made the wine that we drank. We wanted to make them eat the raisin, but having it in their mouth they spit it out and thought (such as Ammianus Marcellinus recounts of our ancient Gauls) that it was poison, such are these people ignorant of the best thing that God has given to man, after bread."[40] The long-term impact of these encounters is difficult to discern, however, and French colonists continued to look to Mi'kmaw communities primarily as a source of wild foods. In the late seventeenth century, for example, the colonial promoter and landowner Nicolas Denys recounted hiring indigenous children to collect raspberries and strawberries so that his laborers could keep to their tasks.[41] Despite the early ambitions of missionaries such as the Jesuit Pierre Biard, there was little success—or indeed little colonial interest—in convincing indigenous peoples to take up agriculture and a more recognizably sedentary lifestyle.[42]

Whatever skill Vallée showed as a surveyor and engineer, there is little in his *Mémoire* to suggest that he had any comparable training in botany. His botanical descriptions were an assemblage of personal observation and information collected from local colonial and indigenous populations. In his first description of the "plante marine," for example, Vallée combined his own study of the plant's morphology and habitat, which he claimed had been repeated several times over the previous two years with knowledge gathered from colonial informants.[43] An exact itinerary is impossible to reconstruct, but Vallée did refer to specific locations in individual descriptions. The "plante marine," for example, had been found in the port of Louisbourg, just as the "herbe à jean hebert" had been found near the "port St. Pierre commonly called port Toulouse."[44] This was the region to which sixty-six Acadian families had come after 1714 and where indigenous people continued to settle during the summer.[45] Other locations such as "milnimikesche" suggested a different sort of travel entirely, entailing a distance as much cultural as geographical, and hinted at the continued presence of indigenous names and knowledge.[46]

While the object of this shipment (and other shipments like it that traveled yearly to Paris in the eighteenth century) was to decontextualize new plants from these new worlds, Vallée's text frequently revealed an effort to immerse its audience in complex Acadian ecologies that were simultaneously natural and cultural.[47] If Vallée's references to his routes were sporadic, his attention to the ecological contexts of his collection was consistent. In nine of his eleven botanical descriptions, Vallée made explicit reference to where the plant grew. Botanical evidence suggests that he focused his research on wetlands and coastal areas of Île Royale. The plant that he called "Kocokar," for instance, was described as growing "commonly on the tidal flats which are along the ocean."[48] However, current populations of *Plantago*, as this plant is now called, grow predominantly in nonwetlands, suggesting that Vallée's collecting trips did not extend beyond the coastal areas where he observed Kocokar growing.[49] More generally, the number of references to aquatic plants suggests that much of his collection came from similar (if not the same) ecosystems. Whether by design or by geographic constraint, it seems likely that the *Mémoire sur les plantes qui sont dans la caise B* was drawn from coastal settlements easily reached from Louisbourg.[50] This strategy suggests an inversion of the sorts of travel imagined in Enlightenment scientific practice.[51] Rather than providing pieces of American environments in Paris, Vallée routinely strove to discursively bring his readers to him and Île Royale.

Some plants, such as "Sarrazine" (a variant of *Sarracenia*, now known as *Sarracenia purpurea*, or purple pitcher plant), were provided with variations on common names familiar in use on both sides of the Atlantic.[52] The Dutch botanist Carolus Clusius had first depicted *Sarracenia* in 1576 after having received the plant from a French apothecary. This apothecary, Claude Gonier, had himself likely received the plant from the fishing fleet that annually traveled to the Grand Banks and what is now maritime Canada.[53] The Récollet missionary Gabriel Sagard had provided the Wendat name "Angyahouiche Orichya" when he had seen it on his travels into the Great Lakes region.[54] That Vallée called the plant "Sarrazine" suggests a familiarity—either his own or that of the people with whom he discussed the plant—with plant names that circulated throughout the Atlantic world.

Just as often, however, the author resisted the temptation to apply European names to American plants. The author connected the otherwise unnamed "plante marine" with "the true coraline" in a written description, for example, but did not equate them. Likewise, "Chicouaäbane" was like but not the same as the water lilies native to France. Novelty was assumed, and facile equivalencies were avoided. Other specimens, such as the "seeds of a plant from this country," were left without any identification at all.[55] Yet other plants were presented with names that embedded them in the lived worlds of colonial or indigenous communities. The "herbe à jean hebert" was named because "one claims that it was him who made the discovery," for example.[56] By this time botanists such as Jean-François Gaultier in Quebec were equally aware of the neologisms that distanced the taxonomies of Acadians from those of New France.[57]

Similarly, even as Vallée sought to demonstrate the utility of American flora to would-be Parisian patrons, this utility was explored through the histories of nearby indigenous and colonial communities. In six of the eleven descriptions, for example, Vallée discussed the medicinal properties of plants such as the "plante marine," "thysaouyarde," and the "herbe à jean hebert."[58] As he described these medicinal properties, however, he embedded discussions of utility in narratives of colonial and indigenous usage that emphasized the distance between the study of the plants in Europe and his firsthand experience of indigenous and colonial communities. The "plante marine" had been used to treat worms in infants "perfectly well," a treatment for an illness "very frequent in this country not only to children but even more to those of an advanced age."[59] These were plants that cured colonial and indigenous populations of illnesses that were of local concern. The plant "thysaouyarde" was a proven cure for scurvy because it had worked in recent memory, relieving the crew of a ship sailing for the Compagnie des Indes of the symptoms of the illness within four to five days.[60]

Although Vallée had only been in Louisbourg for two years when he wrote this text, the evidence that his text provides of botanical, medical, and cultural exchange between local indigenous communities and colonists suggests that these exchanges were relatively common and were already well established. When he described the "seeds of a plant from this country," for instance, he wrote that "I am sending a specimen of a seed of which nobody knows the name and several leaves of this plant in a little paper packet on which is written unknown plant."[61] The author was aware that he lacked information about the plant, however, and indicated that he had also asked indigenous informants for their input as a matter of course; he noted that "the *sauvages* say nothing of this plant."[62] Four plants were sent to France identified by names that seem likely to be indigenous, even where colonial names had become common.

The *Mémoire sur les plantes qui sont dans la caise B* showed particular attention to aboriginal usage of local plants. The Récollet missionary Chrestien Leclercq, who proselytized among the Mi'kmaq of the Gaspé Peninsula, wrote that "They are all naturally surgeons, apothecaries, & doctors, by the familiarity and experience they have of certain simples."[63] Nonetheless, colonial texts frequently described indigenous peoples who were reluctant to share information that was meant to be kept secret or that was the rightful possession of women.[64] When the Sieur de Dièreville, a surgeon who wrote an account of his travel to Acadia in the early eighteenth century, related that the indigenous inhabitants "have an infallible remedy for Epilepsy," he also explained why it remained unknown to colonists. When "A Soldier at the Fort on the St. John River" fell subject to the condition, a nearby indigenous woman sought out and provided "two black doses the size of two broad Beans, scraping of a plant root." The remedy took effect, the soldier's symptoms resided, and he "never had an attack of this malady" again. The commandant of the fort sent out a search for the anonymous woman "but always in vain; he could get no tidings of her, in spite of every inquiry he made."[65] The colonial promoter Nicolas Denys likewise shared hints of knowledge that remained hidden to him as a Frenchman, echoing authors who related similar encounters to the west in New France.[66]

While historians have long commented on the close relationship between French colonists and local Mi'kmaw communities, Vallée's text therefore demonstrates that divisions between indigenous and colonial knowledge and between indigenous and introduced flora at Île Royale had blurred considerably by 1725.[67] Vallée wrote about "thysaouyarde," for example, that "it is with this plant that the *sauvages* cure themselves of ulcers of the mouth by chewing it continually" and that it had also been used to treat French cases of scurvy.[68] Plants with aboriginal names such as "thysaouyarde" were provided with analyses of their medicinal properties that were explained through examples of European use and vice versa.[69] When describing the "herbe à jean hebert," Vallée recorded that this plant was used by the *sauvages* to treat "all sorts of old ulcers, after having ground it and applied it on the wounds." In his description of the plant "Sarrazine," Vallée offered anecdotal evidence that colonial populations had adopted indigenous botanical practices; he explained that aboriginal peoples "who run in the woods" drank rainwater from the leaves of "Sarrazine" and that at the foundation of the colony, French children had likewise drunk the liquid contained inside the leaves after it had been heated.[70]

Establishing the use of plants by indigenous peoples outside of these historical texts is a challenge, as the acidic soils of eastern Canada undermine the preservation of botanical specimens that might otherwise be recovered by archaeologists.[71] Nonetheless, paleoethnobotany has been able to demonstrate indigenous exploitation of a number of wild fruits such as cherries, raspberries, and crab apples.[72] Modern place-names such as Shubenacadie—a Mi'kmaw community during the period under consideration—hint at the significance of this knowledge; the name "Shubenacadie" comes from the Mi'kmaw *segebunakade*, or "place where groundnut [*Apios americana*] abounds."[73] Evidence of the medicinal use of plants is more sporadic still, but recent ethnobotanical studies have shown a vibrant tradition that has adapted to and survived centuries of change and challenge.[74]

The presentation of the plant Kocokar highlights this vitality that is otherwise often invisible. Toward the middle of the *Mémoire*, "Kocokar" was identified in the script running across the top of the page. The name runs quickly into a written description that lays out the plant's local usage and its morphology, a text that runs another page and a half in the thick, curved script common to all the descriptions. A leaf survives pressed against the written page in the area making up a left-hand margin, providing a material counterpart to the described specimen. As mentioned above, "Kocokar" was an "aquatic plant" that grew in "ponds" or "commonly on the shore alongside the ocean." It was a plant that was "unctuous" and was used medicinally by indigenous peoples and known to the French colonial population—called here the "creôles"—as the "herb graisse." This second name, which can be translated as "fat herb," gestures toward the multiple lives of the plant in Acadian and indigenous cultures.[75]

What is most remarkable about this plant, however, is something that is only obvious to us today: this plant was likely a European introduction. A species of *Plantago*, a genus of weeds that had arrived with an earlier generation of colonists in Acadia, Kocokar had become naturalized and so thoroughly assimilated that Vallée sent it back to Europe as an American specimen. The arrival of the plant in North America is undocumented, but recent studies suggest that it likely arrived with crop seeds that the Acadians brought with them.[76] *Plantago* species, like many weeds, grow well at disturbed sites and thrive with the spread of agriculture and the clearing of forests.[77] Once in American environments it spread quickly, acquiring the name "Englishmen's foot" or "White man's foot."[78] English authors who discussed the flora of colonial North America such as John Josselyn and John Clayton were aware that plantain had been introduced from Europe. Josselyn, for example, wrote that the aboriginal peoples of New England called plantain "English-Mans foot, as though produced by their treading," suggesting that native communities also understood that colonization had introduced the plant.[79]

Vallée clearly thought that the plant he called "Kocokar" was indigenous to Île Royale. The leaf was accompanied by seeds, clearly included in the hope that this exotic medicinal could be cultivated in Paris. Beyond proving that Vallée was not a particularly skilled botanist, his description of Kocokar suggested that it was its use by aboriginal communities that led him to assume that the plant was native to Île Royale. Vallée wrote, for example, that the plant was used by nearby native communities to treat hydropsy, an illness that made the body swell with fluid. Today, species of *Plantago* continue to be used by the Mi'kmaq and many other cultures medicinally.[80] As Frieda Knoblich has written, "Plantain was . . . certainly not a harbinger of cultural 'defeat' but became a plant with sustaining material and spiritual uses entirely separate from the geographical and cultural context it came from."[81]

This sort of layering of appropriations and reappropriations makes this plant—a weed that you will likely see growing as readily on sidewalks in Boston as on the beaches of Cape Breton today—interesting enough. Yet tracing out the process by which one plant crossed the Atlantic and took root in American environments makes it clear that it would be a mistake to suggest that each new name was simply a veneer or that we can separate out the cultural and natural histories of this plant. Instead, Vallée's manuscript and his discussion of Kocokar demonstrate that both the ecologies and cultures of Île Royale were emergent phenomena; they were the product and evidence of over a century of sustained cultural and ecological translation.

As important as Vallée's text is for the insights it offers into the circulation of knowledge between indigenous and colonial communities at Île Royale, the history of the text after it left Louisbourg in 1725 also reveals a great deal about the circulation of knowledge in the wider French Atlantic world. The specific trajectory of the text from Louisbourg to Paris is impossible to trace. As it entered into the Atlantic networks of the Ministry of the Marine and the Paris-based Académie Royale des Sciences, Vallée's *Mémoire* was effectively anonymized and ignored, valued more for the specimens that were pressed between the pages than for its written text.[82] If it is true that these networks were indeed incomplete and much less efficient than often assumed, scholars have consistently shown that the indigenous origins of Enlightenment science was effaced in France and throughout Europe.[83] If it has therefore become routine for historians to analyze the process by which indigenous and amateur informants were marginalized in accounts of American environments produced by European naturalists, a closer study of the *Mémoire sur les plantes qui sont dans la caise B* can illustrate how this erasure was accomplished and what was lost in the process.

There is no evidence that Vallée's foray into colonial botany found a favorable response among either Parisian naturalists or the colonial administration. Stored, as it remains to this day, with other plant specimens in the Muséum national d'Histoire naturelle's herbarium rather than with the texts of the museum's library, it seems likely that Vallée's audience at the Royal Garden placed the highest value on the leaves that were pressed between the pages of his *Mémoire*. As the *Mémoire* arrived in France, the balance that Vallée had sought to attain between the presentation of written text and physical specimens was undermined by his Parisian audience. Pressed and dried leaves are present on pages 4, 5, 7, 12, and 14 of the text and represent, in that order, "thysaouyarde," "herbe à jean hebert," "Kocokar," "Pacogire," and "Pettite fougere."[84] From stains that are present on several other pages, it seems likely that when first sent to France most (if not all) botanical descriptions in this *Mémoire* were similarly augmented by a physical specimen pressed between the pages. With the exception of the "herbe à jean hebert," where the leaf is large enough to obscure the text when left in place, these leaves were presented on the page in such a way that they visually complemented and balanced the written descriptions.

As the title of the *Mémoire* suggests, this document was originally intended as an accompaniment to a larger shipment of physical specimens destined for Paris. In the description of Salzepareille, for example, Vallée advised his readers that he had also sent them a specimen of the root of the plant.[85] Likewise, he also sent the leaf, seed, and root of the Pacogire that he had collected in the ponds of Île Royale and that resembled a type of water lily.[86] Collections of plants such as these were a common feature of communication networks in the eighteenth-century French Atlantic world. In 1738, for example, Jean-Baptiste Gosselin, Hubert-Joseph de La Croix, and Benoît Favre among them sent five cases of plants to Paris from Quebec.[87] Abbé Gosselin sent another case in 1739 and more again in 1740, 1741, and 1743.[88] The contents of the cases were rarely specified in administrative correspondence that tracked their shipment. Instead, most refer simply to roots or plants, with little indication of numbers or identity. More verbose accounts provide little in the way of clarification. In 1727, the curé de Terrebonne, Lepage de Sainte-Claire, sent "several plants of a species of wild chicory almost like young artichoke plants."[89] Colonial administrators integrated scientific research into military and economic networks to facilitate the transport of these shipments and to extend the reach of the Académie Royale des Sciences into the interior of the continent.[90] Once they arrived in the Atlantic port cities of France such as Nantes or Rochefort, American plants were likewise inserted into networks of gardens that aimed to preserve or keep them alive until they reached Paris.[91]

If it was the skilled eye that Vallée brought to his analysis of Louisbourg's fortifications and planning that made him useful as an engineer and surveyor, the value of amateur botanical collectors such as Vallée to French botanical science was measured in the number of cases of plants that were sent and the condition in which they arrived in Europe.[92] By the time Vallée sent his *Mémoire* to Paris, the Académie Royale des Sciences had been in existence for fifty-nine years and had become, as it was originally intended to be, an influential arbiter of scientific legitimacy in the service of the French Crown.[93] The foundation of the Académie Royale des Sciences reimagined the contours of scientific community in the French Atlantic world, centralizing scientific authority in Paris and mapping a division of scientific labor onto Atlantic networks. In 1732, the respected botanist and member of the academy Antoine de Jussieu hinted at the limited role imagined for an ideal correspondent and collector. "If the botanist is able," he wrote, "he must send figures and descriptions, and some seeds either dried or maintained at a temperature so that they arrive alive and in a state to be transplanted. After we will have them examined and make comparisons with those of this country which they resemble the most."[94] Reminiscent of what Ralph Bauer has called "epistemic mercantilism" or what Susan Scott Parrish has more bluntly referred to as the "epistemic arrogance" of European naturalists who derided the ability of their colonial counterparts to adequately understand the flora and fauna of the New World, botanists at the academy sought to establish a clear division between themselves and those colonial collectors they credited only with supplying the raw materials on which their work depended.[95]

In 1753, the academician Henri-Louis Duhamel du Monceau outlined the limited expectations of a colonial correspondent more explicitly still. Duhamel du Monceau's *Avis pour le transport par mer des arbres, des plantes vivaces, des semences, et de diverses autres curiosites d'histoire naturelle* advised would-be correspondents on how to create a form with which to frame (and limit) their observations. Told even how to fold the paper used into eight sections, these correspondents were advised to provide only that information desired by Duhamel du Monceau and other Parisian naturalists. This information could include common or indigenous names, the "real names" of the plants, information about where the plant had been collected, and what time of year that specimens had been collected.[96] Meticulous instructions aimed to preserve live plants, herbarium specimens, and seeds so they were usable by French naturalists.[97] Parisian naturalists sought reliable laborers and suppliers, not collaborators.

Despite the discursive dichotomy between metropolitan and colonial science that botanists such as Jussieu evoked, the academy's efforts to establish its own networks in French North America produced more nuanced categories of scientific activity. The academy's presence in North America was centered on Québec and New Orleans, where royal physicians (and one apothecary) served a dual function as skilled correspondents of the academy and medical practitioners. Michel Sarrazin, for example, was named the first corresponding member of the academy in North America in 1699; he was a correspondent of Joseph-Pitton de Tournefort, an influential botanist and professor at the Royal Garden with whom Sarrazin had studied.[98] In New Orleans, royal apothecary Alexandre Vielle and royal physician Jean Prat, although never elected to the academy, became regular correspondents with academicians such as Bernard de Jussieu, the younger brother of Antoine and a respected botanist himself.[99] Yet the role of these correspondents was never imagined to be equal to that of their patrons and counterparts at the Royal Garden and the Académie Royale des Sciences. Instead, while correspondents such as Sarrazin and Vielle established reputations as researchers through the study of American flora and fauna such as, respectively, beavers and the wax myrtle, their primary role was to reliably prepare descriptions and shipments of plants and animals that would survive the trip to France.[100] Whatever scientific research they conducted was understood to be partial and incomplete, subject to the confirmation of more skilled observers at the academy.

These trained and reliable correspondents of the academy were valuable because they made the study of American flora in Paris possible. In essence, they made American plants portable as stable discursive and material objects that could survive transport to Paris intact.[101] This was possible because after receiving training in Paris and working with texts that kept their knowledge and technique up to date, correspondents such as Michel Sarrazin and Jean Prat framed their research in the same registers as the academy.[102] When studying American plants, for example, the academy's American correspondents distanced themselves from amateur collectors through discursive and material practices that framed plants as assemblages of distinct morphological features that they preserved for their Parisian counterparts. While Vallée described *Sanguinaria canadensis* (the plant that he identified as "herbe à jean hebert") as a plant that grew to the height of an elbow and had "a leaf similar to the leaf of the vine," Sarrazin wrote an account that focused attention on the minute details of the plant's morphological features and described them in the standardized language of his Parisian audience. *Sanguinaria*'s fruit, for example, "is a pod around 2 inches long, pointed at the extremities, 5 or 6 lines wide at the middle."[103]

Both Sarrazin and Vallée described aboriginal usage of the plant—Sarrazin described the plant as an abortifacient and Vallée as a treatment for ulcers—but they differed greatly in the credence they gave to indigenous informants. Sarrazin, for example, wrote simply that "I do not believe" aboriginal claims because he had not observed the same effects personally.[104] While Vallée added that "I send some of its roots and its seeds in a little leather sack marked a," Sarrazin sent the plant that he called *Bellarnosia canadensis* as plant number 13 in his shipment of 1698.[105] While the storage practices of Sarrazin's botanical patron at the Royal Garden, Joseph-Pitton de Tournefort, make it difficult to identify the specific plants that Sarrazin sent, it would have been prepared identically to any of the other herbarium specimens that have been identified as Sarrazin's. While Vallée's plants retained the inspiration and idiosyncrasy of their author, those produced by trained correspondents of the academy could be easily inserted into networks of specimen exchange that connected researchers throughout Europe.[106]

Yet Vallée was not alone in weaving indigenous knowledge deeply into his collection of American flora. In 1740, for example, the widow Lepaillieur (Cathérine Jérémie) sent both "a packet containing some roots proper for different uses" and a *mémoire* in which she summarized her study of aboriginal medicine.[107] Likewise, the ensign Daneau de Muy prepared an "instructive *mémoire*" about local plants of the *pays d'en haut* and aboriginal medical use of them.[108] Jesuits such as Joseph-François Lafitau and Pierre-François-Xavier de Charlevoix twinned their study of the moral and natural environments of their American missions; study of plants such as corn, wild rice, and ginseng were thought to offer insights into the mental and moral worlds of aboriginal cultures.[109] While these Jesuit accounts survive, the work of amateur naturalists such as Jérémie and Daneau de Muy have not. Vallée's manuscript *Mémoire* therefore provides substance to recent research that has only been able to demonstrate that such voices were systematically silenced and makes clear that rather than simply seeking to leverage his access to Mi'kmaw cultures into official favor, Vallée had a conception of American environments that had been profoundly influenced by his encounter with indigenous botanical knowledge.

François-Madeleine Vallée's *Mémoire sur les plantes qui sont dans la caise B* demonstrates that amateur naturalists in colonial North America imagined the scientific community of the French Atlantic world in more expansive terms than did Parisian naturalists. The effect of Vallée's botanical descriptions was to emphasize the distance, both geographical and cultural, that separated his readers in Paris from the flora of Île Royale. Although Vallée had arrived in Louisbourg only two years previously, his *Mémoire* was less a paean to the mercantilist possibilities presented by these plants than a glimpse into the complex social and natural ecologies of Île Royale. Indigenous botanical knowledge was not presented as either exotic or suspect but instead was a legitimate source of information about American flora.

Vallée's text emerged from the intersection of multiple networks of knowledge production in the French Atlantic world. Yet it was his imperfect mastery of botany that made his work possible. Had Vallée understood the limitations of his contact with both the Mi'kmaq and local ecosystems, he might never have spoken for indigenous cultures and local environments so confidently. Likewise, had this author understood that naturalist members of the Académie Royale des Sciences considered indigenous knowledge inconsequential to true botanical science, he might never have turned to colonial botany to salvage his reputation with local and imperial administrators. Instead, Vallée's imaginative but imperfect imitation of academic science in the *Mémoire sur les plantes* maintained an unerring confidence in the ultimate commensurability of French and indigenous botanical knowledge. As an optimistic and ultimately unsuccessful effort to introduce both the plants and peoples of Île Royale into the Atlantic networks of the Académie Royale des Sciences, the *Mémoire sur les plantes* is testimony to the possibilities and limits of translation in the eighteenth-century Atlantic world.

Chapter 11

Native Engravings on the Global Enlightenment: Pedro Murillo Velarde's Sea Map and Historical Geography of the Spanish Philippines

Ruth Hill

> In this compendious account, oh Saintly Apostle, I have expressed as
> in a reduced map, . . . a small part of the great amount I owe you. . . .
> Without the microscope of Pride (which tends to represent pygmies as
> Giants) to bulk it up, its brevity . . . shames me.
> —Pedro Murillo Velarde, *Catecismo o Instrucción Christiana* (1752)

As part of the Enlightenment's increasingly global remit, the animal, mineral, and vegetable kingdoms of Spanish Asia and Spanish America played a crucial role in the disciplinization of geography, natural history, physics, and chemistry.[1] They presented to members of western Europe's royal academies and religious orders alike scores of plants, brutes, and human beings never before seen in the Old World. Beyond exoticism, there arose new scientific methods, hypotheses, inventions, and theories derived from exemplars of Spanish Asian and Spanish American nature, as they had since the sixteenth century.[2] An especially vivid example of the global Enlightenment is the Jesuit polymath Pedro Murillo Velarde (1696–1753), who wrote in his *Catecismo o Instrucción Christiana* about a life of "dangers, scares, rations, and toil" spent "going cross the entire surface of the earthly globe and making a complete trip around the entire world, and then some."[3] He lived most of his adult life (1723–1750) in Spanish Asia and produced the first modern sea map of the Philippines (Figure 11.1),

Figure 11.1. Pedro Murillo Velarde, *Carta hydrográphica y chorográphica de las Yslas Filipinas*, engraved by Nicolás de la Cruz Bagay, Manila, 1734. Courtesy of the Newberry Library, Chicago. Call no. map4F G8060 1734 .V4.

which surfaced recently in the international dispute over the South Sea.[4] The map was engraved by the Filipino (*indio*) engraver and publisher Nicolás de la Cruz Bagay in 1732 and published in 1734 and then, with significant modifications, in 1744 and 1749. Commissioned by the Spanish Bourbon Philip V, the Jesuit missionary's sea chart preceded by two decades his narrative rendering of Spanish Asia in the eighth volume of his *Geographía Histórica*.[5] Understanding the relationship between these two works is a prerequisite for analyzing the processes of translation and transculturation that produced both.

The very title *Geographía Histórica* assumed that geography and history—sacred, profane, natural—did not lead separate lives. The most obvious manifestation of interdependence is perhaps Murillo Velarde's promise to readers that his narration would follow his map. Additionally, the map itself narrates a *historia* through both words and illustrations. This obviously reciprocal relationship between the works also has a disciplinary layer. As the editors of this volume remind us, *historia* was a multivalent rubric. Murillo Velarde's *Geographía Histórica* lives up to the twin expectations for the history genre held by the Spanish Royal Academy of Language in 1734. For one thing, it is a narration belonging to the demonstrative branch of classical rhetoric that recounts discoveries, conquests, invasions, and church and Crown activities.[6] For another, it exemplifies the same royal academy's second entry on *historia*: "a description that is done of natural things—animal, vegetable, mineral, etc.—like Pliny's, Acosta's, Dioscorides's, etc."[7] The other half of his title's equation was, of course, *geografía*. The academy's entries on *geographía* and *geográphico* tell us that geography or cosmography (academy members used the two as synonyms) is "the science that deals with the universal description of the entire Earth . . . as well as with knowledge of climes, parallels, and geographical measurements."[8] As in a preracial retable of human, plant, and animal diversity, the 1734 map is framed by illustrations of peoples, flora, fauna, customs, and more detailed maps. Natural and moral *historia* and *geografía* are thus embedded together in the squares that surround the sea chart proper.

The natural history dimension of Murillo Velarde's tour de force lays bare a scientific economy in which plants, brutes, and animals (including humans) are divided and defined according to authority, reason, and experience—his own and that of Armenians, Malabars, Filipinos, Chinese, and many others in Spanish Asia and beyond. Murillo Velarde was convinced that a life spent among natives such as his Filipino engraver Cruz Bagay rendered him more capable than other geographers and historians of navigating and representing nature. In this regard, Murillo Velarde reminds us of a previous generation of historians such as José de Acosta, Bernabé Cobo, and Francisco Hernández who invoked the practices and the lore of the diverse peoples among whom they lived in order to warrant their own claims about and to non-Western nature. Additionally, the Jesuit geographer aimed to show that he could not only converse with natural philosophers, physicians, and theologians in western Europe but could also *exceed* them—hence, the optic of corpuscularism in his taxonomies of the East Indies, where most Western European scientists had never been. It is therefore appropriate and critically productive to approach the Jesuit cartographer's adaptations of Western scientific theory to non-Western experience and the myriad ways in which the latter prompted and altered Western scientific modernity as a kinetic loop of translation, commodification, and circulation.

The motivations and methods of Murillo Velarde's maps and *Geographía Histórica* were in harmony with the early Spanish Bourbon economic and political reforms and reform proposals (*proyectismo*).[9] He sought to accomplish what no other Spaniard had produced and what every civilized people ostensibly required: a historical geography of the known world.[10] He aimed to wrest control of the geographical, historiographical, and more broadly scientific narratives about Spanish Asia—about its vegetable, animal, and mineral kingdoms—from European authorities who enjoyed international acclaim and assent. Still, much more was at stake, as Emma Spary reminds us: "Vast sums of money were involved in colonial trade, for individual and state alike; thus naturalists' discussions about economies were highly political."[11] From the Jesuit naturalist's perspective, knowledge of nature had to be gathered by Spaniards in order to squeeze utility out of agriculture, part and parcel of the bioprospecting that would underwrite the Crown's broader and practical goals such as modernizing the army and navy and expanding commerce. There was intense competition for such knowledge and elaborate subterfuge employed to wrest the secrets of nature from natives and Europeans alike.[12]

As he expounds on the natives' cultivation as well as the medicinal and economic benefits of the cocoa bean (cacao) in New Spain, the inseparability of scientific and economic harvests is instantly legible: "although Foreigners generally find fault with everything Spanish, our chocolate is still admitted, with the general approval of the Royal Academicians—and our silver, even more so."[13] Spanish, African, and indigenous natural knowledge of Spanish America and Spanish Asia was being harvested by naturalists from the same countries that were (often illegally) harvesting pearls and emeralds in Tierra Firme or smuggling gold and silver through the ports of El Callao, Cartagena, Portobelo, and smaller ports in between and from Acapulco to Manila to Liverpool and Dunkirk. Understanding non-European nature involved not only processes of cultural translation but also material appropriation, oftentimes through the mediation of collectors who "played a crucial role in the development of science because they provided the raw materials to allow those in cabinets, libraries, pharmacies, and courts to create both specimens and categories of meaning."[14]

The sine qua non of scientific and imperial projects was navigation. Murillo Velarde penned a review for a groundbreaking manual titled *Navegación especulativa y práctica* (*Speculative and Practical Navigation*), engraved and published by the Filipino Cruz Bagay. The utility of navigation is present in the Jesuit canon law professor's review from start to finish:

> Not one City, not one Province, not one Kingdom alone, but instead the entire World has a share in the useful goods [*utilidades*] of Navigation. The latter circulates basic supplies, merchandise, Treasure, the Arts, machines, and Sciences between one Kingdom and another. It makes sterile Regions fertile; savage Islander pagans, civilized and social, which is to say that it makes men out of wild beasts. Shanties and huts, it converts into Fortresses and Palaces. From jungles of ferocious beasts, it forms Cities of courtiers. The blind and superstitious Pagan world's places of worship have been consecrated as Temples of the true Numen. Grottoes of Vipers, Basilisks, and other monsters of vice have been transformed into a Paradise of Virtues, the bloody cruelty of the Caribs into Christian charity, and, lastly, the entire Orb that was previously divided into many Worlds, due to the lack of connections between their Peoples, has become a great City divided into many Kingdoms, Provinces, and Regions as [a city is divided] into different neighborhoods, streets, and outskirts, the most expansive gulfs now being like small rivers that are connected with each other now by the portable bridges of so many merchant fleets, Battleships, and large Vessels.[15]

In the geographer's rendering, connecting different continents by ships—portable bridges—wrought humanity from brutes and circulated merchandise, peoples, and knowledge around the globe. Navigation spelled globalization.

Navigation was dependent on the intellectual breadth and precision of cartographers, geographers, and natural historians. In this respect, the quantity and the quality of printed sources in *Geographía Histórica* are difficult to fathom in an age without the Internet: they include European and American (Spanish, French, Dutch, British) histories; *ars historicae*; natural histories, herbals, and medical literature; modern works of physics (chemical and mechanical), astronomy, and mathematics; *specula principum*; newspapers; scientific and literary periodicals; maps, geographies, and atlases; dictionaries; works of critique; letters; and collections of Crown and canon laws. Murillo Velarde enjoyed open access to the currents of printed modern science, it may be assumed, because it fell to the professor of theology and canon law to supervise the torrent of foreign books entering Manila via foreign merchants.[16] Right up to the publication date of his ten volumes, the procurator-general was perusing materials in Madrid and Rome. Near the end of an extensive prologue, he explains to his readers that he had just read "some paper" written by Jacques Nicolas Bellin and published in Paris in 1752.[17] Bellin, an engineer with the French Navy as well as royal hydrographer (or cartographer), praised the Jesuit's 1734 *carte hydrographique* and the 1744 edition that was reproduced five years later in *Historia de la Provincia de Philipinas*, a few copies of which had made it to France.[18]

Notwithstanding the French royal cartographer's prestigious seal of approval, Bellin disputed the accuracy of some of the Jesuit's measurements and of English and Dutch maps and sea charts of Asia, after having consulted the *mémoires* of navigators and the findings published in academic journals.[19] The Spaniard countered that he had decades of experience traveling around the world, especially between Spanish America and Spanish Asia. "I have shared my Map with Pilots and Geographers from all Nations, and all of them have praised it, and [George] Anson had it engraved in London."[20] Indeed, "it is the Map which governs all pilots and on the basis of which charges are brought against them in the Courts."[21] The Spanish were excellent navigators, the English and Dutch were excellent map makers, and the French were neither.[22]

The Jesuit canonist's exasperation points up a structural aider and abettor of epistemes and paradigms in the eighteenth century. The culture of academies, prizes, fame, and institutional support—a scientific *economy of prestige*—existed in several west European countries already in the seventeenth century.[23] Scientific economies of prestige in France, England, the Netherlands, and elsewhere implied (when they did not claim outright) that Spanish imperial science was lacking. Even the Spanish monarch Philip V's royal cosmographer in the 1730s was a Frenchman: Antoine-Augustin Buzen La Martinière, "our Catholic Monarch Philip V's Geographer," had given the world the "*Diccionario Geográphico* [*Dictionaire geographique et critique*], the most extensive and accurate of all that have been published to-date."[24] Murillo Velarde was thoroughly familiar with the Prussian geographer Philipp Clüver's immensely popular *Introductionis Universam Geographiam*, to which Bruzen La Martinière had decisively contributed.[25]

However, the latter was not the only French geographer whom Philip V honored with his royal imprimatur; indeed, Bruzen La Martinière is today perhaps the least remembered of the French geographers so honored by Spain's first Bourbon monarch. Far better known then and now, Charles-Marie de La Condamine was commissioned by Philip V, along with a team of French scientists and two Spanish mathematicians and astronomers, to measure the equator as part of the Spanish-French geodesic expedition (1736–1743).[26] La Condamine's prestige as a geographer, cartographer, and natural historian ensured that his publications would carry an imponderable weight among modern scientists of nature. His influence was considerable within what Antonello Gerbi termed the "disputa del Nuovo Mondo" (dispute of the New World): the controversy over the so-called degeneration of animals, plants, and minerals in the New World.[27]

Gerbi acknowledged that theologians, historians, and geographers from the Renaissance onward had claimed that the humid and hot climate in the Torrid Zone doomed animals and plants alike. Still, those early modern conceptions of degeneration did not interest him, nor did alternative climate theories (see Miglietti's chapter in this volume), so he primarily discussed the Comte de Buffon and his interlocutors.[28] In doing so, Gerbi forfeited the opportunity to explore how Spanish Asia was configured within the degeneration debate and, equally significant, how the Republic of Letters in Spanish Asia contributed to the debunking of degeneration myths. In the Philippines, the dispute of the New World transformed itself into idyllic descriptions of an ever-provident nature that insinuates the overwrought descriptions and fallible analysis produced by royal academicians well before Georges-Louis Leclerc, Comte de Buffon.

Murillo Velarde's intervention in the degeneration debate linked up four historiographical and geographical narratives. The first was Enrique Flórez's Clave geográfica, in which he pointed out how wrong the ancients were about the Torrid Zone's supposed unfitness for human habitation. The religious historian corrected this scientific myth by noting the Tropical Zone's variety of climes and affirming its nature reminiscent of the ancients' eternal spring.[29] The second was El Orinoco ilustrado y defendido, a widely disseminated and translated natural history in which the Jesuit Joseph Gumilla employed scientific reasoning and decades of firsthand observation to dismiss the Orinoco region's climate detractors.[30] The third was Relación histórica del viaje a la América Meridional (Historical Relation of the Journey to Middle America), in which the Spanish scientists Jorge Juan and Antonio de Ulloa painted a desultory portrait of the Orinoco region's climate based on their participation in the Spanish-French geodesic expedition.[31] The fourth was a product of the same expedition, *La Figure de la Terre*, in which another French geographer and member of the expedition, Pierre Bouguer, was primarily concerned with "la perfection de la géographie."[32] For all that, he did not neglect natural history or imperial politics while certifying that the tropical climate induced degeneracy in the Indians, mestizos, and Spaniards residing in today's Panama, Colombia, Venezuela, and Ecuador.

In Murillo Velarde's volume on the Americas, he referred to Gumilla's *Orinoco ilustrado y defendido* and embraced La Condamine's principal correction to the same.[33] The Spaniard also recalled the Spanish-French geodesic expedition, Ulloa and Juan's *Relación del viaje a la América Meridional*, and La Condamine's recently published *Histoire des Pyramides de Quito*.[34] The latter work prompted Murillo Velarde to accuse the French geographer of taking credit for the work of his colleagues Louis Godin and Bouguer, plagiarizing his map of Quito Province from the criollo explorer and entrepreneur Pedro de Maldonado, and misrepresenting the dispute between the French and Spanish monarchies over the inscriptions on the pyramids erected by their respective scientists.[35] After observing that Juan and Ulloa's *Relación del viaje* depicted ancient palaces of indigenous emperors standing outside Quito, Murillo Velarde remarked facetiously that "Good thing La Condamine represents Spaniards in Peru as less skilled at these works than the Indians who governed them 200 years ago. We're way ahead of our time!"[36]

As seen through the lens of the New World degeneration dispute, the most influential and understudied of the Spanish-French geodesic expedition's narratives was Bouguer's *Relation* in *La Figure de la Terre*, which was an expanded version of a series of discourses given in 1744 at the Royal Academy of Sciences in Paris, attended by the Comte de Buffon and other members. The discourses took place in the year preceding La Condamine's return from the expedition with hundreds of animal and plant specimens for the author of *Histoire naturelle*. The Parisian *Mémoires pour l'Histoire des Sciences et des Beaux-Arts* published a précis of those 1744 Academy sessions in 1748[37] as well as lengthy abstracts from *La Figure de la Terre* in a critical review in 1749.[38]

Of special interest to *la disputa del Nuovo Mondo*, the 1749 critical review touched on Bouguer's *Relation* in which the French scientist affirmed that the "heat in the country is unbearable for its own inhabitants and it brands them with an almost idiotic indolence."[39] The physical stupor, caused by excessive heat and humidity, was inevitably communicated to the mind. The international prestige and popularity enjoyed by the Parisian periodical guaranteed the circulation of Bouguer's theory of New World degeneration throughout

Europe and Europe's colonies in Asia and the Americas. Just as significant, the applications of tropical degeneration theory exceeded the confines of the Americas: "The unrelenting humidity of the lands here is as exhausting as the continuity of heat in the air. *It's the same in every place situated between the two Tropics, or where there are woodlands. Voilá* the Physical cause that explains everything: *forests*."[40] The degeneration of trees, plants, brutes, and humans in tropical climes, as asserted in *La Figure de la Terre*, published extracts, and the critical review, was to filter through Murillo Velarde's historical geography of Spanish Asia on several levels.

The Jesuit jurist repudiated Spanish Asia's climate declaimers by asseverating that his part of the Torrid Zone, though humid, was tempered by the wind and the sun, all of which resulted in a "benignant and healthy clime."[41] "The winters and summers hardly differ," he continued, "neither the heat nor the cold being excessive, rather it usually appears that the continuous Spring of the Golden Age, *Ver erat aeternum*, moved to this Country."[42] "The land is," he remarked wryly, "as in other matters, fertile to a fault."[43] This *locus amoenus* served the Jesuit in Manila as a bulwark against detractors of the tropics. His chorographic profile of the Philippine Islands underscored that wind, humidity, and rain tempered the heat. The sun, in turn, tempered the humidity of the porous and cavernous land, and a "benign and healthy temperament results from this conjoining of causes."[44] In keeping with the praise and/or blame dictate of demonstrative rhetoric, the geographer-historian modeled how to flip the islands' negatives into positives through his recourse to the mechanical physics and chemistry of the Western scientific revolution.

In Pierre Gassendi's *Syntagma Physicum*, widely disseminated in a French abridged edition, he defined a mixed body as the weaving together and tempering of atoms of different shapes, sizes, and combinations, made up of the four elements theorized by Galen and recognized by Thomist Aristotelian natural philosophy (air, fire, water, earth).[45] Murillo Velarde was well versed in contemporary mechanical physics, although he frequently invoked modern chemistry, which argued for five principles: three active (mercury, sulfur, and salt) and two passive (earth and water). For instance, he observed that the sulfur in the terrain of the Philippine Islands was exhaled through pores (or voids) and caused powerful thunder and lightning storms.[46] His understanding of nature strongly resembled the Valencian humanist Juan Bautista Berni's blending of mechanical and chemical theories and empirical methods. Murillo Velarde's contemporary insisted that almost all bodies including our own give off effluvia, or vapors, through their pores. The phenomenon is invisible to the naked eye, but "we observe it with the microscope."[47] The melding of Gassendi's atomism, Francis Bacon's experimentalism, and Robert Boyle's chemistry in Berni's *Filosofía racional, natural, metafísica i moral* exemplifies the Spanish reconciliation of modern and Aristotelian logic, metaphysics, and physics that took place during the seventeenth and eighteenth centuries.

In the same vein, Murillo Velarde had read the pharmacist and physician Félix Palacios's *Curso Chímico del doctor Nicolas Lémery* (1707), a version of Nicholas Lémery's *Cours de chymie* (first published in 1675), that the Spaniard expanded to include even more medical cases and chemical experiments. Immediately following Palacios's work is pharmacist Joseph Assin y Palacios de Ongoz's *Segundo curso chímico*. It begins with the section "Reflexión Físico-Mecánica sobre los principios próximos y remotos de los mixtos," in which mechanical physics and chemistry are conjoined as if they did not hold disparate views on matter and the active and passive elements of the universe.[48] Significantly, the same scientific modus operandi in other parts of western Europe now commands the attention of historians of natural philosophy and the sciences,[49] confirming that Spain's collage of theories and methods was not exceptional.

Fused with scientific modernity, in *Geographía Histórica* and the sea chart there are visual vignettes of agricultural society in the Philippines engraved by the *indio* Cruz Bagay. The visible patterns of the organic world are known through the prism of local knowledge and experience.[50] Hence, Murillo Velarde's access to the organic world as it was lived by Filipinos, Aetas, Malabars, Spanish mestizos, Sangleys, Sangley mestizos (who were half *indio* and half Sangley), and other peoples in Spanish Asia was paramount to his knowledge of nature and various works. He assembled and assimilated vast quantities of data from such interactions in the port city of Manila:

The conflux of various peoples has no parallel, I believe, anywhere else in the world. In the course of an hour spent in the Tuley, or Port of Manila, you will see nearly all the peoples of Europe, Asia, America, and Africa pass through; you will see their manners of dress; you will hear their languages. The amazing thing is, they all communicate with each other in Spanish. But, how? Each people has put together a gibberish whereby they understand each other. One day I heard a pitched argument between a Sangley, an Armenian, and—I think—a Malabar.

They were all speaking Spanish, and I didn't understand a single one of them, because I hadn't studied the vocabularies [of their languages]. For example, the Chinese, to say *alcalde* [mayor], *español* [Spaniard], and *indio* [Filipino native], say them like this: *alicaya, cancia, juania.*[51]

Spanish was the lingua franca in the Port of Manila and was both a product of and a vehicle for processes of transculturation. The latter encompassed not only amalgamations of language and dress but also epistemological and economic synergies, adaptations, and appropriations that came to constitute the global Enlightenment's core. Data derived from that cluster of languages, customs, and cultures equipped Murillo Velarde to correct the natural-historical record: "The most ubiquitous fruit in both Indies is the Plantain [*Plántano*], called that not from *plantain* in the Holy Scriptures as [José] Acosta thinks, but, rather, from *Palán*, which is the name that the Malabars give it, and the Arabs call it *Muza.*"[52] Murillo Velarde's Filipino engraver grafted the *Plántano* onto the 1734 map's frame (Figure 11.2).

Non-Europeans' local knowledge of nature was a global currency, and from Murillo Velarde's amendments, we glean that the Philippines were a magnet for merchants, porters, and peddlers but also for missionaries. Indeed, Jesuits with whom he was in contact after his arrival in 1723 hailed from the Lowlands, France, Germany, Italy, Portugal, and the Americas. Jesuit missionaries throughout Asia experimented with seeding, grafting, and transplanting fruits and vegetables from Spain, the Americas, China, and India[53] as active agents of bioprospecting.[54] Cacao was brought to the Philippines, Murillo Velarde records, "through the Jesuit Father Juan de Ávila's incessant diligence over many years."[55] Mango trees were brought from India.[56] Thus, quotidian folk knowledge about local nature was conveyed to missionaries located throughout Asia, who integrated, translated, and circulated that native knowledge throughout the globe.[57]

The trade in native epistemologies and knowledge of nature was carried out orally, of course, but also in print. The Bohemian Jesuit Paul Klein (Pablo Clain in Spanish) was a cartographer, historian, botanist, and pharmacist who served for many decades in the Philippine Islands. Murillo Velarde knew him through his authored volume: "*Dilao*, from the looks of it, must be a type of Rhubarb. Father Pablo Clain provides many types of it in a book that he wrote, *Medicamentos fáciles, para consuelo de los Doctrineros y alivio de los Indios destituídos de Medicos.*"[58] Although the Spanish scientist Hernández's posthumous *Tesoro*, analyzed by Marroquín Arredondo in this volume, has

Figure 11.2. Carta hydrográphica y chorográphica de las Yslas Filipinas (detail): "1. *Caimán*, or crocodile, of which these Islands' rivers are full. 2. *Saua*, very large snake. 3. Filipino in a *bajaque* [long white garment with a tail, belted at the waist], tilling with a *carabao*, or buffalo. 4. *Luzón* [mortar, made from tree trunk, and pistol] in which rice is peeled, from which this Island got its name *Luzón*." In the background: "white crow," "cocoa tree," "plantain tree." Courtesy of the Newberry Library, Chicago.

received scholarly attention, the Bohemian Jesuit Klein's *Medicamentos fáciles* has been largely ignored, although both volumes could not have been written without the firsthand knowledge provided by native husbandmen and healers. Indeed, Klein's work brought together the traditions of the Chinese, the Malabars, the Filipinos, the Japanese, and other peoples in Asia who lived and/or worked in Spanish Asia. They transferred their knowledge to Klein and other Jesuits, most often in their respective dialects of Spanish.

Murillo Velarde also praised the Moravian Jesuit George Joseph Kamel, who came to the islands in 1688 and opened Manila's first *botica* (pharmacy). The Jesuit botanist and physician served not only peasants on the Jesuit missions but also well-to-do Spaniards for nearly two decades. He published two books on herbal medicine before his death in 1706.[59] Beyond herbals and the compilations of native remedies directed to missionaries by Jesuits such as

Klein and Kamel, letters written by Jesuits serving in Asia were published and widely read across the globe, as *Geographía Histórica* attests:

> Among medicinal things in the Philippines, Catbalogan seed, which is called *Igasud*, or St. Ignatius's berry, has become renowned. It is good for indigestion, toothache, fevers, seizures, conditions caused by drafts, and numerous other things, of which there are lengthy Catalogues compiled by famous Physicians from Europe. . . . The Chinese in Peking were urgently searching for it since it was the most effective remedy found during a fever epidemic, and not one person who took it died, as I have read in a Letter from Peking from 1745. And in Rome and all of Italy, and even in France, they highly prize it.[60]

Many of the Jesuits' letters were translated into French, Spanish, and other languages, which of course multiplied exponentially their influence and that of the non-Western epistemologies lodged within them.

Colonial cultures of natural history overlapped and interacted thanks to the global trade in natural knowledge accrued by natives and transferred to nonnatives, who thereafter translated it into other conceptual, systematic, visual, and linguistic structures. Native knowledge from one part of the Spanish *Monarquía* was circulated, in person or in print, to another: the Jesuit cartographer reports that what Spaniards called *canela silvestre* (wild cinnamon) natives called *calinga* and was the same herb that natives in Spanish Florida called *sasafras*, "whose powers [virtudes] Cárdenas describes and exhalts in *Historia de la Florida*."[61] "El Palo de Manungal," Murillo Velarde explains, "is as light as cork, yellow, and very bitter. They say that snakes flee from it. It's good for calming the stomach, and I have heard a Physician with many years of practice in the Philippines say that it is better than Quina [from the Viceroyalty of New Granada] for treating fevers."[62]

Numerous chapters in this volume substantiate that native knowledge of medicinal and other herbs and plant life expanded and refined Spanish natural history and natural philosophy—the border between these two was, of course, a porous one. It is less understood, however, that merchants and missionaries in the eighteenth-century Philippines took for granted that monetizing the islands' natural resources was pivotal to the economic and military might of Spain's empire. Moreover, the scholarly record has overlooked the degree to which the same two types of colonists took for granted the role of Filipinos and other peoples from Asia in turning imperial resources into capital. What immediately springs to mind is the importance of tens of thousands of Sangleys and Sangley mestizos (half Chinese/half Spanish residents in Manila), who carried out domestic trade through Manila's port well as the trade between the islands and the rest of Asia. Additionally, Filipino natives engraved maps like Murillo Velarde's, which made further exploration and exploitation possible for Spaniards. Further still, *Geographía Histórica* relays the abundance of a spice that was believed to be the linchpin of the Spanish Empire's economic and military rebirth: the domesticated variety of cinnamon, or *canela*.

The Dutch and the English continued to control the trade in spices such as cinnamon, cardamom, clove, and mace, which abounded in the Philippines well before the first Spanish colonists and missionaries arrived. Indeed, the Spanish continued to import spices from other parts of Asia through Manila at elevated prices, as the islands' procurator in Madrid complained in the middle of the seventeenth century. A century later in an unpublished reform project directed to the king of Spain, a merchant and longtime resident of Manila named Nicolás Norton y Nichols rebuked the Spaniards' refusal to exploit the natives' cultivation of cinnamon. Were cinnamon traded directly between the islands and Spain, he proposed, the Dutch suppliers would suffer, and the Spanish merchants would prosper. Everyone knew how much Spanish silver wound up in Dutch hands, Norton y Nichols wrote. The king would conserve more silver within his dominions with a royal decree regarding the extraction of cinnamon. Besides, doing so would allow residents of New Spain to buy cinnamon at the price set by Spanish merchants in Cádiz. Furthermore, the Spanish Crown would encourage the poor to drink more chocolate—a highly taxed good in Spain—by increasing the availability and affordability of cinnamon, which flavored the drink.[63] Chocolate was made from cacao, a plant native to the islands. It was depicted by Murillo Velarde's Filipino engraver next to the banana tree (*Plántano*) and a Filipino husbandman (see Figure 11.2).

Another autochthonous plant was cotton, of which there were two varieties, Murillo Velarde explained. The first grew on tall trees with few leaves, and natives used the cocoon-like capsules to stuff pillows and mattresses. The second, which grew on bushes was white, delicate, and beautiful and was turned into thread "from which are made the most beautiful, attractive, and useful woven shawls, bedspreads, tablecloths, towels, and other products, which would be useful not only for wearing here but also for sending to New Spain."[64] Because Spaniards failed to capitalize on the natives' knowledge and customs, all residents had to turn to foreigners for their clothes and other textiles. With a comparison that spoke volumes, Murillo Velarde lamented that "those who reside in the land treat it like they treat cinnamon, for they strip it rather than cultivate it."[65]

Murillo Velarde fused knowledge of Thomist Aristotelian and modern physics with native epistemologies and experiences in his classification of trees. Writing of the abundance of palm, bamboo, and bejuco climbing vines, he described them as "the three elements of which various mixed bodies are combined," as if to communicate the atomic structure of animate objects.[66] Palms were numerous, as were their kinds. *Niog* (coconut) was tall and straight like date trees in Africa and Andalusia and was used as roofing material and to make mats: "they are the vines and olive trees of the East Indies."[67] The coconut palm appears in one of Cruz Bagay's engravings of humans, plants, and brutes in the islands (Figure 11.3). "Foreign authors call it *Nux Indica*, they depict it in their maps and accounts," and "there is not a tree in the known world that is of greater utility."[68] Thanks to his *indio* engraver Cruz Bagay, the Jesuit polymath could offer here and elsewhere an authoritative description—in words and in lines—of an object of European naturalists' fascination.

Like the early chroniclers of the Americas, Murillo Velarde perforce assimilated nature to Western European scientific and social practices, translating the organic world of the Indias Orientales. The *Yoro* palm provided *sagú*, consumed like bread in the West. The *Buri* palm bore a little round fruit from which Filipino natives made their rosaries. They combined wine, vinegar, honey, and molasses to make flour and bread from the ground fruit and then used the entire trunk to make *sagú*. A small palm known as *Bonga* bore "a fragrant nut like the acorn, astringent and relaxing, and they make a chew out of it with lime and betel leaf, whose use is popular throughout Asia, and it is the betel leaf and areca nut [i.e., paan] [chewed] in India, and its consumption is enormous."[69] The *Bonga* palm also appears in one of Cruz Bagay's tableaux, the legend of which informs the viewer that *Bonga* is the natives' tobacco (see Figure 11.3). *Yonot* palm produced a wine called *tubá*, which was flavorful and refreshing when it was sweet and made you drunk when it had soured. *Yonote* and *baroc* were the Yonot palm's main products. The first was a kind of black esparto grass, with a coarseness resembling a horse's mane and tail, from which Filipinos made cords that lasted longer underwater than the Europeans' esparto or hemp. The second resembled black wool: the *indios* filled mattresses and pillows with it, and it also served as tinder for a fire.

Figure 11.3. Carta hydrográphica y chorográphica de las Yslas Filipinas (detail): "1. Canes, very long and thick, from which scaffolding and houses are made. 2. *Bonga* palms, from which one makes *el buyo* [a chew from crushed nuts, lime, and betel leaf], which is used by every kind of people, chewing it like tobacco. 3. Very large bat with a head like a dog's. 4. Coconut palms, from which they get water, wine, oil, *tubá* [an alcoholic beverage], etc." In the background: "papaya tree," "jackfruit tree," "albino *machin* [long-tailed macaque]." Courtesy of the Newberry Library, Chicago.

Wine, schnapps, and *tubá* were made from the *Nipa* or *Sasa* palm, whose leaves were roofing material.[70]

The second element was bamboo. "The *Bamboo Trees* of the Indies," according to *Geographía Histórica*, "are the giants of the Species, but not as much as they are built up to be by some, who write lies that are fatter and longer than the Bamboos themselves."[71] The Jesuit's Filipino engraver uses the more generic Spanish term *cañas* in his likeness of a Filipino on a ladder chopping down bamboo canes (see Figure 11.3). "The *Bejuco* is the Indian's third element; it's a type of wicker or reed that grows in the thickets of the countryside. It is solid and flexible; they cut it in half and weave Mats and Baskets in all shapes and sizes; Cots, Chairs, Benches, and a thousand other things. It is used as twine for tying things and as cable for the row-barges."[72]

Chances are that the bejuco hanging vine provided Murillo Velarde's only comfort as he cataloged and expurgated foreign publications arriving on the merchant ships. While other missionaries took their siesta, "he was seen lying on a mattress on the floor in his quarters, like in bed, surrounded by books, with an inkwell and a quill for removing the stains that are typically found in their clauses."[73]

The Filipino natives' utilization of these three elements and of trees and woody plants more broadly were translated into the Jesuit mission's buildings and furniture.[74] Native knowledge and capitalization of natural resources gave Murillo Velarde a further means for validating or invalidating claims found in botanies and natural histories that were usually written, illustrated, and published in Europe. Further, the heat and humidity of the tropics were not presagers of doom but instead were a boon to the trees just described as elemental to natives' lives as well as to the timber forests of cedar, ebano, oak, and pine, which could be harvested for shipbuilding.[75]

"On Animals," the third chapter in the Jesuit cartographer's account, returns to the climate question not, however, to discuss minerals or vegetables but instead to discuss brutes and humans. His fundamental query was how does the clime of a place alter the corpuscular constitution of animal bodies in ways that lead to the formation of *diferencias*? This question should prompt one of our own: what should we make of Murillo Velarde's usage of *diferencia*, from the Latin *differentia*, which Scholastics and Later Scholastics used to distinguish between species of a genus? At first blush, his concept of *diferencia* is Aristotelian through and through. Still, the concept was fundamental to Carolus Linnaeus's binomial taxonomy, and the fact that Murillo Velarde used the term *diferencias* in volumes on the two Indies (Asia and the Americas) suggests that he was familiar with one or more editions of Linnaeus's work published in Paris, Halle, Stockholm, and Leipzig in the 1740s. Additionally, the Jesuit cartographer frequently cites the leading scientific journals of western Europe, and on this score it is significant that the 1747 and 1748 issues of the Parisian *Histoire de l'Académie Royale des Sciences* featured detailed critical engagements with Linnaeus's revised editions.[76] No matter his mode of access, Murillo Velarde was aware of Linnaeus's system.

Beyond all doubt too is the originality of Murillo Velarde's conceptualization of biological differentiation due to climate and his resulting taxonomic gestures. His decades of immersion in the animal, vegetable, and mineral realms of Spanish Asia inevitably influenced his readings of and contributions to scientific modernity in Western Europe. His account of Spanish Asia fits the natural history of East and West together—one informs and transforms the other. The West's preoccupation with albino and piebald animals, for instance, had ignored the Orient in favor of exemplars from European, African, and American locales. Numerous case studies of these so-called *monsters* or *accidents* were published in *Histoire de l'Académie Royale des Sciences* and the *Journal de Trévoux* and its successor, *Mémoires pour l'Histoire des Sciences et des des Beaux-Arts*, during the first four decades of the eighteenth century. Naturally, the Jesuit historian had such venues and their readers in mind when he foregrounded exemplars from Manila.

Murillo Velarde alluded to a successful deer hunt by Indians on the Jesuit mission at Maragondong before describing a white stag sent to Madrid from Manila as well as a piebald (white-and red-spotted) deer that he compared to a chessboard.[77] Cruz Bagay engraved, without labeling, the albino or piebald stag in the background of various human kinds or groups (Figure 11.4). Admittedly, I cannot determine if the stag's dark spine was the native engraver's signaling of piebaldry or his artistic shadowing of albinism. In either case, it is worth pointing out that Murillo Velarde's sea chart was published before the famed anatomist Jacques Bénigne Winslow's "Remarques sur les monstres." In Part 1 of the French Dane's dissertation, featured in *Histoire de l'Académie Royale des Sciences*, he exhaustively detailed the *King's Fawn*, that is, a piebald fawn sent by royal order to a colleague of Winslow's in 1729.[78] Winslow's dissection of this rare specimen comprised Part 2.[79]

Another of the Spanish polymath's exemplars of albinism fused classical Roman literature with British empiricism to accentuate the marvels of nature in Spanish Asia. In an ingeniously scientific and rhetorical *translatio*, Murillo Velarde adapted the satirist Juvenal's "a rare bird in the lands, most resembling a black swan": "Domestic Crows can be found everywhere. They are generally black. Some I have seen that have a white feather here and there, like gray hairs, and one I have seen was perfectly white, like snow, although it's truly *rara avis in terris, alboque simillima Corvo*, and it is rare that animals are white where men are brown."[80] Here I recall that the chemist Boyle had included in his *Experiments and Considerations Touching Colours* (1664) "a perfectly White Raven, as to Bill as well as Feathers, which I attentively considered, for fear of being impos'd upon."[81] Murillo Velarde did the Englishman one turn better: he had Cruz Bagay depict the *Cuervo blanco*, or albino raven, in its Philippine habitat (see Figure 11.2).

The Jesuit also recounted that he had seen monkeys and chimpanzees, which Filipino natives called *machines*, roaming the countryside and

Figure 11.4. Carta hydrográphica y chorográphica de las Yslas Filipinas (detail). Left to right: "High-ranking Spaniard with page," "Brown Negro born in this land," "Indians in cockfight." In the background: "*Aetas*, or black savages, in the mountains." Courtesy of the Newberry Library, Chicago.

swinging from trees. Spaniards called those primates of a larger species *zambos*. According to natives, one of these *machines*, armed with a bamboo rod, once chased a Pampango in Mindanao until the man collapsed and died. Direct observation, on the other hand, allowed Murillo Velarde to claim that "I saw two as white as snow, and one red one."[82] A framing scene on the 1734 sea chart includes an albino monkey or chimp classified as *Machin blanco* (see Figure 11.3). Still another case of albinism surfaces in *Geographía Histórica*, as the Jesuit instructs readers that "There are also certain Rabbits, completely white, kept in homes, but they would not survive in the wild due to the humidity."[83] What immediately comes to mind here is Bouguer's strident *Relation* from 1749. There is nonetheless an equally urgent reminiscence that links the Spanish missionary's daily contact with fauna in the wild and domesticated animals in natives' homes to the the metropoles of Western Europe.

Boyle acknowledged in his *Experiments and Considerations Touching Colours* that the air in a locale could alter the color of terrestrial bodies there.

In fact, air could generate colors *de novo*. He dismissed climate alone, however, as the cause of whiteness in animals and people.[84] The English natural philosopher repeatedly used the term "texture" to account for colors. Likewise, the Valencian Berni, who translated Boyle's work on colors as *Teatro de colores*, contended that color depended on both the surface and the texture (*la textura*), or internal fibers, of mixed bodies. Berni specified that the woven structure or design was not visible to the naked eye and might even be at odds with the visible surface of matter.[85] Murillo Velarde reasoned that white rabbits had to be kept indoors, away from heat and humidity, because their material temperament, which was the cause of their color as well as of their corporeal or material soul's functions (emotions, instincts, movements, etc.), would be altered by the atomic *effluvia*—by the streams or vapors of atoms of fire, heat, air, and earth exhaled on the islands by the soil, plants, brutes, humans, etc.

Murillo Velarde's historical geography of Spanish Asia embodies the enormous and defining influence of corpuscular matter theories on Spanish natural philosophy, or the natural sciences, and at once expands atomism's orbit to encompass Manila. In the following passage, he affirms that climate alters the material or sensitive soul of quadrupeds, causing adaptation and differentiation:

> Filipino Indians had Dogs and Cats, but they were puny. Now there are many, and of various European breeds [*castas*]. Cats and dogs here tend to get along together without quarreling, and they usually even eat from the same plate as brothers. Doubtless here, due to the humidity of the land, they lack the corpuscles, atoms, molecules, and fibers that pit them against each other in other parts of the world.[86]

His mechanical understanding of the feline or canine here evinces that prime matter—not any flavor of Later Scholasticism's *hidden cause*—directs animal emotions, perceptions, knowledge, and movements.[87] Climatic conditions alter particles of matter in such animals. The geographer's foray into the mechanics of the animal soul hearkens back to the corpuscular chemistry and physics discussed earlier in this chapter. According to Berni, effluvia cause animals—including humans—to avert or attract each other.[88] Although European cats and dogs were proverbially fighting, the effluvia in the islands given off by them and by all mixed bodies altered their material souls to such a degree that they were drawn to each other as if they were kin.

Murillo Velarde's 1734 map (see Figure 11.1) showcases exemplars of human and cultural diversity from his three decades of living at and working with the Jesuit mission in Manila. Among them there are a Malabar, an Armenian, a well-dressed black criollo (i.e., black man born in the Philippines), a Spaniard, a family of Chinese Filipino mestizos, a Chinese pagan, a Chinese Christian, Filipino Indians, a Japanese, a Portuguese Mardica, a Lascar from India, a Camarin, and Negritos or Aetas (black pagans living in the surrounding hills). Like the *casta* paintings and illustrations from eighteenth-century Mexico, these engravings offered their largely European audience a set of visual stereotypes. Unlike the Mexican representations, however, Cruz Bagay's engravings are not a catalog of miscegenation sequences; they are far less exoticized, even sparse. A further distinction must be noted: the engraver, unlike the painter or illustrator, was an *indio* charged with translating the Spanish geographer's vision into lines. In a relationship akin to that between an architect or painter and the artisans or disciples who executed his designs, Murillo Velarde and Cruz Bagay were, we might say today, *cocreators* of the 1734 sea chart, with its moral and natural history of framing images. The map must in fact be viewed as a particular artifact of those processes of *transculturación* that marked the global Enlightenment as a whole.

In *Geographía Histórica*, which explicitly hews to that map, the classification of human animals in the Philippines divides them into two *diferencias* based on cultural assimilation to Spanish norms. First, there were the civilized peoples (*Naciones Políticas*): the Tagalos, Pampangos, Ilocos, Pangasinanes, Cagayanes, Camarines, Visayas, and Mindanaos, most of whom are mentioned, along with the religious orders that were charged with overseeing these *nuevos christianos*, in the cartouche of the 1734 map. The Jesuit geographer was convinced that these peoples were descendants of Malaysians, "a civilized, numerous, and spread-out people [*nación*]."[89] He based this on personal contact with them: "upon passing through the Strait of Malaca some Malays came up to the Ship, and they are similar to Filipinos, not only in their color and features, but also in many words, which confirmed me in my opinion."[90] Second, there were pagans (*bárbaros*): *Negros del monte* (Blacks in the hills), who are backgrounded as *Aetas ó cimarrones del monte* on his 1734 map (see Figure 11.4) and appear also in his description of Pangasinan Province[91] as well as Manobos, Igorrots, and numerous other peoples who are not under the Church's control.[92] Further into his account he uses the term *cafres*, meaning "man without religion" (*hombre sin ley*).[93] "In Manila there are many Kafirs," he reports, describing them as pagans who lived in the mountains and

Figure 11.5. Carta hydrográphica y chorográphica de las Yslas Filipinas (detail). Left to right: "Kafirs [men without religion]," "Camarin," "Lascar." Courtesy of the Newberry Library, Chicago.

jungles like wild beasts and with a penchant for witchcraft.[94] The term *Cafres* (Kafirs) is also engraved on the 1734 map's frame (Figure 11.5).

Geographía Histórica bookends those uncivilized peoples in the Philippine Islands with another civilized group: "There are other Negros in Manila, whom they call out of respect *Morenos* or *Criollos* (Browns or Creoles), with sharp minds and more civilized and reasonable habits. These Blacks, I have no doubt, came from Malabar or Coromandel."[95] Among Cruz Bagay's visualizations of the author's taxonomies, there is one (see Figure 11.4) that foregrounds *Español* (Spaniard), *Negro atezado criollo de la tierra* (Black African Creole from here), and *Indios peleando gallos* (Filipinos cockfighting) and relegates *Aetas ó cimarrones del monte* (Aetas, maroons in the hills) to the background, to the right of the unlabeled albino or piebald stag analyzed earlier in this chapter.

As part of natural history, Murillo Velarde's taxonomy of natives cannot avoid phenotype even amid cultural criteria:

Their eyes are big and wide, in which they differ from Sangleys and mestizos de Sangley, who eyes are thickly stitched like eyelets. Their hair is somewhat straight and long, and it is the idol of the Indians, who take care of it and style it with great diligence, and their hair distinguishes them from Blacks, who have raisin heads. Their beards are small and sparse, as in all of Asia, and this distinguishes them from Spaniards, although there are some Spaniards with pitiful beards such that they could pass for Indians.[96]

Further, just as we saw in the Jesuit's conceptualization of adaptation and differentiation in nonhuman animals, we see here in his conceptualization of the human body that skin color, nose shape, eye shape, and hair are features of prime matter—of corpuscular philosophy in the tradition of Gassendi, Boyle, Berni, and others. Hence the following description of the *indios philipinos*:

They are of sturdy body, their color is brown (*bazo*), their noses are all flat, without exception, which is a thing of wonder, that, amid so many thousands of men and across so many ages, no one has seen a pointy nose on an *indio*. I wish moderns would explain why the corpuscles that form the noses for thousands of leagues and in countless persons must always be obtuse and never pointy.[97]

Murillo Velarde was inviting empirical and mechanical natural philosophers to figure out how atoms or molecules of a specific shape were attracted and hooked to each other to form the nose that he considered a defining characteristic of this human *differentia*. Those strands of Western European scientific modernity were paramount to the Jesuit naturalist's taxonomy.

That said, the Spanish Crown's adaptation of precolonial social arrangements also weighed heavily, especially in distinguishing *estamento*, or social rank, within the *differentia* formed by *indios*. The most significant indigenous institution, politically and economically, was the *datu*, or governing nobility, composed of Malay descendants. By dint of transculturation, the Spanish local administration of native towns (*pueblos de indios*) was composed of governors (*gobernadorcillos*) and heads (*cabezas de barangay*). In the geographer's day, *cabezas de barangay* were often wealthy Tagalos, and even they were outnumbered by *mestizos de Sangley*, one of whose parents descended from a *principal* (Filipino noble) and the other from a Chinese.[98] Murillo Velarde tells his readers that the town heads and native nobles in general "dress like Spaniards and wear a lot of gold."[99] Analogous to caciques in colonial Spanish America, *cabezas de barangay* were captains charged with collecting the royal tribute from indigenous plebs assigned to them.[100] Thus, within the variety of human known as *indio*, there were social ranks that distinguished an *indio* from a head and from a *principal*, who was classified as Spanish gentry.

The Jesuit cartographer's contempt for the ruling class in Indian towns is obliquely revealed in *Geographía Histórica*: "The faces of the Spaniards who have some illustrious ancestry from the country soon become the color of olives, with no remedy for this illness ever found in the boticaries, which is part of God's plan, that it serve as a ballast to vanity for some of them who are insufferable when they find themselves appointed to some Crown position."[101] This stinging rebuke was notably as scientific as it was religious. The assertion that God had marked haughty *principales*—members of the Spanish gentry, legal and socially—with an olive-colored stain would have immediately resonated with amateur and academy savants who held that native plebs were born white except for a telltale stain on their backside, which signaled their true complexion.[102] The Spanish geographer flaunted his experimental knowledge of indigenous bodies and at once satirically relegated the *principales*, who belonged to the Spanish nobility, to the social rank of the native plebs, or *indios*.

In sum, Murillo Velarde's two decades of living and working in the midst of non-European peoples enabled the Jesuit in Manila to contest largely academic illustrations and accounts of the nature of Spanish Asia. He conceived his maps and historical geography of the Philippine Islands against a Eurocentric—and, more precisely, Gallocentric—backdrop of academic prestige and imperial utility that marginalized Spanish expertise in cartography, geography, and natural history. By reconciling mechanical and chemical understandings of matter and terrestrial bodies, as many European modern natural philosophers were, he moved within the confines of both Later Scholastic natural philosophy and the *nova philosophia*. His fluency in modern physics and chemistry not only confirmed the arrival of scientific modernity to Spanish Asia but also generated interpretations, applications, and questions wholly unforeseen by *novatores* in western Europe.

Notwithstanding such findings, however, there are issues outstanding in my analysis that have been raised in disparate geographical and temporal contexts by other contributors to this volume. What, for example, remains of the native geographies that undoubtedly contributed to Murillo Velarde's

Geographía Histórica of Spanish Asia and to his 1734 map of the same? How should we approach the mediations between Western European and Filipino epistemologies that produced the maps and historical-geographical account? At the very least, we must strive to refine our tools of analysis and expand our critical vocabularies for confronting cultural synergy and symbiosis. In this vein, the title of Antonio Cornejo Polar's posthumously published essay warned of "the risks of metaphor" following on the indiscriminate and fashionable use of *mestizaje* and hybridity in academic circles.[103] Those risks are real, and they pose a special challenge to historians of science and theorists of race alike. How, then, might we develop a critical language that eschews presentism and at the same time engages both historians of the present and historians of the past? One potential pathway, among many others, is to proceed with an awareness of the necessity of leaving traces, as Maurizio Ferraris has famously phrased it, and of acknowledging their social value.[104] In Murillo Velarde's maps and *Geographía Histórica*, some native traces are immediately legible; others, I admit, shall require sustained investigation, reflection, and collaboration.

Afterword: Lost in Translation

William Eamon

Spanish explorers and missionaries to the New World loved playing tricks on American Indians. It was their way of demonstrating the superiority of Catholicism and European science over native "superstitions." Spaniards recorded lots of them, such as the one Luis Millones Figueroa describes in his chapter in this volume when the Jesuit missionary Bernabé Cobo fooled a group of Incas by secretly using a magnifying glass to light a fire, creating the blaze as if by magic. We can be pretty sure Cobo's trick was a carefully thought-out strategy to achieve his main purpose of converting the Indians to the true faith. By demonstrating his "magic," he wanted to impress the "barbarous" natives and convince them of the superiority of European religion and culture.

But American Indians had some tricks of their own. Juan Pimentel recounts an instance of native trickery that must have happened many times over. When Vasco Núñez de Balboa interrogated natives about the whereabouts of gold and a sea beyond the mountains of Darién, they routinely indicated that they were to be found farther on, much farther on. By assuring Balboa that gold and water existed in abundance but "over there," Pimentel speculates, they "hoped that the foreigners would pass them by and go and harass someone else, preferably their enemies."[1] Concealment and deception were built into the cagey relationship between natives and colonial occupiers.[2] As in Europe, where guarding trade secrets was an economic strategy for survival in a competitive economic climate, concealment, whether of medical or geographical secrets, was a strategy for both cultural survival and cultural domination.

The analogy between trickery and translation may not be obvious. Yet just like a trick, a translation is a performance. Ralph Manheim, the great translator from German, compared the translator to an actor who speaks as the author would if the author spoke English. The translator's challenge, he said, is "to impersonate his author."[3] Just as in a trick, an illusion whose cause is hidden, the actor hides in the character and becomes invisible (that's what actors mean by being "in character"), convincingly connecting with the audience as a bridge connects two distinct places. The translator plays a similar kind of trick, this one on the reader, by attempting to "become" the author and remain invisible. Edith Grossman, the distinguished American translator of Miguel de Cervantes and Gabriel García Márquez, described translation as "a living bridge between two realms of discourse, two realms of experience."[4]

Translation is never literal; it is always a *retelling*. No two languages ever line up perfectly, word for word and phrase for phrase. Just as an actor interpreting a script discovers a play anew and creates something unique in each performance, translating too is an act of discovery and a creation of something new. There is thus an essential congruity between translation and discovery, for it is in these retellings that discovery takes place. But instead of a mystical (and perhaps mythical) eureka moment of discovery, the chapters in this volume demonstrate that the path from translation to discovery is often circuitous, hampered by imperfect communication, impeded by linguistic ignorance, distorted by religious and colonialist agendas, and thwarted by deliberate suppression of sources. Repeatedly we find that censorship was the rule, not the exception, in exchanges between Europeans and Native Americans. It was the informant, not the translator, who was made invisible. Europeans relied on countless native informants such as the cacique Ponquiaco, of Juan Pimentel's stimulating chapter, for information about New World nature. But Ponquiaco is one of the few we know by name. The rest were, so to speak, lost in translation.

Modern translators agree that the goal of a translation is fidelity to the original text. As Grossman expresses it, "Intrinsic to the concept of a translator's fidelity to the effect and impact of the original is making the second version of the work as close to the first writer's intention as possible."[5] Renaissance translators took a different view of their art. They tended to think of translation as a kind of opening of a box containing mysteries locked in a different language. Roger Williams titled his famous dictionary of the Algonquin language *Key into the Language of America* (1643) because, he wrote, it offered a "key" to "open a Box" containing the "rarities concerning the Natives themselves not yet discovered."[6]

The authors of the chapters in this volume helpfully take a more capacious definition of translation, restricting it not just to texts and also including the

movement (*translatio*) of ideas and things across time and space. Daniela Bleichmar's consideration of the *Codex Mendoza*, one of the few Aztec codices to
survive the wholesale destruction of "idolatrous" New World texts, illustrates
the tenuousness of the *physical* translation of texts.[7] But the very process of
physical translation enabled the transformation of indigenous concepts and
the creation of new knowledge, she argues. European scholars, fascinated and
mystified by the text's exotic "Mexican hieroglyphs," avidly reproduced the
images, thereby creating a new *Codex Mendoza*. "Mobility led to mutation
and multiplication," Bleichmar observes. Similarly, as Sara Miglietti shows in
her chapter, the multiple translations of New World climate reports—across
languages, disciplines, geographical spaces, and institutions—changed how
climate was understood.[8] Conceptualizing translation in such broad terms
opens up generous spaces for a consideration of the movement from translation to discovery.

If, as Edith Grossman says, translation is a bridge between two cultures,
it is a bridge that enables travel in both directions, not just a one-way passage from text to translation to reader. That two-way journey occasionally
facilitated a dialogue resulting in, as Marcy Norton shows, a syncretic mar-
riage of the indigenous and the European. To be sure, the dialogue was usually lopsided and tipped in favor of the colonial intruders, as we learn from
Jaime Marroquín Arredondo's meticulous reexamination of the Francisco
Hernández text. Marroquín Arredondo employs the term "transculturation"
to describe the intercultural exchanges that took place between missionaries and colonial administrators and their native informants—including, in
Hernández's case, Creole and native doctors.[9] Hernández, like all European
travelers and traders, brought a lot of intellectual baggage with him to New
Spain, including conventional European medical theories and the religious
ideals and ideological tools of political and economic domination of Spain's
American territories.

Although much was gained in the translation process, a lot was lost too.
"Noise"—or intellectual interference—could be deafening in the transcultural contact zones where European intellectuals interacted with natives and
tried to sort out what was essential from what was just incidental.[10] For colonial travelers such as Hernández, the "essential" meant what might be useful
to the state or profitable as commodities in the marketplace. What natives
thought was essential was not usually the same as what Europeans thought
was essential, as Norton's example of Quetzal, anatomized in her chapter
with surgical precision, suggests.[11] Time and again the intellectual baggage

that Europeans brought with them stood in the way of attempts to grasp native practices.[12]

The weight of tradition may have protected Europeans from the "shock of the new," as historians such as Anthony Grafton describe Europe's reaction to the New World encounter.[13] But it also screened out the richness and variety of native cultures. Nurtured on tales of fantastic beings in faraway lands and buoyed by an eclectic mix of classical, Hermetic, and Scholastic philosophy, Europeans were predisposed to putting New World cultures into pre-programmed epistemological boxes.[14] Cobo stared in disbelief at the Indians' supposed depravity and bestiality, seeing only "savages as uncouth and inept as unfinished logs," never fully comprehending that alien culture.[15]

Nor, for that matter, were things much different at home: the validity of the so-called new philosophy that emerged in the seventeenth century rested on the supposition that "naive" empirical knowledge was inherently incomplete and unreliable, lacking a firm scientific foundation. The experience in French Acadia of the colonial engineer François-Madeleine Vallée, skillfully examined by Christopher Parsons, is a case in point.[16] As Parsons shows, the European virtuosi imagined a limited role for collectors such as Vallée, one analogous to the "Depradators" of Francis Bacon's utopian *New Atlantis*, who would gather data from all corners of the world and send it back to metropolitan "Interpreters of Nature" to be assessed and interpreted. Thus, Vallé's remarkable *Mémoire sur les plantes*, with its detailed descriptions of plants and their medicinal uses based on reports from local Mi'kmaw informants, seems to have been almost completely ignored in the stately halls of the Paris-based Académie Royale des Sciences. Though valued for the specimens pressed between its pages, Vallé's careful descriptions of indigenous plant uses made little impression on the virtuosi. Send seeds and dried leaves, said the Parisian botanist Antoine de Jussieu, we'll do the rest. The snooty manner of metropolitan scientists such as Jussieu recalls the equally haughty view of Galileo, who spoke for the community of learned natural philosophers when he contrasted the "eyes of an idiot" with those of "a careful and practiced anatomist or philosopher."[17] To the new philosophers, the sublime mysteries of the universe were beyond the capacities of ordinary people, let alone Native Americans.[18]

Translation was in any case sketchy, imperfect, and partial. As Vallée, Hernández, and others found out, it wasn't easy to extract empirical knowledge from native informants, who were often secretive and reticent to share information with outsiders. Trickery and deception were constant companions in the fragile relationships of American Indians and colonial intruders, and the duplicity went both ways. Translations were never transparent and were always clouded, like vision blurred by cataracts. But discovery frequently happens in the blurred vision of faulty translation, the imperfect vision that opens up a space for wonder, the catalyst of discovery.

Must we banish discovery from our lexicon of the history of early modern science? It depends on how one understands "discovery." While the editors of this volume (and some of its authors) tend to be skeptical of the usefulness of that concept (and in all the chapters, translation takes center stage), others leave room for a more moderate stance. Juan Pimentel, taking a cue from philosopher of science Augustine Brannigan, cogently argues for Balboa's sighting of the Pacific Ocean as a *discovery* (because "he led the expedition that unleashed the knowledge of the Pacific Ocean") while also acknowledging the role that the *translation* of indigenous knowledge to Europeans played in that discovery.[19] Similarly, Sarah Rivett notes that the *translation* process that took place in learning indigenous languages led over the long run to the *discovery* of "unprecedented Euro-American insights into indigenous linguistic structures and their accompanying cosmologies."[20] There are, in my view, positive signs in current historiography that augur the survival of the idea of discovery.

Usually discovery is understood as some sort of psychological or intellectual gestalt shift involving a radical change in the way a phenomenon or event is understood. As the philosopher Norwood Russell Hanson (anticipating Thomas Kuhn) explains, the discoverer is one "who sees in familiar objects what no one else has seen before."[21] However, recent research has shown that in the early modern period "science" meant more than theory and that the early modern sciences included more than astronomy, physics, and cosmology. Pamela Smith, writing on current trends in the historiography of Renaissance science, suggests a more apt definition of science as "the interaction of humans with their natural environment and their aspirations to understand it."[22] If we accept the definition of science as "human engagement with nature," as Smith urges, then not only is the scope of the history of science enlarged—to include, for example, technology, natural history, alchemy, and medicine—but an entirely new cast of characters enters the stage. Not only educated elites and humanist literati but also craftsmen, women, fishermen, voyagers, missionaries, peasants, and American Indians collected natural knowledge.

New locations of scientific practice also emerged. Vernacular understandings of nature took shape in pharmacies, workshops, gardens, oceangoing ships, warehouses, dockyards, printing houses, Andean forests, and even households and plazas as well as in lecture halls. Suddenly, the places of scientific practice become enlarged to include spaces in colonial settings, thus bringing into the picture transcultural exchanges in a global context. Finally, the new historiography argues for a less stringent separation of head from hand and suggests that things as well as books are the bearers of scientific knowledge.[23]

We can detect in the transcultural contacts so richly described in this volume the nascent emergence of a model of scientific inquiry—and discovery—that would eventually become enshrined as the "Baconian method." In his somewhat idealized scheme, the English philosopher and lord chancellor Sir Francis Bacon imagined a flow of knowledge from gatherers of empirical information to interpreters of data in an orderly process directed by a central authority, a process that he thought would not just generate new data but would also lead to scientific discovery. As we learn from Sara Miglietti's chapter, something similar to Bacon's idea seems to have taken place when empirical reports about New World climates were submitted to the Casa de la Contratación (House of Trade) and later the Royal Society of London.[24] To be sure, interruptions occurred in the translation of knowledge, sometimes accidental, occasionally deliberate. In John Slater's lively chapter, we meet the cantankerous, disagreeable Spanish botanist Bernardo de Cienfuegos, who while insisting on writing in the vernacular and scrupulously avoiding Latin terminology resolutely refused to have his work printed, rather like some of today's digital Luddites. Needless to say, Cienfuegos's massive manuscript remained practically unnoticed until the twentieth century.[25] Cienfuego's anachronistic, "paranoid" style of natural history ran directly counter to the Baconian ideal.

As is the case with many of his ideas, Bacon described his model for advancing scientific discovery in a fable. His utopian tract *New Atlantis*, a fictional story of a community founded by Spanish sailors who become shipwrecked and marooned on the island of Bensalem, described a state-sponsored scientific research institute called Solomon's House. The institute sends out various data collectors, including "Depradators" who collect natural history data and "Mystery-men" who gather experiments of the mechanical arts. Eventually the data gets organized in tables by "Compilers" and finally goes to the "Interpreters of Nature," who "raise discoveries by experiments into greater observations, axioms, and aphorisms." As Michael Hunter and others have shown, Solomon's House, Bacon's idealized scientific research institution, would later become a model for the Royal Society of London.[26]

Where did Bacon get this idea? Recent studies have pointed out that Solomon's House bears an unmistakable resemblance to Spain's colonial institutions for information gathering, such as the Casa de la Contratación and the Consejo de Indias (Council of the Indies).[27] Bacon was well acquainted with the Spanish maritime discoveries, as were most educated Englishmen. Spanish treatises on navigation, natural history, and cosmography were sold in London bookstores and were readily available to merchants, mariners, and curious readers.[28] As Ralph Bauer explains in fascinating detail, English translations of Spanish works on natural history such as Richard Eden's redaction of Gonzalo Fernández de Oviedo y Valdés's popular *Sumario de la natural historia de las Indias* were purposely contextualized for an English audience.[29] Bacon was keenly aware of living in a new age of discovery. It is hardly surprising that as a philosopher and practical man concerned about England's commercial future, he should have paid close attention to the scientific machinery that Spain put in place to achieve its transoceanic power. For a man who compared himself to Christopher Columbus, the Iberian achievement was a compelling metaphor of scientific discovery.

Instead of asking what made discoveries happen, perhaps we need to be asking how they came to be recognized as or labeled discoveries. The philosopher Augustine Brannigan characterizes this approach as the attributional model—a refined way of saying that discovery is a matter of perspective. Not only that, discoveries are discoveries only when they are socially identified as discoveries.[30] That is why discoveries are often seen in retrospect as having been inevitable when in fact they may been simply outcomes of serendipity.

Discovery is about as central to our understanding of science as any concept, whether fact, theory, or experiment. Yet it is clear that the traditional positivist idea of the history of science as the "discovery of objective truth," as George Sarton once described it, no longer bears scrutiny in the cold light of modern historiography.[31] Because accounts of scientific discoveries are retroactive reconstructions in light of the European experience, the history of discovery is almost always written from the perspective of the present, a viewpoint that historians nowadays well nigh unanimously reject.[32]

Historians of early modern science may not agree about whether to abandon or keep the concept of discovery. For some, the very word reeks of the detested positivism that dominated historiography a few generations ago and still lingers in popular science writing. Historians of science nowadays roundly reject that prejudice. The arrogance of discovery repels.

Not so fast, say others. Discovery, while dripping with ideological muck, is still an essential concept because it tells a real and important story about the history of science. We historians weren't meant to simply dissect and nuance the past; we must also to tell good and convincing stories, because story, with its respect for fine-grained detail and plain observation, reveals the truth of history more clearly and distinctly than dissection and nuance while also preserving the ambiguity and uncertainty—that is, the reality and truth—of the past. Narrative is the historian's most powerful tool for translating the foreign past into a story that rings true in the present.

I count myself among the latter. We need not nor should we abandon the narrative of discovery, though our goal should be to tell it in a way that includes all characters and perspectives; only in that way will the story be complex and true. Discovery is inherently a narrative, a story that begins with an encounter and ends with the social recognition of a phenomenon's identity as a discovery. There is no more effective way to describe the intellectual shift that takes place during that process than narrative.

In most cases they are not eureka experiences. Balboa's discovery of the Pacific Ocean was not just one discovery; it was multiple discoveries: not only that a sea lay beyond the mountains but also that judging by tidal changes it was a colossal sea. And in his chance encounter with Ponquiaco, the sagacious *mozo prudente* of Peter Martyr's story, Balboa discovered a truth that was of even greater importance than the discovery of the Pacific Ocean: the discovery that natives were not savages and instead were astute and sagacious observers. As for the reverse, we have no way of knowing what Ponquiaco— the American Indian of whom the Spaniards said "he revealed to them the natural secrets these lands held"—made of the invaders.

Invention or discovery? Either way, the interchanges between observed facts and cultural expectations gave rise to profound experiences of doubt and discovery, the stuff of powerful narratives.

Discovery almost always occurs by chance. Francis Bacon eloquently explained that truth through the myth of Pan, the goat-footed god of hunting and protector of shepherds, who was out hunting in the forest and stumbled upon the lost goddess Ceres (the goddess of agriculture) when all the other higher gods failed in their search her. Bacon interpreted the myth to mean that "the discovery of things useful to life . . . is not to be looked for from the abstract philosophies, as it were the greater gods, but only from Pan; that is from sagacious experience and the universal knowledge of nature, which will often by chance, and as it were while engaged in hunting, stumble upon such discoveries."[33] Bacon called this method "sagacity and a kind of hunting by scent, rather than a science."[34] We would call it serendipity, discoveries made by chance encounters.[35] One might say that the Baconian methodology of discovery, one of Bacon's most important philosophical insights, boils down to a program to codify sagacity.

The role chance that plays in discovery is no secret to practicing scientists. Virtually every one of them will tell you that fortune looms large in discovery, and many have their own tales of serendipitous encounters. Contrary to the opinion of some philosophers of science, testing hypotheses isn't the scientist's goal. Nor is falsification. Some will tell you that most hypotheses aren't worth testing, let alone falsifying. Nor is proving that something isn't true ever going to make the career of a scientist. Discovery is the silver chalice of science, they will tell you, and every scientist knows it.

Understanding discovery is therefore an important task for historians of science. We know there are pitfalls in tacking too closely to the narrative of discovery. But discovery is something that "lies at the heart of the scientific revolution" and is still one of the most difficult and important stories to tell.[36] While discovery should be central to our narrative, the chapters in this volume also teach us that in the early modern knowledge economy, which opened up diverse new spaces for making knowledge, translation was often—and in some cases necessarily—the beginning of discovery.[37] At a moment when natural knowledge was understood as being about things and practices and not speculative answers to "why" questions, the movement of knowledge and practices across cultural and geographical distances sparked unforeseen epistemological changes. Just as discovery is not self-evident (as George Sarton assumed), neither is translation. The chapters in this volume record countless examples of lacunae and erasures in the translation of indigenous knowledge and practices to Europeans, some the result of deliberate suppression and others the accidental outcome of preconceptions, linguistic incompetence, or just simply slippages. But the chapters also furnish ample evidence of translations giving rise to discoveries. The one thing that is consistent about these myriad translations is that they were always (or for the most part) tied to facts, objects, and specimens—always about *how* things occur and rarely about speculative answers as to *why* things are. The fore-grounding of that attribute is also one of the distinguishing marks of the new history of the scientific revolution now being written.[38]

If the early modern period was an age of translation, as we learn from the chapters in this volume, it was also the age of the new.[39] In the period delineated by these studies, Europeans came upon new worlds both East and West, invented new technologies such as printing, encountered new peoples and cultures, observed new stars in the heavens, opened new trade routes, brought back from distant lands a menagerie of exotic plants and animals, propagated new religious faiths, and created new philosophies that challenged long-held beliefs. Long before the European encounter with the New World, the wondrous had been part and parcel of the literature of travel.[40] But the discoveries of the sixteenth century "gave new life to the long tradition of writing on natural wonders."[41] Suddenly the "wonders of the East" were no longer just things read about in books of dubious authenticity. Ivory tusks, African charms, canoes, stuffed birds of paradise, and exotic plants and animals such as tobacco, parrots, and armadillos populated the gardens, zoos, and collections of aristocrats, pharmacists, and merchants.[42] And it was not just exotica from the New World that turned the heads of Europeans. More spectacular were *naturalia* from Asia, many transported or translated to Europe by Jesuits, including the amazingly observant polymath Pedro Murillo Velarde, the subject of Ruth Hill's enlightening chapter.[43] Of course, Europeans knew about plenty of marvels from the East by reading authors such as Pliny, whose passion for the extraordinary led him to imagine mares impregnated by the wind, dog-headed people, and similar fanciful stuff. But Europeans had never actually *seen* any of these things. Suddenly in the Renaissance there were marvels aplenty before their very eyes.

Encounters with the new and exotic led inevitably to translation, because only through translation is the seemingly incomprehensible made intelligible. Translations arose in part out of the need to know for economic and imperialistic reasons—for example, Philip II's driving need to gather information about his colonial territories in order to ascertain their worth, which spawned many of the translation projects described in this book.[44] But translation was also driven by curiosity, for translation is an attempt not just to show the exotic but also to re-create it. That is where translation and discovery meet: bewildering novelty invariably arouses wonder and in turn inflames curiosity, the engine of discovery.

Early modern philosophers insisted to the point of cliché that wonder is not the end but rather the beginning of inquiry. Descartes famously made it "the first of all the passions," which causes the mind "to consider attentively those objects that seem to it rare and extraordinary," thus inflaming the curiosity that leads the mind to discovery.[45] First the senses are bewitched by novelty; then the mind snaps to attention and begins the work of dissection that leads ultimately to the discovery of hidden causes.[46] The paradox is that inquiry, which leads to understanding, inevitably ends wonder. "Wonder entailed a passionate desire for the *scientia* it lacked," observes Carolyn Walker Bynum; "it was the stimulus and incentive to investigation."[47]

Wonder, curiosity, discovery: to these successive moments leading to scientific knowledge we must add translation, which in the early modern era was so often a prelude to the sequence of events that led to discovery. During the sixteenth and seventeenth centuries the knowledge economy underwent a shift to valuing facts over explanations by way of causes, thereby opening up the scientific community to include people all over the globe of all social ranks and backgrounds, from London virtuosi to Dutch merchants to Peruvian shamans.[48] For the global scientific community under the reign of facts, the translation of ideas and things across vast distances and among peoples of myriad languages took center stage. It is no coincidence that "the beginnings of global science occurred during the period of the rise of a global economy," writes Harold Cook.[49] Merchants, rulers, and virtuosi shared many of the same passions, including a passion for collecting and exchanging facts and things. In that global setting, translation was the handmaiden of discovery.

Notes

Introduction

1. Francis Bacon, *The New Organon*, ed. Lisa Jardine and Michael Silverthorne (Cambridge: Cambridge University Press, 2000), 89.

2. On the current crisis of the paradigm of discovery in the natural sciences, see Russell Stannard, *The End of Discovery* (Oxford: Oxford University Press, 2010), 209–222. The classic critiques of the paradigm of discovery as an agent of change are Thomas S. Kuhn, *The Structure of Scientific Revolutions*, 2nd ed. (Chicago: University of Chicago Press, 1970), 35–42; Michel Foucault, *The Order of Things: An Archaeology of the Human Sciences* (New York: Vintage Books, 1994); Alan Chalmers, *What Is This Thing Called Science?*, 4th ed. (Indianapolis: Hackett Publishing, 2013).

3. Enrique Dussel, *El encubrimiento del otro: Hacia el origen del mito de la modernidad* (Quito: ABYA-YALA, 1994); Walter Mignolo, *The Darker Side of the Renaissance: Literacy, Territoriality, and Colonization* (Ann Arbor: University of Michigan Press, 1995); Mabel Moraña, Enrique Dussel, and Carlos A. Jáuregui, eds., *Coloniality at Large: Latin America and the Postcolonial Debate* (Durham, NC: Duke University Press, 2008).

4. See James Maffie, *Aztec Philosophy: Understanding a World in Motion* (Boulder: University Press of Colorado, 2014); Eduardo Viveiros de Castro, *Cannibal Metaphysics: For a Post-Structural Anthropology*, trans. and ed. Peter Skafish (Minneapolis: Univocal and the University of Minnesota Press, 2014); Eduardo Viveiros de Castro, *From the Enemy's Point of View: Humanity and Divinity in an Amazonian Society*, trans. Catherine Howard (Chicago: University of Chicago Press, 1992); *Entangled Trajectories: Indigenous and European Histories*, ed. Ralph Bauer and Marcy Norton, special issue of *Colonial Latin American Review* 26, no. 1 (March 2017).

5. For important recent forays into the cross-cultural history of science in the early modern Atlantic world, see Simon Varey et al., eds., *Searching for the Secrets of Nature: The Life and Works of Dr. Francisco Hernández* (Stanford, CA: Stanford University Press, 2000), 127–134; José Pardo-Tomás, "'Antiguamente vivían más sanos que ahora': Explanations of the native mortality in the *Relaciones Geográficas de Indias*," in *Medical Cultures of the Early Modern Spanish Empire*, ed. John Slater, María Luz López-Terrada, and José Pardo-Tomás, 41–65 (Surrey, UK: Ashgate, 2014); José Pardo-Tomás and Mauricio Sánchez Menchero, eds., *Geografías Médicas: Orillas y fronteras culturales de la medicina (siglos XVI y XVII)* (Mexico City: UNAM/Centro de Investigaciones Interdisciplinarias en Ciencias y Humanidades, 2014); Marcy Norton, *Sacred Gifts, Profane Pleasures: A History of Tobacco and Chocolate*

in the Atlantic World (Ithaca, NY: Cornell University Press, 2008); Jaime Marroquín Arredondo, *Diálogos con Quetzalcóatl: Humanismo, etnografía y ciencia (1492–1577)* (Madrid: Iberoamericana Vervuert, 2014); Pablo Gómez, *The Experiential Caribbean: Creating Knowledge and Healing in the Early Modern Atlantic* (Chapel Hill: University of North Carolina Press, 2017).

6. On the notion of a transcultural hermeneutics, see Helen Watson-Verran and David Turnbull, "Science and Other Indigenous Knowledge Systems," in *Handbook of Science and Technology Studies*, ed. Sheila Jasanoff, Gerald E. Marble, James C. Peterson, and Trevor Pinch, 115–139 (Thousand Oaks, CA: Sage, 1995); David Turnbull, *Masons, Trickster and Cartographers: Comparative Studies in the Sociology of Scientific and Indigenous Knowledge* (London: Routledge, 2000).

7. Scott L. Montgomery, *Science in Translation: Movements of Knowledge Through Cultures and Time* (Chicago: University of Chicago Press, 2000), 2.

8. See, for example, Stephen Gaukroger, *The Emergence of a Scientific Culture: Science and the Shaping of Modernity, 1210–1685* (Oxford, UK: Clarendon, 2006); Ann Blair, "Natural Philosophy," in *The Cambridge History of Science*, Vol. 3, *Early Modern Science*, ed. Katherine Park and Lorraine Daston, 365–406 (Cambridge: Cambridge University Press, 2006).

9. Peter Harrison, *The Bible, Protestantism, and the Rise of Natural Science* (Cambridge: Cambridge University Press, 1998), 8.

10. See Víctor Navarro Brotóns and William Eamon, eds., *Beyond the Black Legend: Spain and the Scientific Revolution* (Valencia: Institute of the History of Science, 2007).

11. Important examples include José María López Piñero and María Luz López Terrada, eds., *La influencia española en la introducción en Europa de las plantas americanas: 1493–1623* (Valencia: Instituto De Estudios Documentales e Históricos Sobre La Ciencia, Universitat De València-C.S.I.C, 1997); José María López Piñero and José Pardo-Tomás, *La influencia de Francisco Hernández (1517–1587) en la constitución de la botánica y la materia médica modernas* (Valencia: Instituto de Estudios Documentales e Históricos sobre la Ciencia, 1996); Pardo-Tomás, "'Antiguamente vivían más sanos que ahora'"; Jorge Cañizares-Esguerra, *Nature, Empire, and Nation: Explorations of the History of Science in the Iberian World* (Stanford, CA: Stanford University Press, 2006); Antonio Barrera-Osorio, *Experiencing Nature: The Spanish American Empire and the Early Scientific Revolution* (Austin: University of Texas Press, 2006); Nicolás Wey-Gómez, *The Tropics of Empire: Why Columbus Sailed South to the Indies* (Cambridge, MA: MIT Press, 2008); Daniela Bleichmar, *Visible Empire: Botanical Expeditions and Visual Culture in the Hispanic Enlightenment* (Chicago: University of Chicago Press, 2012); Daniela Bleichmar, *Visual Voyages: Images of Latin American Nature from Columbus to Darwin* (New Haven, CT: Yale University Press, 2017); Maria Portuondo, *Secret Science: Spanish Cosmography and the New World* (Chicago: University of Chicago Press, 2009); Arndt Brendecke, *Imperium und Empirie: Funktionen des Wissens in der spanischen Kolonialherrschaft* (Cologne: Böhlau, 2009); Londa Schiebinger and Claudia Swan, eds., *Colonial Botany: Science, Commerce, and Politics in the Early Modern World* (Philadelphia: University of Pennsylvania Press, 2005).

12. For an important exception, see David Freedberg, *The Eye of the Lynx: Galileo, His Friends, and the Beginnings of Modern Natural History* (Chicago: University of Chicago Press, 2002), esp. 198-350.

13. Francis Bacon, *The Works of Francis Bacon, New Edition*, 15 vols., ed. James Spedding, Robert Leslie Ellis, and Douglas Denon Heath (Boston: Houghton, Mifflin, 1900), 6:46.

14. Richard Hakluyt, *The Principal Navigations, Voyages, Traffiques & Discoveries of the English Nation*, 12 vols. (Glasgow: James McLehose and Sons, 1903), 1: xxxv.

15. See Portuondo, *Secret Science*. On alchemy, see Mar Rey Bueno, *Los señores del fuego: Destiladores y espagíricos en la corte de los Austrias* (Madrid: Corona Borealis, 2002). On science under Philip II more generally, see David Goodman, *Power and Penury: Government, Technology, and Science in Philip II's Spain* (Cambridge: Cambridge University Press, 1988).

16. On Sigüenza y Góngora, see Ralph Bauer, *The Cultural Geography of Colonial American Literatures: Empire, Travel, Modernity* (Cambridge: Cambridge University Press, 2003), 157–178. On Kircher, see Paula Findlen, *Athanasius Kircher: The Last Man Who Knew Everything* (New York, Routledge, 2004).

17. On scientific networks, see Bruno Latour, *Science in Action: How to Follow Scientists and Engineers Through Society* (Milton Keynes, UK: Open University Press, 1987), esp. 215–257. On the Jesuit network, see Luis Millones Figueroa and Domingo Ledesma, eds., *El saber de los jesuitas, historias naturales y el Nuevo Mundo* (Frankfurt: Vervuert-Iberoamericana, 2005).

18. On Spanish and Spanish American "patriotic epistemology" in the production of knowledge about the New World, see Jorge Cañizares Esguerra, *How to Write the History of the New World* (Stanford, CA: Stanford University Press, 2001).

19. See Margarita Zamora, *Reading Columbus* (Berkeley: University of California Press, 1993), 21–38 and 95–151; Portuondo, *Secret Science*.

20. See Katherine Park and Lorraine Daston, "Introduction," in *The Cambridge History of Science*, 3:1–20. See also in the same volume Peter Dear's "The Meanings of Experience," 106–132.

21. See Marroquín Arredondo, *Diálogos*.

22. See Georges Baudot, *Utopia and History in Mexico: The First Chroniclers of Mexican Civilization* (Boulder: University Press of Colorado, 1995), 110–115.

23. See Maffie, *Aztec Philosophy*.

24. See Alfredo López Austin and Leonardo López Luján, *Monte sagrado: Templo Mayor* (Mexico City: Instituto Nacional de Antropología e Historia/Universidad Nacional Autónoma de México/Instituto de Investigaciones Antropológicas, 2009); Elizabeth Hill Boone, *Cycles of Time and Meaning in the Mexican Books of Fate* (Austin: University of Texas Press, 2007); Miguel León Portilla, *Los antiguos Mexicanos: A través de sus crónicas y cantares* (Mexico City: Fondo de Cultura Económica, 1961); Miguel León Portilla, *La Filosofía náhuatl estudiada en sus fuentes* (Mexico City: Universidad Nacional Autónoma de México, 1966); Angel María Garibay Kintana, *Historia de la literatura náhuatl* (Mexico City: Porrúa, 1953).

25. The phrase "contact zones" was first introduced by Rolena Adorno. For its history, see her *The Polemics of Possession in Spanish American Narrative* (New Haven, CT: Yale University Press, 2007), 329. On "cultural borders," see Gloria Anzaldúa, *Borderlands: La Frontera; The New Mestiza* (San Francisco: Aunt Lute Books, 1987).

26. See Fernando Ortiz, *Contrapunteo cubano del tabaco y el azúcar*, reprint ed. (Madrid: Cátedra, 2002), 102–103.

27. Homi Bhabha, *The Location of Culture* (New York: Routledge, 1994), 114. See also Serge Gruzinski, *The Mestizo Mind: The Intellectual Dynamics of Colonization and Globalization* (New York: Routledge, 2002), 23.

28. See Marroquín Arredondo, *Diálogos*.

29. See Anthony Grafton, "The Identities of History in Early Modern Europe: Prelude to a Study of the *Artes Historicae*," in Gianna Pomata and Nancy G. Siraisi, eds., *Historia: Empiricism and Erudition in Early Modern Europe* (Cambridge, MA: MIT Press, 2005), 53; Karl Kohut, "Las crónicas de Indias y la teoría historiográfica: Desde los comienzos hasta mediados del siglo XVI," in *Narración y Reflexión: Las crónicas de Indias y la teoría historiográfica*, ed. Karl Kohut (Mexico City: El Colegio de México, 2007), 19–20; Sarah H. Beckjord, *Territories of History: Humanism, Rhetoric, and the Historical Imagination in the Early Chronicles of Spanish America* (University Park: Pennsylvania State University Press, 2007), 30–36; Gianna Pomata and Nancy G. Siraisi, "Introduction," in *Historia: Empiricism and Erudition*, 4–5.

30. Pomata and Siraisi, "Introduction," in *Historia: Empiricism and Erudition*, 5, 15. See also Peter Dear, *Revolutionizing the Sciences: European Knowledge and Its Ambitions, 1500–1700* (Princeton, NJ: Princeton University Press, 2009), 31; Gregorio A. Hinojo, "Nebrija y la historiografía renacentista: La fortuna," in *Antonio de Nebrija: Edad Media y Renacimiento*, ed. Carmen Codoñer and Juan Antonio González Iglesias (Salamanca: Ediciones Universidad de Salamanca, 1997), 31–32.

31. See Richard W. Serjeantson, "Proof and Persuasion," in *The Cambridge History of Early Modern Science*, 3:132–175. For the Iberian case, see Brendecke, *Imperium und Empirie*; Roberto González Echevarría, "Humanismo, Retórica y las Crónicas de la Conquista," in *Isla a su Vuelo Fugitiva: Ensayos Críticos sobre Literatura Hispanoamericana*, 9–26 (Madrid: José Porrúa Turanzas, 1983); González Echevarría, *Myth and Archive: A Theory of Latin American Narrative* (Cambridge: Cambridge University Press, 1990); Walter Mignolo, "El Métatexto Historiográfico y la Historiografía Indiana," *MLN* 96, no. 2 (1981): 358–402, esp. 389; Walter Migolo, "Cartas, crónicas y relaciones del descubrimiento y la conquista," in *Historia de la literatura hispanoamericana: Época colonial*, ed. Luis Iñigo Madrigal, 57–116 (Madrid: Ediciones Cátedra, 1982).

32. See Marroquín Arredondo, *Diálogos*, and his chapter in this volume.

33. See Angélica Morales et al., eds., *De la circulación del conocimiento a la inducción de la ignorancia* (Mexico City: UNAM, 2017). See also Norton, *Sacred Gifts*.

Chapter 1

This research is supported by the Spanish Ministry of Science and Innovation, National Research Project HAR 2014-52157-P.

1. Gonzalo Fernández de Oviedo, *Historia general y natural de las Indias*, Vol. 3 (Madrid: BAE, Atlas, 1959), 210–215. From the abundant secondary literature on Balboa and the sighting of the South Sea, I rely mainly on Feliciano Correa et al., *Vasco Núñez de Balboa, descubridor de la Mar del Sur: Edición conmemorativa del V Centenario del Descubrimiento del Océano Pacífico, 1513–2013* (Madrid: Ediciones Círculo Científico, 2013); Luis Blas Aritio, *Vasco Núñez de Balboa y los cronistas de Indias* (Panama: Ediciones Balboa, 2012); Carmen Mena, *El Oro del Darién: Entradas y cabalgadas en la conquista de Tierra Firme, 1509–1525* (Madrid: CSIC, 2011); Bethany Aram, *Leyenda negra y leyendas doradas en la conquista de América: Pedrarias y Balboa* (Madrid: Marcial Pons, 2008).

2. Oviedo, *Historia general*, 214.

3. For an overall view of the process, see Carl O. Sauer, *Descubrimiento y dominación española en el Caribe* (Mexico City: FCE, 1984).

4. On the invisibility and the ghostly nature of natives in American history, see Renée L. Bergland, *The National Uncanny: Indian Ghosts and American Subjects* (Hanover, NH: University Press of New England, 2000); Matthew Restall, *Seven Myths of the Spanish Conquest* (Oxford: Oxford University Press, 2004).

5. Helene Watson-Verran and David Turnbull, "Science and Other Indigenous Knowledge Systems," in *Handbook of Science and Technology Studies*, ed. S. Jasanoff, G. Markle, T. Pinch, and J. Petersen, 115–139 (Thousand Oaks, CA: Sage, 1995); David Turnbull, *Maps Are Territories: Science Is an Atlas* (Chicago: University of Chicago Press, 1989); Barbara E. Mundy, *The Mapping of New Spain: Indigenous Cartographies and the Maps of the Relaciones Geográficas* (Chicago: University of Chicago Press, 1996); Alessandra Russo, *El realismo circular: Tierras, espacios y paisajes de la cartografía hispana, siglos XVI y XVII* (Mexico City: UNAM Instituto de Investigaciones Estéticas, 2005); Alessandra Russo, *The Untranslatable Image: A Mestizo History of the Arts in New Spain, 1500–1600* (Austin: University of Texas Press, 2014); Alexander Hidalgo and John F. López, eds., *The Ethnohistorical Map in New Spain*, special issue of *Ethnohistory* 61, no. 2 (Spring 2014).

6. Bruno Latour, "Visualization and Cognition: Drawing Things Together," in *Knowledge and Society Studies in the Sociology of Culture Past and Present*, ed. Henrika Kuklick (Bingley, UK: JAI, 1986), 5–6.

7. Omar Jaén, *La población del Istmo de Panamá: Estudio de Geohistoria* (Madrid: Agencia Española de Cooperación Internacional, 1998), 44–78; Richard Cooke and Luis Alberto Sánchez Herrera, "Panamá indígena, 1501–1550," in *Historia general de Panamá*, Vol. 1, pt. 1, *Las sociedades originarias: El orden colonial*, ed. Alfredo Castillero Calvo, 47–78 (Panama: Comité Nacional del Centenario de la República, 2004).

8. Kathleen Romoli, *Los de la lengua de cueva: Los grupos indígenas del istmo oriental en la época de la conquista española* (Bogotá: Instituto Colombiano de Antropología, 1987).

9. Neil L. Whitehead, "Indigenous Cartography in Lowland South America and the Caribbean," in *Cartography in the Traditional African, American, Arctic, Australian, and Pacific Societies*, Vol. 2, Book 3, *The History of Cartography*, ed. David Woodward and Malcolm G. Lewis (Chicago: University of Chicago Press, 1998), 301.

10. Oviedo, *Historia general*, 327.

11. On Balboa's indigenous policy, see Mena, *El Oro del Darién*, 262; Blas Aritio, *Vasco Núñez de Balboa*, 188–254. On native alliances with the conquerors in both Americas, see Laura E. Matthew and Michel R. Oudijk, eds., *Indian Conquistadors: Indigenous Allies in the Conquest of Mesoamerica* (Norman: University of Oklahoma Press, 2007); Wayne E. Lee, ed., *Empires and Indigenes: Intercultural Alliance, Imperial Expansion and Warfare in the Early Modern World* (New York: New York University Press, 2011).

12. Ricardo Piqueras, *Entre el hambre y El Dorado: Mito y contacto alimentario en las huestes de la conquista del XVI* (Sevilla: Diputación de Sevilla, 1997), 175–200. See also Ricardo Piqueras, "Un indio vale casi como un caballo: Utilización indígena en las huestes del siglo XVI," *Boletín Americanista* 46 (1996): 275–297.

13. On cultural mediation, see Louise Bénat-Tachot and Serge Gruzinski, eds., *Passeurs culturels: Mécanismes de métissage* (Paris: Presses Universitaires de Marne-la-Vallée/Editions de la Maison des Sciences de l'homme, 2001); Simon Schaffer, Lissa Roberts, Kapil Raj, and James Delbourgo, eds., *The Brokered World: Go-Betweens and Global Intelligence, 1770–1820* (Sagamore Beach, MA: Science History Publications/USA, 2009).

14. Bartolomé de Las Casas, "Historia de las Indias, III," in *Obras completas*, Vol. 5, Book 3 (Madrid: Alianza, 1994), chap. 41, 1927.

15. Pedro Mártir de Anglería, "Década segunda," chapter 3 in *Décadas del Nuevo Mundo* (Madrid: Polifemo, 1989), 117.

16. Ibid.

17. Piqueras, *Entre el hambre y El Dorado*.

18. Pablo Sánchez León, *Abundancia y frustración: Por una historia conceptual de la economía en la modernidad latinoamericana (I)* (Madrid: Postmetrópolis, 2015).

19. See Theodor de Bry, *América 1590–1634* (Madrid: Siruela, 1992), 178. For a discussion on the role of the editions and illustrations of de Bry in the context of the Black Legend, see Patricia Gravatt, "Rereading Theodore de Bry's Black Legend," in *Rereading the Black Legend: The Discourses of Religious and Racial Differences in Renaissance Empires*, ed. Margaret R. Greer, Maureen Quilligan, and Walter Mignolo, 225–243 (Chicago: University of Chicago Press, 2008); Bernadette Bucher, *Icon and Conquest: A Structural Analysis of the Illustrations of de Bry's Great Voyages* (Chicago: University of Chicago Press, 1981).

20. Anglería, "Década segunda," 117.

21. Las Casas, "Historia de las Indias, III," 1929.

22. Ibid. For the sharing of the booty among the conquering army, see Mena, *El Oro del Darién*, 316–332.

23. Mena, *El Oro del Darién*, 477–492.

24. The assignment of scientific discoveries to individuals and their attribution to mental processes both have a long tradition, going back to the nineteenth-century idea so graphically expressed by Thomas Carlyle: "The *history of the world* is but the biography of great men." In the history of science, this viewpoint is still widespread despite what sociology and the history of science itself have shown, thanks to Robert K. Merton, Thomas Kuhn, Charles Coulston Gillispie, Michel Serres, Bruno Latour, Steve Woolgar, Steven Shapin, Simon Schaffer, Peter Dear, Mario Biagioli, Peter Galison, and many, many others.

25. Augustine Brannigan, *The Social Basis of Scientific Discoveries* (Cambridge: Cambridge University Press, 1981), 120–142, chap. 7, "Perspective, Reflexivity, and the Apparent Objectivity of Discovery," a fundamental text for any discussion on the notion of discovery.

26. Felipe Fernández-Armesto, *Civilizations: Culture, Ambition, and the Transformation of Nature* (New York: Free Press, 2001), 384. There is an immense bibliography on the invention of the Pacific and the Hispanic vision of the great ocean. Among them are Ricardo Padrón, "A Sea of Denial: The Early Modern Spanish Invention of the Pacific Rim," *Hispanic Review* 77, no. 1 (2009): 1–27; Rainer F. Buschmann, Edward R. Slack Jr., and James B. Tueller, *Navigating the Spanish Lake: The Pacific in the Iberian World, 1521–1898* (Honolulu: University of Hawai'i Press, 2014); Rainer F. Buschmann, *Iberian Visions of the Pacific Ocean, 1507–1899* (London: Palgrave Macmillan, 2014); Mercedes Maroto, *Exploring the Explorers: Spain and Oceania, 1519–1794* (Manchester, UK: Manchester University Press, 2009); Salvador Bernabéu, ed., *El Pacífico español: Mitos, viajeros y rutas oceánicas* (Madrid: Sociedad Geográfica Española, 2003).

27. Padrón, "A Sea of Denial," 1–27. The expression "the Spanish Lake" was popularized in Oskar H. K. Spate's classic work, *The Spanish Lake* (Canberra: ANU, 1979). See also Ricardo Padrón, *The Spacious Word: Cartography, Literature, and Empire in Early Modern Spain* (Chicago: University of Chicago Press, 2004).

28. On the knowledge of tides and their importance for medieval navigation, see Charles O. Frake, "Cognitive Maps of Time and Tide Among Medieval Seafarers," *Man*, new series, 20, no. 2 (June 1985): 254–270.

29. See, for example, Ángel de Altolaguirre y Duvale, *Vasco Núñez de Balboa* (Madrid: Real Academia de la Historia, 1914); Kathleen Romoli, *Núñez de Balboa: Descubridor del Pacífico* (Madrid: Espasa-Calpe, 1967); Manuel Lucena Salmoral, *Vasco Núñez de Balboa: Descubridor de la Mar del Sur* (Madrid: Anaya, 1989).

30. Bethany Aram, "Distance and Misinformation in the Conquest of America," in *The Limits of Empire: European Imperial Formations in Early Modern World History; Essays in Honor of Geoffrey Parker*, ed. Tonio Andrade and William Reger, 223–235 (Farnham, UK: Ashgate, 2012); Bethany Aram, *Leyenda negra y leyendas doradas en la conquista de América: Pedrarias y Balboa* (Madrid: Marcial Pons, 2008).

31. Nicolás Wey-Gómez, *The Tropics of Empire: Why Columbus Sailed South to the Indies* (Cambridge, MA: MIT, 2008).

32. Padrón, "A Sea of Denial"; Thomas Suárez, *Early Mapping of the Pacific: The Epic Story of Seafarers, Adventurers, and Cartographers Who Mapped the Earth's Greatest Ocean* (Singapore: Periplus, 2004). See also Martin Waldseemüller, *Introducción a la cosmografía y las cuatro navegaciones de Américo Vespucio*, ed. Miguel León-Portilla (Mexico City: Instituto de Investigaciones Históricas-UNAM, 2007).

33. Padrón, "A Sea of Denial," 5–6; Norman J. W. Thrower, "New Geographical Horizons: Maps," in *First Images of America: The Impact of the New World on the Old*, Vol. 2, ed. Fredi Chiapelli, Michael J. B. Allen, and Robert L. Benson, 659–674 (Berkeley: University of California Press, 1976).

34. Armando Cortesao, *"Descobrimento" e descobrimentos* (Coimbra: Junta de Investigações do Ultramar, 1972), 3–6.

35. Juan Gil, *Mitos y utopías del descubrimiento*, 3 vols. (Madrid: Alianza, 1989).

36. Constantino Bayle, *El Dorado fantasma* (Madrid: Consejo de la Hispanidad, 1943). In the context of a broader investigation, I am interested in applying the concepts of ghost and specter to a group of images and episodes from Iberian science.

37. See Correa et al., *Vasco Núñez de Balboa*; Aram, *Leyenda negra y leyendas doradas*.

38. Herzog August Bibliothek, Wolfenbüttel, Cod. Guelf. 103, Aug. 2.

39. Richard Uhden, "Die Kartenschätze der Herzog August Bibliothek zu Wolfenbüttel," *Niedersachsen* 36 (1931): 65–74; Richard Uhden, "An Unpublished Portolan Chart of the New World, A. D. 1519," *Geographical Journal* 91, no. 1 (January 1938): 44–50; Yorck Alexander Haase and Harold Jantz, *Die neue Welt in den Schätzen einer alten europäischen Bibliothek*, Exhibition catalog of the Herzog August Bibliothek, Vol. 17 (Wolfenbüttel: Herzog August Bibliothek, 1976); Maria Luisa Martín-Merás, "La cartografía de los descubrimientos en la época de Carlos V," in *Carlos V: La náutica y la navegación*, ed. José Ignacio González-Aller, 75–94 (Barcelona: Sociedad Estatal para la Conmemoración de los Centenarios de Felipe II y Carlos V-Lunwerg, 2000); José María Sanz-Heredia, "El portulano del Pacífico de la Herzog August Bibliothek," in *Vasco Núñez de Balboa*, 167–194; Antonio Sánchez, *La espada, la cruz y el Padrón: Soberanía, fe y representación cartográfica en el mundo ibérico bajo la Monarquía hispánica* (Sevilla: CSIC, 2013), 169–170; Joaquim Alves Gaspar, "The Representation of the West Indies in Early Iberian Cartography: A Cartometric Approach," *Terra Incognitae* 47, no. 1 (April 2015): 10–32.

40. On portolan charts, see Joaquim Alves Gaspar and Henrique Leitão, "What Is a Nautical Chart, Really? Uncovering the Geometry of Early Modern Nautical Charts," *Journal of Cultural Heritage* 29 (2018): 130–136; Tony Campbell, "Portolan Charts from the Late Thirteenth Century to 1500," in *The History of Cartography*, Vol. 1, ed. John B. Harley and David Woodward, 371–463 (Chicago: University of Chicago Press, 1987); Sandra Sáenz-López, "El portulano, arte y oficio," in *Cartografía medieval hispánica: Imagen de un mundo en construcción*, ed. Mariano Cuesta y Alfredo Surroca, 111–135 (Madrid: Real Sociedad Geográfica-Real Liga Naval Española, 2009); Richard Pflederer, *Finding Their Way at Sea: The Story of Portolan Charts, the Cartographers Who Drew Them and the Mariners Who Sailed by Them* (Houten: HES & De Graaf, Houten, 2012); Fortunato Lepore, Marco Piccardi and Enzo Pranzini, "The Autumn of Mediaeval Portolan Charts: Cartometric Issues," *e-Perimetron* 7, no. 1 (2012): 16–27.

41. See the classic work of the great historian of cartography J. Brian Harley, "Silences and Secrecy: The Hidden Agenda of Cartography in Early Modern Europe," *Imago Mundi* 40, (1988): 57–76.

42. Pascual de Andagoya, *Relación y documentos*, ed. Adrián Blázquez (Madrid: Historia 16, 1986), 88: "provincia que llamamos las Behetrías por no haber en ella ningún señor, se llama Cueva" (another province we call Behetrías for not having any Lord).

43. Juan Gil, *Mitos y utopías del descubrimiento*, Vol. 3, *El Dorado* (Madrid: Alianza, 1989), 52–58.

44. There is an extensive bibliography on Iberian cartography in the age of discovery. As in other subjects of such magnitude, we shall only list some of the reference works that have helped us learn the main points: Alison Sandman, "Spanish Nautical Cartography in the Renaissance," in *The History of Cartography*, Vol. 3, *Cartography in the European Renaissance*, ed. David Woodward, 1095–1142 (Chicago: University of Chicago Press); María Luisa Martín-Merás, *Cartografía marítima hispana: La imagen de America* (Barcelona: Lunwerg, 1993); Ursula Lamb, *Cosmographers and Pilots of the Spanish Maritime Empire* (Aldershot, UK: Variorum, 1995); Padrón, *The Spacious Word*; María Portuondo, *Secret Science: Spanish Cosmography and the New World* (Chicago: University of Chicago Press, 2009); Sánchez, *La espada, la cruz y el Padrón*.

45. I refer to the namesake title of María Portuondo's book *Secret Science* (2009).

46. Alves Gaspar, "The Representation of the West Indies," 24; Lepore, Piccardi, and Pranzini, "The Autumn of Mediaeval Portolan Charts," 17.

47. On the important role played by traditional technologies in the history of science, see David Edgerton, *The Shock of the Old: Technology and Global History Since 1900* (London: Profile Books, 2006). The survival of the *portulanos* and the amazing accuracy achieved by some of them, still hard to equal, is a commonplace accepted by all the specialized bibliography (see note 40 above).

48. "Ferdinandus hispanae Rex cum uellet huius terre optimam cognitionem habere circiter quingentos expertos et rei bellice peritos iuros in hanc terram misit ut diligenter omnia perquirerent, qui cum circiter sexaginta millia passuum introgressi inuenerunt aliud seuissimum uelut inmensum mare cuius cursus undarum ab australibus plagis ad litora uoluebatur. Vnde clare liquet hanc terram minime ese continentem ut non nulli cosmographi uoluerunt." The translation is from my colleague Eduardo Fernández Guerrero.

49. Tony Campbell gave a figure of 180 surviving maps and atlases from the fourteenth and fifteenth centuries, a very small number and perhaps not even representative material. See Campbell, "Portolan Charts," 373.

50. "*Oceanus Occi qui cum Meridionali cojungitur*."

51. Padrón, "A Sea of Denial," 2.

Chapter 2

1. The most authoritative botanical book at the time, Dioscorides's *Materia Medica*, did not have more than six hundred classified plants. See John Riddle, *Dioscorides on Pharmacy and Medicine* (Austin: University of Texas Press, 1985); Germán Somolinos D'Ardois, "La fusión indoeuropea en la medicina mexicana del siglo XVI," in *Historia general de la medicina en México*, Vol. 2, *Medicina Novohispana: Siglo XVI* (Mexico City: UNAM, 1984), 127–132; Carlos Viesca Treviño and Fernando Martínez Cortés, "Plantas medicinales americanas: Su injerto en la medicina hipocrática," in *Historia general de la medicina en México*, 2:175–202; José María López Piñero and José Luis Fresquet Febrer, "El mestizaje cultural de la medicina novohispana del siglo XVI y su influencia en Europa," in *El Mestizaje Cultural y la Medicina Novohispana del siglo XVI*, ed. J. L. Fresqeut Febrer and J. M. López Piñero, 9–23 (Valencia: Instituto de Estudios Documentales e Históricos sobre la Ciencia, 1995); Juan Comas, "La influencia indígena en la medicina hipocrática en la Nueva España del siglo XVI," in *El Mestizaje Cultural*, 91–123.

2. Hernández returned to Spain with those fifteen volumes plus another one of dried specimens. See David Freedberg, *The Eye of the Lynx: Galileo, His Friends, and the Beginnings of Modern Natural History* (Chicago: University of Chicago Press, 2002), 246. See also "Letter to Philip II After Francisco Hernández's Return to Seville in 1577," in José Toribio Medina, *Biblioteca Hispano-Americana 1493–1810*, Vol. 2 (Amsterdam: N. Israel, 1968), 292.

3. "Letter to Philip II After Francisco Hernández's Return to Seville," 292.

4. See José Enrique Campillo Álvarez, *Francisco Hernández: El Descubrimiento Científico del Nuevo Mundo* (Toledo: Diputación Provincial de Toledo, 2000) 131–150; Germán Somolinos D'Ardois, "Vida y obra de Francisco Hernández," in *Obras completas*, **XX** vols. (Mexico City: UNAM, 1960), 1:259–269.

5. See Simon Varey, "A Note on Texts and Translations," in *The Mexican Treasury: The Writings of Dr. Francisco Hernández*, ed. Simon Varey, trans. Rafael Chabrán, Cynthia L. Chamberlin, and Simon Varey, xvi–xviii (Stanford, CA: Stanford University Press, 2000); José María López Piñero and José Pardo-Tomás, *Nuevos materiales y noticias sobre la* Historia de las plantas de Nueva España *de Francisco Hernández* (Valencia: Instituto de Estudios Documentales e Históricos sobre la Ciencia, 1994), 136–142, 145–147; José María López Piñero and José Pardo-Tomás, *La influencia de Francisco Hernández (1517–1587) en la constitución de la botánica y la materia médica modernas* (Valencia: Instituto de Estudios Documentales e Históricos sobre la Ciencia, 1996), 24; José María López Piñero and José Pardo-Tomás, "The Contribution of Hernández to European Botany and Materia Medica," in *Searching for the Secrets of Nature: The Life and Works of Dr. Francisco Hernández*, ed. Simon Varley et al., 127–134 (Stanford, CA: Stanford University Press, 2000); Freedberg, *The Eye of the Lynx*, 198–350. See also Marcy Norton, "The Quetzal Takes Flight: Microhistory, Mesoamerican Knowledge, and Early Modern Natural History," this volume.

6. The *Rerum medicarum* final version came out in 1649–1651. See Freedberg, *The Eye of the Lynx*, 255–256, 8, 198.

7. The complete title of Ximenez's work is *Quatro libros de la naturaleza y virtudes de las plantas, y animales que estan recebidos en el uso de Medicina en la Nueva España* (Mexico City: Casa de la viuda de Diego López Dávalos, 1615). See also José Pardo-Tomás, "¿Viajes de ida

o de vuelta? La circulación de la obra de Francisco Hernández en México (1576–1672)," in *Il Tesoro Messicano: Libri E Saperi Tra Europa E Nuovo Mondo*, ed. Maria Eugenia Cadeddu and Marco Guardo, 39–66 (Rome: Leo S. Olschki, 2013).

8. See Roy MacLeod, "Introduction," in *Nature and Empire: Science and the Colonial Enterprise*, ed. Roy MacLeod, *Osiris* 15, (2000): 15; Londa Schiebinger, *Plants and Empire: Colonial Bioprospecting in the Atlantic World* (Cambridge, MA: Harvard University Press, 2004), esp. 73–93; Londa Schiebinger and Claudia Swan, *Colonial Botany: Science, Commerce, and Politics in the Early Modern World* (Philadelphia: University of Pennsylvania Press, 2005); Steven Shapin and Simon Schaffer, *Leviathan and the Air-Pump: Hobbes, Boyle, and the Experimental Life* (Princeton, NJ: Princeton University Press, 2011), 1–5.

9. For the use of "ethnographic history," see Rolena Adorno, *The Polemics of Possession in Spanish American Narrative* (New Haven, CT: Yale University Press, 2007).

10. "History, which may be called just and perfect history, is of three kinds. . . . The first we call chronicles, the second lives, and the third narrations or relations. Of these, . . . the third [excels] in verity and sincerity." Francis Bacon, *The Advancement of Learning*, Book 2 (London: J. M. Dent, 1958), II:5.

11. Pomata and Siraisi also notice that this trend culminated in the Baconian identification of *historia* and *experientei*, which gave the *historia* of nature unprecedented significance as the foundation of a true natural philosophy. Gianna Pomata and Nancy G. Siraisi, "Introduction," in *Historia: Empiricism and Erudition in Early Modern Europe*, ed. Gianna Pomata and Nancy G. Siraisi (Cambridge: MIT Press, 2005), 4–8.

12. See "Introducción," in *Constructores de otredad: Una introducción a la Antropología Social y Cultural*, ed. Mauricio Boivin, Ana Rosato, and Victoria Arribas, 7–13 (Buenos Aires: Antropofagia, 2004); Margaret Hodgen, *Early Anthropology in the Sixteenth and Seventeenth Centuries* (Philadelphia: University of Pennsylvania Press, 1964), 8; Anthony Pagden, *The Fall of Natural Man: The American Indian and the Origins of Comparative Ethnology* (Cambridge: Cambridge University Press, 1982).

13. Some examples are Ramón Pané, *Relación acerca de las antigüedades de los indios* (1494–1496); Andrés de Olmos, *Historia de los mexicanos por sus pinturas* (1533–1536); Toribio de Benavente Motolinía, *Historia de los indios de Nueva España* (ca. 1536); Bernardino de Sahagún, *Historia general de las cosas de Nueva España* (ca. 1577); Francisco Hernández, *Antigüedades de la Nueva España* (ca. 1576); Inca Garcilaso de la Vega, *Comentarios reales de los Incas* (1609).

14. Bacon, *The Advancement of Learning*, VII:6.

15. See Pomata and Siraisi, "Introduction," 1–38; Jaime Marroquín Arredondo, *Diálogos con Quetzalcóatl: Humanismo, etnografía y ciencia (1492–1577)* (Madrid: Iberoamericana Vervuert, 2014), 22–27.

16. See Tullio Gregory, "Translatio Studiorum," in *Translatio Studiorum: Ancient, Medieval and Modern Bearers of Intellectual History*, ed. Marco Sgarbi, 1–21 (Leiden: Brill Academic Publishers, 2012).

17. Giacinta Spinosa, "Translatio Studiorum Through Philosophical Terminology," in *Translatio Studiorum*, 73–80.

18. See Schiebinger and Swan, "Introduction," in *Colonial Botany*, 1–16.

19. See José Pardo-Tomás, "Antiguamente vivían más sanos que ahora: Explanations of Native Mortality in the *Relaciones Geográficas de Indias*," in *Medical Cultures of the Early*

Modern Spanish Empire, ed. John Slater, María Luz López-Terrada, and José Pardo-Tomás, 4–16 (Surrey, UK: Ashgate, 2014); see also Pardo-Tomás, "¿Viajes de ida o de vuelta? La circulación de la obra de Francisco Hernández en México (1576–1672)," 39–66.

20. The definition of the constitutional parts of sciences comes from Alan Chalmers, *What Is This Thing Called Science?* (Indianapolis: Hackett, 2013) 157.

21. Pomata and Siraisi, "Introduction," 4–5, 15; Brian Ogilvie, *The Science of Describing: Natural History in Renaissance Europe* (Chicago: University of Chicago Press, 2006), 8; Katherine Park and Lorraine Daston, "Introduction: The Age of the New," in *The Cambridge History of Science*, Vol. 3, *Early Modern Science*, ed. Katherine Park and Lorraine Daston, 1–17 (Cambridge: Cambridge University Press, 2006); Paula Findlen, *Possessing Nature: Museums, Collecting, and Scientific Culture in Early Modern Italy* (Berkeley: University of California Press, 1996), 11.

22. Somolinos D'Ardois, "Vida y obra de Francisco Hernández," 100–101.

23. Harold Cook, *Matters of Exchange: Commerce, Medicine, and Science in the Dutch Golden Age* (New Haven, CT: Yale University Press, 2007), 2–3.

24. The *princeps* edition of Pliny's natural history was published in Venice in 1469. See Brian Ogilvie, "Natural History, Ethicas, and Physico-Theology," in *Historia*, 76.

25. Other influential botanical works of the first half of the sixteenth century were Otto Brunfels and Hans Weiditz's *Herbarum vivae eicones* (1532), Hieronymus Boch's *Kreütterbuch* (1539), Conrad Gessner's *Historia plantarum et vires* (1541), and Leonhart Fuch's *De historia stirpium commentarii insignes* (1542). See Brian Ogilvie, "Natural History, Ethics, and Physico-Theology," in *Historia*, 80–81.

26. Some of the most prominent places for the study of medicine and botany were the universities of Valencia, Alcalá de Henares, and Salamanca as well as the Monastery of Guadalupe. See Somolinos D'Ardois, "Vida y obra de Francisco Hernández," 111; Víctor Navarro Brotóns, "Humanismo y ciencia en el siglo XVI," in *Antonio de Nebrija: Edad Media y Renacimiento*, ed. Carmen Codoñer y Juan Antonio González Iglesias (Salamanca: Ediciones Universidad de Salamanca, 1997), 364; Navarro Brotóns, "Humanismo," 363–365.

27. Hernández herborized the fields of Seville along with surgeon Juan Fragoso, author of *De succedaneis medicamentis*, published in Madrid in 1575. See Somolinos D'Ardois, "Vida y obra de Francisco Hernández," 117.

28. Somolinos D'Ardois, "Vida y obra de Francisco Hernández," 122–123, 132–133.

29. Ann Blair, "Natural Philosophy," in *The Cambridge History of Science*, 3:366.

30. See Ogilvie, *The Science of Describing*, 99, 298; Park and Daston, "Introduction," 4; Daniel Garber, "Physics and Foundations," in *The Cambridge History of Science*, 3:21–22; Peter Dear, *Revolutionizing the Sciences: European Knowledge and Its Ambitions, 1500–1700* (Princeton, NJ: Princeton University Press, 2009), 107.

31. See John G. T. Anderson, *Deep Things Out of Darkness: A History of Natural History* (Berkeley: University of California Press, 2012), 32.

32. See Nicolás Wey-Gómez, "Memorias de la zona tórrida: El naturalismo clásico y la «tropicalidad» americana en el Sumario de la natural historia de las Indias de Gonzalo Fernández de Oviedo (1526)," *Revista de Indias* 73, no. 259 (2013): 620, 627.

33. Anderson, *Deep Things Out of Darkness*, 42.

34. Cook, *Matters of Exchange*, 31–32; Schiebinger and Swan, *Colonial Botany*, 227.

35. Schiebinger and Swan, *Colonial Botany*, 228.

36. Cook, *Matters of Exchange*, 9.

37. This interest did not translate into economic success. See John Slater, "The Green Gold Fallacies: Myth and Reality in the Transatlantic Trade in Medicinal Plants," in *Geografías médicas: Fronteras culturales de la medicina hispanoamericana, siglos XVI y XVII*, ed. Mauricio Sánchez-Menchero and José Pardo-Tomás, 99–122 (Mexico City: CEIICH-UNAM, 2014).

38. In Madrid, Hernández cultivated good relationships with humanists such as Juan de Herrera and Andreas Vesalius. See Somolinos D'Ardois, "Vida y obra de Francisco Hernández," 128–133. Apparently Hernández also was on good terms with Juan de Ovando and Cardinal Diego Espinosa, president of the Council of Castille, who were the two fundamental architects of an "informed reform" in the government of the Indies. See José Pardo-Tomás, "Médecine et histoire naturelle," *Histoire, médecine et santé* 2 (2017): 77–97; Somolinos D'Ardois, "Vida y obra de Francisco Hernández," 136–141.

39. Campillo, *Francisco Hernández*, 142.

40. "The Instructions of Philip II to Dr. Francisco Hernández" (January 11, 1570), in *The Mexican Treasury*, 46.

41. See Pardo-Tomás, "Médecine et histoire naturelle."

42. "[la] perfección a lo moderno de España y de todos los demás de sus reinos, lo cual, si el resto de los príncipes hiciese en los suyos, gozaría nuestra edad de lo que no gozaron los que nos precedieron." Enrique López, "Historiar la naturaleza: Reflexiones sobre la traducción a la *Historia natural* de Plinio por Francisco Hernández," *Delaware Review of Latin American Studies* 11, no. 1 (2010): 8.

43. "The Instructions of Philip II to Francisco Hernández," in *The Mexican Treasury*, 46. See also Carlos Viesca Treviño, "Reflexiones epistemológicas en torno a la medicina náhuatl," *Estudios de Cultura Náhuatl* 20 (1990): 214.

44. "The Instructions of Philip II to Francisco Hernández," in *The Mexican Treasury*, 46. Upon arrival in Mexico City, Hernández befriended the University of Mexico's humanists Francisco Cervantes de Salazar and Juan de la Fuente, the chairs of rhetoric and medicine, respectively. Enrique González González, "La enseñanza médica en la ciudad de México durante el siglo XVI," in *El Mestizaje Cultural y la Medicina*, 134.

45. See "Relación de méritos y servicios," Archivo General de Indias P-262, R.9, and P22 R.11.

46. Viesca Treviño and Martínez Cortés, "Plantas medicinales americanas," 185.

47. Gunther B. Risse, "Shelter and Care for Natives and Colonists: Hospitals in Sixteenth-Century New Spain," in *Searching for the Secrets of Nature*, 65–70; Somolinos D'Ardois, "Vida y obra de Francisco Hernández," 169–179; Rafael Chabrán and Simon Varley, "Entr'acte," in *Searching for the Secrets of Nature*, 102–105.

48. Somolinos D'Ardois, "Vida y obra de Francisco Hernández," 202, 203; Viesca Treviño and Martínez Cortés, "Plantas medicinales americanas," 184.

49. Raquel Álvarez Pelaez, *La Conquista de la naturaleza americana* (Madrid: Consejo Superior de Investigaciones Científicas, 1993), 181–215; Jesús Bustamante, "El conocimiento como necesidad de Estado: Las encuestas oficiales sobre Nueva España durante el reinado de Carlos V," *Revista de Indias* 60, no. 218 (2000): 33–55.

50. In Luz A. Martínez, "El quiebre epistemológico y el nacimiento del nuevo sujeto de conocimiento en la 'Historia General y Natural de las Indias' de Gonzalo Fernández de Oviedo," *Revista Chilena de Literatura* 77 (2010): 236–250.

51. José Pardo-Tomás, "Making Natural History in New Spain, 1525–1590," in *Medical Cultures of the Early Modern Spanish Empire* (Surrey, UK: Ashgate, 2014), 46–47.

52. Ibid.

53. Bustamante, "El conocimiento como necesidad de Estado," 41.

54. Ibid.; Miguel León Portilla, "Sebastián Ramírez de Fuenleal y las Antigüedades Mexicanas," *Estudios de Cultura Náhuatl* 8 (1969): 15–18.

55. The term "epistemological setting" comes from Arnd Brendecke, "Introducción," in *Imperio e información: Funciones del saber en el dominio colonial español* (Madrid: Iberoamericana Vervuert, 2012), 15–42.

56. Miguel León Portilla, "Ramírez de Fuenleal," *Estudios de Cultura Náhuatl* 8 (1969): 14, 20–23.

57. Fuenleal worked as inquisitor in Seville and as *oidor* of Granada's chancellery before being appointed as bishop of Santo Domingo. See José Luis Sáez, *Don Sebastián Ramírez de Fuenleal: Obispo y legislador* (Santo Domingo: Banco de Reservas de la República Dominicana, 1996), "Carta de Sebastián Ramírez de Fuenleal a la emperatriz sobre la Visita Pastoral y otros asuntos eclesiásticos" (Santo Domingo, August 11, 1531), 131. About Erasmian influence in early sixteenth-century Valladolid, see *Humanismo Cristiano*, ed. Francisco Martín Hernández, Alfonso Ortega, and Ramón Hernández Martín (Salamanca: Caja de Ahorros y Monte de piedad de Salamanca, 1989), 7.

58. León Portilla, "Ramírez de Fuenleal," 25.

59. Ibid., 20–22.

60. See Pardo-Tomás, "Making Natural History in New Spain," 46–50.

61. Álvarez, "La conquista de la naturaleza Americana," 187–207.

62. About the Spanish Crown's development of empirical methods for obtaining and managing information, see Antonio Barrera Osorio, *Experiencing Nature: The Spanish American Empire and the Early Scientific Revolution* (Austin: University of Texas Press, 2006); Brendecke, "Introducción."

63. See R. W. Serjeantson, "Proof and Persuasion," in *The Cambridge History of Science*, 3:158; Rolena Adorno, "The Discursive Encounter of Spain and America: The Authority of Eyewitness Testimony in the Writing of History," *William and Mary Quarterly* 49, no. 2 (1992): 210–228.

64. Cook, *Matters of Exchange*, 81. See also Mary Poovey, *A History of the Modern Fact: Problems of Knowledge in the Sciences of Wealthhand Society* (Chicago: University of Chicago Press, 1998).

65. Gerónimo de Mendieta, *Historia Eclesiástica Indiana* (Mexico City: Porrúa, 1980), 35.

66. Marroquín Arredondo, *Diálogos con Quetzalcóatl*.

67. Sáez, *Don Sebastián Ramírez de Fuenleal*, 14.

68. Joaquín García Icazbalceta, *Don fray Juan de Zumárraga: Primer obispo y arzobispo de México* (Mexico City: Antigua Librería de Andrade y Morales, 1881), 8–9.

69. Joseph Pérez, *Breve Historia de la Inquisición en España* (Barcelona: Martínez Roca, 2002), 121–122.

70. Georges Baudot, *Utopia and History in Mexico: The First Chroniclers of Mexican Civilization (1520–1569)* (Niwot: University Press of Colorado, 1995), 126–127.

71. Ibid., 131–135.

72. From "Historia de los mexicanos por sus pinturas," in Joaquín García Icazbalceta, *Nueva colección de documentos para la historia de México*, Vol. 3 (Mexico City: Salvador Chávez Hayhoe, 1941), 210.

73. Bernardino de Sahagún, *Historia general de las cosas de Nueva España* (Mexico City: Porrúa, 1999), 73.

74. Alfredo López Austin, "Estudio acerca del método de investigación de fray Bernardino de Sahagún," *Estudios de Cultura Náhuatl* 42 (2011): 360–361.

75. Ann Blair, *Too Much to Know: Managing Scholarly Information Before the Modern Age* (New Haven, CT: Yale University Press, 2010), 73–77. See also Ann Blair, "Note Taking as an Art of Transmission," *Critical Inquiry* 31, no. 1 (2004): 85–107; Lorraine Daston, "Taking Note(s)," *Isis* 95, no. 3 (2004): 443–448.

76. Daston, "Taking Note(s)," 445.

77. Ann M. Blair, *Too Much to Know: Managing Scholarly Information Before the Modern Age* (New Haven, CT: Yale University Press, 2010), 95.

78. He also stayed at *encomenderos*' houses. See Somolinos D'Ardois, "Vida y obra de Francisco Hernández," 197.

79. Ibid., 198.

80. Francisco Hernández, "Epistle to Arias Montano," in *The Mexican Treasury*, 262–263. Somolinos D'Ardois, "Vida y obra de Francisco Hernández," 195.

81. Francisco Hernández, "Memorial al Virrey Martín Enríquez," in *Biblioteca Hispano-Americana 1493–1810*, ed. José Toribio Medina, Vol. 2 (Amsterdam: N. Israel, 1968), 290–291.

82. José Toribio Medina writes that a royal bill of 1574 decreed that "the interpreter assisted him [Hernández] all day." Toribio Medina, *Biblioteca Hispano-Americana*, 271; Hernández, "Epistle to Arias Montano," 262–263.

83. Hernández, "Epistle to Arias Montano," 262–263; "Will of Francisco Hernández," in *The Mexican Treasury*, 61–62.

84. The same 1574 royal bill also determined that Hernández should be provided with "a scribe to serve him." Toribio Medina, *Biblioteca Hispano-Americana*, 271.

85. Francisco Hernández writes to Viceroy Martín Enríquez that during his expeditions he risks his life "and that of his slaves." "Last Memorial to Viceroy Martín Enríquez," in Toribio Medina, *Biblioteca Hispano-Americana*, 291. Hernández mentions a numerous group of servants he wanted to be compensated in his will. The problem was that "there were so many of them and so varied that they cannot be identified." "Will of Francisco Hernández," in *The Mexican Treasury*, 62.

86. Somolinos D'Ardois also speculates that some *ticiti* could have been part of the expeditions. Somolinos D'Ardois, "Vida y obra de Francisco Hernández," 195.

87. Their Christian names were "Juan Pérez de San Pablo, Pedro Pérez de San Juan, Miguel García de San Sebastión, Francisco de la Cruz de Xihuitenco, Balthasar Juárez de San Sebastián, Antonio Martínez de San Juan." Miguel León Portilla, *Bernardino de Sahagún: Pionero de la Antropología* (Mexico City: UNAM/El Colegio Nacional, 1999), 137.

88. See Carlos Viesca Treviño, "El médico mexica," in *Medicina Novohispana: Historia general de la medicina en México*, Vol. 2, ed. Gonzalo Aguirre Beltrán and Roberto Moreno de los Arcos (Mexico City: Universidad Nacional Autónoma de México/Academia Nacional de Medicina, 1990), 223.

89. Francisco Hernández's "Letter to the King of March, 31, 1573," in *The Mexican Treasury*, 52. Hernández explicitly states that he gathers *relaciones* from Indian doctors in

his "Letter to Philip II" of December 1547, where he lets the king know that with relation to the new medicines, there is a need to verify "the experiences known from the Indians through *relación*." Toribio Medina, *Biblioteca Hispano-Americana*, 282. In his "Last Memorial to Viceroy Martín Enríquez," Hernández also suggests that his herbalists travel different regions including "coastal and hot regions and so sweep everything and bring plants and *relaciones*" (291).

90. Miguel León Portilla, "Las comunidades mesoamericanas ante la institución de los hospitales para indios," in *Medicina novohispana siglo XVI: Historia general de la medicina en México*, Vol. 2, ed. Gonzalo Aguirre-Beltrán and Roberto Moreno de los Arcos, 219–221 (Mexico City: Universidad Nacional Autónoma de México/Academia Nacional de Medicina, 1990); Roberto Campos Navarro and Adriana Ruiz-Llanos, "Adecuaciones interculturales en los hospitales para indios en la Nueva España," *Gaceta Médica de México* 137, no. 6 (2001): 600–603.

91. In his "Letter to Philip II, March 31, 1573," in *The Mexican Treasury*, 53, Francisco Hernández wrote that the "Viceroy orders, w[i]th some urgency, all the governors of New Spain to send [Hernández] the best people who can be found in their provinces." The royal bill of March 9, 1574, ordered that "governors send to Mexico the most notable [things] of their provinces." Toribio Medina, *Biblioteca Hispano-Americana*, 271. In his "Last Memorial to Viceroy Martín Enríquez," Hernández requests funds to pay all those Indians who bring him plants, *relaciones*, and sketches to Mexico City (291). In Hernández's 1576 "Letter to Juan de Ovando" he tells the president of the Council of Indies that he is still waiting for herbalists to collect plants from the highlands. See *Documentos inéditos para la historia de España*, Vol. 1 (Madrid: Viuda de Calero, 1842), 378.

92. Francisco Hernández wrote in his "Letter to Philip II, December 1, 1574" that he would move to a hospital in Mexico City, where he would work every day with "four doctors from this city, which are the ones of note, and that, once seen the medicines to be experimented and the sick to whom they will be administered, that they are given to them and see the effect of them, this will be done in other hospitals and around the city, as it has been done so far, and in common accord there will be composed the book of substitutes." Toribio Medina, *Biblioteca Hispano-Americana*, 282.

93. In his "Letter to Philip II, December 12, 1572," in *The Mexican Treasury*, 51, Hernández wrote that it was necessary to order "native and Spanish doctors" from "the Canary Islands, Santo Domingo and China" to provide him with "pictures in miniature of everything natural . . . , which can be done easily, with an account of their virtues and qualities."

94. Francisco Hernández, "Letter to Philip II, March 31, 1573," in *The Mexican Treasury*, 52.

95. See Ignacio Bernal, "La obra de Sahagún, otra carta inédita de Francisco del Paso y Troncoso," *Estudios de Cultura Náhuatl* 16 (1983): 273–275. See also "Entr'acte," in *Searching for the Secrets of Nature: The Life and Works of Dr. Francisco Hernández*, ed. Simon Varley, Rafael Chabrán, and Dora B. Weiner (Stanford, CA: Stanford University Press, 2000), 102–103.

96. Alfredo López Austin, "De las plantas medicinales y de otras cosas medicinales," *Estudios de Cultura Náhuatl* 9 (1971): 127.

97. A brief account of the qualities of plants that Hernández looked for can be read in his "Epistle to Arias Montano," in *The Mexican Treasury*, 263–264, where he let his friend know that while composing his natural history he had taken into account "the fruits, the leaves, and

292   Notes to Pages 57–61

any of the names of the species as they vary from region to region, their medicinal powers, the native soil, the method of cultivation, and their taste, . . . which diseases can be cured by it, what is the limit of heat, what color it is, and whatever substance grows beneath the bark." 98. Ibid., 263.

99. "Letter of Francisco Hernández to Philip II, November/December 1571," in *The Mexican Treasury*, 48. Similar enthusiasm for the realist quality of Hernández's illustrations can be read in Baltasar Porreño's *Los dichos y hechos del Rei Felipe II* (1628), where he stated that the illustrations "represent all the [plants'] parts and measures with greater and newer curiosity than what has been done to this time." Of the great value that Hernández assigned to his illustrations, perhaps there is no more eloquent testimony than his will. The first people he ordered to receive any money were the three painters who worked with him in Mexico: Pedro Vásquez and Antón and Baltasar Elías. See Francisco Hernández, "Will," in *The Mexican Treasury*, 62.

100. *Obras del licenciado José Fernando Ramírez*, Vol. 2 (Mexico City: V. Agüeros, 1898), 318–330; José Eusebio Nieremberg, *Historia naturae, maxime peregrinae* (Antwerp: Balthasaris Moreti, 1635), 306, 310; Francisco Bravo, *Opera Medicinalia* (Mexico City: Pedro Ocharte, 1570), 573; Francisco Guerra, "Biographical and Bibliographical Introduction," in *The Opera Medicinalia* (Folkestone, UK: Dawsons of Pall Mall, 1970), 18–22.

101. "The Instructions of Philip II to Francisco Hernández," in *The Mexican Treasury*, 46.

102. See Lorraine E. Daston and Elizabeth Lunbeck, "Introduction: Observation Observed," *Histories of Scientific Observation*, ed. Lorraine E. Daston and Elizabeth Lunbeck (Chicago: University of Chicago Press, 2011), 12–13; Katharine Park, "Observations in the Margins," in *Histories of Scientific Observation*, 17–18; Gianna Pomata, "Observation Rising: Birth of an Epistemic Genre, 1500–1650," in *Histories of Scientific Observation*, 46; José María López Piñero, "Prologue," in *Más allá de la Leyenda Negra: España y la Revolución Científica*, ed. Víctor Navarro Brotóns and William Eamon (Valencia: Instituto de Historia de la Ciencia y documentación López Piñero & Universitat de Valencia, 2007), 20; Peter Dear, "The Meanings of Experience," in *The Cambridge History of Science*, 3:106.

103. Park, "Observations in the Margins," 17; Pomata, "Observation Rising," 55.

104. Gianna Pomata, "*Praxis Historialis*: The Uses of *Historia* in Early Modern Medicine," in *Historia*, 115–116. See also Dear, "The Meanings of Experience," 112–113.

105. See Marroquín Arredondo, "Sensual abuela: La historiografía de Gonzalo Fernández de Oviedo en los orígenes de la ciencia moderna," *Alteridades* 25, no. 50 (2015): 77–89; Luz Ángela Martínez, "El quiebre epistemológico y el nacimiento del nuevo sujeto de conocimiento en la *Historia general y natural de las Indias* de Gonzalo Fernández de Oviedo," *Revista Chilena de Literatura* 77 (2010): 236–250.

106. Martínez, "El quiebre epistemológico," 15.

107. Ibid., 11.

108. Examples abound in his *Historia general y natural*. See Gonzalo Fernández de Oviedo y Valdés, *Historia general y natural de las Indias, Islas y Tierra-Firme del mar océano*, Vols. 1–3 (Asunción: Editorial Guarania, 1944–1945), 2:218–230, 2:210–211, 2:286–287, 3:13–22.

109. Ibid., 1:230.

110. Sahagún, *Historia general de las cosas de Nueva España*, 694–695.

111. See Sáez, *Don Sebastián Ramírez de Fuenleal*, "Carta de Sebastián Ramírez de Fuenleal a la emperatriz sobre encomiendas, enseñanza y otros asuntos de gobierno" (Mexico, August 8, 1533), 184.

112. Sahagún, *Historia general de las cosas de Nueva España*, 583.

113. Ibid., 20.

114. Viesca Treviño and Martínez Cortés, "Plantas medicinales americanas," 184.

115. Laín Entralgo notices that *dynamis* was considered during the Renaissance as *potentia, virtus, qualitas, facultas*, or *vis*. Pedro Laín Entralgo, *Historia de la Medicina* (Barcelona: Salvat, 1978), 252.

116. In one of his letters to the king, he writes that after having finished with the expeditions in the interior of Mexico, it was time "to take to heart making experiences of all that I could, especially of the purges and the most important medicines." Viesca Treviño and Martínez Cortés, "Plantas medicinales americanas," 186. In the same article they quote Alonso López de Hinojosos, surgeon at the Hospital Real de Indios, who wrote that "the doctor Francisco Hernández . . . was at present doing *experience* of the medicinal and purgative herbs and other natural things of this New Spain" (186–187, my emphasis). To deal with his kidney problems, Hernández experimented with Mexican plants such as *quapatli* (unidentified), *tlapati* (ricinus communis), *ocpatli* (probably acacia angustifolia), and *mexixquilitl* (nasturtium). Hernández, *Obras completas*, Vol. 3, *Historia natural de la Nueva España*, pt. 2, 43, 119.

117. See "La polémica sobre la dicotomía frío-calor," in *La medicina invisible: Introducción al estudio de la medicina tradicional de México*, ed. Xavier Lozoya and Carlos Zolla, 73–90 (Mexico: Folios Ediciones, 1986).

118. Alfredo López Austin analyzes the importance of the *tonalli* for Mesoamerican medicine in *Cuerpo humano e ideología: Las concepciones de los antiguos nahuas* (Mexico City: Universidad Nacional Autónoma de México, Instituto de Investigaciones Antropológicas, 1984), 223–251.

119. Harold J. Cook notices that university-trained medical doctors, or "physics," were against the mere "empiricists" and were vigilant in regard to surgeons and apothecaries' practices and credentials. See Harold J. Cook, "Medicine," in *The Cambridge History of Science*, 3:420.

120. Hernández, *Antigüedades de la Nueva España*, 118; Viesca Treviño and Martínez Cortés notice Hernández's abundant and constant rebuttals of the Mexican Indian doctor's therapeutic ideas that contradicted Galen's humoral theory. See Viesca Treviño and Martínez Cortés, "Plantas medicinales americanas," 195–197.

121. Hernández, *Obras completas*, Vol. 3, *Historia natural de la Nueva España*, pt. 2, 183.

122. Ibid., 3:323–324.

123. Somolinos D'Ardois, "Vida y obra de Francisco Hernández," 125.

124. Ibid., 156–157.

125. Ibid., 43–45.

126. Michel de Montaigne, *Ensayos completos* (Mexico City: Editorial Porrúa, 1999) 167.

127. See Anthony Grafton, *Defenders of the Text: The Traditions of Scholarship in an Age of Science, 1450–1800* (Cambridge, MA: Harvard University Press, 1991), 3–5; James Bono, *The Word of God and the Languages of Man: Interpreting Nature in Early Modern Science and Medicine*, Vol. 1. (Madison: University of Wisconsin Press, 1995), 7–10.

128. Francisco Hernández, *Obras completas*, Vol. 4, *Historia natural de Cayo Plinio Segundo: Trasladada y anotada por el docor Francisco Hernández*, pt. 1, 6 (my emphasis).

129. Ibid., 4:8.

130. "Letter to Philip II (November/December 1571)" in *The Mexican Treasury*, 48.

131. Francisco Hernández, "Epistle to Arias Montano," in *The Mexican Treasury*, 263–264.

132. Hernández, *Obras completas*, Vol. 6, *Historia natural de Cayo Plinio Segundo*, pt. 2a, 305.

133. Hernández, *Antigüedades de la Nueva España*, 155.

134. Hernández, *Obras completas*, Vol. 2, *Historia natural de la Nueva España*, pt. 1, 6. Motolinía had noticed in his *Memoriales* (ca. 1541) that the names of the plants indicated their medicinal uses. See Toribio de Benavente Motolinía, *Memoriales*, ed. Nancy J. Dyer (Mexico City: El Colegio de México, 1996), 520.

135. In *De los nombres de Cristo*, ed. Cristobal Cuevas (Madrid: Cátedra, 1984), 160.

136. Jesús Bustamante, "Francisco Hernández, Plinio del Nuevo Mundo: Tradición clásica, teoría nominal y sistema terminológico indígena en una obra renacentista," in *Entre dos mundos: Fronteras culturales y agentes mediadores*, ed. Berta Ares Queija and Serge Gruzinski, 243–268 (Sevilla: Escuela de Estudios Hispano-Americanos, 1997).

137. Hernández, *Obras completas*, Vol. 2, *Historia natural de la Nueva España*, pt. 1, 90.

138. Somolinos D'Ardois, "Vida y obra de Francisco Hernández," 177. He likely used Alonso de Molina's *Arte de la lengua mexicana y castellana* and *Vocabulario de la lengua mexicana y castellana*, both published in Mexico in 1571, and perhaps also Andrés de Olmos's earlier *Arte de la lengua mexicana*.

139. Peter Dear, *Revolutionizing the Sciences: European Knowledge and Its Ambitions, 1500–1700* (Princeton, NJ: Princeton University Press, 2009), 31.

140. See Anthony Grafton, "The Identities of History in Early Modern Europe: Prelude to a Study of the *Artes Historicae*," in *Historia*, 53; Karl Kohut, "Las crónicas de Indias y la teoría historiográfica: Desde los comienzos hasta mediados del siglo XVI," in *Narración y Reflexión: Las crónicas de Indias y la teoría historiográfica*, ed. Karl Kohut (Mexico City: El Colegio de México, 2007), 19–20.

141. Karl Kohut, "Las crónicas de Indias y la teoría historiográfica: Desde los comienzos hasta mediados del siglo xvi," in *Narración y Reflexión: Las crónicas de Indias y la teoría historiográfica*, ed. Karl Kohut, 14–21 (Mexico City: El Colegio de México, 2007).

142. Marcel Bataillon, *Erasmo y España: Estudios sobre la historia espiritual del siglo XVI* (Mexico City: Fondo de Cultura Económica, 2007), 12–22; Francisco Hernández Martín, "Campo universitario," in *Humanismo Cristiano*, ed. Francisco Martín Hernández et al. (Salamanca: Caja de Ahorros y Monte de piedad de Salamanca, 1989), 201.

143. Nancy Struever, *Rhetoric, Modality, Modernity* (Chicago: University of Chicago Press, 2009), 119.

144. Ibid., 17. Mexican Indians' rhetorical mastery proved by itself their intellectual worth. On a related note, in May 1533 Fuenleal once again praised the natives' intellectual capacity in a letter to the emperor. "If by the exterior deeds one is to judge understanding," Fuenleal wrote, they "exceed the Spaniards" (34).

145. Calepino first published his work in 1502 in Reggio nell'Emilia. A 1590s Basil edition included eleven languages. See Albert Labarre, *Bibliographie du dictionarium d'Ambrogio Calepino (1502–1779)* (Baden-Baden: Koerner, 1975).

146. Ibid., 17–21.

147. Sahagún, *Historia general de las cosas de Nueva España*, 21.

148. See Jesús Bustamante, "Retórica, Traducción y Responsabilidad Histórica: Claves Humanísticas en la Obra de Bernardino de Sahagún," in *Humanismo y visión del otro en la*

España Moderna, ed. Berta Ares, Jesús Bustamante, Francisco Castilla, and Fermín del Pino (Madrid: Consejo Superior de Investigaciones Científicas, 1993), 345; Marroquín Arredondo, *Diálogos con Quetzalcóatl*, 144–152.

149. Bernardino de Sahagún, *Historia general de las cosas de Nueva España*, Vol. 2, ed. Alfredo López Austin y Josefina García Quintana (Madrid: Alianza, 1988), 597.

150. Jorge Cañizares Esguerra, *Nature, Empire, and Nation: Explorations of the History of Science in the Iberian World* (Stanford, CA: Stanford University Press, 2006), 8–9; Ignacio Bernal, "La obra de Sahagún, otra carta inédita de Francisco del Paso y Troncoso," *Estudios de Cultura Náhuatl* 16 (1983): 265–325; Iris Montero Sobrevilla, "Lessons from a Sleeping Beauty: Hummingbird Torpor and Natural Historical Knowledge in the Early Modern Period" (forthcoming).

151. López Piñero and Pardo-Tomás, *La influencia de Francisco Hernández*, 21–34.

152. Bustamante, "Francisco Hernández, Plinio del Nuevo Mundo," 243–268.

153. One version of this Mesoamerican recipe can actually be found in the *Libellus de Medicinalibus Indorum Herbis* (Mexico City: Fondo de Cultura Económica and Instituto Mexicano de Seguro Social, 1991), 49.

154. Hernández, *Obras completas*, Vol. 2, *Historia natural de la Nueva España*, pt. 1, 217.

155. Ibid., 2:217–218.

156. Francisco Hernández, *Obras completas*, Vol. 4, *Historia natural de Cayo Plinio Segundo*, pt. 1, 5–6.

157. Hernández, *Antigüedades de la Nueva España*, 107.

158. Walter Mignolo, *The Darker Side of the Renaissance: Literacy, Territoriality, and Colonization* (Ann Arbor: University of Michigan Press, 1995), 44–46, 199–202.

159. Tzvetan Todorov, *La conquista de América, el problema del otro* (Mexico City: Siglo XXI, 1987), 105–106.

160. George E. Marcus and Michael M. J. Fischer summarize: human sciences recognize today "that social life must fundamentally be conceived as the negotiation of meanings." George E. Marcus and Michael M. J. Fischer, *Anthropology as Cultural Critique: An Experimental Moment in the Human Sciences* (Chicago: University of Chicago Press, 1999), 26.

161. Marroquín Arredondo, "Introducción," in *Historia de los prejuicios en América: La Conquista* (Mexico City: Porrúa, 2007), xiii.

Chapter 3

1. Bernabé Cobo, *Historia del Nuevo Mundo*, ed. Marcos Jiménez de la Espada, 4 vols. (Sevilla: Sociedad de Bibliófilos Andaluces, 1890–1895), 1:64–65.

2. Inca Garcilaso de la Vega, *Comentarios reales de los Incas*, Vol. 2, ed. Ángel Rosenblat (Buenos Aires: Emece, 1943), 276–277.

3. Luis Millones Figueroa, "Una edición por terminar: La *Historia del Nuevo Mundo* de Bernabé Cobo," in *Edición y anotación de textos andinos*, ed. Ignacio Arellano and José Antonio Mazzotti (Navarra: Universidad de Navarra/Vervuert–Iberoamericana, 2000), 55–59.

4. Luis Millones Figueroa, "La historia natural del padre Bernabé Cobo: Algunas claves para su lectura," *Colonial Latin American Review* 12, no. 1 (2003): 90–95.

5. Millones Figueroa, "La historia natural," 92–93; Luis Millones Figueroa, "La *intelligentsia* jesuita y la naturaleza del Nuevo Mundo en el siglo XVII," in *El saber de los jesuitas,*

historias naturales y el Nuevo Mundo, ed. Luis Millones Figueroa and Domingo Ledezma, 36–43 (Madrid: Iberoamericana-Vervuert, 2005).

6. Cobo, *Historia del Nuevo Mundo*, 1:65–66. All translations are my own.

7. Millones Figueroa, "La historia natural," 87–88.

8. William B. Ashworth, "Natural History and the Emblematic World View," in *Reappraisals of the Scientific Revolution*, ed. David Lindberg and Robert S. Westman (Cambridge: Cambridge University Press, 1990), 318–319.

9. Cobo, *Historia del Nuevo Mundo*, 1:333–334.

10. Luis Millones Figueroa, "El lenguaje y la naturaleza en la *Historia del Nuevo Mundo* de Bernabé Cobo," in *La impronta humanística (SS. XV–XVIII): Saberes, visiones e interpretaciones*, ed. A. Castro Santamaría and J. García Nistal, 317–321 (Palermo: Officina di Studi Medievali, 2013).

11. Brian W. Ogilvie, *The Science of Describing: Natural History in Renaissance Europe* (Chicago: University of Chicago Press, 2006), 192–203.

12. Cobo, *Historia del Nuevo Mundo*, 1:334.

13. Ibid., 1:333–334.

14. J. A. Cavanilles, "Sobre algunos botánicos españoles del siglo XVI," *Anales de Ciencias Naturales* 20 (1804): 126–140.

15. Steven Harris, "Mapping Jesuit Science: The Role of Travel in the Geography of Knowledge," in *The Jesuits: Culture, Science, and the Arts, 1540–1773*, ed. John O'Malley et al. (Toronto: University of Toronto Press, 1999), 228–233.

16. Luis Martín, *The Intellectual Conquest of Peru: The Jesuit College of San Pablo, 1568–1767* (New York: Fordham University Press, 1968).

17. Andrés I. Prieto, *Missionary Scientists: Jesuit Science in Spanish South America, 1570–1810* (Nashville: Vanderbilt University, 2011), 105–115.

18. Prieto, *Missionary Scientists*, 169–194.

19. Cobo, *Historia del Nuevo Mundo*, 1:7–8.

20. Roland Hamilton, "El padre Bernabé Cobo y las lenguas indígenas de América," *Lexis* 2, no. 1 (1978): 91–96.

21. Cobo, *Historia del Nuevo Mundo*, 4:155–156.

22. Millones Figueroa, "El lenguaje y la naturaleza," 318–320.

23. Cobo, *Historia del Nuevo Mundo*, 4:187.

24. Cobo, *Historia del Nuevo Mundo*, 1:194–200.

25. Cobo, *Historia del Nuevo Mundo*, 4:187–188.

26. Ibid., 4:200.

27. Sabine Anagnostou, "Jesuits in Spanish America: Contributions to the Exploration of the American Materia Medica," *Pharmacy in History* 47, no. 1 (2005): 7–10.

28. Cobo, *Historia del Nuevo Mundo*, 2:99–100.

29. Cobo, *Historia del Nuevo Mundo*, 1:476.

30. Cobo, *Historia del Nuevo Mundo*, 4:201–202.

31. Cobo, *Historia del Nuevo Mundo*, 2:102–103.

32. Luis Millones Figueroa, "The Bezoar Stone: A Natural Wonder in the New World," *Hispanófila* 171 (2014): 139–156.

33. Cobo, *Historia del Nuevo Mundo*, 1:275–276.

34. Ibid., 1:426.

35. Ibid., 1:249.

36. Cobo, *Historia del Nuevo Mundo*, 2:10.

37. Luis Millones Figueroa, "The Staff of Life: Wheat and 'Indian Bread' in the New World," *Colonial Latin American Review* 19, no. 2 (2010): 313–317.

38. Cobo, *Historia del Nuevo Mundo*, 2:429–431.

39. Cobo, *Historia del Nuevo Mundo*, 1:361–362.

Chapter 4

An earlier version of this chapter appeared as "History in Pictures: Translating the *Codex Mendoza*," *Art History*, 38, no. 4 (Fall 2015): 682–701.

1. Latin Americanists use the word "codex" for any work connected to Amerindian traditions of pictorial writing and understood to have involved indigenous makers, regardless of its format, support, date, absence or presence of European elements, or use of alphabetic text—it is the indigenous referent that is crucial. The classic work on Mesoamerican pictorial documents in the colonial period is Donald Robertson, *Mexican Manuscript Painting of the Early Colonial Period: The Metropolitan Schools* (1959; reprint, Norman: University of Oklahoma Press, 1994). Also indispensable are the works of Elizabeth Hill Boone, among them *Stories in Red and Black: Pictorial Histories of the Aztecs and Mixtecs* (Austin: University of Texas Press, 2000); Elizabeth Hill Boone and Walter Mignolo, eds., *Writing Without Words: Alternative Literacies in Mesoamerica and the Andes* (Durham, NC: Duke University Press, 1994); Elizabeth Hill Boone and Thomas B. F. Cummins, eds., *Native Traditions in the Post Conquest World* (Washington, DC: Dumbarton Oaks, 1998); Elizabeth Hill Boone, ed., *Painted Books and Indigenous Knowledge in Mesoamerica: Manuscript Studies in Honor of Mary Elizabeth Smith* (New Orleans: Middle American Research Institute, 2005). In this chapter I use the terms "Aztec" and "Mexica" interchangeably.

2. The standard source is the magnificent edition by Frances Berdan and Patricia Rieff Anawalt, *The Codex Mendoza*, 4 vols. (Berkeley: University of California Press, 1992); since January 2015 a superb online scholarly edition is available at http://codicemendoza.inah.gob.mx. The codex's manufacture is investigated in detail in Jorge Gómez-Tejada, "Making the *Codex Mendoza*, Constructing the *Codex Mendoza*: A Reconsideration of a Sixteenth-Century Mexican Manuscript," PhD dissertation, Yale University, 2012. See also Todd P. Olson, "Reproductive Horror: Sixteenth-Century Mexican Pictures in the Age of Mechanical Reproduction," *Oxford Art Journal* 34, no. 3 (2011): 449–469.

3. The codex does not address the number or ethnicity of the painters and scribes, though scholars have assumed on stylistic grounds that the artists were indigenous. Based on meticulous formal analysis, Gómez-Tejada, "Making the *Codex Mendoza*," chap. 2, suggests that two artists worked on the images. Scholarly speculation about the possible identity of artists and scribes is discussed in H. B. Nicholson, "The History of the *Codex Mendoza*," in Berdan and Anawalt, *The Codex Mendoza*, 1:1–2, and Gómez-Tejada, "Making the *Codex Mendoza*," 37–39.

4. On style, see Kathleen Stewart Howe, "The Relationship of Indigenous and European Styles in the *Codex Mendoza*: An Analysis of Pictorial Style," in Berdan and Anawalt, *The Codex Mendoza*, 1:25–33; Gómez-Tejada, "Making the *Codex Mendoza*," chaps. 1 and 2.

5. Clavijero described it as "la raccolta di Mendoza" (Mendoza's collection) in *Storia antica del Messico* (Cesena, 1780–1781), 1:22. The connection is questioned by Nicholson, "The History of the *Codex Mendoza*," 1–5, and Gómez-Tejada, "Making the *Codex Mendoza*."

6. Among the vast literature on this issue, see especially Carolyn Dean and Dana Leib-sohn, "Hybridity and Its Discontents: Considering Visual Culture in Colonial Spanish Amer-ica," *Colonial Latin American Review* 12, no. 1 (2003): 5–35; Serge Gruzinski, *The Mestizo Mind: The Intellectual Dynamics of Colonization and Globalization* (New York: Routledge, 2002).

7. On early colonial Mexican art and translation, see Alessandra Russo, *The Untrans-latable Image: A Mestizo History of the Arts in New Spain, 1500–1600* (Austin: University of Texas Press, 2014).

8. She is prominently depicted as an interpreter in the *Relación de Tlaxcala*, the *Codex Durán*, and the *Florentine Codex*, among others. See Frances Karttunen, "Rethinking Malinche," in *Indian Women of Early Mexico*, ed. Susan Schroeder, Stephanie Wood, and Robert Stephen Haskett (Norman: University of Oklahoma Press, 1997), 291–312.

9. The classic work on the early Franciscans is Robert Ricard, *The Spiritual Conquest of Mexico* (1933; reprint, Berkeley: University of California Press, 1966).

10. The original reads "llevar de un lugar a otro alguna cosa, o encaminarla . . . el bolver la sentencia de una lengua en otra." Covarrubias's *Tesoro de la lengua castellana o española* is unpaginated.

11. *Codex Mendoza*, 1r–18r; see Berdan and Anawalt, *The Codex Mendoza*, 1:25–54, 2:3–25, 3:9–43, 4:7–41.

12. *Codex Mendoza*, 18v–56r; see Berdan and Anawalt, *The Codex Mendoza*, 1:55–79, 2:32–141, 3:44–119, 4:42–117.

13. The second section is related to the *Matrícula de Tributos* (*Codex Moctezuma*), com-mentary by Frances F. Berdan and Jacqueline de Durand-Forest (Graz: Akademische Druck-und Verlagsanstalt, 1980).

14. Samuel Purchas, *Hakluytus posthumus: Or Purchas his pilgrimes*, 4 vols. (London: Printed by William Stansby for Henrie Fetherstone, 1625), 3:1066. I have modernized the original spelling throughout.

15. The use of black and red ink is highly suggestive, as the Nahua expression *in tlilli in tlapalli* (meaning "the black ink, the red ink") refers to writing and more broadly to knowledge.

16. Richard Kagan, *Urban Images of the Hispanic World, 1493–1793* (New Haven, CT: Yale University Press, 2000), 1–44.

17. Berdan and Anawalt, *The Codex Mendoza*, 1:81–92, 2:143–238.

18. Two early examples of codices used as evidence in legal trials are discussed in Thomas B. F. Cummins, "From Lies to Truth: Colonial Ekphrasis and the Act of Crosscultural Transla-tion," in *Reframing the Renaissance: Visual Culture in Europe and Latin America, 1450–1650*, ed. Claire Farago (New Haven, CT: Yale University Press, 1995), 152–174; María del Carmen Herrera Meza and Ethelia Ruiz Medrano, *El códice de Tepeucila: El entintado mundo de la fijeza imaginaria* (Mexico City: Instituto Nacional de Antropología e Historia, 1997).

19. The statement calls out some mistranslations, noting that it was a mistake for the interpreter to use the Moorish words *alfaqui* (a Muslim cleric or expert in Islamic law) and *mezquitas* (mosques) instead of *sacerdote* (priest) and *templos* (temples), thus remarking on another act of translation by which New World religiosity was rendered through the vocabu-lary of Old World idolatry and the Christian Reconquista of Spain.

20. See Nicholson, "The History of the *Codex Mendoza*."

21. Richard Hakluyt, *Divers Voyages Touching the Discoverie of America* (London: Wood-cocke, 1582); Richard Hakluyt, *The Principal Navigations, Voiages, Traffiques & Discoueries of the English Nation* (London: By George Bishop, Ralph Newberie, and Robert Barker, 1589–1600). The inscription reads "D[ue]: yourselfe in gold rydinge to London ye 7th of september 1587 / V^t [£5]." The exact date and means of Hakluyt's acquisition are debated in the scholarship. On Hakluyt, see Peter C. Mancall, *Hakluyt's Promise: An Elizabethan's Obsession for an English America* (New Haven, CT: Yale University Press, 2007).

22. G. J. Toomer, *John Selden: A Life in Scholarship*, 2 vols. (Oxford: Oxford University Press, 2009), 2:793–799.

23. See John B. Glass, "A Census of the Native Middle American Pictorial Manuscripts," in *Handbook of Middle American Indians*, Vol. 14, ed. Howard F. Cline (Austin: University of Texas Press, 1975), 81–252. Their trajectories tended to be complex and are often quite difficult to document with detail or certainty; see, for instance, Lauran Toorians, "Some Light in the Dark Century of Codex Vindobonensis Mexicanus 1," *Codices manuscripti* 9, no. 1 (1983): 26–69; Lauran Toorians, "Codex Vindobonensis Mexicanus 1: Its History Completed," *Codices manuscripti* 10, no. 3 (1984): 87–97.

24. See, for instance, Ole Worm, *Museum Wormianum* (Leiden: Apud Iohannem Elsevirivm, 1655), 383–384.

25. "Contiene questo libro non altro che GEROGLIFICI del MESSICO, i quali sono figure stravagantissime, e per la Maggio parte esprimono huomini, & animali stranamente monstruosi." Lorenzo Legati, *Museo Cospiano* (Bologna: Per Giacomo Monti, 1677), 191.

26. "Che cosa significhino, non m'è noto, nè sò che sia noto ad altri nell'Europa. . . . Sò che s'accingerebbe ad una bella, e curiosa impresa, chi prendesse ad illustrare le tenebre di questi misterii letterarii, non per anco spiegati nell'Europa." Legati, *Museo Cospiano*, 192.

27. Purchas, *Hakluytus posthumus*, 3:1065–1117. Purchas briefly alluded to what he called a "Mexican historie" and "Mexican picture historie" in an earlier publication but did not reproduce the codex; see *Purchas His Pilgrimage: Or, Relations of the World and the Religions Observed in All Ages and Places Discovered, from the Creation unto This Present*, 2nd rev. ed. (London: Printed by William Stansby for Henrie Fetherstone, and Are to Be Sold at His Shop in Pauls Church-Yard at the Signe of the Rose, 1614), 803–804, 811.

28. Purchas, *Hakluytus posthumus*, 3:1065.

29. On the importance of history as a genre, see Gianna Pomata and Nancy G. Siraisi, eds., *Historia: Empiricism and erudition in Early Modern Europe* (Cambridge, MA: MIT Press, 2005).

30. Purchas, *Hakluytus posthumus*, 3:1066, 1065.

31. It is not known whether anyone consulted the original codex between Purchas and Kingsborough, who gave the *Mendoza* pride of place as the very first item in his *Antiquities of Mexico*. Edward Bernard did mention it in his published catalog of manuscripts in British collections, *Catalogi librorum manuscriptorum Angliae et Hiberniae in unum collecti, cum indice alphabetico*, Vol. 1 (Oxford, UK: E Theatro Sheldoniano, 1697), pt. 1, 157, item number 3134: "Historia Mexicana Hispanice cum Figuris & Iconibus & explicatione Lingua Mexicana partim, partimque Hispanica" (A Spanish Mexican History with Figures and Icons and Explanations Partly in the Mexican Language, Partly in Spanish).

32. This is an important intervention, given early modern European debates about the correlation between alphabetic language and civility. On the colonial role of the written word,

see Boone and Mignolo, *Writing Without Words*; Walter Mignolo, *The Darker Side of the Renaissance: Literacy, Territoriality, and Colonization* (Ann Arbor: University of Michigan Press, 1995), esp. pts. 1 and 2.

33. Purchas, *Hakluytus posthumus*, 3:1070–1071, figure E on 1070.

34. Ibid., 3:1071, end of the italicized textual interpretation of the figures.

35. "l'art descrire," "par certaines peintures, qui estoyent comme hieroglyphiques." Johannes de Laet, *L'Histoire du Nouveau Monde ou description des Indes* (Leiden: Chez Bonauenture & Abraham Elseuiers, Imprimeurs Ordinaires De L'Vniversité, 1640), bk. 5, chap. 10, 154.

36. "Succession des Rois de Mexique selon leurs Annales peintes." De Laet, *L'Histoire*, bk. 5, chap. 13, 160–162.

37. Nicholas Dew, "Reading Travels in the Culture of Curiosity: Thévenot's Collection of Voyages," *Journal of Early Modern History* 10, nos. 1–2 (2006): 39–59.

38. Daniel Stolzenberg, *Egyptian Oedipus: Athanasius Kircher and the Secrets of Antiquity* (Chicago: University of Chicago Press, 2013). See also Brian Curran, *The Egyptian Renaissance: The Afterlife of Ancient Egypt in Early Modern Italy* (Chicago: University of Chicago Press, 2007); Byron Ellsworth Hamann, "How Maya Hieroglyphs Got Their Name: Egypt, Mexico, and China in Western Grammatology Since the Fifteenth Century," *Proceedings of the American Philosophical Society* 152, no. 1 (March 2008): 1–68.

39. For example, *Treasures of the Bodleian*, Bodleian Library, Oxford, September 30–December 23, 2011; *Marks of Genius: Treasures from the Bodleian Library*, The Morgan Library and Museum, New York, June 6–September 28, 2014, http://www.themorgan.org/exhibitions/marks-of-genius.

40. This is in opposition to Bruno Latour's influential idea of "immutable mobiles." See, for instance, Bruno Latour, *Science in Action: How to Follow Scientists and Engineers Through Society* (Cambridge, MA: Harvard University Press), 1987, 215–257.

Chapter 5

I am grateful to the scholars who have read drafts and/or shared insights or material from their research with me, including Paula Alonso, Ralph Bauer, Elizabeth Boone Hill, William Eamon, Domingo Ledezma, José Ramón Marcaida López, Jaime Marroquín Arredondo, Iris Montero Sobrevilla, María Olivdo Moreno, and Barbara Mundy, as well as the feedback I received from audiences at the Centro de Investigaciones Interdisciplinarias en Ciencias y Humanidades at the Universidad Nacional Autónoma de México, particularly Haydeé García Bravo and Angélica Morales Sarabia (2015), the Southwest Seminar on Colonial Latin American History (2017), and the History of Science Seminar at Harvard University (2018).

1. Francis Willughby and John Ray, *Ornothologiæ libri tres* (London: John Martyn, 1676); Francis Willughby and John Ray, *The Ornithology of Francis Willughby* (London: John Martyn, 1678).

2. Willughby and Ray, *Ornithology*, preface (unpaginated).

3. Charles E. Raven, *John Ray, Naturalist: His Life and Works* (Cambridge: Cambridge University Press, 1950), 322–325; Tim R. Birkhead, Paul J. Smith, Megan Doherty, and Isabelle Charmantier, "Willughby's Ornithology," in *Virtuoso by Nature: The Scientific Worlds of Francis Willughby FRS (1635–1672)*, ed. Tim Birkhead, 268–304 (Boston: Brill, 2016); Isabelle

Charmantier, Dorothy Johnston, and Paul J. Smith, "The Legacies of Francis Willughby," in *Virtuoso by Nature*, 360–385.

4. Michel Foucault, *The Order of Things: An Archaeology of the Human Sciences* (London: Tavistock Publications, 1970); William B. Ashworth, "Natural History and the Emblematic World View," in *Reappraisals of the Scientific Revolution* (Cambridge: Cambridge University Press, 1990), 317; Brian W. Ogilvie, *The Science of Describing: Natural History in Renaissance Europe* (Chicago: University of Chicago Press, 2006), 262–263.

5. José María López Piñero and José Pardo-Tomás, *La influencia de Francisco Hernández (1512–1587) en la constitución de la botánica y la* materia médica *modernas* (Valencia: Universitat de València, 1996), 164, 199–203; José María López Piñero and José Pardo-Tomás, *Nuevos materiales y noticias sobre la* Historia de las plantas de Nueva España *de Francisco Hernández* (Valencia: Instituto de Estudios Documentales, 1994).

6. Miguel de Asúa and Roger French, *A New World of Animals: Early Modern Europeans on the Creatures of Iberian America* (Alershot, UK: Ashgate, 2005), 215. Dr. Mariana de Campos Françozo of the University of Leiden is conducting research on indigenous knowledge in the *Historia naturalis brasiliae*.

7. Lara Putnam, "To Study the Fragments/Whole: Microhistory and the Atlantic World," *Journal of Social History* 39 (2006): 615–630; Carlo Ginzburg, "Microhistory and Global History," in *The Cambridge World History*, Vol. 6, *The Construction of a Global World, 1400–1800 CE*, ed. Jerry H. Bentley, Sanjay Subrahmanyam, and Merry E. Wiesner-Hanks, 446–473 (Cambridge: Cambridge University Press, 2015).

8. Florike Egmond, *The Mammoth and the Mouse: Microhistory and Morphology* (Baltimore: Johns Hopkins University Press, 1997); Juan Pimentel, *The Rhinoceros and the Megatherium* (Cambridge, MA: Harvard University Press, 2017).

9. Marcy Norton, *Sacred Gifts, Profane Pleasures: A History of Tobacco and Chocolate in the Atlantic World* (Ithaca, NY: Cornell University Press, 2008).

10. Ibid., 10; Marcy Norton, "Subaltern Technologies and Early Modernity in the Atlantic World," *Colonial Latin American Review* 2, no. 1 (2017): 20.

11. Iris Montero Sobrevilla, "Indigenous Naturalists," In *New Cultures of Natural History*, ed. Helen Curry, Emma Spary, James Secord, and Nick Jardine (Cambridge: Cambridge University Press, forthcoming 2018).

12. Diana Magaloni-Kerpel, "Real and Illusory Feathers: Pigments, Painting Techniques, and the Use of Color in Ancient Mesoamerica," Nuevo Mundo Mundos Nuevos, January 25, 2006, http://nuevomundo.revues.org/1462; Karl A. Taube, "Flower Mountain: Concepts of Life, Beauty, and Paradise Among the Classic Maya," *RES: Anthropology and Aesthetics*, no. 45 (2004): 69–98.

13. Elizabeth Hill Boone, *Cycles of Time and Meaning in the Mexican Books of Fate* (Austin: University of Texas Press, 2007), 114–116, see also 123, 129.

14. *Codex Borgia*, plates 49–53; *Codex Vaticanus* 3733, plates 17–18. The Vatican Library provides digital scans of the *Borgia*, https://digi.vatlib.it/view/MSS_Borg.mess.1. A facsimile of the *Codex Vaticanus* 3733 is at http://www.famsi.org/research/loubat/Vaticanus%203773 /thumbs0.html. My interpretations are indebted to the groundwork of Eduard Seler, *Comentarios al Códice Borgia* (Mexico City: Fondo de Cultura Económica, 1963), and Boone, *Cycles of Time*.

15. *Codex Borgia*, plates 53, 49.

16. Frances Berdan and Patricia Rieff Anawalt, eds., *The Essential Codex Mendoza* (Berkeley: University of California Press, 1997), fols. 43, 45, 46, 47, 48; Frances Berdan, "Circulation of Feathers in Mesoamerica," Nuevo Mundo Mundos Nuevos, January 21, 2006, http://nuevomundo.revues.org/1387.

17. *Codex Borgia*, plates 61–70. See also Eduard Seler, *Codex Vaticanus No. 3773 (Codex Vaticanus B): An Old Mexican Pictorial Manuscript in the Vatican Library* (Berlin: Printed by T. and A. Constable, 1903), e.g., 249, 253, 265, 294.

18. Alessandra Russo, "Plumes of Sacrifice: Transformations in Sixteenth-Century Mexican Feather Art," *RES: Anthropology and Aesthetics*, no. 42 (October 1, 2002): 226–250; Magaloni-Kerpel, "Real and Illusory Feathers"; Alessandra Russo et al., eds., *El vuelo de las imágenes: Arte plumario en México y Europa* (Mexico City: Instituto Nacional de Bellas Artes, Instituto Nacional de Antropología e Historia, 2011); Sabine Haag, Alfonso de Maria y Campos, Lilia Rivero Weber, and Christian Feest, eds., *El Penacho de Moctezuma: Plumaria del México antiguo* (Altenstadt: ZFK Publishers, 2012).

19. Elizabeth H. Boone, "Incarnations of the Aztec Supernatural: The Image of Huitzilopochtli in Mexico and Europe," *Transactions of the American Philosophical Society* 79, pt. 2 (1988): 4. See also Arild Hvidtfeldt, *Teotl and *Ixiptlatli: Some Central Conceptions in Ancient Mexican Religion* (Copenhagen: Munksgaard, 1958), 98–99; Molly H. Bassett, *The Fate of Earthly Things: Aztec Gods and God-Bodies* (Austin: University of Texas Press, 2015), 53–78.

20. Russo, "Plumes of Sacrifice," 232.

21. Bernardino de Sahagún, *The Florentine Codex: General History of the Things of New Spain*, 12 books in 13 vols., trans. Arthur J. O. Anderson and Charles Dibble (Santa Fe: School of American Research and the University of Utah Press, 1950), bk. 2, pp. 82, 86, 113, 149, 196 (hereafter *FC*).

22. Haag et al., *El Penacho de Moctezuma*.

23. Magaloni-Kerpel, "Real and Illusory Feathers"; Haag et al., *El Penacho de Moctezuma*.

24. Bernardino de Sahagún, *Primeros Memoriales*, trans. Thelma D. Sullivan and H. B. Nicholson (Norman: University of Oklahoma Press, 1997), 206; see also Justyna Olko, *Insignia of Rank in the Nahua World: From the Fifteenth to the Seventeenth Century* (Boulder: University Press of Colorado, 2014).

25. *FC*, bk. 8, chap. 8.

26. Thelma D. Sullivan, "Nahuatl Proverbs, Conundrums, and Metaphors, Collected by Sahagún," *Estudios de Cultura Náhuatl* 4 (1963): 160–161, 156–157, also 138–139; *FC*, bk. 6, chap. 24.

27. *FC*, bk. 9, chaps. 18–21, pp. 89–93; Magaloni-Kerpel, "Real and Illusory Feathers."

28. John Bierhorst, trans., *Cantares Mexicanos: Songs of the Aztecs* (Stanford, CA: Stanford University Press, 1985). References to the quetzal can be found throughout.

29. Louise M. Burkhart, "Flowery Heaven: The Aesthetic of Paradise in Nahuatl Devotional Literature," *RES: Anthropology and Aesthetics*, no. 21 (1992): 90.

30. Burkhart, "Flowery Heaven." See also Louise M. Burkhart, *Before Guadalupe: The Virgin Mary in Early Colonial Nahuatl Literature* (Austin: University of Texas Press, 2001); Russo, "Plumes of Sacrifice."

31. Quoted in Burkhart, *Before Guadalupe*, 43, see also 37, 42; Burkhart, "Flowery Heaven," 106; Russo, "Plumes of Sacrifice," 237.

32. Russo, "Plumes of Sacrifice"; Olko, *Insignia of Rank in the Nahua World*.

33. Barbara E. Mundy, *The Death of Aztec Tenochtitlan, the Life of Mexico City* (Austin: University of Texas Press, 2015), 105.

34. Olko, *Insignia of Rank in the Nahua World*, 353.

35. Ibid., 342–349; Russo, "Plumes of Sacrifice."

36. See also Norton, *Sacred Gifts*; Mundy, *The Death of Aztec Tenochtitlan.*

37. Quoted in Lluís Nicolau d'Olwer, *Fray Bernardino de Sahagún, 1499–1590*, trans. Mauricio J. Mixco (Salt Lake City: University of Utah Press, 1987 [1952]), 32–33.

38. This paragraph follows d'Olwer, *Fray Bernardino de Sahagún*; Miguel Leon-Portilla, *Bernardino de Sahagún: First Anthropologist* (Norman: University of Oklahoma Press, 2012); Jesús Bustamante, *Fray Bernardino de Sahagún: Una revisión crítica de los manuscritos y de su proceso de composición* (Mexico City: Universidad Nacional Autónoma de México, 1990).

39. *FC*, bk. 2, chap. 37, p. 147.

40. *FC*, bk. 2, chap. 26, p. 86.

41. Alfredo López Austin, "Estudio acerca del método de investigación de fray Bernardino de Sahagún," *Estudios de Cultura Náhuatl* 42(2011), 353–400; Ilaria Palmieri Capesciotti, "La fauna del libro XI del Códice Florentino de fray Bernardino de Sahagún," *Estudios de Cultura Náhuatl* 32 (2001): 189–221.

42. "Historia universal de las cosas de la Nueva España repartida en doce libros: En lengua mexicana y Española," Real Academia de Historia (Madrid) mss 9/5524[1], fol. 264r. Digitized at http://bibliotecadigital.rah.es/dgbrah/es/consulta/registro.cmd?id=57663. Bustamante, *Fray Bernardino de Sahagún*, 301–305; Charles E. Dibble, "Los manuscritos de Tlatelolco y México y el Códice Florentino," *Estudios de Cultura Náhuatl* 29 (1999), 27–64. I explore the production of this text in relationship to Mesoamerican ontologies and animals in Norton, *The Tame and the Wild: A History of People and Animals in the Atlantic World After 1492* (Cambridge, MA: Harvard University Press, forthcoming).

43. *FC*, bk. 11, p. 19. Dibble and Anderson note when Nahuatl differs between the RAH ms and the *Florentine Codex.*

44. There were (and are) a number of different places with this name in New Spain, but contextual clues suggest that the one in Veracruz was intended.

45. *FC*, bk. 11, p. 19–20.

46. RAH mss 9/5524[1]; *FC*, bk. 11.

47. *FC*, bk. 11, p. 19.

48. Bierhorst, *Cantares Mexicanos*, 39–41.

49. Jeanette Favrot Peterson, "Perceiving Blackness, Envisioning Power: Chalma and the Black Christs in Colonial Mexico," in *Seeing Across Cultures in the Early Modern World*, ed. Dana Leibsohn and Jeanette Favrot Peterson (Farnham, UK: Ashgate, 2012), 59, 62.

50. *FC*, bk. 11, p. 20.

51. Germán Somolinos d'Ardois, *Vida y obra de Francisco Hernández* (Mexico City: UNAM, 1960); López Piñero and Pardo-Tomás, *La influencia de Francisco Hernández*; López Piñero and Pardo-Tomás, *Nuevos materiales*; Simon Varey, ed., *The Mexican Treasury: The Writings of Dr. Francisco Hernández* (Stanford, CA: Stanford University Press, 2000); Simon Varey and Rafael Chabrán, eds., *Searching for the Secrets of Nature: The Life and Works of Dr. Francisco Hernández* (Stanford, CA: Stanford University Press, 2000); Jaime Marroquín Arredondo, *Diálogos con Quetzalcóatl: Humanismo, etnografía y ciencia (1492–1577)* (Madrid: Iberoamericana, 2014).

52. Quoted in López Piñero and Pardo-Tomás, *La influencia*, 41, 42.

53. Jaime Marroquín Arredondo, "The Method of Francisco Hernández: Early Modern Science and the Translation of Mesoamerica's Natural History," this volume; Somolinos, *Vida y obra de Francisco Hernández*, 194–196.

54. Bustamante, *Fray Bernardino de Sahagún*, 300–305, 353–358.

55. Based on comparison of *FC*, bk. 11, p. 19; Francisco Hernández, *Historia natural de Nueva España*, 2 vols., trans. José Rojo Navarro (Mexico City: UNAM, 1960), 2:318. To my knowledge no one has previously noted that Hernández used Book 11 for his "Natural History of Animals." For a discussion of the relationship between the "Historia universal" and Hernández's natural histories in relationship to chapters on animals more broadly, see Norton, *The Tame and the Wild*. Two different versions survive of Hernández's chapter on the quetzal bird: that in the 1651 edition, which was based on a copy made of the Escorial manuscript (Hernández, "Historiae animalium et mineralium novae hispaniae," in *Rerum medicarum Novae Hispaniae Thesaurus*, 13), and his original manuscript, which he continued to annotate after sending the "clean" copy to Spain (Biblioteca Nacional de España, ms 22438, fols. 22–23). Excepting the cross-outs (of which there are many), the quetzal entry in the draft and the published version are nearly identical but, as discussed below, were ordered differently.

56. The Latin is *divorum*, which Navarro translated as "gods," but in this context I think "divine things" makes more sense, as discussed below.

57. Hernández, *Historia natural de Nueva España*, 2:318–319.

58. *FC*, bk. 11, chap. 2, p. 19.

59. For the Spanish text of the *Florentine Codex*, I have used Bernardino de Sahagún, *Códice florentino* (Mexico City: Secretaría de Gobernación, 1979), 237, and the digital facsimile available at "General History of the Things of New Spain by Fray Bernardino de Sahagún: The Florentine Codex," World Digital Library, https://www.wdl.org/en/item/10096/.

60. Hernández, "Historiae animalium," 13; Hernández, *Historia natural de Nueva España*, 2:318.

61. Christine E. Jackson, *Peacock* (London: Reaktion Books, 2006).

62. Hernández, "Historiae animalium," 13; Hernández, *Historia natural de Nueva España*, 2:318.

63. Biblioteca Nacional de España, ms 22438, fol. 22.

64. Quoted in Magaloni-Kerpel, "Real and Illusory Feathers" (my emphasis). See also *FC*, bk. 9, pp. 89–90.

65. López Piñero and Pardo-Tomás, *La influencia*, 44–45.

66. Quoted in ibid., 45.

67. Today these are in the Biblioteca Nacional de España. Francisco Hernández, "De historia plantarum, animalium et mineralium Novae Hispanae," Biblioteca Nacional de España, mss 22436–22439. See also Jesús Bustamante, "Natural History of New Spain," in *The Mexican Treasury*, 27–30.

68. López Piñero and Pardo-Tomás, *La influencia*; Varey and Chabrán, *Searching for the Secrets of Nature*. For animals, see my forthcoming book *The Tame and the Wild*.

69. Three seventeenth-century books were based directly or indirectly (via Recchi) on Hernández's manuscripts: Francisco Ximenes, *Quatro libros de la naturaleza y virtudes de las plantas y animales* (Mexico, 1615), Juan Eusebio Nieremberg's *Historia naturae, maxime*

peregrinae (Antwerp, 1635), and the *Rerum medicarum Novae Hispaniae Thesaurus, seu, Plantarum animalium mineralium Mexicanorum historia* (Rome, 1648–1651).

70. Nieremberg, *Historia naturae*, 206–243.

71. Domingo Ledezma, "Una legitimación imaginativa del Nuevo Mundo: La *Historia naturae, maxime peregrinae* del jesuita Juan Eusebio Nieremberg," in *El saber de los jesuitas, historias naturales y el Nuevo Mundo*, ed. Luis Millones Figueroa and Domingo Ledezma (Madrid: Iberoamericana, 2005), 55–57. For a study of Nieremberg and "science of the baroque," see José Ramón Marcaida López, *Arte y ciencia en el Barroco Español* (Seville: Fundación Focus-Abengoa, Marcial Pons Historia, 2014).

72. Ledezma, "Una legitimación imaginativa," 67.

73. Translated and quoted in ibid., 59, 67, 66, 56. See also Marcaida López, *Arte y ciencia*.

74. Nieremberg, *Historia naturae*, 229, translated in Willughby and Ray, *Ornithology*, 385. I am also grateful to Domingo Ledezma for sharing his translation of Nieremberg's entry, which will appear in a forthcoming published translation of the *Historia naturae*.

75. Nieremberg, *Historia naturae*, 230; Willughby and Ray, *Ornithology*, 385.

76. Nieremberg, *Historia naturae*, 230; Willughby and Ray, *Ornithology*, 385.

77. Biblioteca Nacional de España, ms 22438, fol. 35; Hernández, "Historiae animalium," 23.

78. *FC*, bk. 11, pp. 19–20.

79. Willughby and Ray, *Ornithology*, preface.

80. Ibid.

81. On expeditions, see Mark Greengrass, Daisy Hillyard, Christopher D. Preston, and Paul. J. Smith, "Science on the Move: Francis Willughby's Expedition," in *Virtuoso by Nature*, 142–226.

82. Willughby and Ray, *Ornithology*, preface.

83. Ibid.

84. Norton, *The Tame and the Wild*.

85. On these views, see Dorothy Johnston, "The Life and Domestic Context of Francis Willughby," in *Virtuoso by Nature*, 1–43; Greengrass et al., "Science on the Move," 175, 177–178.

86. Quoted in Greengrass et al., "Science on the Move," 178.

87. See the introduction to this volume.

88. Willughby and Ray, *Ornithology*, 128, 140, 161, 184; see also 68, 289, 296, 318–319, 339.

89. Ibid., 385–396; Willughby and Ray, *Ornothologiæ libri tres*, 297.

90. Asúa and French contend that Ray found "the fair amount of Aztec lore" in Hernández "utterly uncongenial" and therefore had difficulty incorporating his natural history into *Ornithology: A New World of Animals*, 214–218.

91. Willughby and Ray, *Ornithology*, 385–386.

92. Library of Congress shelf mark: Kislak Coll. FOL. QH41.N6 copy 2.

93. Dorothy Johnston, former keeper of manuscripts at the University of Nottignham, wrote about Ray's marginalia in the dealer's note for Nieremberg's *Historia naturae* in the Kislak Collection at the Library of Congress, kindly provided to me by Arthur Dunkelman of the Kislak Family Foundation. I am grateful to Dr. Johnston for comparing these hash marks with others known to be made by Willughby and making this provisional identification.

94. Compare the italicized annotations in *Ornothologiæ libri tres*, 297, 298, and marginalia in Nieremberg, *Historia naturae* 208, 209 (Kislak Coll. FOL. QH41.N6 copy 2).

95. Willughby and Ray, *Ornithology*, 385–386.

96. Nieremberg, *Historia naturae*, Library of Congress Kislak Coll. FOL. QH41.N6 copy 2, pp. 229–230.

97. This judgment is based on a comparison with Ledezma's modern Spanish translation.

98. Nieremberg, *Historia naturae*, 230; Hernández, "Historiae animalium," 13.

Chapter 6

1. Description based on my own examination of the manuscript. Jacques Gravier, *Dictionary of the Algonquian-Illinois Language*, Watkinson Library, Trinity College, Hartford, CT. The dictionary is now also available online through the Watkinson Library Internet Archive. Information on the circumstances of the dictionary's production comes from "John F. Swenson to Mr. Jeffrey H. Kaimowitz, 13 March 1989," in John F. Swenson, *John F. Letters re Gravier Dictionary*, American Indian Vocabulary Collection, Watkinson Library, Trinity College.

2. "Brief Relation of the Journey to New France," in *Jesuit Relations and Allied Documents: Travels and Explorations of the Jesuit Missionaries in New France*, 71 vols, ed. Reuben Gold Thwaites (Cleveland: Burrows Brothers, 1896–1901), 5:91.

3. Other scholars have noted this increase in linguistic expertise by the third generation of French Jesuits. See: Robert Michael Morrissey, "'I Speak It Well': Language, Cultural Understanding, and the End of a Missionary Middle Ground in Illinois Country, 1673–1712," *Early American Studies* Fall (2011): 617–648; Tracy Neale Leavelle, *The Catholic Calumet: Colonial Conversions in French and Indian North America* (Philadelphia: University of Pennsylvania Press, 2012), 97–125; Brett Rushforth, *Bonds of Alliance: Indigenous and Atlantic Slaveries in New France* (Chapel Hill: University of North Carolina Press for the Omohundro Institute for Early American History and Culture, 2012), 15–73. Similar expertise has also been attributed to third and fourth generation Puritan missionaries, most notably in Douglas Winiarski's excellent work on Josiah Cotton. "'A Question of Plain Dealing: Josiah Cotton, Native Christians, and the Quest for Security in Eighteenth-Century Plymouth County," *New England Quarterly* 77, no. 3 (2004): 368–413.

4. Experience Mayhew, *Observations on the Indian Language*, ed. John S. H. Fogg (Boston: D. Clapp & Son, 1884), 8.

5. Gravier, *Dictionary of the Algonquian-Illinois Language*; Sebastian Rale, "A Dictionary of the Abnaki Language, in North America," in *Memoirs of the American Academy of Arts and Sciences* I (Cambridge, MA: Printer to the University, 1833), 370–575; Antoine-Robert Le Boullenger, *French and Miami-Illinois Dictionary*, John Carter Brown Library, Providence, RI; Josiah Cotton, "Vocabulary of the Massachusett (Or Natick) Indian Language," in *Collections of the Massachusetts Historical Society*, 147–257 (Cambridge, MA: Printed by E. W. Metcalf, 1830); Mayhew, *Observations on the Indian Language*.

6. The print archive is fairly substantial, including the seventeenth-century texts in John Eliot's Indian Library, for which he imported a specific printer by the name of Marmaduke Johnson. Of relevance to this time period, see also *The Massachusetts Psalter: Or, Psalms of David* (Boston: Printed by B. Green and J. Printer, 1709). Several sermons and catechisms exist in manuscript. See Josiah Cotton, Sermon, Massachusetts, 1710, Ayer Collection, Newberry Library, Chicago; Experience Mayhew, Sermons, Papers of Experience Mayhew,

Massachusetts Historical Society, Boston; Prayer Book, Abnaki, American Indian Vocabulary Collection, Watkinson Library, Hartford, CT.

7. On natural philosophy and scriptural history from 1680 to 1720, see William Poole, *The World Makers: Scientists of the Restoration and the Search for the Origins of the Earth* (Oxford, UK: Peter Lang, 2010), esp. 75–84. On the breakdown of biblical linguistics, see Thomas R. Trautman, *Languages and Nations: The Dravidian Proof in Colonial Madras* (Berkeley: University of California Press, 2006), 1–41.

8. The quote is from Joseph-François Lafitau, *Customs of the American Indians Compared with the Customs of Primitive Times*, 2 vols., ed. and trans. William N. Fenton and Elizabeth L. Moore (Toronto: Champlain Society, 1974), 2:267.

9. For a theorization of this process during the Enlightenment, see Johannes Fabian, *Time and the Other: How Anthropology Makes Its Object* (New York: Columbia University Press, 2014).

10. Giambattista Vico, Jean Jacques Rousseau, Adam Smith, Johann Gottfried Herder, Wilhelm von Humboldt, and Lord Monboddo, just to name a few.

11. On connections between Locke and missionary linguistics, see Sarah Rivett, "Learning to Write Algonquian Letters: The Indigenous Place of Language Philosophy in the Seventeenth-Century Atlantic World," *William and Mary Quarterly* 71, no. 4 (2014): 549–588. Matthew Hale's *Primitive Origin of Mankind* (1677) shows the beginnings of the disintegrating ability of philosophers to unite linguistics with biblical and world history. I am not ascribing an entirely causal role to Locke's *Essay*. Indeed, I argue against this in "Learning to Write Algonquian Letters." Instead, I propose Locke as codifying some of the insights about language already in circulation, particularly due to colonial language encounters.

12. Lafitau, *Customs of the American Indians*, 2:253.

13. Ibid.

14. Ibid., 1:53.

15. Ibid., 2:268.

16. Ibid.

17. Ibid., 2:261.

18. "It was only towards the end of the fifteenth century that these immense regions [North and South America] were discovered" (Lafitau, *Customs of the American Indians*, 1:42). "When two peoples who speak languages so far apart as Iroquois and French meet for the needs of trade or for their common defense, they are forced equally on both sides, to approach each other in their own language" (Lafitau, *Customs of the American Indians*, 2:261).

19. Lafitau, *Customs of the American Indians*, 2:261.

20. Dewi W. Evans and Brynley F. Roberts, eds., *Edward Lhwyd Archaeologia Britannica: Texts and Translations* (Aberystwyth: Celtic Studies Publications, 2009), 6–7.

21. For connections between John Eliot and the Royal Society, see Sarah Rivett, "Empirical Desire: Converstion, Ethnography, and the New Science of the Praying Indian," *Early American Studies* 4, no. 1 (2006): 16–45.

22. Nancy Edwards, "Edward Lhuyd and the Origins of Early Medieval Celtic Archaeology," *Antiquaries Journal* 87 (2007): 165–196.

23. For an account of the Druidical fascination, see Ronald Hutton, *Blood & Mistletoe: The History of the Druids in Britain* (New Haven, CT: Yale University Press, 2009), 49–124.

24. IMAGINES seu Figurae variorum Inscriptionum praecipue Sepulchralium, Stowe ms 1023, British Library, London, 3–6.

25. For an account of practices of rereading the land from the perspective of Christian history, see Alexandra Walsham, *Reformation of the Landscape: Religion, Identity, & Memory in Early Modern Britain & Ireland* (Oxford: Oxford University Press, 2011).

26. David Malcolme and Edward Lhwyd, *A Collection of Letters, in Which the Imperfection of Learning, Even Among Christians, and a Remedy for It, Are Hinted* (Edinburgh, UK, 1739), 14, 41.

27. Ibid., 36.

28. On philology and nostalgia, see Allen J. Frantzen, *Desire for Origins: New Language, Old English, and Teaching the Tradition* (New Brunswick, NJ: Rutgers University Press, 1990); Christopher Cannon, *The Grounds of English Literature* (Oxford: Oxford University Press, 2004); Michael Modarelli, "The Struggle for Origins: Old English in Nineteenth-Century America," *Modern Language Quarterly* 73, no. 4 (2012): 527–543.

29. William Baxter, *Glossarium Antiquitatum Britannicarum* (London: J. Watts, 1719), 78.

30. Much has been written about Jesuit linguistic skill, beginning with Victor E. Hanzeli, *Missionary Linguistics in New France: A Study of Seventeenth and Eighteenth-Century Descriptions of American Indian Languages* (Mouton: The Hague, 1969). See also Peter A. Dorsey, "Going to School with the Savages: Authorship and Authority Among the Jesuits of New France," *William and Mary Quarterly* 55, no. 3 (1998): 399–420; Tracy Neale Leavelle, "'Bad Things' and 'Good Hearts': Mediation, Meaning, and the Language of Illinois Christianity," *Church History* 76, no. 2, 363–394; Peter Burke, "The Jesuits and the Art of Translation in Early Modern Europe," in *The Jesuits II: Cultures, Sciences, and the Arts*, ed. by Peter Burke, John O'Malley, Gauvin Alexander Bailey, Steven J. Harris, and Frank T. Kennedy, 24–32 (Toronto: University of Toronto Press, 2006); Marc Fumaroli, "The Fertility and Shortcomings of Renaissance Rhetoric: The Jesuit Case," in *The Jesuits: Cultures, Sciences, and the Arts, 1540–1773*, ed. John W. O'Malley, Gauvin Alexander Bailey, Steven J. Harris, and T. Frank Kennedy, 90–106 (Toronto: University of Toronto Press, 1999). Recently, Micah True has written about Jesuit linguistic expertise as an ideal expressed throughout the *Relations* in order to emphasize both the efficacy of the Jesuit mission in New France and the "bidirectional" flow of knowledge between priests and indigenous populations. Micah True, *Masters and Students: Jesuit Ethnography in Seventeenth-Century New France* (Montreal: McGill Queens University Press, 2015), 51.

31. Julien Binneteau, "Letter of Father Julien Binneteau, of the Society of Jesus, to a Father of the Same Society," in *Jesuit Relations and Allied Documents*, 65:69–71.

32. John W. O'Malley explains that the *Spiritual Exercises* functioned as a basic course of movement that the Jesuits strove to make operative in whatever they did. The structure of the *Spiritual Exercises* can thus be discerned in the course of their quotidian activities and in the annual reports. The year 1548 is the publication date with official papal approval. *The First Jesuits* (Cambridge, MA: Cambridge University Press, 1993), 37–50, 87–90.

33. Mary R. Calvert, *Black Robe on the Kennebec* (Monmouth, ME: Monmouth Press, 1991), 229, 231, and 238–239. The letters of October 30, 1689, and August 26, 1690, are printed as the appendix.

34. Scott Stevens, a native speaker of Mohawk, explained to me that the figure 8 is meant to designate a sound that approximates the pronunciation of the French word *huit*.

35. Sebastian Rasles, *A Dictionary of the Abnaki Language, in North America* (Cambridge, UK: Printer to the University, 1833), 566–567.

36. Antonio de Nebrija, *Gramática castellana: Texto establecido sobre la ed. "princeps" de 1492, por Pascual Galindo Romeo y Luis Ortiz Muñoz, con una introd., notas y facsímil: Prólogo del Sr. D. José Ibáñez Martín* (Madrid, 1946). The statement appears at the beginning of the prologue, "siempre la lengua fue companera del imperio" (5). For an analysis of Nebrija's grammar as establishing a key relationship between Renaissance theories of writing and the colonization of Amerindian languages, see Walter D. Mignolo, "Nebrija in the New World: The Question of the Letter, the Colonization of Amerindian Languages, and the Discontinuity of the Classical Tradition," *L'Homme* 32, no. 122/124 (1992): 185–207.

37. On primitiveness as a crucial component of language ideologies, see Richard Bauman and Charles L. Briggs, *Voices of Modernity: Language Ideologies and the Politics of Inequality* (New York: Cambridge University Press, 2003). On ideas of the deficiency of native languages, see Julie Tetel Andresen, *Linguistics in America, 1769–1924* (London: Routledge, 1990), 83–119; Anthony Pagden, *European Encounters with the New World* (New Haven, CT: Yale University Press, 1993), 126–140; Edward G. Gray, *New World Babel: Languages and Nations in Early America* (Princeton, NJ: Princeton University Press, 1999); Rüdiger Schreyer, "'Savage' Languages in Eighteenth-Century Theoretical History of Language," in *The Language Encounter in the Americas, 1492–1800*, ed. Edward G. Gray and Norman Fiering (New York: Berghahn Books, 2000), 310–326; David B. Paxman, "Language and Difference: The Problem of Abstraction in Eighteenth-Century Language Study," *Journal of the History of Ideas* 54 (1993): 19–36.

38. David Silverman, *Faith and Boundaries: Colonists, Christianity, and Community Among the Wampanoag Indians of Martha's Vineyard, 1600–1871* (Cambridge: Cambridge University Press, 2005), 141.

39. Gravier, "Letter by Father Jacques Gravier in the form of a Journal of the Mission of l'Immacule Conception de Notre Dame in the Illinois Country," in *Jesuit Relations and Allied Documents*, 64:195, 215, 225, 227.

40. David J. Costa, *The Miami-Illinois Language* (Lincoln: University of Nebraska Press, 2003), 14.

41. For two recent studies of Jesuit dictionaries from this time period, see Robert Michael Morrissey, "'I Speak It Well': Language, Cultural Understanding, and the End of a Missionary Middle Ground in Illinois Country, 1673–1712," *Early American Studies* (Fall 2011): 617–648; Tracy Neale Leavelle, *The Catholic Calumet: Colonial Conversions in French and Indian North America* (Philadelphia: University of Pennsylvania Press, 2012), 97.

42. Calvert, *Black Robe on the Kennebec*, 239.

43. For an analysis of this shift, see Jennifer Monaghan, *Learning to Read and Write in Colonial America* (Amherst: University of Massachusetts Press, 2005), 169–188.

44. "Proposals for Propagating the Gospel in All Pagan Countries," Society for the Propagation of the Gospel Papers, Vol. VII, 4–7, Lambeth Palace, London, United Kingdom.

45. Society for the Propagation of Christian Knowledge, Cambridge University Library, SPCK.MS.CN3/5.

46. Randall Balmer, "Freeman, Bernardus," American National Biography Online, February 2000; Monaghan, *Learning to Read and Write in Colonial America*, 173.

47. "Society of the Propagation of the Gospels Papers," Series A:7, 203–204, Rhodes House, Oxford, United Kingdom.

48. Monaghan, *Learning to Read and Write in Colonial America*, 176.

49. In a letter to Sir William Ashurst dated December 10, 1712, Mather clearly recognizes the SPG's goal of instructing the proselytes in English but with the following caveat:

> The grand concern of reprinting the Indian Bible often comes under our consideration. The most of your commissioners are averse to doing it at all, and rather hope to bring the rising generation by schools and other ways, to a full acquaintance with the English tongue, in which they will have a key to all the treasures of knowledge which we ourselves are owners of. My own poor opinion is that the projection of anglicising our Indians is much more easy to be talked of than to be accomplished. It will take more time than the commissioners who talk of it can imagine.

Quoted in *Selected Letters of Cotton Mather*, ed. Kenneth Silverman (Baton Rouge: Louisiana State University Press, 1971), 127.

50. Quoted in Mayhew, *Observations on the Indian Language*, 8.

51. Ibid., 9–11.

52. See David Silverman, "Indians, Missionaries, and Religious Translation: Creating Wampanoag Christianity in Seventeenth-Century Martha's Vineyard," *William and Mary Quarterly* 6, no. 2 (2005): 141–174.

53. Mayhew *Observations on the Indian Language*.

54. Josiah Cotton, "Vocabulary of the Massachusett (Or Natick) Indian Language." The appendix to this printed edition of Cotton's Indian vocabulary explains that he used the *Indian Primer* and the *Eliot Bible* to study the orthography of Massachusett.

55. Ibid., 242–244.

56. See Ives Goddard, "The Description of the Native Languages of North America Before Boas," in *Handbook of North American Indians*, Vol. 17, edited by Ives Goddard, 17–42 (Washington, DC: Smithsonian Institution, 1996); Hilary E. Wyss and Kristina Bross, *Early Native Literacies in New England: A Documentary History* (Amherst: University of Massachusetts Press, 2008), 1–11; Anna Ash, Jessie Little Doe Fermino, Ken Hale, and Leanne Hinton, "Diversity in Local Language Maintenance and Restoration: A Reason for Optimism," in *The Green Book of Language Revitalization in Practice*, edited by Ken Hale, 19–39 (New York: Academic Press, 2001).

57. See Silverman, "Indians, Missionaries, and Religious Translation," 141.

58. James Hammond Trumbull, *Natick Dictionary: A New England Indian Lexicon; Introduction by Edward Everett Hale* (Lincoln: University of Nebraska Press, 2009), 35.

59. Ibid., 22.

60. Ibid., 19.

61. Josiah Cotton's phrase is "Negonne kuhquttumoonk," with "negonne" meaning "old, ancient, and so first in the order of time" and "kuhquttumoonk" meaning "he thirsts." Ibid., 42, 82.

62. Cotton, *Vocabulary of the Massachusetts (Or Natick) Indian Language*, 242.

63. Claudio R. Salvucci, "Introduction," in John Gilmary Shea, ed., *Elements of a Miami-Illinois Grammar*, 1–8 (1890; reprint, Bristol, PA: Evolution Publishing, 1890), 1–8.

64. Fermino, Hale, and Hinton, "Diversity in Local Language Maintenance and Restoration."

65. Colin G. Calloway, *The Abenaki* (New York: Chelsea House Publishers, 1989), 85–87.

66. This is Bernard Perley's insight in "Aboriginality at Large: Varieties of Resistance in Maliseet Language Instruction," in *Identities: Global Studies in Culture and Power* 13 (2006): 187–208.

67. For an analysis of this discourse of modernity, see Jean M. O'Brien, *Firsting and Lasting: Writing Indians Out of Existence in New England* (Minneapolis: University of Minnesota Press, 2010).

Chapter 7

1. Raymond Phineas Stearns, *Science in the British Colonies of America* (Urbana: University of Illinois Press, 1970), 32.

2. See David Freedberg, *The Eye of the Lynx: Galileo, His Friends, and the Beginnings of Modern Natural History* (Chicago: University of Chicago Press, 2013).

3. See Victor Navarro Brotóns and William Eamon, eds., *Más allá de la Leyenda Negra: España y la Revolución Científica* [Beyond the Black Legend: Spain and the Scientific Revolution] (Valencia: Instituto de Historia de la Ciencia y Documentación López Piñero, Universitat de València, 2007). See also Jorge Cañizares-Esguerra, *Puritan Conquistadors: Iberianizing the Atlantic, 1550–1700* (Stanford, CA: Stanford University Press, 2006); Daniela Bleichmar, Paula De Vos, Kristin Huffine, and Kevin Sheehan, eds., *Science in the Spanish and Portuguese Empires, 1500–1800* (Stanford, CA: Stanford University Press, 2009); Juan Pimentel, "The Iberian Vision: Science and Empire in the Framework of a Universal Monarchy, 1500–1800," *Osiris* 15, no. 1 (2000): 17–21. On the important role that Spain played especially in New World natural history, see José María López Piñero and Maríaluz López Terrada, eds., *La influencia española en la introducción en Europa de las plantas americanas: 1493–1623* (Valencia: Instituto de Historia de la Ciencia y Documentación López Piñero, Universitat de València, C.S.I.C., 1997); Maríaluz López Terrada and José Pardo-Tomás, *Las primeras noticias sobre plantas americanas en las relaciones de viajes y crónicas de Indias, 1493–1553* (Valencia: Instituto de Historia de la Ciencia y Documentación López Piñero, Universitat de València, C.S.I.C., 1993); Antonio Barrera Osoria, *Experiencing Nature: The Spanish American Empire and the Early Scientific Revolution* (Austin: University of Texas Press, 2006).

4. Bruno Latour, *We Have Never Been Modern*, trans. Catherine Porter (Cambridge, MA: Harvard University Press, 1993), 10. See also Kellie Robertson, "Medieval Materialism: A Manifesto," *Exemplaria* 22, no. 2 (Summer 2010): 99–118, esp. 103.

5. Augustine, *The Confessions*, ed. Albert Cook Outler (Louisville, KY: Westminster, 1955), 233. See also Hans Blumenberg, *The Legitimacy of the Modern Age*, trans. Robert M. Wallace (Cambridge, MA: MIT Press, 1999), 240, 282, 249. For Löwith's account of the connection between Christian apocalyptic eschatology and scientific "progress," see Karl Löwith, *Meaning in History* (Chicago: University of Chicago Press, 1949), esp. 188–190. For more recent studies of the history of curiosity, see Susan Scott Parrish, *American Curiosity: Cultures of Natural History in the Colonial British American World* (Chapel Hill: University of North Carolina Press for the Omohundro Institute of Early American History and Culture, 2006); Barbara Benedict, *Curiosity: A Cultural History of Early Modern Inquiry* (Chicago: University of Chicago Press, 2001); Toby Huff, *Intellectual Curiosity and the Scientific Revolution: A Global Perspective* (Cambridge: Cambridge University Press, 2011).

6. Heiko Oberman, *"Contra vanam curiositatem": Ein Kapitel der Theologie zwischen Seelenwinkel und Weltall* (Zürich: Theologischer Verlag, 1974), 17–18.

7. Stephen Gaukroger, *The Emergence of a Scientific Culture: Science and the Shaping of Modernity, 1210–1685* (Oxford, UK: Clarendon, 2006), 3.

8. Ibid., 18–19.

9. For an annotated bibliography of Oviedo's works, see Daymond Turner, *Gonzalo Fernández de Oviedo y Valdés: An Annotated Bibliography* (Chapel Hill: University of North Carolina Press, 1966). For a comprehensive study of Oviedo's works, see Antonello Gerbi, *Nature in the New World: From Christopher Columbus to Gonzalo Fernández de Oviedo* (Pittsburg: University of Pittsburg Press, 1985); Kathleen Myers, *Fernández de Oviedo's Chronicle of America* (Austin: University of Texas Press, 2007).

10. This first part was republished in Salamanca in 1547 together with an account of the conquest of Peru by Francisco de Xérez. This edition was titled *Coronica delas Indias: La hystoria general de las Indias agora nueuamente impressa corregida y emendada; 1547: y con la conquista del Peru* (Salamanca: Printed for Iuan de Iunta, 1547).

11. Bartolomé de Las Casas, *Las Casas on Columbus: Background and the Second and Fourth Voyages*, trans. Nigel Griffin, ed. Anthony Pagden; Reportorium Colombianum VII (Turnhout: Brepols, 1999), 25.

12. Gonzalo Fernández de Oviedo y Valdés, *Oviedo de la Natural hystoria de las Indias* (Toledo: Printed for Go[n]çalo Ferna[n]dez de Ouiedo al[ia]s e Valdes, 1526), 43.

13. Oviedo, *Oviedo de la Natural hystoria*, 9.

14. For a description and discussion of this work, see Thomas Day Goodrich, "Ottoman Americana: The Search for the Sources of the Sixteenth-Century Tarih-I Hind-I Garbi," *Bulletin of Research in the Humanities* 85 (Autumn 1982): 269–294.

15. Oviedo, *Oviedo de la Natural hystoria*, "Proemio," fol. Ii.

16. Ibid., 11.

17. Anthony Pagden, *European Encounters with the New World: From Renaissance to Romanticism* (New Haven, CT: Yale University Press, 1993), 43.

18. Stuart Clark, *Vanities of the Eye: Vision in Early Modern European Culture* (Oxford: Oxford University Press, 2007), 9.

19. I develop this argument in more detail in *The Alchemy of Conquest: Science, Religion, and the Secrets of the New World* (Charlottesville: University of Virginia Press, forthcoming).

20. For a discussion of the role that the medieval and Renaissance "art" of memory played in the composition of the *Sumario*, see Antonio Sánchez Jiménez, "Memoria y utilidad en el *Sumario de la natural historia de las Indias*," *Colonial Latin American Review* 13, no. 2 (2004): 263–273; Andrés Prieto, "Classification, Memory, and Subjectivity in Gonzalo Fernández de Oviedo's *Sumario de la natural historia* (1526)," *MLN* 124, no. 2 (March 2009): 329–349.

21. See Jeremy Paden, "The Iguana and the Barrel of Mud: Memory, Natural History, and Hermeneutics in Oviedo's *Sumario de la natural historia de las Indias*," *Colonial Latin American Review* 16 (2007): 203–226. On Renaissance natural history more generally, see Brian Ogilvie, *The Science of Describing: Natural History in Renaissance Europe* (Chicago: University of Chicago Press, 2006); Henry Lowood, "The New World and the European Catalogue of Nature," in *American in European Consciousness, 1493–1750*, ed. Karen Ordahl Kupperman, 295–323 (Chapel Hill: University of North Carolina Press for the Institute of Early American History and Culture, Williamsburg, 1995).

22. Francis Bacon, *New Atlantis*, ed. Brian Vickers (Oxford: Oxford University Press, 1996). On Lucretius and his subterranean life during the Renaissance, see Gerard Passannante, *The Lucretian Renaissance: Philology and the Afterlife of Tradition* (Chicago: University of Chicago Press, 2011).

23. See David Gwyn, "Richard Eden Cosmographer and Alchemist," *Sixteenth Century Journal* 15, no. 1 (1984): 12–34; C. J. Kitching, "Alchemy in the Reign of Edward VI: An

Episode in the Career of Richard Whalley and Richard Eden," *Bulletin of the Institute of Historical Research* 44 (1971): 308–315.

24. On Aeneas Silvius's influence on Columbus, see Nicolás Wey Gómez, *The Tropics of Empire: Why Columbus Sailed South to the Indies* (Cambridge, MA: MIT Press, 2008).

25. William Newman, *Promethean Ambitions: Alchemy and the Quest to Perfect Nature* (Chicago: University of Chicago Press, 2004), 23. On Albertus Magnus and Aquinas, see especially 44–52.

26. See Richard Eden, "To the Reader," in Sebastian Münster, *A Treatyse of the Newe India, with Other New Founde Lands and Islandes, as Well Eastwarde as Westwarde*, trans. R. Eden (London: n.p., 1553), n.p.

27. Ibid., A8.

28. Richard Eden, *The Decades of the Newe Worlde or West India* (London: William Powell, 1555), 326.

29. Ibid., 215.

30. Ibid., 184.

31. Ibid.

32. Ibid., 185.

33. Ibid., 214.

Chapter 8

I thank Maríaluz López-Terrada, Mar Rey Bueno, James Amelang, and William Eamon for their helpful suggestions.

1. Andreas Vesalius, *The China Root Epistle*, trans. Daniel H. Garrison (Cambridge: Cambridge University Press, 2015), 18. Vesalius exaggerates slightly; guaiacum was still used as a milder alternative to mercury treatments for the pox a century afterward. See Cristian Berco, *From Body to Community: Venereal Disease and Society in Baroque Spain* (Toronto: University of Toronto Press, 2016), 101–103.

2. José Pardo-Tomás, "East Indies, West Indies: Garcia de Orta and the Spanish Treatises on Exotic *Materia Medica*," in *Medicine, Trade and Empire: Garcia de Orta's Colloquies on the Simples and Drugs of India (1563) in Context*, ed. Palmira Fontes da Costa (Farnham, UK: Ashgate, 2015), 195.

3. See, for example, Marcy Norton, "The Quetzal Takes Flight: Microhistory, Mesoamerican Knowledge, and Early Modern Natural History," this volume; Enrique Álvarez López, "Las plantas de América en la botánica europea del siglo XVI," *Revista de Indias* 6 (1945): 221–288; José María López Piñero and José Pardo-Tomás, *Nuevos materiales y noticias sobre la* Historia de las plantas de Nueva España *de Francisco Hernández* (Valencia: Universitat de València/CSIC, 1994); José María López Piñero and Maríaluz López-Terrada, *La influencia española en la introducción en Europa de las plantas americanas (1493–1623)* (Valencia: Universitat de València/CSIC, 1997).

4. José María López Piñero, *Medicina e historia natural en la sociedad española de los siglos XVI y XVII* (Valencia: Universitat de València, 2007), 115.

5. José Pardo-Tomás, "Two Glimpses of America from a Distance," in *Carolus Clusius*, ed. Florike Egmond et al., (Amsterdam: Koninklijke Nederlandse Akademie van Wetenschappen, 2007), 177.

6. Daniela Bleichmar, "The Trajectories of Natural Knowledge in the Spanish Empire (ca. 1550–1650)," in *Mas allá de la Leyenda Negra: España y la Revolución Científica*, ed. Victor

Navarro Brotóns and William Eamon (Valencia: Universitat de Valéncia/CSIC, 2007), 142; Daniela Bleichmar, "Books, Bodies, and Fields: Sixteenth-Century Transatlantic Encounters with New World *Materia Medica*," in *Colonial Botany: Science, Commerce, and Politics in the Early Modern World*, ed. Londa Schiebinger and Claudia Swan (Philadelphia: University of Pennsylvania Press, 2005), 96.

7. In his study of Garcia de Orta's *Colóquios*, Pardo-Tomás underscores the importance of distinguishing between the European circulation of knowledge about exotic flora in Latin and "the particular Iberian circulation in Spanish." Pardo-Tomás, "East Indies, West Indies," 198.

8. Brian Ogilvie, *The Science of Describing: Natural History in Renaissance Europe* (Chicago: University of Chicago Press, 2006), 270.

9. Ibid.

10. Lucia Binotti, *Cultural Capital, Language and National Identity in Imperial Spain* (London: Támesis, 2012), 17–50.

11. Although it was first published in 1540, with subsequent editions in 1551 and 1564, Fernández and Ramón Laca speculate that *De Citriis* was written sometime around 1533. See Florentino Fernández González and Luis Ramón-Laca Menéndez de Luarca, "El tratado sobre los cítricos de Nicolás Monardes," *Asclepio* 54, no. 2 (2002): 151. As I discuss below, *De Citriis* must have been written sometime after 1536 and probably closer to 1540. For more about Monardes's short works in Latin, see José María López Piñero, *Medicina e historia natural en la sociedad española de los siglos XVI y XVII* (Valencia: Universitat de València, 2007), 111.

12. Fernández and Ramón-Laca, "El tratado sobre los cítricos," 153. I cite Fernández and Ramón-Laca's edition, although there is another modern edition: Humberto Julio Paoli, "Tre rari opusculi di Nicolás Monárdes: III, De citriis aurantiis et limonis," *Archeion* 24, no. 2 (1942): 168–189.

13. Fernández and Ramón Laca note Monardes's debt to the proem of Book 1 of Celsus's *De Medicina*, but it seems clear that Monardes also draws on the proem to Book 7 of *De Medicina*.

14. Fernández and Ramón Laca guess that this citation is taken from Ruel's 1516 edition of Dioscorides. I have not found it there, but it does appear verbatim in Ruel's *De Natura Stirpium* (Paris: ex officina Simonis Colinae, 1536), 191–192. This indicates that Monardes wrote *De Citriis* after 1536. In his edition of the *De Citriis*, Paoli mentions both works by Ruel but does not use them to date Monardes's composition of *De Citriis*. Paoli, "Tre rari opusculi," 179.

15. Athenaeus, *Athēnaiou Deipnosophistou tēn polymathestatēn pragmateian nyn exesti soi philologou mikrou priamenōi pollōn te kai megalōn [Deipnosophistae]* (Venice: apud Aldum, et Andream socerum, mense, 1514), preface (unpaginated).

16. Angela Nuovo, *The Book Trade in the Italian Renaissance* (Leiden: Brill, 2013), 423. On Manuzio's influence in Spain, see Binotti, *Cultural Capital*, 51–94; Clive Griffin, *Aldus Manutius's Influence in the Hispanic World* (Florence: L. S. Olschki, 1998).

17. Nuovo, *The Book Trade in the Italian Renaissance*, 6.

18. Neither Monardes's *De Citriis* nor Manuzio's preface are paginated. However, the fact that Monardes's opening lines in *De Citriis* echo the first sentence in Manuzio's preface makes the borrowing easy to spot.

19. Desiderius Erasmus, *Opera omnia* (Amsterdam: Koninklijke Nederlandse Akademie van Wetenschappen, 1969), 351. None of Erasmus's "Protean" greetings in Book 33 of *De copia* are identical to either Monardes's or Manuzio's salutations.

20. Ignacio Díaz-Delgado Peñas calls attention to this shift in register, focusing on the academic nature of Monardes's content in his Latin texts rather than his stylistic aspirations. Ignacio Díaz-Delgado Peñas, *Entre el comercio, la ciencia . . . y la sospecha: Vida y obra de Nicolás Monardes Alfaro* (Madrid: Biblioteca Virtual Ignacio Larramendi de Polígrafos, 2015), 29.

21. José María López Piñero and María Luz Terrada Ferrandis, *Introducción a la terminología médica* (Barcelona: Masson, 2005), 192.

22. On Monardes's writing about the New World as part of a strategy of imperial appropriation, see Bleichmar, "Books, Bodies, and Fields," 83; Pardo-Tomás, "Two Glimpses of America from a Distance," 175.

23. Nicolás Monardes, *Dos libros: El uno trata de todas las cosas que traen de nuestras Indias occidentales . . . El otro libro trata de las dos medicinas maravillosas que son contra todo veneno . . .* (Sevilla: Sebastian Trugillo, 1565), n.p.

24. Ibid., n.p. On the importance of cheap American substitutes for expensive Asian medicines, see José María López Piñero and José Pardo-Tomás, *La influencia de Francisco Hernández (1515–1587) en la constitución de la botánica y la ateria médica modernas* (Valencia: Universitat de València/CSIC, 1996), 66; López Piñero and López-Terrada, *La influencia española*, 57–58; José Pardo-Tomás, *Oviedo, Monardes, Hernández: El tesoro natural de América; Colonialismo y ciencia en el siglo XVI* (Madrid: Nivola, 2002), 120; Michael Solomon, *Fictions of Well-Being: Sickly Readers and Vernacular Medical Writing in Late Medieval and Early Modern Spain* (Philadelphia: University of Pennsylvania Press, 2010), 86.

25. Both physic nut and the castor oil plant are from the same family (Euphorbiaceae). I follow Pardo-Tomás and López Terrada's identification of the "higuera del infierno" as *Jatropha curcas* L. Michael Solomon identifies "higuera del infierno" as *Datura stramonium* L. See José Pardo-Tomás and Maríaluz López-Terrrada, *Las primeras noticias sobre plantas americanas* (Valencia: Universitat de València/CSIC, 1993), 197; Solomon, *Fictions of Well-Being*, 79.

26. Ralph Bauer, "The Blood of the Dragon: Alchemy and Natural History in Nicolás Monardes's *Historia medicinal*," in *Medical Cultures of the Early Modern Spanish Empire*, ed. John Slater, Maríaluz López-Terrada, and José Pardo-Tomás (Farnham, UK: Ashgate, 2014), 70.

27. Daniela Bleichmar, "The Trajectories of Natural Knowledge in the Spanish Empire (ca. 1550–1650)," in *Mas allá de la Leyenda Negra: España y la Revolución Científica*, ed. Victor Navarro Brotòns and William Eamon (Valencia: Soler, 2007), 142; Bleichmar, "Books, Bodies, and Fields," 96.

28. Pardo-Tomás, "East Indies, West Indies," 208–209.

29. John Slater, "The Green Gold Fallacies: Myth and Reality in the Transatlantic Trade in Medicinal Plants," in *Geografias médicas: Fronteras culturales de la medicina hispanoamericana, siglos XVI y XVII*, ed. Mauricio Sánchez-Menchero and José Pardo-Tomás, 99–122 (Mexico: CEIICH-UNAM, 2014).

30. He later became Philip's surgeon as well. José Luis Fresquet, *Juan Fragoso y los Discursos de las cosas aromáticas . . . (1572)* (Valencia: Universitat de València, 2002), 7.

31. Fresquet notes that Fragoso alloyed Paracelsian ideas to his Hippocratic medicine. Ibid., 8.

32. Antonio Hernández Morejón, *Historia Bibliográfica de la Medicina Española*, Vol. 3 (Madrid: Viuda de Jordán e Hijos, 1843), 151–165.

33. On Spanish contributions to the study of the supernova in 1572, see Víctor Navarro, *Jerónimo Muñoz: Introducción a la Astronomía y la Geografía* (Valencia: Consell Valencià de Cultura, 2004), 19–26.

34. Pardo-Tomás, "East Indies, West Indies," 201–202, reexamines this political context.

35. Fresquet, *Juan Fragoso y los* Discursos . . . *(1572)*, 11.

36. Fragoso may have been prompted to find royal patronage and publish his *Discursos* (1572) upon learning that Monardes dedicated the second part of his *Historia medicinal* (1571) to Philip II. Although Monardes never formed part of the courtly world and spent his life in Seville, the *Historia medicinal* was translated many more times than the *Discursos*. On Monardes, translation, and the importance of Spanish as a medical language, see López Piñero and Terrada Ferrandis, *Introducción a la terminología médica*, 191–215.

37. Juan Fragoso, *Discursos de las cosas aromáticas* . . . (Madrid: en casa de Francisco Sánchez, 1572), unpaginated dedicatory titled "Epistola Dedicatoria A la muy alta y muy poderosa señora Doña Iuana de Austria."

38. López Piñero's assessment of Fragoso's plagiarism is devastating in its understatement: "[incluye] algunas descripciones parcialmente originales." See López Piñero, *Medicina e historia natural*, 144.

39. Fresquet, *Juan Fragoso y los* Discursos . . . *(1572)*, 10. On Fragoso in general, see José Luis Fresquet Febrer, "La difusión inicial de la materia médica americana en la terapéutica europea," in *Medicinas, drogas y alimentos vegetales del Nuevo Mundo: Textos e imágenes españolas que los introdujeron en Europa*, 317–388 (Madrid: Ministerio de Sanidad y Consumo, 1992); José Luis Fresquet Febrer, "Los inicios de la asimilación de la materia médica americana por la terapéutica europea," in *Viejo y nuevo continente: La medicina en el encuentro entre dos mundos*, ed. José María López Piñero (Madrid: Saned, 1992), 280–307.

40. C. P. Jones, *Culture and Society in Lucian* (Cambridge, MA: Harvard University Press, 1986), 61.

41. Fragoso's mastery of the sound of natural history is reflected in the fact that he is one of the authorities on usage included in the *Diccionario de Autoridades* (1726–1739). In fact, the *Discursos* is one of the principal sources for botanical terms in the landmark dictionary.

42. Zaragoza (Saragossa in Catalan) and Siracusa are more or less homophonous but do not share an etymology. For a brief discussion of "Zaragoza de Sicilia," see Robert Ricard, "Saragosse et Syracuse," *Bulletin Hispanique* 54, no. 1 (1952): 70–71.

43. Lucian of Samosata, *Selected Dialogues*, trans. C. D. N. Costa (Oxford: Oxford University Press, 2005), 182; Fragoso, *Discursos de las cosas aromáticas*, "Epistola Dedicatoria."

44. For many during the sixteenth century, translating Lucian was understood as an act of "beligerancia ideológica y/o religiosa" (ideological and/or religious belligerence), perhaps even tinged with Protestantism; it seems unlikely that Fragoso is invoking the Erasmist tendencies of Lucian's Spanish translators Juan de Jarava and Andrés de Laguna. Ana Vian Herrero, "Fábula y diálogo en el Renacimiento: Confluencia de géneros en el Coloquio de la mosca y la hormiga de Juan de Jarava," *Dicenda* 7 (1988): 456.

45. Michael O. Zapalla, *Lucian of Samosata in the Two Hesperias: An Essay in Literary and Cultural Transformation* (Potomac, MD: Scripta Humanistica, 1990), 234.

46. Antonio Vives Coll, *Luciano de Samosata en España (1500–1700)* (Valladolid: Sever-Cuesta, 1959), 19–22.

47. Zapalla, *Lucian of Samosata in the Two Hesperias*, 118.

48. Ibid., 235.

49. Ibid., 237.

50. Mary M. Gaylord, "The True History of Early Modern Writing in Spanish: Some American Reflections," *Modern Language Quarterly* 57, no. 2 (1996): 222.

51. Celso Arévalo, "Bernardo de Cienfuegos y la Botánica de su época," in *Estudios sobre la ciencia española del siglo XVII*, ed. Asociación Nacional de Historiadores de la Ciencia Española, 324–335 (Madrid: Gráfica Universal, 1935); Emilio Blanco Castro, Ramón Morales Valverde, and Pedro M. Sánchez Moreno, "Bernardo Cienfuegos y su aportación a la botánica en el siglo XVII," *Asclepio* 46, no. 1 (1994): 37–123.

52. I thank Mar Rey Bueno and Maríaluz López-Terrada for their help in compiling this list. On Porres, see Rey Bueno's "Concordias medicinales de entrambos mundos: El proyecto sobre materia médica peruana de Matías de Porres (fl. 1621)," *Revista de Indias* 66, no. 237 (2006): 347–362. On titles such as "historia de las plantas" and natural history as history, see Bauer and Marroquín Arredondo's introduction to this volume.

53. Juan Fragoso, *Catalogus simplicium medicamentorum, quae in usitatis huius temporis compositionibus presertim Mesuaei et Nicolai . . . Quid pro quo . . .* (Compluti: Apud petrum Robles e Ioannem de Villanova, 1566), n.p.

54. Matías de Porras [Porres], *Breves advertencias para beber frio con nieve* (Lima: Geronymo de Contreras, 1621), 33r.

55. Bernardo de Cienfuegos, *Historia de las plantas*, 7 vols.(Manuscript from the Biblioteca Nacional de España, ca. 1630), 3:483r–495r.

56. Cienfuegos, *Historia de las plantas*, 2:741.

57. Ibid., 2:i, "Al lector."

58. Pardo-Tomás, "Two Glimpses of America from a Distance," 176; John Slater, "The Terrible Embrace of the Incipient Baroque: Textually Enacting the Union of Crowns," *ellipsis* 12 (2014): 200.

59. Florike Egmond, "Names of Naturalia in the Early Modern Period: Between the Vernacular and Latin, Identification and Classification," in *Translating Knowledge in the Early Modern Low Countries*, ed. Harold J. Cook and Sven Dupré (Berlin: Lit, 2012), 151.

60. Florike Egmond, "Figuring Exotic Nature in Sixteenth-Century Europe: Garcia de Orta and Carolus Clusius," in *Medicine, Trade and Empire: Garcia de Orta's Colloquies on the Simples and Drugs of India (1563) in Context*, 173–176; Ogilvie, *The Science of Describing*, 247–248.

61. Slater, "The Terrible Embrace of the Incipient Baroque," 200.

62. This skepticism was not misplaced, nor was it unique to Cienfuegos. Fernando Bouza, "Para qué imprimir: De autores, público y manuscritos en el Siglo de Oro," *Cuadernos de Historia Moderna* 18 (1997), 31–50; Anthony Grafton, *The Culture of Correction in Renaissance Europe* (London: British Library, 2011).

63. Cienfuegos, *Historia de las plantas*, 4:362.

64. López Pinero and López-Terrada, *La influencia española*, 88.

65. Cienfuegos, *Historia de las plantas*, 1:97–98, 2:1124.

66. Cienfuegos, *Historia de las plantas*, 4:404.

67. Cienfuegos, *Historia de las plantas*, 2:1124.

68. Cienfuegos, *Historia de las plantas*, 1:97–98, 2:586, 4:227.

69. Cienfuegos, *Historia de las plantas*, 2:96.

70. Ibid.

71. Cienfuegos, *Historia de las plantas*, 2:396–397; Carolus Clusius, *Rariorum aloquot stirpium per Hispanias observatarum Historia, libris duobus expressa* (Antwerp: ex officina Christophori Plantini, 1576), 151.

72. "Siempre que los estrangeros (como tan amigos nuestros) pueden quitar honra, gloria, reputacion, o fama a España lo hazen, digolo por Carlo Clusio." Cienfuegos, *Historia de las plantas*, 2:396–397.

73. Cienfuegos, *Historia de las plantas*, 1:1; Clusius, *Rariorum aloquot stirpium*, 11.

74. Marcelo Aranda et al., "The History of Atlantic Science: Collective Reflections," *Atlantic Studies* 7, no. 4 (2010): 495.

75. Mar Rey Bueno, "Herbolaria de Indias: Apuntes para una materia médica del Nuevo Mundo (1516–1526)," *Azogue* 7 (2010–2013): 255.

Chapter 9

Earlier versions of this chapter were presented at the University of Maryland at College Park in December 2015 and at the Renaissance Society of America annual conference in Boston in April 2016. I would like to thank the volume's editors as well as Andrea Frisch and David Lines for helpful comments on earlier drafts. I am also grateful to the Institute of Historical Research in London, which funded part of the research presented in this chapter, and to Rupert Baker, library manager at the Royal Society, who greatly facilitated my research in the society's archives.

1. See, Ralph Bauer and Jaime Marroquín Arredondo, "Introduction: An Age of Translation," this volume.

2. Of common use among scholars since the late nineteenth century, the term "climate theory" has recently come under criticism on account of the semantic shift of the term "climate" from premodern times to the present. See Franz Mauelshagen, "Ein neues Klima im 18. Jahrhundert," *Zeitschrift für Kulturwissenschaften* 1 (2016): 39–57. In the absence of a better alternative, the term will be retained here for the sake of convenience though in full awareness of the methodological issues involved in its use.

3. Mary Floyd-Wilson, *English Ethnicity and Race in Early Modern Drama* (Cambridge: Cambridge University Press, 2003).

4. Richard Grove, *Green Imperialism: Colonial Expansion, Tropical Island Edens and the Origins of Environmentalism, 1600–1860* (Cambridge: Cambridge University Press, 1995); Mark Harrison, *Climates and Constitutions: Health, Race, Environment and British Imperialism in India, 1600–1850* (Oxford: Oxford University Press, 1999); Rebecca Earle, *The Body of the Conquistador: Food, Race and the Colonial Experience in Spanish America, 1492–1700* (Cambridge: Cambridge University Press, 2012); Anya Zilberstein, *A Temperate Empire: Making Climate Change in Early America* (Oxford: Oxford University Press, 2016); Sara Miglietti and John Morgan, eds., *Governing the Environment in the Early Modern World: Theory and Practice* (Abingdon, UK: Routledge, 2017).

5. Edward W. Said, "Traveling Theory," in *The World, the Text, and the Critic* (Cambridge, MA: Harvard University Press, 1983), 226. For a "longue durée" history of climate theories, see Clarence Glacken, *Traces on the Rhodian Shore: Nature and Culture in Western Thought from Ancient Times to the End of the Eighteenth Century* (Berkeley: University of California Press, 1967).

6. The meaning of the terms "cosmological" and "chorological" is explained in section 2 below.

7. See, for instance, Daniel Carey, "Compiling Nature's History: Travellers and Travel Narratives in the Early Royal Society," *Annals of Science* 54, no. 3 (1997): 269–292; Antonio Barrera-Osorio, *Experiencing Nature: The Spanish American Empire and the Early Scientific Revolution* (Austin: University of Texas Press, 2006); María M. Portuondo, *Secret Science: Spanish Cosmography and the New World* (Chicago: University of Chicago Press, 2009); Andrés Prieto, *Missionary Scientists: Jesuit Science in Spanish South America, 1570–1810* (Nashville: Vanderbilt University Press, 2011); Paul Nelles, "Cosas y cartas: Scribal Production and Material Pathways in Jesuit Global Communication (1547–1573)," *Journal of Jesuit Studies* 2 (2015): 421–450. Other studies will be cited below.

8. Some important first steps in this direction include Conor Reilly, "A Catalogue of Jesuitica in the 'Philosophical Transactions of the Royal Society of London' (1665–1715)," *Archivum Historicum Societatis Iesu* 27 (1958): 339–362; Victor Navarro, "Tradition and Scientific Change in Early Modern Spain: The Role of the Jesuits," in *Jesuit Science and the Republic of Letters*, ed. Mordechai Feingold (Cambridge, MA: MIT Press, 2006), 331–388; Jorge Cañizares-Esguerra, "The Colonial Iberian Roots of the Scientific Revolution," in *Nature, Empire, and Nation: Explorations of the History of Science in the Iberian World* (Stanford, CA: Stanford University Press, 2006), 14–45.

9. See Frank Lestringant, *Mapping the Renaissance World: The Geographical Imagination in the Age of Discovery*, trans. David Fausett (Cambridge, UK: Polity, 1994), 3–4; Matthew McLean, *The Cosmographia of Sebastian Münster: Describing the World in the Reformation* (Aldershot, UK: Ashgate, 2007), 94–99.

10. On the Macrobian world map and its origins and influence, see Nicolás Wey Gómez, *The Tropics of Empire: Why Columbus Sailed South to the Indies* (Cambridge, MA: MIT Press, 2008), 71–92.

11. Marsilio Cagnati, *De Romani aëris salubritate* (Rome: Luigi Zanetti, 1599), 55. This map has been studied by Saul Jarcho, "Two Maps in an Early Treatise on Epidemiology (Cagnati, 1599)," *Journal of Urban Health: Bulletin of the New York Academy of Medicine* 61, no. 8 (1985): 763–766. For other similar examples, see Saul Jarcho, "Some Early Italian Epidemiological Maps," *Imago Mundi* 35 (1983): 9–19.

12. Portuondo, *Secret Science*.

13. Aristotle, *Politics* 7.7 (1327b, 23–33).

14. Francisco Carriscondo Esquivel, "El valor de la *Apologética historia sumaria* para el análisis de la neología astronómica y cosmográfica renacentista," *Revista de filología española* 89, no. 1 (2009): 163–174.

15. See Jean Bodin, *Method for the Easy Comprehension of History* [*Methodus ad facilem historiarum cognitionem*], trans. Beatrice Reynolds (New York: Columbia University Press, 1945), 84–86.

16. For instance, Montesquieu's discussion of climate theory in Books 14–19 of the *Spirit of the Laws* (1748) features an interesting mix of cosmological and chorological views, thus testifying to a revival of cosmological climate theory during the Enlightenment.

17. See, for instance, Karen Kupperman, "The Puzzle of the American Climate in the Early Colonial Period," *American Historical Review* 87, no. 5 (1982): 1262–1289; Karen Kupperman, "Fear of Hot Climates in the Anglo-American Colonial Experience," *William and Mary Quarterly* 41, no. 2 (1984): 213–240.

18. Zilberstein, *A Temperate Climate*; Kupperman, "The Puzzle of the American Climate," 1287–1288. Kupperman focuses on seventeenth-century British travelers, but similar

observations with regard to the climatic impact of animal farming were made by Gonzalo Fernández de Oviedo (1478–1557) in his *Historia general y natural de las Indias*. See Antonello Gerbi, *Nature in the New World: From Christopher Columbus to Gonzalo Fernández de Oviedo* (Pittsburgh: University of Pittsburgh Press, 1985), 289.

19. James R. Fleming, *Historical Perspectives on Climate Change* (Oxford: Oxford University Press, 1998), 21–32.

20. Anthony Grafton, April Shelford, and Nancy Siraisi, *New Worlds, Ancient Texts: The Power of Tradition and the Shock of Discovery* (Cambridge, MA: Harvard University Press, 1995). See also Bauer and Marroquín Arredondo, "Introduction," this volume. For some interesting remarks regarding the value and potential limits of Grafton's work, see Andrea Frisch, *The Invention of the Eyewitness: Witnessing and Testimony in Early Modern France* (Chapel Hill: University of North Carolina Press, 2004), 77n1.

21. See, for instance, Bodin, *Method for the Easy Comprehension of History*, 102, where we find one of very few references to the New World and its peoples in Bodin's works (compare with Grafton, Shelford, and Siraisi, *New Worlds, Ancient Texts*, 126).

22. Prieto, *Missionary Scientists*, 149–152.

23. See Bauer and Marroquín Arredondo, "Introduction," this volume. For a classic overview, see Margaret T. Hodgen, *Early Anthropology in the Sixteenth and Seventeenth Centuries* (Philadelphia: University of Pennsylvania Press, 1964).

24. Stephanie Leitch, *Mapping Ethnography in Early Modern Germany: New Worlds in Print Culture* (New York: Palgrave Macmillan, 2010); Daniel Carey and Claire Jowitt, eds., *Richard Hakluyt and Travel Writing in Early Modern Europe* (Farnham, UK: Ashgate, 2012).

25. Portuondo, *Secret Science*. On secrecy and competition, see also Bauer and Marroquín Arredondo, "Introduction," this volume.

26. Barrera-Osorio, *Experiencing Nature*, 82–99.

27. On Ovando, see Stafford Poole, *Juan de Ovando: Governing the Spanish Empire in the Reign of Philip II* (Norman: University of Oklahoma Press, 2004).

28. Quoted and translated in Barrera-Osorio, *Experiencing Nature*, 81.

29. Ibid.

30. The text of Santa Cruz's *Memorial* is published in *Relaciones Geográficas de Indias—Perú*, 2 vols., ed. Marcos Jiménez de la Espada (Madrid: Atlas, 1965), 2:xvi–xxi. The passage quoted here ("tengan cuidado de saber el sitio della, si es montuosa ó llana, ó si es llena de anegadizos ó lagunas") is taken from question 3 of the *Memorial* (xix).

31. "Memoria de las cosas a que se ha de responder y de que se han de hacer las relaciones," in *Relaciones Geográficas del siglo XVI: Nueva Galicia*, ed. René Acuña (Mexico City: UNAM, 1988), 18 ("3. Y, generalmente, el temperamento y calidad de la dicha provincia o comarca, si es muy fría o caliente, o húmeda o seca, de muchas aguas o pocas y cuándo son, más o menos, y los vientos que corren en ella qué tan violentos y de qué parte son, y en qué tiempos del año"; "4. Si es tierra llana o áspera, rasa o montuosa, de muchos o pocos ríos o fuentes, y abundosa o falta de aguas, fértil o falta de pastos, abundosa o estéril de frutos y de mantenimientos"; "6. El altura o elevación del polo ... o en qué días del año el sol no echa sombra ninguna al punto del medio día"; "5. De muchos o pocos indios, y si ha tenido más o menos en otro tiempo que ahora, y las causas que dello se superien; y, si los hay, [si] están poblados en pueblos formados y permanentes; y el talle y suerte de sus entendimientos, inclinaciones y manera de vivir").

32. "Descripcion fecha de la provincia de Vilcas Guaman por el illustre señor Don Pedro de Carabajal ... en el año de 1586," in *Relaciones Geográficas de Indias—Perú*, 1:209; see throughout in response to question 17 of Ovando's thirty-seven-chapter questionnaire of 1569.

33. "Descripcion de la tierra de la tierra del repartimiento de San Francisco de Atunrucana y Laramati ... año de 1586," in *Relaciones Geográficas*, Vol. 1, ed. Jiménez de la Espada, 233.

34. Markus Friedrich, "Government and Information-Management in Early Modern Europe: The Case of the Society of Jesus (1540–1773)," *Journal of Early Modern History* 12 (2008): 539–563. As J. Gabriel Martínez-Serna has recently observed, it would be highly desirable to see more "comparative studies of secular imperial networks and the Jesuit organization." J. Gabriel Martínez-Serna, "Procurators and the Making of the Jesuits' Atlantic Network," in *Soundings in Atlantic History: Latent Structures and Intellectual Currents, 1500–1830*, ed. Bernard Bailyn and Patricia L. Denault (Cambridge, MA: Harvard University Press, 2009), 181. In particular, more information will be necessary to establish whether interactions between secular and Jesuit networks played any role in promoting the rise of questionnaires as a privileged form of data collecting in the latter half of the sixteenth century.

35. Martínez-Serna, "Procurators and the Making of the Jesuits' Atlantic Network," 190–191.

36. François de Dainville, *La Géographie des humanistes* (Geneva: Slatkine Reprints, 1969); Stephen Harris, "Mapping Jesuit Science: The Role of Travel in the Geography of Knowledge," in *The Jesuits: Cultures, Sciences, and the Arts, 1540–1773*, ed. John W. O'Malley et al. (Toronto: University of Toronto Press, 1999), 212–240. For the role of geography in the Jesuit *ratio studiorum*, see *The Ratio Studiorum: The Official Plan for Jesuit Education* [Ratio atque Institutio Studiorum Societatis Iesu], trans. Claude Pavur (St. Louis: Institute of Jesuit Sources, 2005), 109.

37. Prieto, *Missionary Scientists*; Glacken, *Traces on the Rhodian Shore*, 450.

38. On Botero's *Relationi universali*, see Romain Descendre, *L'Etat du monde: Giovanni Botero entre raison d'état et géopolitique* (Geneva: Droz, 2009). On the architecture of the *Relationi* and its ties to climate theory, see Federico Chabod, "Giovanni Botero," in *Scritti sul Rinascimento* (Turin: Einaudi, 1967), 342–343. On Botero and his sources for the American sections of the *Relationi*, see Aldo Albonico, *Il mondo americano di Giovanni Botero* (Rome: Bulzoni, 1990). Botero also discusses climate theory in his treatise on the reason of state, *Della ragion di Stato* (Venice: Giolito de' Ferrari, 1589), 5.2.

39. On the genres and readership of early modern travel writing, including the Jesuit missionaries' reports to Rome, see Andreas Motsch, "Relations of Travel: Itinerary of a Practice," *Renaissance and Reformation/Renaissance et Réforme* 34, nos. 1–2 (2011): 207–236; Matthew Day, "Western Travel Writing, 1450–1750," in *The Routledge Companion to Travel Writing*, ed. Carl Thompson (Abingdon, UK: Routledge, 2015), 161–172; Adrien Paschoud, *Le Monde amérindien au miroir des* Lettres édifiantes et curieuses (Oxford, UK: Voltaire Foundation, 2008), 145–168.

40. Harris, "Mapping Jesuit Science," 231. See also Paul Nelles, "Seeing and Writing: The Art of Observation in the Early Jesuit Missions," *Intellectual History Review* 20, no. 3 (2010): 317–333.

41. Ignatius of Loyola to Father Gaspar Berze (Barceo), Rome, February 24, 1554, in *Obras completas de San Ignacio de Loyola* (Madrid: Editorial Catolica, 1963), 854–855 ("que se escriviese algo de la cosmografía de las regiones donde andan los nuestros, como sería

cuán luengos son los días de verano y de invierno, cuándo comienza el verano, si las ombras van sinistras, o a la mano diestra. Finalmente, si otras cosas hay que parezcan extraordinarias, se dé aviso, como de animales y plantas no conocidas, o no in tal grandeza, etc.."). See Harris, "Mapping Jesuit Science."

42. Letter of November 22, 1547, quoted in Dainville, *La Géographie des humanistes*, 113.

43. Nelles, "Seeing and Writing."

44. Nelles, "Cosas y cartas," 425.

45. Friedrich, "Government and Information-Management," 547.

46. Ibid., 549.

47. Paul Nelles ("Seeing and Writing," 329) has identified a similar shift from continued narrative to fragmented description in some seventeenth-century *litterae annuae*, such as those that the French missionary Paul Le Jeune sent from New France in the 1630s.

48. Carey, "Compiling Nature's History."

49. John Gascoigne, "The Royal Society, Natural History and the Peoples of the 'New World[s],' 1660–1800," *British Journal for the History of Science* 42, no. 4 (2009): 541.

50. Henry Oldenburg, "Preface," *Philosophical Transactions* 11, no. 123 (March 1676): 552–553. On Oldenburg, see Marie Boas Hall, *Henry Oldenburg: Shaping the Royal Society* (Oxford: Oxford University Press, 2002).

51. Oldenburg, "Preface," 553.

52. Ibid., 555.

53. Michael Hunter, "Robert Boyle and the Early Royal Society: A Reciprocal Exchange in the Making of Baconian Science," *British Journal for the History of Science* 40, no. 1 (2007): 1–23.

54. See, for instance, Reilly, "A Catalogue of Jesuitica"; Cañizares-Esguerra, "The Colonial Iberian Roots"; John Gascoigne, "Crossing the Pillars of Hercules: Francis Bacon, the Scientific Revolution and the New World," in *Science in the Age of Baroque*, ed. Ofer Gal and Raz Chen-Morris, 217–237 (Dordrecht: Springer, 2013).

55. London, Royal Society, Classified Papers, 19/44 and 19/46. Various sets of answers to this questionnaire are also preserved (Classified Papers, 19/75, 19/76, 19/77).

56. Thomas Hill to Henry Oldenburg, July 13, 1671, in Henry Oldenburg, *Correspondence*, Vol. 8, ed. Alfred Rupert Hall and Marie Boas Hall (Madison: University of Wisconsin Press, 1971), 155–156. The original list of queries is preserved in Classified Papers, 19/73 (transcribed and translated in Oldenburg, *Correspondence*, 8:220–251); Oldenburg sent them to Hill on August 19, 1671.

57. Hunter, "Robert Boyle and the Early Royal Society."

58. I draw this list of questions from Oldenburg's "Queries for His Excellencie the Lord Henry Howard of Norfolk, Embassador for His Majesty to Marocco [*sic*]," London, Royal Society, Classified Papers, 19/33 (ca. 1669).

59. Robert Boyle, "General Heads for a Natural History of a Countrey, Great or Small," *Philosophical Transactions* 1, no. 11 (April 1666): 186–189. For the history of this text, see Hunter, "Robert Boyle and the Early Royal Society." Boyle's "General Heads" were extremely popular and long-lived and were reprinted several times in the seventeenth and eighteenth centuries either as a stand-alone piece or within collections of travel writings.

60. Boyle, "General Heads," 186.

61. London, Royal Society, Classified Papers, 19/43 (dated October 6, 1669). See Hunter, "Robert Boyle and the Early Royal Society," 19–20.

62. According to a note in the manuscript, the list was sent shortly afterward to Martyn Lo, vice consul of Iskenderun, along with a list of particular inquiries for Turkey. Hunter ("Robert Boyle and the Early Royal Society"), who first attracted attention to this document, does not seem to realize that it is Oldenburg's list, not Boyle's, that most closely reflects the template of individual lists of queries drafted after 1666.

63. See Thomas Tenison's letter to Oldenburg of November 7, 1671 (Oldenburg, *Correspondence*, 8:344–348), where the future archbishop of Canterbury apologizes for inadvertently reshuffling the order of his answers to questions in the "Enquiries Concerning Agriculture" section previously printed in *Philosophical Transactions* 1, no. 5 (July 1665): "A[nswer] to Q[uestion] 9, misplac'd by me" (346).

64. For a case in point, see Oldenburg's insertion of the connecting phrase "So much of the Baths" (in italics) to transition from the section on baths to the section on quarries in the printed version of Edward Browne's "Accompt Concerning the Baths of Austria and Hungary; as Also Some Stone-Quarries, Talcum Rocks, &c. in Those Parts," *Philosophical Transactions* 5, no. 59 (May 1670): 1050. Browne's original text can be read in Henry Oldenburg, *Correspondence*, Vol. 5, ed. Alfred Rupert Hall and Marie Boas Hall (Madison: University of Wisconsin Press, 1968), 484.

65. Harriet Knight, *Organising Natural Knowledge in the Seventeenth Century: The Works of Robert Boyle* (Saarbrücken: Lambert Academic Publishing, 2011), 33.

66. For the concept of "matter of fact," its Baconian origins, and its role and implications for the scientific mentality of the early Royal Society, see Lorraine Daston, "Perché i fatti sono brevi?," *Quaderni storici* 36, no. 3 (2001): 745–770; Knight, *Organising Natural Knowledge*, 32–52.

67. Joan-Pau Rubiès, "Instructions for Travellers: Teaching the Eye to See," *History and Anthropology* 9, nos. 2–3 (1996): 139–189.

68. In this sense, my approach is similar to that of other scholars who have investigated the connection between rhetoric and epistemology in early modern natural science. See, for instance, Peter Dear, "Totius in Verba: Rhetoric and Authority in the Early Royal Society," *Isis* 76, no. 2 (1985): 144–161; Hunter, "Robert Boyle and the Early Royal Society"; Neil Safier, "Transformations de la zone torride: Les répertoires de la nature tropicale à l'époque des Lumières," *Annales: Histoire, Sciences Sociales* 66, no. 1 (2011): 143–172.

69. A good case in point is Inca Garcilaso de la Vega's history of the Incas, *Comentarios reales de los Incas*, first published in Lisbon in 1609. As Neil Safier ("Transformations de la zone torride," 17) has noted, the two opening chapters, which situate Peru within the framework of cosmological climate theory, disappear in eighteenth-century French translations of the work.

Chapter 10

1. Pehr Kalm, *Voyage de Pehr Kalm au Canada en 1749*, ed. Jacques Rousseau, Guy Béthune, and Pierre Morisset (Montreal: P. Tisseyre, 1977), 3.

2. James Delbourgo and Nicholas Dew, "Introduction: The Far Side of the Ocean," in *Science and Empire in the Atlantic World*, ed. James Delbourgo and Nicholas Dew (New York: Routledge, 2008), 5.

3. Kalm, *Voyage de Pehr Kalm au Canada en 1749*, 3. See also Lisbet Koerner, *Linnaeus: Nature and Nation* (Cambridge, MA: Harvard University Press, 1999).

4. For a broader Atlantic perspective on these cultural encounters, see the other chapters in this volume. For overviews of the history of botanical and ecological exchange in French

North America, see Alain Asselin, Jacques Cayouentte, and Jacques Mathieu, *Curieuses histoires de plantes du Canada*, Vols. 1–2 (Quebec: Septentrion, 2014–2015)

5. On the Columbian Exchange, see Alfred W. Crosby, *The Columbian Exchange: Biological and Cultural Consequences of 1492* (Westport, CT: Greenwood, 1972). On the planned neo-Columbian exchanges of the eighteenth and nineteenth centuries, see Stuart McCook, "The Neo-Columbian Exchange: The Second Conquest of the Greater Caribbean," *Latin American Research Review* 46 (2011): 11–31.

6. Staffan Müller-Wille, "Walnuts at Hudson Bay, Coral Reefs in Gotland: The Colonialism of Linnaean Botany," in *Colonial Botany: Science, Commerce, and Politics in the Early Modern World*, ed. Londa Schiebinger and Claudia Swan (Philadelphia: University of Pennsylvania Press, 2005), 37–38. This is not unlike those colonial naturalists analyzed in Kathleen S. Murphy, "Translating the Vernacular: Indigenous and African Knowledge in the Eighteenth-Century British Atlantic," *Atlantic Studies* 8, no. 1 (2011): 29–48.

7. Kalm evidently considered indigenous knowledge more akin to a technological skill than a true science. Clara Sue Kidwell argues that this is how indigenous knowledges are still understood to this day. Clara Sue Kidwell, "Native Knowledge in the Americas," *Osiris* 1 (1985): 209.

8. Kalm, *Voyage de Pehr Kalm au Canada en 1749*, 332. Numerous scholars have explained the distinction between the French *sauvages* (which translates better as "wild men") and the English savages. I have retained the usage of *sauvage*. Thomas G. M. Peace, "Deconstructing the Sauvage/Savage in the Writing of Samuel de Champlain and Captain John Smith," *French Colonial History* 7, no. 1 (2006): 1–20.

9. Kalm, *Voyage de Pehr Kalm au Canada en 1749*, 359.

10. This narrative of scientific centralization is most fully elaborated in James E. McClellan and François Regourd, *The Colonial Machine: French Science and Overseas Expansion in the Old Regime* (Turnhout: Brepols, 2011).

11. There is only one instance in the text where a year is specifically mentioned. In his description of the "plante marine," the author advised his readers that the specimen he sent had been collected in 1725. "Mémoire sur les plantes qui sont dans la caise B," Laboratoire de phanérogamie, Muséum national d'Histoire naturelle, n.p.

12. "Mémoire de F. Vallée sur la construction à Louisbourg," C11C, 16:59, Archives nationales d'outre-mer (hereafter ANOM). Antoine-Gaspard Boucher d'Argis wrote in the *Encyclopédie* that a lettre de cachet, while ostensibly any sealed order of the king, was often intended to "send somebody into exile, or to have them arrested and made a prisoner." See "Lettres de cachet" in *Encyclopédie, ou dictionnaire raisonné des sciences, des arts et des métiers*, ed. Denis Diderot and Jean le Rond D'Alembert, University of Chicago ARTFL Encyclopédie Project, Spring 2010, http://encyclopedie.uchicago.edu/. Peter Moogk writes that many exiles were sent to New France during this period and that "During the 1720s seventy exiles [were] 'fils de famille'—a general term for debauched sons sent abroad to save their worthy families further embarrassment. Influential families could obtain a royal *lettre de cachet* to send the offending child to prison or into exile without a trial." *La Nouvelle France: The Making of French Canada; A Cultural History* (East Lansing: Michigan State University Press, 2000), 111.

13. For the effects of the War of the Spanish Succession and the Treaty of Utrecht, see Dale Miquelon, *New France, 1701–1744: A Supplement to Europe* (Toronto: McClelland and Stewart, 1987), chap. 3.

14. For examples of this work, see J. Sherman Bleakney, *Sods, Soil, and Spades: The Acadians at Grand Pré and Their Dykeland Legacy* (Montreal: McGill-Queen's University Press, 2004); Gregory M. W. Kennedy, *Something of a Peasant Paradise? Comparing Rural Societies in Acadie and the Loudunais, 1604–1755* (Montreal: McGill-Queen's University Press, 2014); Matthew G. Hatvany, "The Origins of the Acadian Aboiteau: An Environmental Historical Geography," *Historical Geography* 30 (2002): 121–137; A. J. B. Johnston, "Défricheurs d'eau: An Introduction to Acadian Land Reclamation in a Comparative Context," *Material Culture Review/Revue de la culture matérielle* 66 (2007): 32–41.

15. Wicken provides an estimate of a 3.75 percent annual growth rate or, over the period 1671–1755, a thirtyfold increase. William C. Wicken, "Encounters with Tall Sails and Tall Tales: Mi'kmaq Society, 1500–1760," PhD dissertation, McGill University, 1994, 217.

16. James Pritchard provides an estimate of 30,000 hectares of salt marsh in the region. James Pritchard, *In Search of Empire: The French in the Americas, 1670–1730* (Cambridge: Cambridge University Press, 2004), 34. A. J. B. Johnston puts the number of claimed acres at 13,000 and estimates that twenty-six times more land was claimed from the sea than from the forest. Johnston, "Défricheurs d'eau," 33.

17. Kenneth Donovan, "Imposing Discipline upon Nature: Gardens, Agriculture and Animal Husbandry in Cape Breton, 1713–1758," *Material Culture Review/Revue de la culture matérielle* 64, (2006): 20–37; Miquelon, *New France*, 108–110.

18. Miquelon, *New France*, 121–123; N. E. S. Griffiths, *From Migrant to Acadian: A North American Border People, 1604–1755* (Montreal: McGill-Queen's University Press, 2005), chap. 10.

19. Miquelon, *New France*, 119; Thomas G. M. Peace, "Two Conquests: Aboriginal Experiences of the Fall of New France and Acadia," PhD dissertation, York University, 2011, 180–184.

20. On the construction of the fortifications and the growth of the town, see A. J. B. Johnston, "From *Port de Pêche* to *Ville Fortifiée*: The Evolution of Urban Louisbourg, 1713–1758," *Proceedings of the Meeting of the French Colonial Historical Society* 17 (1993): 24–43.

21. "Mémoire de F. Vallée sur la construction à Louisbourg," C11C, 16:59, ANOM.

22. Ibid.

23. Ibid.

24. F. J. Thorpe, "François Madeleine Vallée," Dictionary of Canadian Biography, http://biographi.ca/en/bio/vallee_francois_madeleine_3E.html.

25. Ibid.

26. It was during this time, writes historian A. J. B. Johnston, that the organization of the fortified city "reached a new level of sophistication." A. J. B. Johnston, *Control and Order in French Colonial Louisbourg, 1713–1758* (East Lansing: Michigan State University Press, 2001), 85.

27. Laurent Lavoie, "La vie intellectuelle et les activités culturelles à la forteresse de Louisbourg 1713–1758," *Man and Nature* 4 (1985): 130.

28. Londa Schiebinger, *Plants and Empire: Colonial Bioprospecting in the Atlantic World* (Cambridge, MA: Harvard University Press, 2004), 7; Emma C Spary, "'Peaches Which the Patriarchs Lacked': Natural History, Natural Resources, and the Natural Economy in France," *History of Political Economy* 35, no. 5 (2003): 16–20.

29. "Monsieur Vallée au ministre," C11B, 14:414, ANOM.

30. Ibid. Maurepas took a keen interest in colonial science throughout the French Atlantic world. See Roland Lamontagne, "L'influence de Maurepas sur les sciences: Le botaniste Jean Prat à La Nouvelle-Orléans, 1735–1746," *Revue d'histoire des sciences* (1996): 113–124.

31. "Monsieur Vallée au ministre," C11B, 14:414, ANOM.

32. Ibid., 415.

33. The work of historians such as Bill Wicken demonstrates the inadequacy of using the term "nomadic" to refer to communities that continuously occupied areas over the span of centuries as was once common. Bill Wicken, "26 August 1726: A Case Study in Mi'kmaq-New England Relations in the Early 18th Century," *Acadiensis* 23, no. 1 (1993): 6–7; Wicken, "Encounters with Tall Sails and Tall Tales," 97–115.

34. These seem to have grown and expanded in the era of early contact. See Bruce J. Bourque and Ruth Holmes Whitehead, "Tarrentines and the Introduction of European Trade Goods in the Gulf of Maine," *Ethnohistory* 32, no. 4 (1985): 327–341.

35. David Demeritt, "Agriculture, Climate, and Cultural Adaptation in the Prehistoric Northeast," *Archaeology of Eastern North America* 19 (1991): 183–202; James B. Petersen and Ellen R. Cowie, "From Hunter-Gatherer Camp to Horticultural Village: Late Prehistoric Indigenous Subsistence and Settlement," in *Northeast Subsistence-Settlement Change: AD 700–1300,* ed. John P. Hart and Christina B. Rieth (Albany: New York State Museum, 2002), 277.

36. The influence of European foods on Mi'kmaw health is suggested as a major factor in declining health in the seventeenth century. Peace, "Two Conquests," 55–56.

37. Wicken, "Encounters with Tall Sails and Tall Tales," 230. See also Peace, "Two Conquests," 89–90, 101.

38. Wicken, "Encounters with Tall Sails and Tall Tales," 228.

39. Griffiths, *From Migrant to Acadian,* 34–37, 259; Peace, "Two Conquests," 57–58, 90; Wicken, "Encounters with Tall Sails and Tall Tales," 235–236.

40. Marc Lescarbot, *Histoire de la Nouvelle-France* (Paris: Chez Adrian Perier, 1617), 555.

41. Nicolas Denys, *Description geographique et historique des costes de l'Amerique Septentrionale avec l'Histoire naturelle du païs* (Paris: L. Billaine, 1672), 108–109.

42. Ramsay Cook, *1492 and All That: Making a Garden Out of a Wilderness* (North York, Ontario: Robarts Centre for Canadian Studies, 1993); Peace, "Two Conquests," 124. This was part of a broader program aimed at converting "errant" peoples to sedentary lifestyles and Christianity. See Alain Beaulieu, *Convertir les fils de Caïn: Jésuites et Amérindiens nomades en Nouvelle-France, 1632–1642* (Quebec: Nuit blanche, 1990).

43. "Mémoire sur les plantes qui sont dans la caise B," n.p.

44. Ibid.

45. Bernard Pothier, "Acadian Settlement on Ile-Royale, 1713–1734," MA thesis, University of Ottawa, 1967, 56–57.

46. "Mémoire sur les plantes qui sont dans la caise B," n.p.

47. On the transport of botanical and zoological specimens in the Atlantic world, see Christopher M. Parsons and Kathleen S. Murphy, "Ecosystems Under Sail: Specimen Transport in the Eighteenth-Century French and British Atlantics," *Early American Studies: An Interdisciplinary Journal* 10, no. 3 (2012): 503–529.

48. Ibid.

49. This is based on the identification of the leaf specimen for Kocokar by Ruth Newell, curator of the E. C. Smith Herbarium at the Harriet Irving Botanical Gardens at Acadia

University in Wolfville, Nova Scotia. Plantain species grow widely but are not solely coastal plants. *Plantago lanceolata* "prefers dry sites . . . and gravelly slopes." P. B. Cavers, I. J. Bassett, and C. W. Crompton, "The Biology of Canadian Weeds: 47. Plantago lanceolata L," *Canadian Journal of Plant Science* 60, no. 4 (1980): 1271. *Plantago* "Usually occurs in non-wetlands (estimated probability 67%–99%), but is occasionally found in wetlands (1%–33%)." "Plantago major L.: Common Plantain," U.S. Department of Agriculture, http://plants.usda.gov /java/profile?symbol=PLMA2.

50. Complaints about the limitations that geography imposed on the activities of colonial collectors were frequent. See, for example, Arthur Vallée, *Michel Sarrazin, 1659–1735: Sa vie, ses travaux, et son temps* (Quebec: Le Quotidien Levis, 1927), 219.

51. For a sophisticated analysis of how French naturalists sought to convey American environments to Enlightenment audiences, see Neil Safier, *Measuring the New World: Enlightenment Science and South America* (Chicago: University of Chicago Press, 2008).

52. "Mémoire sur les plantes qui sont dans la caise B," n.p. Recent work by Canadian historians have erred in assuming that the French botanist Joseph Pitton de Tournefort named the plant after Michel Sarrazin. Kathryn A. Young, "Crown Agent-Canadian Correspondent: Michel Sarrazin and the Académie Royale des Sciences, 1697–1734," *French Historical Studies* 18, no. 2 (1993): 426.

53. Bernard Boivin, "La flore du Canada en 1708: Étude et publication d'un manuscrit de Michel Sarrasin et Sébastien Vaillant," *Études littéraires* 10, nos. 1–2 (1977): 234; A. Ubrizsy and J. Heniger, "Carolus Clusius and American Plants," *Taxon* 32, no. 3 (1983): 433. On the coastal exchanges between Native Americans and French fishermen, see Laurier Turgeon, "French Fishers, Fur Traders, and Amerindians During the Sixteenth Century: History and Archaeology," *William and Mary Quarterly* 55, no. 4 (1998): 585–610.

54. Gabriel Sagard, *Le Grand Voyage du pays des Hurons: Suivi du Dictionnaire de la langue huronne* (Montreal: Presses de l'Université de Montreal, 1998), 314.

55. "Mémoire sur les plantes qui sont dans la caise B," n.p.

56. Ibid.

57. Jean-François Gaultier, "Description de plusieurs plantes du Canada par M Gaultier," Cote: P91, D3, Fonds Jean-François Gaultier, Bibliothèque et Archive nationale de Québec, 117. For a broader discussion of plant names in French North America, see Marthe Faribault, "L'apios tubéreux d'Amérique: Histoire de mots," *Recherches amérindiennes au Québec* 21, no. 3 (1991): 65–75; Marthe Faribault, "Les phytonymes de l'Histoire naturelle des Indes Occidentales de Louis Nicolas: Image du lexique botanique canadien à la fin du XVIIe siècle," in *Français du Canada, Française de France: Actes du quatrième Colloque international de Chicoutimi, Québec, du 21–24 septembre 1994*, ed. Thomas Lavoie, 99–120 (Tübingen: Max Niemayer Verlag, 1996).

58. "Mémoire sur les plantes qui sont dans la caise B," n.p.

59. Ibid.

60. Ibid.

61. Ibid.

62. Ibid.

63. Chrestien Leclercq, *Nouvelle relation de la Gaspésie*, ed. Réal Ouellet (Montreal: Presses de l'Université de Montréal, 1999), 563.

64. For an example of the gendering of ecological knowledge in indigenous societies, see Barbara Mann, "The Lynx in Time: Haudenosaunee Women's Traditions and History,"

American Indian Quarterly 21, no. 3 (1997): 423–449; Bruce M. White, "The Woman Who Married a Beaver: Trade Patterns and Gender Roles in the Ojibwa Fur Trade," *Ethnohistory* 46, no. 1 (1999): 123–127.

65. Diéreville, *Relation of the Voyage to Port Royal in Acadia or New France*, ed. John Clarence Webster, trans. Alice de Kessler Lusk Webster (Toronto: Champlain Society, 1933), 181.

66. Nicolas Denys, *Histoire naturelle des peuples, des animaux, des arbres & plantes de l'Amérique septentrionale* (Paris: Chez Claude Barbin, 1672), 365; Pierre Margry, *Découvertes et établissements des Français dans l'ouest et dans le sud de l'Amérique Septentrionale, 1614–1754*, Vol. 5 (Paris: Maisonneuve et cie., 1879–1888), 110–111.

67. Wicken, "Encounters with Tall Sails and Tall Tales," 385–411; John Mack Faragher, *A Great and Noble Scheme: The Tragic Story of the Expulsion of the French Acadians from Their American Homeland*, (New York: Norton, 2005), chaps. 2 and 3.

68. "Mémoire sur les plantes qui sont dans la caise B," n.p.

69. Ibid.

70. Ibid.

71. Michael Deal, "Palaeoethnobotanical Research at Port au Choix," *Newfoundland and Labrador Studies* 20, no. 1 (2005): 132.

72. See Sara J. Halwas, "Where the Wild Things Grow: A Palaeoethnobotanical Study of Late Woodland Plant Use at Clam Cove, Nova Scotia," MA thesis, Memorial University, 2006, 37–48, 67–70.

73. Michael Deal and Elaine L. Thomas, "Late Prehistoric Plant Use in the Western Minas Basin Area, Nova Scotia," in *Current Northeast Paleoethnobotany II*, ed. John P. Hart (Albany: New York State Museum, 2008), 180.

74. Ibid.; Halwas, "Where the Wild Things Grow," 65–68. For more recent studies of contemporary Mi'kmaw ethnobotany, see R. Frank Chandler, Lois Freeman, and Shirley N Hooper, "Herbal Remedies of the Maritime Indians," *Journal of Ethnopharmacology* 1, no. 1 (1979): 49–68; Laurie Lacey, *Micmac Medicines: Remedies and Recollections* (Halifax, Nova Scotia: Nimbus Publishing, 1993).

75. "Mémoire sur les plantes qui sont dans la caise B," n.p.

76. Wayne R. Hawthorn, "The Biology of Canadian Weeds: 4. Plantago Major and P. Rugelii," *Canadian Journal of Plant Science* 54, no. 2 (1974): 387.

77. John H. McAndrews, "Human Disturbance of North American Forests and Grasslands: The Fossil Pollen Record," in *Vegetation History*, ed. B. Huntley and T. Webb (Utrecht: Kluwer, 1988), 683–685.

78. For "Englishmen's foot," see Colin G. Calloway, *New Worlds for All: Indians, Europeans, and the Remaking of Early America* (Baltimore: Johns Hopkins University Press, 1997), 14; Alfred W. Crosby, *Ecological Imperialism: The Biological Expansion of Europe, 900–1900* (New York: Cambridge University Press, 2004), 169. For "White man's foot," see Hawthorn, "The Biology of Canadian Weeds," 387.

79. Crosby, *Ecological Imperialism*, 156.

80. Lacey, *Micmac Medicines*, 73, 90; "Plaintain" text search string, Native American Ethnobotany Database, http://naeb.brit.org/uses/search/?string=plantain.

81. Frieda Knobloch, *The Culture of Wilderness: Agriculture as Colonization in the American West* (Chapel Hill: University of North Carolina Press, 1996), 123.

82. For more information on the scientific networks of the French Atlantic, see McClellan and Regourd, *The Colonial Machine*; François Regourd, "Capitale savante, capitale

coloniale: Sciences et savoirs coloniaux à Paris aux XVIIe et XVIIIe siècles," *Revue d'histoire moderne et contemporaine* 55, no. 2 (2008): 121–151. On the information networks of the French Atlantic world more generally, see Kenneth J. Banks, *Chasing Empire Across the Sea: Communications and the State in the French Atlantic, 1713–1763* (Montreal: McGill-Queen's University Press, 2002).

83. On the inefficiency of the "colonial machine," see Loïc Charles and Paul Cheney, "The Colonial Machine Dismantled: Knowledge and Empire in the French Atlantic," *Past & Present* 219, no. 1 (2013): 127–163. On the erasure of indigenous knowledge in French science, see Christopher M. Parsons, "The Natural History of Colonial Science: Joseph-François Lafitau's Discovery of Ginseng and Its Afterlives," *William and Mary Quarterly* 73, no. 1 (2016): 37–72; Kapil Raj, *Relocating Modern Science: Circulation and the Construction of Knowledge in South Asia and Europe, 1650–1900* (New York: Palgrave Macmillan, 2007).

84. "Mémoire sur les plantes qui sont dans la caise B," n.p.

85. Ibid.

86. Ibid.

87. "Lettre de Hocquart au ministre," C11A, 70:113, ANOM.

88. Ibid., 72:64; "Lettre de Hocquart au ministre," C11A, 73:414v, ANOM; "Lettre de Hocquart au ministre," C11A, 76:22, ANOM; "Lettre de Hocquart au ministre," C11A, 80:70, ANOM.

89. "Lettre non signee," C11A, 49:519, ANOM.

90. Young, "Crown Agent-Canadian Correspondent."

91. For discussion of these networks, see Lamontagne "L'influence de Maurepas," 116; M. Wong and P. Huard, "Les enquêtes scientifiques françaises et l'exploration du monde exotique aux XVIIe et XVIIIe siècles," *Bulletin de l'École française d'Extrême-Orient* 52, no. 1 (1964): 143–155.

92. By 1753, the academician and naturalist Henri-Louis Duhamel du Monceau had collaborated with the former governor of New France, Roland-Michel Barrin, marquis de La Galissonière, to produce a set of instructions for would-be correspondents aimed at minimizing losses. Duhamel du Monceau, *Avis pour le transport par mer des arbres, des plantes vivaces, des semences, et de diverses autres curiosites d'histoire naturelle* (Paris: L'Imprimerie Royale, 1753).

93. Roger Hahn, *The Anatomy of a Scientific Institution: The Paris Academy of Sciences, 1666–1803* (Berkeley: University of California Press, 1971), 46–47, 58–60. See also James E. McClellan, *Specialist Control: The Publications Committee of the Académie Royale des Sciences (Paris), 1700–1793* (Philadelphia: American Philosophical Society, 2003), 61–76.

94. Antoine de Jussieu, "Des avantages d'un commerce litteraire avec les botanistes etrangers," ms 1116, Bibliothèque centrale Muséum national d'Histoire naturelle, Paris, 1.

95. Ralph Bauer, *The Cultural Geography of Colonial American Literatures: Empire, Travel, Modernity* (Cambridge: Cambridge University Press, 2003), 4; Susan Scott Parrish, *American Curiosity: Cultures of Natural History in the Colonial British Atlantic World* (Chapel Hill: University of North Carolina Press, 2006), 114.

96. Duhamel du Monceau, *Avis pour le transport par mer des arbres*, 158–160.

97. Ibid. See also Silvia Collini and Antonella Vannoni, *Les instructions scientifiques pour les voyageurs: XVIIe–XIXe siècle* (Paris: l'Harmattan, 2005), 15–54; Lorelaï Kury, "Les instructions de voyage dans les expéditions scientifiques françaises (1750–1830)," *Revue d'histoire des sciences* 51, no. 1 (1998): 65–91.

98. On Sarrazin, see Arthur Vallée, *Un biologiste canadien, Michel Sarrazin, 1659–1735: Sa vie, ses travaux et son temps* (Quebec: LS-A. Proulx, 1927); Young, "Crown Agent-Canadian Correspondent."

99. On Prat, see Roland Lamontagne, "Le dossier biographique de Jean Prat," *Revue d'histoire de l'Amérique française* 16, no. 2 (1962): 219–224. For a broader introduction to colonial science in Louisiana, see Gilles-Antoine Langlois, "Deux fondations scientifiques à la Nouvelle-Orléans (1728–30): La connaissance à l'épreuve de la réalité coloniale," *French Colonial History* 4, no. 1 (2003): 99–115.

100. See "Diverses Observations Anatomiques," *Histoire et Mémoire de l'Académie Royale des Sciences* (1704): 36; Alexandre Vielle, "Description de l'arbrisseau qui porte la cire," ms 196, Bibliothèque centrale, Muséum national d'Histoire naturelle, Paris, 3.

101. These plants became in effect what the science studies scholar Bruno Latour has referred to as "immutable and combinable mobiles." Bruno Latour, *Science in Action: How to Follow Scientists and Engineers Through Society* (Cambridge, MA: Harvard University Press, 1987), 215–257.

102. Often, this could be as simple as using a standardized and properly calibrated instrument. When the royal physician Jean-François Gaultier recorded his observations about Canadian weather, for example, he used a thermometer provided by his correspondent Réaumur for conducting experiments on the raising of chickens. See Arthur Vallée, "Cinq lettres inédites de Jean François Gaultier à M. de Rhéaumur de l'Académie des sciences," *Mémoire de la Société Royale du Canada* 24 (1930): 31–43.

103. Boivin, "La flore du Canada en 1708," 244.

104. Ibid.

105. Ibid. "Mémoire sur les plantes qui sont dans la caise B," n.p.

106. Plants that arrived from the extra-European world soon entered a continental network of individual naturalists, gardens, and scientific institutions. See Staffan Müller-Wille, "Joining Lapland and the Topinambes in Flourishing Holland: Center and Periphery in Linnaean Botany," *Science in Context* 16, no. 4 (2003): 461–488.

107. "Lettre de Hocquart au ministre," C11A, 73:416, ANOM.

108. "Lettre de Beauharnois au ministre," October 17, 1736, C11A, 65:140, ANOM.

109. See Pierre-François-Xavier de Charlevoix, *Journal d'un voyage fait par ordre du Roi dans l'Amérique septentrionale*, ed. Pierre Berthiaume (Montreal: Presses de l'Université de Montréal, 1994); Joseph-François Lafitau, *Mémoire presenté a son altesse royale . . . concernant la précieuse plante du gin-seng de Tartarie* (Paris: chez Joseph Mongé, 1718).

Chapter 11

The epigraph is from Pedro Murillo Velarde, *Catecismo o Instrucción Christiana, en que se explican los Mysterios de nuestra Santa Fé y se exhorta a huir los vicios y abrazar las Virtudes* (Madrid: En la Imprenta de los Herederos de Francisco del Hierro, 1752).

1. On the global Enlightenment, see Dorinda Outram, *The Enlightenment*, 3rd ed. (Cambridge: Cambridge Universitiy Press, 2013).

2. See Ralph Bauer, *The Cultural Geography of Colonial American Literatures: Empire, Travel, Modernity* (Cambridge: Cambridge University Press, 2003); Antonio Barrera Osorio, *Experiencing Nature: The Spanish American Empire and the Early Scientific Revolution* (Austin: University of Texas Press, 2006); Daniela Bleichmar and Paula De Vos, eds., *Science and*

Medicine in the Spanish and Portuguese Empires (Stanford, CA: Stanford University Press, 2008).

3. Murillo Velarde, *Catecismo o Instrucción Christiana*, n.p.

4. On Murillo Velarde's biography, see Bernardo Pazuengos, *Carta edificante sobre la vida, virtudes y muerte del P. Pedro Murillo Velarde, Religioso de la Compañía de Jesús*, ed. Manuel Antonio Murillo Velarde (Murcia: Por Nicolas Joseph Villargordo Y Alcaraz, 1756); Luis Díaz de la Guardia y López, "Datos para una biografía del jurista Pedro Murillo Velarde y Bravo," *Espacio, tiempo y forma*, Serie IV, Historia Moderna, 14 (2001): 407–471. On Murillo Velarde's 1734 map, see Antonio López Gómez and Carmen Manso Porto, *Cartografía del siglo XVIII: Tomás López en la Real Academia de la Historia* (Madrid: Real Academia De La Historia, Departamento De Cartografía Y Artes Gráficas, 2006); Ricardo Padrón, "From Abstraction to Allegory: The Imperial Cartography of Vicente de Memije," in *Early Modern Cartographies*, ed. Martin Brückner, 35–66 (Chapel Hill: University of North Carolina Press, 2012).

5. Pedro Murillo Velarde, *Geographía Histórica*, Vol. 8, *De las Islas Philipinas, del Africa y de sus islas adyacentes* (Madrid: En la Oficina de D. Gabriel Ramirez, 1752). All translations from *Geographía Histórica* are mine.

6. In Real Academia Española de la Lengua, *Diccionario de la lengua castellana*, Vol. 4 (Madrid, 1734), *historia* is defined as "a relation written with the rules of the art; a description of things the way that they happened through a sequential and faithful narration of the most memorable events and the most famous deeds" (162) (my translation).

7. Real Academia Española de la Lengua, *Diccionario de la lengua castellana*, 162.

8. Ibid., 46.

9. See Jerónimo de Ustáriz y Hermiaga, *Theórica y práctica y de Marina* (Madrid: n.p., 1724); Bernardo de Ulloa, *Restablecimiento de las fábricas y el comercio español* (Madrid: Antonio Marín, 1740). I note a significant influence of both works on Murillo Velarde's proposed reforms of commerce and navigation in both Indies.

10. He writes that "In any event, there remains at least the sterile consolation of having tried to present my Country with a work that, besides being enjoyable, useful, upright, and necessary to a Civilized People, no Spaniard has taken on with such a broad scope." Pedro Murillo Velarde, *Geographía Histórica*, Vol. 1, *Donde se describen los reynos, provincias, ciudades, fortalezas, mares, montes, ensenadas, cabos, ríos y puertos, con la mayor individualidad y exactitud, y se refieren las guerras, las batallas, las Paces, y Sucessos memorables, los Frutos, los Animales, los Comercios, las Conquistas, la Religión, los Concilios, las Sectas, los Goviernos, las Lenguas, las Naciones, su genio y su carácter* (Madrid: En la Oficina de D. Gabriel Ramirez, 1752), "Prólogo y razon de la obra," n.p.

11. Emma Spary, "Political, Natural and Bodily Economies," in *Cultures of Natural History*, ed. N. Jardine, J. A. Secord, E. C. Spary, 178–197 (Cambridge: Cambridge University Press, 1996).

12. Londa Schiebinger, *Plants and Empire: Colonial Bioprospecting in the Atlantic World* (Cambridge, MA: Harvard University Press, 2004), 89–92.

13. Pedro Murillo Velarde, *Geographía Histórica*, Vol. 9, *De la América, y de las Islas adyacentes, y de las Tierras Árcticas y Antárcticas, y Islas de los Mares del Norte y Sur* (Madrid: En la Imprenta de Don Aguftin de Gosdejuela y Sierra, 1752), 31.

14. Daniela Bleichmar and Peter C. Mancall, *Collecting Across Cultures: Material Exchanges in the Early Modern Atlantic World* (Philadelphia: University of Pennsylvania Press, 2011), 3.

15. Murillo Velarde, "Censura," in Joseph González Cabrera Bueno, *Navegación especulativa y práctica con la explicación de algunos instrumentos que están más en uso en los Navegantes, con las reglas necesarias para su verdadero uso* (Manila: En El Convento De Nuestra Señora De Los Angeles, 1734), Prólogo, n.p.

16. See Pazuengos, *Carta edificante*, 73. This presents a formidable challenge to the scholarly record, which does not account for the very robust circulation of scientific and other texts to which the Spanish Jesuit had unfettered access. Matthew J. K. Hill's excellent study "Intercolonial Currents: Printing Press and Book Circulation in the Spanish Philippines, 1571–1821," PhD dissertation, University of Texas, Austin, 2015, has taken a fine-tooth comb to the Spanish Inquisition's archives. Apart from two documented shipments of books on religious topics by religious orders in the 1720s, there is a sixty-year gap in the Inquisition's records on official book shipments from, say, Veracruz to Manila. However, in the late 1660s, book shipments from Spain to religious orders in the Philippines included legal, moral, geographical, and even fictional works (ibid. 230–231). Although the Crown's 1767 inventories of the exiled Jesuit libraries have been published, it is impossible to determine when most of the titles were bought. See María Dolores García Gómez, *Testigos de la memoria: los inventarios de las bibliotecas de la Compañía de Jesús en la expulsión de 1767* (Alicante, Spain: Publicaciones De La Universidad De Alicante, 2010).

17. Murillo Velarde, *Geographía Histórica*, Vol. 1, "Prólogo y razon de la obra," n.p.

18. Bellin's sea chart of the Philippines, *Carte réduit des Isles Philippines pour servir aux Vaisseaux du Roy*, was commissioned by the French secretary of state and the navy and first published in 1752. Bellin was referring to Pedro Murillo Velarde, *Historia de la Provincia de Philipinas de la Compañía de Jesús* (Manila: En La Imprenta De La Compan ia De Jesus, Por D. Nicolas De La Cruz Bagay, 1749).

19. Murillo Velarde, *Geographía Histórica*, Vol. 1, "Prólogo y razon de la obra," n.p.

20. Ibid.

21. Ibid.

22. Ibid.

23. I apply James English's model, as set down in *The Economy of Prestige: Prizes, Awards, and the Circulation of Cultural Value* (Cambridge, MA: Harvard University Press, 2005), in a vastly different context, I admit.

24. Enrique Flórez, *Clave geográfica para aprender geografía los que no tienen maestro* (Barcelona: J. F. Piferrer, 1817), "Discurso previo," 37 (my translation). *Clave geográfica* was part of a much larger work published in 1747. In the 1750s, the Inquisition records for book shipments to Manila included Flórez's works; see J.K. Hill, "Intercolonial Currents," 234.

25. Murillo Velarde frequently cites *Introductionis Universam Geographiam, tam Veterem quam Novam, Libri VI: Cum integris Johan; Bunonis, Joh. Fried. Hekelii et Joh. Riskii & selectis Londinensibus notis*, revised, expanded, and annotated ed. with preface by Aug. Bruzen La Martinière (Amsterdam: Apud J. Pauli, 1729), by his last name only or refers to "los Adicionadores de Cluvier."

26. See Antonio Lafuente and Antonio Mazuecos, *Los caballeros del punto fijo: Ciencia, política y aventura en la expedición geodésica hispanofrancesa al virreintao del Perú en el siglo XVIII* (Barcelona: Ediciones Del Serbal, 1987); Neil Safier, *Measuring the New World: Enlightenment Science and South America* (Chicago: University of Chicago Press, 2008).

27. Antonello Gerbi, *La Disputa del Nuovo Mondo: Storia di una polemica, 1750–1900* (1955; reprint, Milan: R. Ricciardi, 1983).

28. See Murillo Velarde's protracted engagement with degeneration theories from the Spanish Renaissance and baroque in his volume on the Americas, *Geographía Histórica*, 9:48–49.

29. Flórez, *Clave geográphica*, 60.

30. José Gumilla, *El Orinoco ilustrado y defendido: Historia natural, civil y geográphica de este gran Río y de sus caudalosas vertientes*, 2 vols., 2nd revised and expanded ed. (Madrid: M. Aguilar, 1745). On Gumilla's account, see Margaret Ewalt, *Peripheral Wonder: Nature, Knowledge, and Enlightenment in the Eighteenth-Century Orinoco* (Lewisburg, PA: Bucknell University Press, 2009).

31. Jorge Juan and Antonio de Ulloa, *Relación histórica del viaje a la América Meridional*, 4 vols. (Madrid: Por A. Marin, 1748).

32. Pierre Bouguer, *La Figure de la Terre déterminée par les Observations des Messieurs Bouguer & de La Condamine de l'Académie Royale des Sciences, envoyés par ordre du Roy au Pérou pour observer aux environs de l'Equateur: Avec une Relation abregée de le Voyage, que contient la description du Pays dans lequel les Opérations ont été faites par M. Bouguer* (Paris: C. A. Jombert, 1749), xii.

33. Murillo Velarde, *Geographía Histórica*, 9:214. The correction appeared in "Lettre de M. de La Condamine aus Auteurs de ce *Journal*." *Mémoires pour l'Histoire des Sciences et des Beaux-Arts: Feb. 1748* (Paris, 1748), 370–383.

34. Charles Marie de La Condamine, *Histoire des Pyramides de Quito élevées par les Académiciens envoyés sous l'Equateur par ordre du Roi* (Paris: De L'Imprimerie Royale, 1751).

35. Murillo Velarde, *Geographía Histórica*, 9:257.

36. Ibid.

37. Author unknown, "Hist. et Mémoires de l'Académie Royale des Sciences pour 1744" (Article CXXXI), in *Mémoires pour l'Histoire des Sciences et des Beaux-Arts* (Paris, December 1748), 2663–2692.

38. Author unknown, "*La Figure de la Terre*" (Article CXXX), in *Mémoires pour l'Histoire des Sciences et des Beaux-Arts* (Paris, November 1749), 2220–2235.

39. Ibid., 2326–2327 (my translation).

40. Ibid., 2327 (emphasis in original; my translation).

41. Murillo Velarde, *Geographía Histórica*, 8:4.

42. Ibid.

43. Ibid., 8:6.

44. Ibid., 8:4.

45. On Gassendi's physics, see Barry Brundell, *Pierre Gassendi: From Aristotelianism to a New Natural Philosophy* (Dordrecht, Holland: D. Reidel, 1987); Luis Díaz Martín, *Pierre Gassendi: La afirmación de una nueva epistemología* (Granada: Universidad De Granada, 1989); Marco Messeri, *Causa e spiegazione: La fisica di Pierre Gassendi* (Milan: F. Angeli, 1985); Antonia LoLordo, *Pierre Gassendi and the Birth of Early Modern Philosophy* (Cambridge: Cambridge University Press, 2009); Thomas Lennon, *The Battle of the Gods and Giants: The Legacies of Descartes and Gassendi, 1655–1715* (Princeton, NJ: Princeton University Press, 1993); Gordon Sidney Brett, *The Philosophy of Gassendi* (London: Macmillan, 1908). On Gassendi's science in early modern Spain, Portugal, Mexico, and Peru, see Ruth Hill, *Sceptres and Sciences in the Spains: Four Humanists and the New Philosophy (ca. 1680–1740)* (Liverpool: Liverpool University Press, 2000).

46. Murillo Velarde, *Geographía Histórica*, 8:5.

47. Juan Bautista Berni, *Filosofía racional, natural, metafísica i moral*, 3 vols. (Valencia, 1736), 2:191. See also 2:315.

48. Nicolás Léméry, *Curso Chímico del doctor Nicolas Léméry*, trans. and expanded by Félix de Palacios ... Joseph Assin y Palacios de Ongoz, Segundo Curso Chímico (Saragossa, Spain: Por Diego De Larvmbe, 1707).

49. Against "radical rupture," Christoph Lüthy reminds us of "the spirit of the multiple and complex transformations that characterized the evolution of physics in the early modern period." Christoph Herbert Lüthy, *David Gorlæus (1591–1612): An Enigmatic Figure in the History of Philosophy and Science*, History of Science and Scholarship in the Netherlands, Vol. 13. (Amsterdam: Amsterdam University Press, 2012), 158. Margaret J. Osler argues that scholars have ignored the nonmechanical aspects of Gassendi's thought, which are readily accessible through his natural philosophy. See "How Mechanical Was the Mechanical Philosophy? Non-Epicurean Aspects of Gassendi's Philosophy of Nature," in *Late Medieval and Early Modern Corpuscular Matter Theories*, ed. Christoph Lüthy, John E. Murdoch, and William R. Newman, 423–439 (Leiden: Brill, 2001). Similarly, Dennis Des Chene offers a nuanced view of the French Jesuit Fabri's physics, which circulated widely outside of France, in "Wine and Water: Honoré Fabri on Mixtures," in *Late Medieval and Early Modern Corpuscular Matter Theories*, 363–379. Fabri's matter theory was corpuscular although not mechanical, Des Chene explains, and "the term 'corpuscular' does not succeed in distinguishing *novator* from *scolasticus*" (378). Indeed, "the terms 'mechanical' and 'chemical' have ambiguities of their own in this period" (378). Likewise, the mechanization of nature in matter theories from the seventeenth century has been grossly overstated, according to Antonio Clericuzio, "Gassendi, Charleton and Boyle on Matter and Motion," in *Late Medieval and Early Modern Corpuscular Matter Theories*, 467–482. "Indeed, non-mechanical corpuscular theories of matter played a prominent part in science. . . . Aristotelian forms and qualities . . . often coexisted with corpuscles" (467).

50. On local knowledge and experience, see Scott Atran, *Cognitive Foundations of Natural History: Towards an Anthropology of Science* (Cambridge: Cambridge University Press, 1996); Scott Atran, "Origin of the Species and Genus Concepts: An Anthropological Perspective," *Journal of the History of Biology* 20, no. 2 (Summer 1987): 195–279.

51. Murillo Velarde, *Geographía Histórica*, 8:52.

52. Ibid., 8:7.

53. Ibid., 8:6.

54. See Schiebinger, *Plants and Empire*; Antonio Barrera Osorio, *Experiencing Nature: The Spanish American Empire and the Early Scientific Revolution* (Austin: University of Texas Press, 2006); Daniela Bleichmar and Paula De Vos, eds., *Science and Medicine in the Spanish and Portugese Empires* (Stanford, CA: Stanford Universitiy Press, 2008).

55. Murillo Velarde, *Geographía Histórica*, 8:8.

56. Ibid.

57. Examples abound in John W. O'Malley, *The Jesuits II: Cultures, Sciences, and the Arts, 1540–1773* (Toronto: University of Toronto Press, 2007); Luis Millones Figueroa and Domingo Ledezma, *El saber de los jesuitas, historias naturales y el Nuevo Mundo* (Madrid: Iberoamericana, 2005); Ewalt, *Peripheral Wonder*; Andrés Prieto, *Missionary Scientists: Jesuit Science in Spanish South America, 1570–1810* (Nashville: Vanderbilt University Press, 2011); Alexandre Coello de la Rosa, *Jesuits at the Margins: Missions and Missionaries in the Marianas, 1668–1769* (New York: Routledge, Taylor & Francis Group, 2015).

58. Murillo Velarde, *Geographía Histórica*, 8:13.

59. Murillo Velarde, *Historia de la Provincia de Philipinas*, 393–394.

60. Murillo Velarde, *Geographía Histórica*, 8:12.

61. Ibid., 8:9.

62. Ibid., 8:12.

63. See procurator Juan Grau y Monfalcon's report, *Justificación de la conservación y comercio de las Islas Filipinas* (1640?), Newberry Library of Chicago, #76637; Nicolás Norton y Nicols, *Comercio de las Islas Philipinas e conveniencias que pueden dar a S. M. Carlos III* (Manila, 1759), Manuscript, Newberry Library of Chicago, #76585.

64. Murillo Velarde, *Geographía Histórica*, 8:31.

65. Ibid.

66. Ibid., 8:9.

67. Ibid.

68. Ibid., 8:10.

69. Ibid.

70. Ibid., 8:10–11.

71. Ibid., 8:11.

72. Ibid.

73. Pazuengos, *Carta edificante*, 73 (my translation).

74. Murillo Velarde, *Geographía Histórica*, 8:11.

75. Ibid., 8:13.

76. The majority of Linnaeus's taxonomic system is considered to be Aristotelian or Galenist. See A. J. Bain, "Logic and Memory in Linnaeus's Sytem of Taxonomy," *Proceedings of the Linnean Society of London* 169, nos. 1–2 (1958): 144–163; Staffan Müller-Wille, "Linnaeus and the Four Corners of the World," in *The Cultural Politics of Blood, 1500–1900*, ed. Ralph Bauer, Kim Coles, Zita Nunes, and Carla Peterson, 191–209 (Houndmills, Basingstoke, Hampshire, UK: Palgrave, 2015). In *Nature's Body: Gender in the Making of Modern Science* (Boston, MA: Beacon, 1993, 1993), Londa Schiebinger labels Linnaeus's alignment of the four humors (corresponding to the four elements), the four continents, and the four races "starkly premodern" (119). Moreover, Enlightenment French botanists used the Aristotelian/Linnaen *differentia* in periodicals that Murillo Velarde read regularly. See, for example, Jean-Étienne Guettard, "Second Mémoire sur les Glandes des Plantes," *Histoire de l'Académie Royale des Sciences* (Paris, 1747), 515–555.

77. Murillo Velarde, *Geographía Histórica*, 8:16.

78. Jacques Bénigne Winslow, "Remarques sur les monstres avec des observations sur les marques de naissance," in *Year 1733 de Histoire de l'Academie Royale des Sciences* (Paris, 1736), 366–389.

79. Jacques Bénigne Winslow, "Remarques sur les monstres: Seconde partie," in *Year 1734 de Histoire de l'Academie Royale des Sciences* (Paris, 1736), 453–490, esp. 453–468 and plates I–III.

80. Murillo Velarde, *Geographía Histórica*, 8:19.

81. Robert Boyle, *Experiments and Considerations Touching Colours* (London, 1664), Experiment XI, at 162–163.

82. Murillo Velarde, *Geographía Histórica*, 8:17.

83. Ibid., 8:16.

84. Boyle, *Experiments and Considerations Touching Colours*, Experiment XI, 152–158.

85. Berni, *Filosofía racional, natural, metafísica i moral*, 2:159.

86. Murillo Velarde, *Geographía Histórica*, 8:16–17.

87. The usage of "fibers" (*fibras*) probably signals his debts to Boyle, Gassendi, Berni and even the French Jesuit Honoré Fabri, who fused tenets of physics drawn from *novatores* with Aristotle's substantial forms, as Des Chene has shown. More broadly, before seventeenth-century atomism went to war with Scholastic substantial forms, "there existed some currents within Aristotelianism itself which . . . combined atomic with hylemorphic notions" (Lüthy, *David Gorlæus*, 159).

88. Berni, *Filosofía racional, natural, metafísica i moral* 2:191–192.

89. Murillo Velarde, *Geographía Histórica*, 8:33.

90. Ibid.

91. Ibid., 8:61.

92. Ibid., 8:33.

93. Ibid., 8:199.

94. Ibid., 8:200.

95. Ibid., 8:33.

96. Ibid., 8:35–36.

97. Ibid.

98. Jusep M. Fradera, *Filipinas, la colonia más peculiar: La hacienda pública en la definición de la política colonial, 1762–1868* (Madrid: Consejo Superior De Investigaciones Científicas, 1999), 148, 181. On the wealth and influence of the Catholic Chinese merchant community, see Joshua Eng Sin Kueh, "The Manila Chinese: Community, Trade, and Empire, C. 1570–C. 1770," PhD dissertation, Georgetown University, 2014.

99. Murillo Velarde, *Geographía Histórica*, 8:35.

100. On the history of the *datu* and its early cultural translation by the Spanish Crown and the Spanish Church, see Patricio Hidalgo Nuchera, *Encomienda, tributo y trabajo en Filipinas (1570–1608)* (Madrid: Universidad Autónoma De Madrid, 1995); Luis Ángel Sánchez Gómez, *Las principalías indígenas y la administración española en Filipinas* (Madrid: Editorial de la Universidad Complutense, 1991); Fradera, *Filipinas, la colonia más peculiar*. See also Margarita Menegus Bornemann and Rodolfo Aguirre Salvador, eds., *El cacicazgo en Nueva España y Filipinas* (Mexico City: Plaza y Valdés, 2005).

101. Murillo Velarde, *Geographía Histórica*, 8:36.

102. See Ruth Hill, "Entering and Exiting Blackness: A Color Controversy in Eighteenth-Century Spain," *Journal of Spanish Cultural Studies* 10, no. 1 (March 2009): 43–58.

103. Antonio Cornejo Polar, *Mestizaje e hibridez: Los riesgos de las metáforas*, Cuadernos de la Literatura, no. 6 (La Paz, Bolivia: Carrera de Literatura, Facultad de Humanidades y Ciencias de la Educación, UMSA, 1997).

104. Maurizio Ferraris, *Documentalità: Perché è necessario lasciar tracce* (Rome: Laterza, 2009).

Afterword

1. Juan Pimentel, "Sighting and Haunting of the South Sea: On Ponquiaco, Balboa, and What Maps Conceal," this volume.

2. Londa Schiebinger, *Plants and Empire: Colonial Bioprospecting in the Atlantic World* (Cambridge, MA: Harvard University Press, 2004), 90.

3. Quoted in Edith Grossman, *Why Translation Matters* (New Haven, CT: Yale University Press, 2010), 11.

4. Ibid.

5. Ibid., 31.

6. Roger Williams, *A Key into the Language of America* (London: Printed by Gregory Dexter, 1643), A2r-v.

7. Daniela Bleichmar, "Pictorial Knowledge on the Move: The Translations of the *Codex Mendoza*," this volume.

8. Sara Miglietti, "New Worlds, Ancient Theories: Reshaping Climate Theory in the Early Colonial Atlantic," this volume.

9. Jaime Marroquín Arredondo, "The Method of Francisco Hernández: Early Modern Science and the Translation of Mesoamerica's Natural History," this volume.

10. Schiebinger, *Plants and Empire*, 84.

11. Marcy Norton, "The Quetzal Takes Flight: Microhistory, Mesoamerican Knowledge, and Early Modern Natural History," this volume.

12. Pimentel notes that the Indians "are not totally deleted" from Oviedo's account. "They simply appear blurred and are depicted according to the cultural stereotypes of their observers." See Pimental, "Sighting and Haunting of the South Sea: On Ponquiaco, Balboa, and What Maps Conceal," this volume.

13. Anthony Grafton, *New Worlds, Ancient Texts: The Power of Tradition and the Shock of Discovery* (Cambridge, MA: Harvard University Press, 1995).

14. J. H. Elliott, *The Old World and the New, 1492–1650* (Cambridge: Cambridge University Press, 1970). In addition, see Wilma George, "Sources and Background to Discoveries of New Animals in the Sixteenth and Seventeenth Centuries," *History of Science* 18 (1980): 79–104; Brian Ogilvie, *The Science of Describing: Natural History in Renaissance Europe* (Chicago: University of Chicago Press, 2006), 143.

15. Bernabé Cobo, *History of the Inca Empire*, trans. Roland Hamilton (Austin: University of Texas Press, 1979), 20.

16. Christopher Parsons, "Columbian Circulations in the North Atlantic World: François-Madeleine Vallée in Eighteenth-Century Île Royale," this volume.

17. Galileo Galilei, "Letter to the Grand Duchess Christina," in *Discoveries and Opinions of Galileo*, trans. Stillman Drake (Garden City, NY: Doubleday, 1957), 196.

18. William Eamon, *Science and the Secrets of Nature: Books of Secrets in Medieval and Early Modern Culture* (Princeton, NJ: Princeton University Press, 1994), chap. 7.

19. Pimentel, "Sighting and Haunting of the South Sea."

20. Sarah Rivett, "Local Linguistics and Indigenous Cosmologies of the Early Eighteenth-Century Atlantic World," this volume.

21. Norwood Russell Hanson, *Patterns of Discovery: An Inquiry into the Conceptual Foundations of Science* (Cambridge: Cambridge University Press, 1965), 5.

22. Pamela Smith, "Science on the Move: Recent Trends in the History of Early Modern Science," *Renaissance Quarterly* 62 (2009): 346.

23. Pamela H. Smith, *The Body of the Artisan: Art and Experience in the Scientific Revolution* (Chicago: University of Chicago Press, 2004). On things as bearers of knowledge, see Pamela Smith and Benjamin Schmidt, eds., *Making Knowledge in Early Modern Europe* (Chicago: University of Chicago Press, 2007); Paula Findlen, ed., *Early Modern Things: Objects and Their Histories* (London: Routledge, 2013).

24. Miglietti, "New Worlds, Ancient Theories."

25. John Slater, "Flora's Fate: Spanish Materia Medica in Manuscript," this volume.

26. On the influence of Bacon's *New Atlantis* on the founding of the Royal Society, see Michael Hunter, *Science and Society in Restoration England* (Cambridge: Cambridge University Press, 1981); Deborah Harkness, *The Jewel House: Elizabethan London and the Scientific Revolution* (New Haven, CT: Yale University Press, 2007), 213–214.

27. Antonio Barrera-Osorio, *Experiencing Nature: The Spanish American Empire and the Early Scientific Revolution* (Austin: University of Texas Press, 2006); John Gascoigne, "Crossing the Pillars of Hercules: Francis Bacon, the Scientific Revolution and the New World," in *Science in the Age of Baroque*, ed. Ofer Gal and Raz Chen-Morris, 217–237 (Amsterdam: Springer, 2013).

28. Andrew Hadfield, *Literature, Travel, and Colonial Writing in the English Renaissance, 1545–1625* (Oxford: Oxford University Press, 1998), 70–110.

29. Ralph Bauer, "The Crucible of the Tropics: Alchemy, Translation, and the English Discovery of America," this volume.

30. Augustine Brannigan, *The Social Basis of Scientific Discoveries* (Cambridge: Cambridge University Press, 1981), 133.

31. Harold J. Cook, *Matters of Exchange: Commerce, Medicine, and Science in the Dutch Golden Age* (New Haven, CT: Yale University Press, 2007), 5.

32. Brannigan, *The Social Basis of Scientific Discoveries*, 121.

33. Bacon, "De Sapientia Veterum," in *The Works of Francis Bacon, Baron of Verulam, Viscount of St. Alban, and Lord Chancellor of England*, 14 vols., ed. James Spedding, Robert Leslie Ellis, and Douglas Denon Heath (New York: Garrett, 1968), 6:713.

34. Bacon, "De augmentis scientiarum," in *The Works of Francis Bacon*, 1:633, trans. 4:421.

35. Sean Silver, "The Prehistory of Serendipity, from Bacon to Walpole," *Isis* 106 (2015): 235–256.

36. Cook, *Matters of Exchange*, 5.

37. For a perceptive discussion of the early modern knowledge economy, see Daniel Jütte, *The Age of Secrecy: Jews, Christians, and the Economy of Secrets, 1400–1800*, trans. Jeremiah Riemer (New Haven, CT: Yale University Press, 2015), 235–349.

38. Cook, *Matters of Exchange*, 6; Smith, "Science on the Move."

39. Katharine Park and Lorraine Daston, "Introduction: The Age of the New," in *The Cambridge History of Science*, Vol. 3, *Early Modern Science* (Cambridge: Cambridge University Press, 2006), 1.

40. Lorraine Daston and Katharine Park, *Wonders and the Order of Nature, 1150–1750* (New York: Zone Books, 1998); Mary Blaine Campbell, *Wonder & Science: Imagining Worlds in Early Modern Europe* (Ithaca, NY: Cornell University Press, 1999).

41. Daston and Park, *Wonders and the Order of Nature*, 147.

42. Daniela Bleichmar and Peter C. Mancall, eds., *Collecting Across Cultures: Material Exchanges in the Early Modern Atlantic World* (Philadelphia: University of Pennsylvania Press, 2011); Paula Findlen, *Possessing Nature: Museums, Collecting, and Scientific Culture in Early Modern Italy* (Stanford, CA: Stanford University Press, 1994); Benjamin Schmidt, *Inventing the Exotic: Geography, Globalism, and Europe's Early Modern World* (Philadelphia: University of Pennsylvania Press, 2015).

43. Ruth Hill, "Native Engravings on the Global Enlightenment: Pedro Murillo Velarde's Sea Map and Historical Geography of the Spanish Philippines," this volume.

44. Arndt Brendecke, *The Empirical Empire: Spanish Colonial Rule and the Politics of Knowledge*, trans. Jeremiah Riemer (Berlin: Walter de Gruyter, 2016).

45. René Descartes, *The Passions of the Soul*, trans. Stephen Voss (Indianapolis: Hackett Publishing, 1989), 52, 56.

46. Daston and Park, *Wonders and the Order of Nature*, 303–304.

47. Carolyn Walker Bynum, "Wonder," *American Historical Review* 102 (1997): 24.

48. Lorraine Daston, "The Factual Sensibility," *Isis* 79 (1988): 452–467.

49. Cook, *Matters of Exchange*, 416.

C o n t r i b u t o r s

Ralph Bauer is an associate professor of English and comparative literature at the University of Maryland, College Park. He is the author of *The Cultural Geography of Colonial American Literatures: Empire, Travel, Modernity* (Cambridge University Press 2003, 2008) and *An Inca Account of the Conquest of Peru* (University of Colorado Press, 2005). Bauer coedited with José Antonio Mazzotti *Creole Subjects in the Colonial Americas: Empires, Texts, Identities* (Omohondro Institute and the University of North Carolina Press, 2009) and also coedited with Marcy Norton *Entangled Trajectories: Indigenous and European Histories,* a special issue of *Colonial Latin American Review* 26 (Spring 2017). Bauer's new monograph is titled *The Alchemy of Conquest: Science, Religion, and the Secrets of the New World* (University of Virginia Press, forthcoming 2019).

Daniela Bleichmar is an associate professor of art history and history at the University of Southern California. She is the author of *Visible Empire: Colonial Botany and Visual Culture in the Hispanic Enlightenment* (University of Chicago Press, 2012) and *Visual Voyages: Images of Latin American Nature from Columbus to Darwin* (Yale University Press, 2017) as well as the coeditor of *Collecting Across Cultures: Material Exchanges in the Early Modern Atlantic World* (University of Pennsylvania Press, 2011) and *Science in the Spanish and Portuguese Empires, 1500–1800* (Stanford University Press, 2008).

William Eamon is a Regents and Distinguished Achievement Professor Emeritus at New Mexico State University. His research focuses on the history of science and medicine in Renaissance Italy and Spain and on science and popular culture in early modern Europe. Eamon's publications include *Science and the Secrets of Nature: Books of Secrets in Medieval and*

Early Modern Europe (Princeton University Press, 1994) and *The Professor of Secrets: Mystery, Medicine, and Alchemy in Renaissance Italy* (National Geographic, 2010). His new projects are titled *Science and Everyday Life in Early Modern Europe, 1500–1750* (under contract with Cambridge University Press) and *Conquistadors of Nature: How the Spanish Explorers Paved the Way to Modern Science.*

Ruth Hill is a professor of Spanish and also the Andrew W. Mellon Chair of the Humanities at Vanderbilt University, where she researches and teaches the critical histories of science, race, and class from the early modern period to the twentieth century, with a particular emphasis on the trans-American and transatlantic engagements of the social and life sciences. Hill is the author of *Sceptres and Sciences in the Spains: Four Humanists and the New Philosophy* (Liverpool University Press, 2000) and *Hierarchy, Commerce, and Fraud in Bourbon Spanish America* (Vanderbilt University Press, 2005) as well as the editor of the special issue *Categories and Crossings: Critical Race Studies and the Spanish World* of the *Journal of Spanish Cultural Studies* (2009) and of the special issue *Other Enlightenments: Spain, from the Atlantic to the Pacific* of *The Eighteenth Century: Theory and Interpretation* (2018).

Jaime Marroquín Arredondo is an associate professor of Spanish at Western Oregon University, where he specializes in Latin American culture, history, and literature with a focus on early modern Mexico. He is the author of *La Historia de los Prejuicios en América: La Conquista* (Porrúa, 2007) and *Diálogos con Quetzalcóatl: Humanismo, etnografía y ciencia (1492–1577)* (Iberoamericana-Vervuert, 2014). He has also coedited *Borders to a Revolution: Culture, Politics and Migration* (Smithsonian Institution Scholarly Press, 2013).

Sara Miglietti is a Senior Lecturer at the Warburg Institute, London, where she focuses on the intellectual history of France and Europe from the Renaissance to the Enlightenment with particular attention to intersections between political thought, moral philosophy, and the natural sciences. She is currently working on a monograph titled "The Empire of Climate: Mastering Environmental Influence in the Early Modern Period," which investigates perceptions and manipulations of climate across early modern Europe and the colonial world.

Luis Millones Figueroa is the Charles A. Dana Professor of Spanish at Colby College. Millones Figueroa's research interests include pre-Columbian and colonial studies with an emphasis on the Andes; early modern science and natural histories of the New World; and Jesuits writings from a transatlantic perspective. He is the author of *Pedro de Cieza de León y su crónica de Indias: La entrada de los incas en la historia universal* (Instituto Francés de Estudios Andinos & Pontificia Universidad Católica, 2001) and the coeditor of *El saber de los jesuitas, historias naturales y el Nuevo Mundo* (Iberoamericana-Vervuert, 2005).

Marcy Norton is an associate professor of history at the University of Pennsylvania. She is the author of *Sacred Gifts, Profane Pleasures: A History of Tobacco and Chocolate in the Atlantic World* (Cornell University Press, 2008) and the coeditor (with Ralph Bauer) of *Entangled Trajectories: Indigenous and European Histories*, a special issue of *Colonial Latin American Review* 26 (Spring 2017). Norton is currently completing a book about colonialism and human-animal relationships in early modern Europe and America that will be published by Harvard University Press.

Christopher Parsons is an assistant professor of history at Northeastern University specializing in the interdisciplinary histories of science and the environment in the French Atlantic world. He has recently completed "A Not-So-New World: Europe and Environment in French Colonial North America" (University of Pennsylvania Press, 2018).

Juan Pimentel is a historian of science at the Institute of History of the Spanish National Research Council. Among his books are *La física de la Monarquía: Alejandro Malaspina, 1754–1810* (Doce Calles, 1998), *Testigos del mundo: Ciencia, literatura y viajes en la Ilustración* (Marcial Pons, 2003), and *El Rinoceronte y el Megaterio* (Abada, 2010).

Sarah Rivett is a professor of English at Princeton University. She is the author of *The Science of the Soul in Colonial New England* (Omohundro Institute of Early American History and Culture by the University of North Carolina Press, 2011) and *Unscripted America: Indigenous Languages and the Origins of Literary Nation* (Oxford University Press, 2017). Rivett has also coedited *Religious Transformations in the Early Modern Americas* (University of Pennsylvania Press, 2014).

John Slater is an associate professor in the Department of Spanish and Portuguese at the University of California, Davis. His research interests include early modern Spanish natural history, medicine, and alchemy; seventeenth-century Spanish drama; translation and the circulation of natural knowledge; and historiography and early modern historiographic theories. Slater is the author of *Todos son hojas: Literatura e historia natural en el barroco español* (Spanish National Research Council, 2010) and the coeditor of *Medical Cultures of the Early Modern Spanish Empire* (Ashgate, 2014).

Index

A c k n o w l e d g m e n t s

We wish to thank the Kislak Family Foundation, the Mexican Cultural Institute, and the Early Americas Working Group in Washington, D.C., for cosponsoring the symposium at which this collection originated. Also, thanks to Bob Lockhart and Peter Mancall for their initial interest in and continued support of the project as well as to the readers for the University of Pennsylvania Press for their helpful comments.